Expository Thoughts on the Gospels

MATTHEW

J. C. Ryle

THE BANNER OF TRUTH TRUST

THE BANNER OF TRUTH TRUST
3 Murrayfield Road, Edinburgh EH12 6EL
P.O. Box 621, Carlisle, Pennsylvania, 17013, U.S.A.

*

First published 1856
First Banner of Truth Trust edition 1986
Reprinted 1995
ISBN 0 85151 483 9

*

Printed and bound in Great Britain by
BPC Paperbacks Ltd
A member of
The British Printing Company Ltd

PREFACE.

In sending forth the first volume of a new Expository work upon the Gospels, I feel it necessary, in order to prevent misapprehension, to offer some explanation of the character and design of the work.

The "Expository Thoughts," which are now before the reader, are not a learned critical commentary. I do not profess to expound every verse of the Gospels, to grapple with every difficulty, to attempt the solution of every hard text, and to examine every disputed reading or translation.

The "Expository Thoughts" are not a continuous and homiletic exposition, containing practical remarks on every verse, like the commentaries of Brentius and Gaulter.

The plan I have adopted in drawing up the "Expository Thoughts" is as follows: I have divided the sacred text into sections or passages, averaging about twelve verses in each. I have then supplied a continuous series of short, plain "Expositions" of each of these passages. In each Exposition I have generally begun by stating as briefly as possible the main scope and purpose of the passage under consideration. I have then selected two, three, or four prominent points in the passage, singled them out from the rest, dwelt exclusively on them, and endeavoured to enforce them plainly and vigorously on the reader's attention. The points selected will be found to be sometimes doctrinal, and sometimes practical. The only rule in selection has been to seize on the really leading points of the passage.

In style and composition I frankly avow that I have studied, as far as possible, to be plain and pointed, and to choose what an old divine calls "picked and packed" words. I have tried to place myself in the position of one who is *reading aloud to others*, and must arrest their attention, if he can. I have said to myself in writing each Exposition, "I am addressing a mixed company, and I have but a short time."—Keeping this in view, I have constantly left unsaid many things that might have been said, and have endeavoured to dwell chiefly on the things needful to salvation. I have deliberately passed over many subjects of secondary importance, in order to say something that might strike and stick in consciences. I have felt that a few points, well remembered and fastened down, are better than a quantity of truth lying loosely, and thinly scattered over the mind.

A few foot notes, explaining difficult passages, have occasionally been added to the Exposition. I have thought it good to add these notes for the information of readers who may feel a wish to know what can be said about the "deep things" of Scripture, and may have no Commentary of their own.

I cannot, of course, expect that the opinions expressed in these Expositions, whether about doctrine, practice, or prophecy, will be satisfactory and acceptable to every one. I can only say, I have spoken out freely, and kept back nothing that seemed to me true. I have set down nothing but what I conscientiously believe to be the real meaning of the inspired writer, and the mind of the Spirit. I have always held that truth is most likely to be reached when men on all sides conceal nothing, but tell out all their minds. Right or wrong, I have endeavoured to tell out my own mind. It is my firm conviction that I have said nothing in these Expositions which is not in perfect harmony with the Thirty-nine Articles of my own Church, and does not agree in the main with all the Protestant Confessions of Faith. The words of an old divine will explain the kind of theology to which I ever desire to adhere and conform: "I know no true religion but Christianity; no true Christianity but the Doctrine of Christ; of His divine person (Col. i. 15), of His divine office (1 Tim. ii. 5), of His divine righteousness (Jer.

xxiii. 6), and of His divine Spirit, which all that are His receive (Rom. viii. 9). I know no true ministers of Christ but such as make it their business, in their calling, to commend Jesus Christ, in His saving fulness of grace and glory, to the faith and love of men. I know no true Christian but one united to Christ by faith, and abiding in Him by faith and love, to the glorifying of the name of Jesus Christ, in the beauties of Gospel holiness. Ministers and Christians of this spirit have for many years been my brethren and companions, and I hope ever shall be, whithersoever the hand of the Lord may lead me." *

I am deeply sensible of the many imperfections and defects of the volume which is now sent forth. No one perhaps will see them more clearly than I do myself. At the same time I think it only fair to say, that no Exposition in this volume has been composed without deliberate reflection, and laborious examination of other men's opinions. There are very few passages handled in these Expositions, concerning which I have not at least *looked* at the views of the following writers: Chrysostom, Augustine, Theophylact, Euthymius, Calvin, Brentius, Bucer, Musculus, Gualter, Beza, Bullinger, Pellican, Ferus, Calovius, Cocceius, Baxter, Poole, Hammond, Lightfoot, Hall, Du Veil, Piscator, Paræus, Jansenius,

* Traill's Preface to "Throne of Grace."

Leigh, Ness, Mayer, Trapp, Henry, Whitby, Gill, Doddridge Burkitt, Quesnel, Bengel, Scott, A. Clarke, Pearce, Adams, Watson, Olshausen, Alford, Barnes, Stier. I can truly say, that I have spent hours, days, and weeks in examining the opinions of these writers, and that when I differ from them it is not because I do not know their views.

Commentaries and Expositions of Scripture are so numerous in the present day, that I feel it necessary to say something about the class of readers whom I have specially had in view in putting forth these EXPOSITORY THOUGHTS.

In the first place, I indulge the hope that the work may be found *suitable for use at family prayers.* The supply of works adapted for this purpose has never yet been equal to the demand.

In the next place, I cannot help hoping that the work may prove *an aid to those who visit the sick and the poor.* The number of persons who visit hospitals, sick-rooms, and cottages, with an earnest desire to do spiritual good, is now very great. There is reason to believe that proper books for reading on such occasions are much wanted.

Last, but not least, I trust that the work may not be found unprofitable *for private reading, as a companion to the Gospels.* There are not a few whose callings and engagements make it impossible for them to read large commentaries and expositions of God's Word. I have thought that such may find it helpful to their memories to have a few leading points set before their minds in connection with what they read.

I now send forth the volume, with an earnest prayer that it may tend to the promotion of pure and undefiled religion, help to extend the knowledge of Christ, and be a humble instrument in aid of the glorious work of converting and edifying immortal souls.

J. C. RYLE.

TABLE OF CONTENTS.

EXPOSITORY THOUGHTS

ON THE GOSPELS.

MATTHEW I. 1—17.

1 The book of the generation of
Jesus Christ, the son of David, the
son of Abraham.
2 Abraham begat Isaac; and
Isaac begat Jacob; and Jacob begat Judas and his brethren;
3 And Judas begat Phares and
Zara of Thamar; and Phares begat
Esrom; and Esrom begat Aram;
4 And Aram begat Aminadab;
and Aminadab begat Naasson;
and Naasson begat Salmon;
5 And Salmon begat Booz of
Rachab; and Booz begat Obed of
Ruth; and Obed begat Jesse;
6 And Jesse begat David the
king: and David the king begat
Solomon of her *that had been the
wife* of Urias;
7 And Solomon begat Roboam;
and Roboam begat Abia; and Abia
begat Asa;
8 And Asa begat Josaphat; and
Josaphat begat Joram; and Joram
begat Ozias;
9 And Ozias begat Joatham; and
Joatham begat Achaz; and Achaz
begat Ezekias;
10 And Ezekias begat Manasses;
and Manasses begat Amon; and
Amon begat Josias;
11 And Josias begat Jechonias
and his brethren, about the time
they were carried away to Babylon:
12 And after they were brought
to Babylon, Jechonias begat Salathiel; and Salathiel begat Zorobabel;
13 And Zorobabel begat Abiud;
and Abiud begat Eliakim; and
Eliakim begat Azor;
14 And Azor begat Sadoc: and
Sadoc begat Achim; and Achim
begat Eliud;
15 And Eliud begat Eleazar;
and Eleazar begat Matthan; and
Matthan begat Jacob;
16 And Jacob begat Joseph the
husband of Mary, of whom was
born Jesus, who is called Christ.
17 So all the generations, from
Abraham to David *are* fourteen
generations; and from David until
the carrying away into Babylon
are fourteen generations; and from
the carrying away into Babylon
unto Christ *are* fourteen generations.

THESE verses begin the New Testament. Let us always read them with serious and solemn feelings.—The book before us contains "not the word of men, but of God." Every verse in it was written by inspiration of the Holy Ghost. (1 Thess. ii. 13.)

Let us thank God daily for giving us the Scriptures. The poorest Englishman who understands his Bible, knows more about religion than the wisest philosophers of Greece and Rome.

Let us never forget the deep responsibility which possession of the Bible entails on us. We shall be judged at the last day according to our light. To whomsoever much is given, of them much will be required.

Let us read the Bible reverently and diligently, with an honest determination to believe and practise all we find in it. It is no light matter how we use this book. Above all, let us never read the Bible without praying for the teaching of the Holy Spirit. He alone can apply truth to our hearts, and make us profit by what we read.

The New Testament begins with the history of the life, death, and resurrection of our Lord Jesus Christ. No part of the Bible is so important as this, and no part is so full and complete. Four distinct Gospels tell us the story of Christ's doings and dying. Four times we read the precious account of His works and words. How thankful we ought to be for this! To know Christ is life eternal. To believe in Christ is to have peace with God. To follow Christ is to be a true Christian. To be with Christ will be heaven itself. We can never hear too much about the Lord Jesus Christ.

The Gospel of St. Matthew begins with a long list of names. Sixteen verses are taken up with tracing a pedigree from Abraham to David, and from David to the family in which Jesus was born. Let no one think that these verses are useless. Nothing is useless in creation. The least mosses, and the smallest insects, serve some good end.—Nothing is useless in the Bible. Every word of it is inspired. The chapters and verses which seem at first sight unprofitable, are all given for some good purpose. He that looks carefully at these sixteen verses, will not fail to see in them useful and instructive lessons.

We learn, for one thing, from this list of names, that *God always keeps His word.* He had promised, that "in Abraham's seed all the nations of the earth should be blessed." He had promised to raise up a Saviour of the family of David. (Gen. xii. 3; Is. xi. 1.) These sixteen verses prove that Jesus was the Son of David and the Son of Abraham, and that God's promise was fulfilled.—Thoughtless and ungodly people should remember this lesson, and be afraid. Whatever they may think, God will keep His word. If they repent not, they will surely perish.—True Christians should remember this lesson, and take comfort. Their Father in heaven will be true to all His engagements. He has said that He will save all believers in Christ. If He has said it, He will certainly do it. "He is not a man, that He should lie."—"He abideth faithful: He cannot deny Himself." (Num. xxiii. 19; 2 Tim. ii. 13.)

We learn, for another thing, from this list of names, *the sinfulness and corruption of human nature.* It is instructive to observe how many godly parents in this catalogue had wicked and ungodly sons. The names of Roboam, and Joram, and Amon, and Jechonias, should teach us humbling lessons. They had all pious fathers. But they were all wicked men. Grace does not run in families. It needs something more than good examples and good advice to make us children of God. They that are born again are not born of blood, nor of the will of the flesh, nor of the will of man, but of God. (John i. 13.) Praying parents should pray night and day, that their children may be born of the Spirit.

We learn, lastly, from this list of names, *how great is the mercy and compassion of our Lord Jesus Christ.* Let us think how defiled and unclean human nature is, and then think what a condescension it was in Him to be born of a woman, and made in the "likeness of men." (Phil. ii. 7.) Some of the names we read in this catalogue remind us of shameful and sad histories. Some of the names are those of persons never mentioned elsewhere in the Bible. But at the end of all comes the name of the Lord Jesus Christ. Though He is the eternal God, He humbled Himself to become man, in order to provide salvation for sinners. "Though He was rich, yet for your sakes He became poor." (2 Cor. viii. 9.)

We should always read this catalogue with thankful feelings. We see here that no one who partakes of human nature can be beyond the reach of Christ's sympathy and compassion. Our sins may have been as black and great as those of any whom St. Matthew names. But they cannot shut us out of heaven, if we repent and believe the Gospel. If the Lord Jesus was not ashamed to be born of a woman whose pedigree contained such names as those we have read to-day, we need not think that He will be ashamed to call us brethren, and to give us eternal life.

MATTHEW I. 18–25.

18 Now the birth of Jesus Christ was on this wise: When as his mother Mary was espoused to Joseph, before they came together, she was found with child of the Holy Ghost.

19 Then Joseph her husband, being a just *man*, and not willing to make her a public example, was minded to put her away privily.

20 But while he thought on these things, behold, the angel of the Lord appeared unto him in a dream, saying, Joseph, thou son of David, fear not to take unto thee Mary thy wife; for that which is conceived in her is of the Holy Ghost.

21 And she shall bring forth a son, and thou shalt call his name JESUS: for he shall save his people from their sins.

22 Now all this was done, that it might be fulfilled which was spoken of the Lord by the prophet, saying,

23 Behold, a virgin shall be with child, and shall bring forth a son, and they shall call his name Emmanuel, which being interpreted is, God with us.

24 Then Joseph being raised from sleep did as the angel of the Lord had bidden him, and took unto him his wife:

25 And knew her not till she had brought forth her firstborn son: and he called his name JESUS.

THESE verses begin by telling us two great truths. They tell us how the Lord Jesus Christ took our nature upon Him, and became man. They tell us also that His birth was miraculous. His mother Mary was a virgin.

These are very mysterious subjects. They are depths, which we have no line to fathom. They are truths, which we have not mind enough to comprehend. Let us not attempt to explain things which are above our feeble reason. Let us be content to believe with reverence, and let us not speculate about matters which we cannot understand. Enough for us to know that with Him who made the world nothing is impossible. We may safely rest in the words of the Apostles' Creed: "Jesus Christ was conceived by the Holy Ghost, and born of the Virgin Mary."

Let us observe *the conduct of Joseph* described in these verses. It is a beautiful example of godly wisdom, and tender consideration for others. He saw the "appearance of evil" in her who was his espoused wife. But he did nothing rashly. He waited patiently to have the line of duty made clear. In all probability he laid the matter before God in prayer. "He that believeth shall not make haste." (Isai. xxviii. 16.)

The patience of Joseph was graciously rewarded. He received a direct message from God upon the subject of his anxiety, and was at once relieved from all his fears. How good it is to wait upon God! Who ever cast his cares upon God in hearty prayer, and found Him fail? "In all thy ways acknowledge Him, and He shall direct thy paths." (Prov. iii. 6.)

Let us observe in these verses, *the two names given to our Lord.* One is "Jesus:" the other "Emmanuel." One describes His office: the other His nature. Both are deeply interesting.

The name Jesus means "Saviour." It is the same name as Joshua in the Old Testament. It is given to our Lord because "He saves His people from their sins." This is His special office. He saves them from the guilt of sin, by washing them in His own atoning blood. He saves them from the dominion of sin, by putting in their hearts the sanctifying Spirit. He saves them from the presence of sin, when He takes them out of this world to rest with Him. He will save them from all the consequences of sin, when He shall give them a glorious body at the last day. Blessed and holy are Christ's people! From sorrow, cross, and conflict they are not saved; but they are "saved from sin" for evermore. They are cleansed from guilt by Christ's blood. They are made meet for heaven by Christ's Spirit. This is salvation! He who cleaves to sin is not yet saved.

"Jesus" is a very encouraging name to heavy-laden sinners. He who is King of kings and Lord of lords might lawfully have taken some more high-sounding title. But He did not do so. The rulers of this world have often called themselves Great, Conqueror, Bold, Magnificent, and the like. The Son of God was content to call Himself "Saviour." The souls which desire salvation may draw nigh to the Father with boldness, and have access with confidence through Christ. It is His office and His delight to show mercy. "God sent not His Son into the world to condemn the world, but that the world through Him might be saved." (John iii. 17.)

Jesus is a name which is peculiarly sweet and precious to believers. It has often done them good, when the favour of kings and princes would have been heard of with unconcern. It has given them what money cannot buy, even inward peace. It has eased their weary consciences, and given rest to their heavy hearts. The Song of Solomon speaks the experience of many, when it says, "Thy name is as ointment poured forth." (Cant. i. 3.) Happy is that person who trusts not merely in vague notions of God's mercy and goodness, but in "Jesus."

The name "Emmanuel" is seldom found in the Bible. But it is scarcely less interesting than the name "Jesus." It is the name which is given to our Lord from His nature as God-man, as "God manifest in the flesh." It signifies, "God with us."

Let us take care that we clearly understand that there was a union of two natures, the divine and human, in the person of our Lord Jesus Christ. It is a point of the deepest importance. We should settle it firmly in our minds, that our Saviour is perfect man as well as perfect God, and perfect God as well as perfect man. If we once lose sight of this great foundation truth, we may run into fearful heresies. The name Emmanuel takes in the whole mystery. Jesus is "God with us." He had a nature like our own in all things, sin only excepted. But though Jesus was "with us" in human flesh and blood, He was at the same time very God.

We shall often find, as we read the Gospels, that our Saviour could be weary and hungry and thirsty,—could weep and groan and feel pain like one of ourselves. In all this we see "*the man*" Christ Jesus. We see the nature He took on Him, when He was born of the Virgin Mary.

But we shall also find in the same Gospels that our Saviour knew men's hearts and thoughts,—that He had power over devils, that He could work the mightiest miracles with a word,—that He was ministered to by angels,—that He allowed a disciple to call Him "my God,"—and that He said, "Before Abraham was I am," and "I and my Father are one." In all this we see "*the eternal God.*" We see Him "who is over all, God blessed for ever. Amen." (Rom. ix. 5.)

If we would have a strong foundation for our faith and hope, we must keep constantly in view our Saviour's *divinity.* He in whose blood we are invited to trust is the Almighty God. All power is in heaven and earth. None can pluck us out of His hand. If we are true believers in Jesus, our heart need not be troubled or afraid.

If we would have sweet comfort in suffering and trial, we must keep constantly in view our Saviour's *humanity.* He is the man Christ Jesus, who lay on the bosom of the Virgin Mary as a little infant, and knows the heart of a man. He can be touched with the feeling of our infirmities. He has Himself experienced Satan's temptations. He has endured hunger. He has shed tears. He has felt pain. We may trust Him unreservedly with our sorrows. He will not despise us. We may pour out our hearts before Him in prayer boldly, and keep nothing back. He can sympathize with His people.

Let these thoughts sink down into our minds. Let us bless God for the encouraging truths which the first chapter of the New Testament contains. It tells us of One who "saves His people from their sins." But this is not all. It tells us that this Saviour is "Emmanuel," God Himself, and yet God with us,—God manifest in human flesh like our own. This is glad tidings. This is indeed good news. Let us feed on these truths in our hearts by faith with thanksgiving.

MATTHEW II. 1—12.

1 Now when Jesus was born in Bethlehem of Judæa in the days of Herod the king, behold, there came wise men from the east to Jerusalem,

2 Saying, Where is he that is born King of the Jews? For we have seen his star in the east, and are come to worship him.

3 When Herod the King had heard *these things*, he was troubled, and all Jerusalem with him.

4 And when he had gathered all the chief priests and scribes of the people together, he demanded of them where Christ should be born.

5 And they said unto him, In Bethlehem of Judæa; for thus it is written by the prophet,

6 And thou Bethlehem, *in* the land of Juda, art not the least among the princes of Juda: for out of thee shall come a Governor, that shall rule my people Israel.

7 Then Herod, when he had privily called the wise men, enquired of them diligently what time the star appeared.

8 And he sent them to Bethlehem, and said, Go and search diligently for the young child; and when ye have found *him*, bring me word again, that I may come and worship him also.

9 When they had heard the king, they departed; and, lo, the star, which they saw in the east, went before them, till it came and stood over where the young child was.

10 When they saw the star, they rejoiced with exceeding great joy.

11 And when they were come into the house, they saw the young child with Mary his mother, and fell down, and worshipped him: and when they had opened their treasures, they presented unto him gifts; gold, and frankincense, and myrrh.

12 And being warned of God in a dream that they should not return to Herod, they departed into their own country another way.

It is not known who these wise men were. Their names and dwelling-place are alike kept back from us. We are only told that they came "from the East." Whether they were Chaldeans or Arabians, we cannot say. Whether they learned to expect Christ from the ten tribes who went into captivity, or from the prophecies of Daniel, we do not know. It matters little who they were. The point which concerns us most is the rich instruction which their history conveys.

These verses show us *that there may be true servants of God in places where we should not expect to find them.* The Lord Jesus has many "hidden ones," like these wise men. Their history on earth may be as little known as that of Melchizedek, and Jethro, and Job. But their names are in the book of life, and they will be found with Christ in the day of His appearing. It is well to remember this. We must not look round the earth and say hastily, "All is barren." The grace of God is not tied to places and families. The Holy Ghost can lead souls to Christ without the help of any outward means. Men may be born in dark places of the earth, like these wise men, and yet like them be made "wise unto salvation." There are some travelling to heaven at this moment, of whom the Church and the world know nothing. They flourish in secret places like the "lily among thorns," and seem to "waste their sweetness on the desert air." But Christ loves them, and they love Christ.

These verses show us, secondly, *that it is not always those who have most religious privileges, who give Christ most honour.* We might have thought that the scribes and Pharisees would have been the first to hasten to

Bethlehem, on the slightest rumour that the Saviour was born. But it was not so. A few unknown strangers from a distant land were the first, except the shepherds mentioned by St. Luke, to rejoice at His birth. "He came unto His own, and His own received Him not." (John i. 11.) What a mournful picture this is of human nature! How often the same kind of thing may be seen among ourselves! How often the very persons who live nearest to the means of grace are those who neglect them most! There is only too much truth in the old proverb, "The nearer the church the further from God." Familiarity with sacred things has an awful tendency to make men despise them. There are many, who from residence and convenience ought to be first and foremost in the worship of God, and yet are always last. There are many, who might well be expected to be last, who are always first.

These verses show us, thirdly, *that there may be knowledge of Scripture in the head, while there is no grace in the heart.* We are told that king Herod sent to inquire of the priests and elders, "where Christ should be born." We are told that they returned a ready answer to him, and showed an accurate acquaintance with the letter of Scripture. But they never went to Bethlehem to seek for the coming Saviour. They would not believe in Him, when He ministered among them. Their heads were better than their hearts.—Let us beware of resting satisfied with head-knowledge. It is an excellent thing, when rightly used. But a man may have much of it, and yet perish everlastingly. What is the state of our hearts? This is the great question. A little grace is better than many gifts. Gifts alone save no one; but grace leads on to glory.

These verses show us, fourthly, *a splendid example of spiritual diligence.* What trouble it must have cost these wise men to travel from their homes to the house where Jesus was born! How many weary miles they must have journeyed! The fatigues of an Eastern traveller are far greater than we in England can at all understand. The time that such a journey would occupy must necessarily have been very great. The dangers to be encountered were neither few nor small.—But none of these things moved them. They had set their hearts on seeing Him "that was born King of the Jews;" and they never rested till they saw Him. They prove to us the truth of the old saying, "Where there is a will there is a way."

It would be well for all professing Christians if they were more ready to follow the example of these good men.—Where is our self-denial? What pains do we take about means of grace? What diligence do we show about following Christ? What does our religion cost us?—These are serious questions. They deserve serious consideration. The truly "wise," it may be feared, are very few.

These verses show us, lastly, a *striking example of faith.* These wise men believed in Christ when they had never seen Him; but that was not all. They believed in Him when the scribes and Pharisees were unbelieving;—but that again was not all. They believed in Him when they saw Him a little infant on Mary's knees, and worshipped Him as a King. This was the crowning point of their faith.—They saw no miracles to convince them. They heard no teaching to persuade them. They beheld no signs of divinity and greatness to overawe them. They saw nothing but a new-born infant, helpless and weak, and needing a mother's care, like any one of ourselves. And yet when they saw that infant, they believed that they saw the divine Saviour of the world! "They fell down and worshipped Him."

We read of no greater faith than this in the whole volume of the Bible. It is a faith that deserves to be placed side by side with that of the penitent thief. The thief saw one dying the death of a malefactor, and yet prayed to Him, and "called Him Lord." The wise men saw a new-born babe on the lap of a poor woman, and yet worshipped Him, and confessed that he was Christ. Blessed indeed are they that can believe in this fashion!

This is the kind of faith that God delights to honour. We see the proof of that at this very day. Wherever the Bible is read the conduct of these wise men is known, and told as a memorial of them. Let us walk in the steps of their faith. Let us not be ashamed to believe in Jesus and confess Him, though all around us remain careless and unbelieving. Have we not a thousand-fold more evidence than the wise men had, to make us believe that Jesus is the Christ? Beyond doubt we have. Yet where is our faith?

MATTHEW II. 13—23.

13 And when they were departed, behold, the angel of the Lord appeareth to Joseph in a dream, saying, Arise, and take the young child and his mother, and flee into Egypt, and be thou there until I bring thee word: for Herod will seek the young child to destroy him.

14 When he arose, he took the young child and his mother by night, and departed into Egypt:

15 And was there until the death of Herod: that it might be fulfilled which was spoken of the Lord by the prophet, saying, Out of Egypt have I called my son.

16 Then Herod, when he saw that he was mocked of the wise men, was exceeding wrath, and sent forth, and slew all the children that were in Bethlehem, and in all the coasts thereof, from two years old and under, according to the time which he had diligently enquired of the wise men.

17 Then was fulfilled that which was spoken by Jeremy the prophet, saying,

18 In Rama was there a voice heard, lamentation, and weeping, and great mourning, Rachel weeping *for* her children, and would not be comforted, because they are not.

19 But when Herod was dead, behold, an angel of the Lord appeareth in a dream to Joseph in Egypt,

20 Saying, Arise, and take the young child and his mother, and go into the land of Israel: for they are dead which sought the young child's life.

21 And he arose, and took the young child and his mother, and came into the land of Israel.

22 But when he heard that Archelaus, did reign in Judæa in the room of his father Herod, he was afraid to go thither: notwithstanding, being warned of God in a dream, he turned aside into the parts of Galilee:

23 And he came and dwelt in a city called Nazareth: that it might be fulfilled which was spoken by the prophets, He shall be called a Nazarene.

LET us observe in this passage, how true it is that *the rulers of this world are seldom friendly to the cause of God.* The Lord Jesus comes down from heaven to save sinners, and at once we are told that Herod the king "seeks to destroy Him."

Greatness and riches are a perilous possession for the soul. Those who seek to have them know not what they seek. They lead men into many temptations. They are likely to fill the heart with pride, and to chain the affections down to things below. "Not many mighty, not many noble are called." "How hardly shall they that have riches enter into the kingdom of God." (1 Cor. i. 26. Mark x. 23.)

Do we envy the rich and great? Does our heart sometimes say, "Oh, that I had their place, and rank, and substance"? Let us beware of giving way to such feelings The very wealth which we admire may be gradually sinking its possessors down into hell. A little more money might be our ruin. Like Herod, we might run into every excess of wickedness and cruelty. "Take heed, and beware of covetousness." "Be content with such things as ye have." (Luke xii. 15. Heb. xiii. 5.)

Do we think that Christ's cause depends on the power

and patronage of princes? We are mistaken. They have seldom done much for the advancement of true religion: they have far more frequently been the enemies of the truth. "Put not your trust in princes." (Psa. cxlvi. 3.) They who are like Herod are many. They who are like Josiah and Edward the Sixth of England are few.

Let us observe, for another thing, how the *Lord Jesus was "a Man of Sorrows," even from His infancy.* Trouble awaits Him as soon as He enters into the world. His life is in danger from Herod's hatred. His mother and Joseph are obliged to take Him away by night, and "flee into Egypt."—It was only a type and figure of all His experience upon earth. The waves of humiliation began to beat over Him, even when He was a sucking child.

The Lord Jesus is just the Saviour that the suffering and sorrowful need. He knows well what we mean when we tell Him in prayer of our troubles. He can sympathize with us, when we cry to Him under cruel persecution. Let us keep nothing back from Him. Let us make Him our bosom friend. Let us pour out our hearts before Him. He has had great experience of affliction.

Let us observe, for another thing, how *death can remove the kings of this world like other men.* The rulers of millions have no power to retain life, when the hour of their departure comes. The murderer of helpless infants must himself die. Joseph and Mary hear the tidings that "Herod is dead;" and at once they return in safety to their own land.

True Christians should never be greatly moved by the persecution of man. Their enemies may be strong, and they may be weak; but still they ought not to be afraid. They should remember that "the triumphing of the wicked is but short." (Job xx. 5.) What has become of the Pharaohs and Neros and Diocletians, who at one time fiercely persecuted the people of God? Where is the enmity of Charles IX. of France, and bloody Mary of England? They did their utmost to cast the truth down to the ground. But the truth rose again from the earth, and still lives; and they are dead, and mouldering in the grave. Let not the heart of any believer fail. Death is a mighty leveller, and can take any mountain out of the way of Christ's Church. "The Lord liveth" for ever. His enemies are only men. The truth shall always prevail.

Let us observe, in the last place, *what a lesson of humility is taught us by the dwelling place of the Son of God*, when He was on earth. He dwelt with His mother and Joseph "in a city called Nazareth."

Nazareth was a small town in Galilee. It was an obscure, retired place, not so much as once mentioned in the Old Testament. Hebron, and Shiloh, and Gibeon, and Ramah, and Bethel, were far more important places. But the Lord Jesus passed by them all, and chose Nazareth. This was humility!

In Nazareth the Lord Jesus lived thirty years. It was there He grew up from infancy to childhood, and from childhood to boyhood, and from boyhood to youth, and from youth to man's estate. We know little of the manner in which those thirty years were spent. That He was "subject to Mary and Joseph," we are expressly told. (Luke ii. 41.) That He worked in the carpenter's shop with Joseph, is highly probable. We only know, that almost five-sixths of the time that the Saviour of the world was on earth, was passed among the poor of this world and passed in complete retirement. Truly this was humility!

Let us learn wisdom from our Saviour's example. We are most of us far too ready to "seek great things" in this world: let us "seek them not." (Jer. xlv. 5.) To have a place and a title and a position in society is not nearly so important as people think. It is a great sin to be covetous and worldly and proud: but it is no sin to be poor. It matters not so much what money we have, and where we live, as what we are in the sight of God. Where are we going when we die? Shall we live for ever in heaven? These are the main things to which we should attend.

Above all, let us daily strive to copy our Saviour's humility. Pride is the oldest and commonest of sins: humility is the rarest and most beautiful of graces. For humility let us labour; for humility let us pray. Our knowledge may be scanty, our faith may be weak, our strength may be small; but if we are disciples of Him who "dwelt at Nazareth," let us at any rate be humble.

MATTHEW III. 1—12.

1 In those days came John the
Baptist, preaching in the wilderness of Judæa,
2 And saying, Repent ye: for the
kingdom of heaven is at hand.
3 For this is he that was spoken
of by the prophet Esaias, saying,
The voice of one crying in the wilderness, Prepare ye the way of the
Lord, make his paths straight.
4 And the same John had his
raiment of camel's hair, and a
leathern girdle about his loins;
and his meat was locusts and wild
honey.
5 Then went out to him Jerusalem, and all Judæa, and all the
region round about Jordan.
6 And were baptized of him in
Jordan, confessing their sins.
7 But when he saw many of the
Pharisees and Sadducees come to
his baptism, he said unto them,
O generation of vipers, who hath
warned you to flee from the wrath
to come?
8 Bring forth therefore fruits
meet for repentance:
9 And think not to say within
yourselves, We have Abraham to

our father: for I say unto you, that God is able of these stones to raise up children unto Abraham.

10 And now also the axe is laid unto the root of the trees: therefore every tree which bringeth not forth good fruit is hewn down, and cast into the fire.

11 I indeed baptize you with water unto repentance: but he that cometh after me is mightier than I, whose shoes I am not worthy to bear: he shall baptize you with the Holy Ghost, and *with* fire:

12 Whose fan *is* in his hand, and he will thoroughly purge his floor, and gather his wheat into the garner: but he will burn up the chaff with unquenchable fire.

THESE verses describe the ministry of John the Baptist, the forerunner of our Lord Jesus Christ: it is a ministry that deserves close attention. Few preachers ever produced such effects as John the Baptist: "There went out to him Jerusalem, and all Judæa, and all the region round about Jordan."—None ever received such praise from the great Head of the Church: Jesus called him "a burning and a shining light" (John v. 35); the great Bishop of souls Himself declared, that "among them that are born of women there hath not risen a greater than John the Baptist." Let us then study the leading features of his ministry.

John the Baptist spoke plainly *about sin.* He taught the absolute necessity of "repentance," before any one can be saved; he preached that repentance must be proved by its "fruits;" he warned men not to rest on outward privileges, or outward union with the Church.

This is just the teaching that we all need. We are naturally dead, and blind, and asleep in spiritual things; we are ready to content ourselves with a mere formal religion, and to flatter ourselves that if we go to church we shall be saved: we need to be told, that except we "repent and are converted," we shall all perish.

John the Baptist spoke plainly *about our Lord Jesus Christ.* He taught people that One "mightier than himself" was coming among them. He was nothing more than a servant: the Coming One was the King. He himself could only baptize with water:" the Coming One could "baptize with the Holy Ghost," take away sins, and would one day judge the world.

This again is the very teaching that human nature requires. We need to be sent direct to Christ: we are all ready to stop short of this; we want to rest in our union with the Church, our regular use of the sacraments, and our diligent attendance on an established ministry. We need to be told the absolute necessity of union with Christ Himself by faith: He is the appointed fountain of mercy, grace, life, and peace; we must each have personal dealings with Him about our souls. What do we know of the Lord Jesus? What have we got from Him? These are the questions on which our salvation hinges.

John the Baptist spoke plainly *about the Holy Ghost.* He preached that there was such a thing as the baptism of the Holy Ghost. He taught that it was the special office of the Lord Jesus to give this baptism to men.

This again is a teaching which we greatly require. We need to be told that forgiveness of sin is not the only thing necessary to salvation. There is another thing yet; and that is the baptizing of our hearts by the Holy Ghost. There must not only be the work of Christ *for* us, but the work of the Holy Ghost *in* us; there must not only be a title to heaven purchased for us by the blood of Christ, but a preparedness for heaven wrought in us by the Spirit of Christ. Let us never rest till we know something by experience of the baptism of the Spirit. The baptism of water is a great privilege: but let us see to it that we have also the baptism of the Holy Ghost.

John the Baptist spoke plainly *about the awful danger of the impenitent and unbelieving.* He told his hearers that there was a "wrath to come:" he preached of an "unquenchable fire," in which the "chaff" would one day be burned.

This again is a teaching which is deeply important. We need to be straitly warned that it is no light matter whether we repent or not; we need to be reminded that there is a hell as well as a heaven, and an everlasting punishment for the wicked as well as everlasting life for the godly. We are fearfully apt to forget this: we talk of the love and mercy of God, and we do not remember sufficiently His justice and holiness. Let us be very careful on this point. It is no real kindness to keep back the terrors of the Lord: it is good for us all to be taught that it is possible to be lost for ever, and that all unconverted people are hanging over the brink of the pit.

In the last place, John the Baptist spoke plainly *about the safety of true believers.* He taught that there was "a garner" for all who are Christ's "wheat," and that they would be gathered together there in the day of His appearing.

This again is a teaching which human nature greatly requires. The best of believers need much encouragement: they are yet in the body; they live in a wicked world: they are often tempted by the devil. They ought to be often reminded that Jesus will never leave them nor forsake them: He will guide them safely through this life, and at length give them eternal glory. They shall be hid in the day of wrath; they shall be as safe as Noah was in the ark.

Let these things sink down deeply into our hearts. We live in a day of much false teaching: let us never forget the leading features of a faithful ministry. Happy would it have been for the Church of Christ, if all its ministers had been more like John the Baptist!

MATTHEW III. 13–17.

13 Then cometh Jesus from Galilee to Jordan unto John, to be baptized of him.

14 But John forbad him, saying, I have need to be baptized of thee, and comest thou to me?

15 And Jesus answering said unto him, Suffer *it to be* so now: for thus it becometh us to fulfil all righteousness. Then he suffered him.

16 And Jesus, when he was baptized, went up straightway out of the water: and lo, the heavens were opened unto him, and he saw the Spirit of God descending like a dove, and lighting upon him:

17 And lo, a voice from heaven, saying, This is my beloved Son, in whom I am well pleased.

WE have here the account of our Lord Jesus Christ's baptism. This was His first step when He entered on His ministry. When the Jewish priests took up their office they were washed with water (Ex. xxix. 4): when our great High Priest begins the great work He came into the world to accomplish He is publicly baptized.

We should notice, firstly, in these verses, *the honour placed upon the sacrament of baptism.* An ordinance of which the Lord Jesus Himself partook is not to be lightly esteemed; an ordinance to which the great Head of the Church submitted ought to be ever honourable in the eyes of professing Christians.

There are few subjects in religion on which greater mistakes have arisen than baptism: there are few which require so much fencing and guarding. Let us arm our minds with two general cautions.

Let us beware, on the one hand, that we do not attach a superstitious importance to the water of baptism. We must not expect that water to act as a charm: we must not suppose that all baptized persons, as a matter of course, receive the grace of God in the moment that they are baptized. To say that all who come to baptism obtain like and equal benefit, and that it matters not a jot whether they come with faith and prayer or in utter carelessness,—to say such things appears to contradict the plainest lessons of Scripture.

Let us beware, on the other hand, that we do not dishonour the sacrament of baptism. It is dishonoured when it is hastily slurred over as a mere form, or thrust out of sight, and never publicly noticed in the congregation. A sacrament ordained by Christ Himself ought not to be treated in this way. The admission of every new member into the visible Church, whether young or grown up, is an event which ought to excite a lively interest in a Christian assembly: it is an event that ought to call forth the fervent prayers of all praying people. The more deeply we are convinced that baptism and grace are not inseparably tied together, the more we ought to feel bound to join in prayer for a blessing, when ever any one is baptized.

We should notice, secondly, in these verses, *the peculiarly solemn circumstances by which the baptism of our Lord Jesus Christ was attended.* Such a baptism never will be again, so long as the world stands.

We are told of the presence of all Three Persons of the blessed Trinity. God the Son, manifest in the flesh, is baptized; God the Spirit descends like a dove, and lights upon Him; God the Father speaks from heaven with a voice. In a word, we have the manifested presence of Father, Son, and Holy Ghost. We may regard this as a public announcement that the work of Christ was the result of the eternal counsels of all the Three Persons of the blessed Trinity. It was the whole Trinity, which at the beginning of the creation said, "Let us make man;" it was the whole Trinity again, which at the beginning of the Gospel seemed to say, "Let us save man."

We are told of "a voice from heaven" at our Lord's baptism: the "heavens were opened," and words were heard. This was a most significant miracle. We read of no voice from heaven before this, except at the giving of the law on Sinai. Both occasions were of peculiar importance; it therefore seemed good to our Father in heaven to mark both with peculiar honour. At the introduction both of the Law and Gospel He Himself spoke. "God spake these words." (Exod. xx. 1.)

How striking and deeply instructive are the Father's words: "This is my beloved Son, in whom I am well pleased." He declares, in these words, that Jesus is the Divine Saviour sealed and appointed from all eternity to carry out the work of redemption: He proclaims that He accepts Him as the Mediator between God and man; He publishes to the world that He is satisfied with Him as the propitiation, the Substitute, the ransom-payer for the lost family of Adam, and the Head of a redeemed people. In Him He sees His holy "law magnified and made honourable:" through Him He can "be just and yet the justifier of the ungodly." (Isa. xlii. 21; Rom. iii. 26.)

Let us carefully ponder these words. They are full of rich food for thought; they are full of peace, joy, comfort, and consolation, for all who have fled for refuge to the Lord Jesus Christ, and committed their souls to Him for salvation. Such may rejoice in the thought, that though in themselves sinful, yet in God's sight they are counted righteous. The Father regards them as members of His beloved Son: He sees in them no spot, and for His Son's sake is "well pleased." (Eph. i. 6.)

MATTHEW IV. 1—11.

1 Then was Jesus led up of the spirit into the wilderness to be tempted of the devil.

2 And when he had fasted forty days and forty nights, he was afterward an hungered.

3 And when the tempter came to him, he said, If thou be the Son of God, command that these stones be made bread.

4 But he answered and said, It is written, Man shall not live by bread alone, but by every word that proceedeth out of the mouth of God.

5 Then the devil taketh him up into the holy city, and setteth him on a pinnacle of the temple,

6 And saith unto him, If thou be the Son of God, cast thyself down: for it is written, He shall give his angels charge concerning thee: and in *their* hands they shall bear thee up, lest at any time thou dash thy foot against a stone.

7 Jesus said unto him, It is written again, Thou shalt not tempt the Lord thy God.

8 Again, the devil taketh him up into an exceeding high mountain, and sheweth him all the kingdoms of the world, and the glory of them;

9 And saith unto him, All these things will I give thee, if thou wilt fall down and worship me.

10 Then saith Jesus unto him, Get thee hence Satan: for it is written, Thou shalt worship the Lord thy God, and him only shalt thou serve.

11 Then the devil leaveth him, and, behold, angels came and ministered unto him.

THE first event in our Lord's ministry which St. Matthew records after His baptism, is His temptation. This is a deep and mysterious subject: there is much in the history of it which we cannot explain; but there lie on the face of the history plain practical lessons, to which we shall do well to take heed.

Let us learn, in the first place, *what a real and mighty enemy we have in the devil.* He is not afraid to assault even the Lord Jesus Himself. Three times over he attacks God's own Son: our Saviour was "tempted of the devil."

It was the devil who brought sin into the world at the beginning. This is he who vexed Job, deceived David, and gave Peter a heavy fall: this is he whom the Bible calls a "murderer," a "liar," and a "roaring lion" (John viii. 44; 1 Pet. v. 8); this is he whose enmity to our souls never slumbers and never sleeps; this is he who for nearly 6000 years has been working at one work,—to ruin men and women, and to draw them to hell; this is he whose cunning and subtlety pass man's understanding, and who often appears "an angel of light." (1 Cor. xi. 14.)

Let us watch and pray daily against his devices. There is no enemy worse than an enemy who is never seen and never dies, who is near us wherever we live, and goes with us wherever we go. Not least let us beware of that habit of foolish talking and jesting about the devil, which is so unhappily common. Let us remember that if we would be saved we must not only crucify the flesh and overcome the world, but also "resist the devil."

Let us learn, in the next place, *that we must not count temptation a strange thing.* "The disciple is not greater than his master, nor the servant than his lord." If Satan came to Christ, he will also come to Christians.

It would be well for believers if they would remember this: they are too apt to forget it. They often find evil thoughts arising within their minds, which they can truly say they hate; doubts, questions, and sinful imaginings are suggested to them, against which their whole inward man revolts: but let not these things destroy their peace, and rob them of their comforts. Let them remember there is a devil, and not be surprised to find him near them. To be tempted is in itself no sin: it is the yielding to temptation, and the giving it a place in our hearts, which we must fear.

Let us learn, in the next place, *that the chief weapon we ought to use in resisting Satan, is the Bible.* Three times the great enemy offered temptations to our Lord. Three times his offer was refused, with a text of Scripture as the reason: "It is written."

Here is one among many reasons why we ought to be diligent readers of our Bibles: the Word is the "sword of the Spirit:" we shall never fight a good fight if we do not use it as our principal weapon.—The Word is the "lamp" for our feet: we shall never keep the King's highway to heaven if we do not journey by its light. (Eph. vi. 17: Psa. cxix. 105.)—It may well be feared that there is not enough Bible-reading amongst us. It is not sufficient to have the Book: we must actually read it, and pray over it ourselves. It will do us no good if it only lies still in our houses: we must be actually familiar with its contents, and have its texts stored in our memories and minds. Knowledge of the Bible never comes by intuition; it can only be got by hard, regular, daily, attentive, wakeful reading. Do we grudge the time and trouble this will cost us? If we do we are not yet fit for the kingdom of God.

Let us learn, in the last place, *what a sympathizing Saviour the Lord Jesus Christ is.* "In that He Himself hath suffered being tempted, He is able to succour them that are tempted." (Heb. ii. 18.)

The sympathy of Jesus is a truth which ought to be peculiarly dear to believers: they will find in it a mine of strong consolation. They should never forget that they have a mighty Friend in heaven, who feels for them in all their temptations, and can enter into all their spiritual anxieties. Are they ever tempted by Satan to distrust God's care and goodness? So was Jesus.—Are they ever tempted to presume on God's mercy, and to run into danger without warrant? So also was Jesus.—Are they ever tempted to commit some one private sin for the sake of some great seeming advantage? So also was Jesus.—Are they ever tempted to listen to some misapplication of Scripture, as an excuse for doing wrong? So also was Jesus.—He is just the Saviour that a tempted people require. Let them flee to Him for help, and spread before Him all their troubles; they will find His ear ever ready to hear, and His heart ever ready to feel: He can understand their sorrows.

May we all know the value of a sympathizing Saviour by experience! There is nothing to be compared to it in this cold and deceitful world. Those who seek their happiness in this life only, and despise the religion of the Bible, have no idea what true comfort they are missing.

MATTHEW IV. 12—25.

12 Now when Jesus had heard that John was cast into prison, he departed into Galilee:

13 And leaving Nazareth, he came and dwelt in Capernaum, which is upon the sea coast, in the borders of Zabulon and Nepthalim:

14 That it might be fulfilled which was spoken by Esaias the prophet, saying,

15 The land of Zabulon, and the land of Nepthalim, *by* the way of the sea, beyond Jordan, Galilee of the Gentiles:

16 The people which sat in darkness saw great light; and to them which sat in the region and shadow of death light is sprung up.

17 From that time Jesus began to preach, and to say, Repent: for the kingdom of heaven is at hand.

18 And Jesus, walking by the sea of Galilee, saw two brethren, Simon called Peter, and Andrew his brother, casting a net into the sea: for they were fishers.

19 And he saith unto them, Follow me, and I will make you fishers of men.

20 And they straightway left *their* nets, and followed him.

21 And going on from thence, he saw other two brethren, James *the son* of Zebedee, and John his brother, in a ship with Zebedee their father, mending their nets; and he called them.

22 And they immediately left the ship and their father, and followed him.

23 And Jesus went about all Galilee, teaching in their synagogues, and preaching the Gospel of the kingdom, and healing all man-

ner of sickness and all manner of disease among the people.

24 And his fame went throughout all Syria: and they brought unto him all sick people that were taken with divers diseases and torments, and those which were possessed with devils, and those which were lunatick, and those that had the palsy; and he healed them.

25 And there followed him great multitudes of people from Galilee, and *from* Decapolis, and *from* Jerusalem, and *from* Judæa, and *from* beyond Jordan.

WE have in these verses the beginning of our Lord's ministry among men. He enters on His labours among a dark and ignorant people; He chooses men to be His companions and disciples: He confirms His ministry by miracles, which rouse the attention of "all Syria," and draw multitudes to hear Him

Let us notice *the way in which our Lord commenced His mighty work.* "He began to preach."

There is no office so honourable as that of the preacher: there is no work so important to the souls of men. It is an office which the Son of God was not ashamed to take up: it is an office to which He appointed His twelve apostles; it is an office to which St. Paul in his old age specially directs Timothy's attention; he charges him with almost his last breath to "preach the Word." (2 Tim. iv. 2.) It is the principal means which God has always been pleased to use for the conversion and edification of souls. The brightest days of the Church have been those when preaching has been honoured; the darkest days of the Church have been those when it has been lightly esteemed. Let us honour the Sacraments and public prayers of the Church, and reverently use them; but let us beware that we do not place them above preaching.

Let us notice the *first doctrine which the Lord Jesus proclaimed to the world.* He "began to say, Repent."

The necessity of repentance is one of the great foundation stones which lie at the very bottom of Christianity: it is a truth which needs to be pressed on all mankind without exception. High or low, rich or poor, all have sinned, and are guilty before God; and all must repent and be converted, if they would be saved.—It is a truth which does not receive the attention it deserves. True repentance is no light matter: it is a thorough change of heart about sin, a change showing itself in godly sorrow for sin,—in heart-felt confession of sin,—in a complete breaking off from sinful habits, and an abiding hatred of all sin. Such repentance is the inseparable companion of saving faith in Christ.—Let us prize the doctrine highly. No Christian teaching can be called sound, which does not constantly bring forward "repentance toward God, and faith toward our Lord Jesus Christ." (Acts xx. 21.)

Let us notice *the class of men whom the Lord Jesus chose to be His disciples.* They were of the poorest and humblest rank in life. Peter, and Andrew, and James, and John, were all "fishermen."

The religion of our Lord Jesus Christ was not intended for the rich and learned alone: it was intended for all the world: and the majority of all the world will always be the poor. Poverty and ignorance of books, excluded thousands from the notice of the boastful philosophers of the heathen world: they exclude no one from the highest place in the service of Christ. Is a man humble? Does he feel his sins? Is he willing to hear Christ's voice and follow Him? If this be so, he may be the poorest of the poor, but he shall be found as high as any in the kingdom of heaven. Intellect, and money, and rank, are worth nothing without grace.

The religion of Christ must have been from heaven, or it never could have prospered and overspread the earth as it has done. It is vain for infidels to attempt to answer this argument: it cannot be answered. A religion which did not flatter the rich, the great, and the learned,—a religion which offered no license to the carnal inclinations of man's heart,—a religion whose first teachers were poor fishermen, without wealth, rank, or power,—such a religion could never have turned the world upside down, if it had not been of God. Look at the Roman Emperors and the heathen priests with their splendid temples on the one side! Look at a few unlearned working men with the Gospel on the other! Were there ever two parties so unequally matched? Yet the weak proved strong, and the strong proved weak. Heathenism fell, and Christianity took its place. Christianity must have been of God.

Let us notice, in the last place, *the general character of the miracles by which our Lord confirmed His mission.* Here we are told of them in the mass; hereafter we shall find many of them described particularly: and what is their character? They were miracles of mercy and kindness. Our Lord "went about doing good."

These miracles are meant to teach us our Lord's power. He that could heal sick people with a touch, and cast out devils with a word, is "able to save all them to the uttermost that come unto God by Him." He is Almighty.

These miracles are meant to be types and emblems of our Lord's skill as a spiritual physician. He, before whom no bodily disease proved incurable, is mighty to cure every ailment of our souls: there is no broken heart that He cannot heal; there is no wound of conscience that He cannot cure. Fallen, crushed, bruised, plague-stricken as we all are by sin, Jesus by His blood and Spirit can make us whole. Only let us apply to Him.

These miracles, not least, are intended to show us Christ's heart. He is a most compassionate Saviour: He rejected no one who came to Him; He refused no one, however loathsome and diseased: He had an ear to hear all, and a hand to help all, and a heart to feel for all. There is no kindness like His. His compassions fail not.

May we all remember that the Lord Jesus is "the same yesterday, and to-day, and for ever." (Heb. xiii. 8.) High in heaven at God's right hand, He is not in the least altered. He is just as able to save, just as willing to receive, just as ready to help, as He was 1800 years ago. Should we have spread out our wants before Him then? Let us do the same now. He can "heal all manner of sickness and all manner of disease."

MATTHEW V. 1—12.

1 And seeing the multitudes, he went up into a mountain: and when he was set, his disciples came unto him:

2 And he opened his mouth, and taught them, saying,

3 Blessed *are* the poor in spirit: for their's is the kingdom of heaven.

4 Blessed *are* they that mourn: for they shall be comforted.

5 Blessed *are* the meek: for they shall inherit the earth.

6 Blessed *are* they which do hunger and thirst after righteousness: for they shall be filled.

7 Blessed *are* the merciful: for they shall obtain mercy.

8 Blessed *are* the pure in heart: for they shall see God.

9 Blessed *are* the peacemakers: for they shall be called the children of God.

10 Blessed are they which are persecuted for righteousness' sake: for their's is the kingdom of heaven.

11 Blessed are ye, when *men* shall revile you, and persecute *you*, and shall say all manner of evil against you falsely, for my sake.

12 Rejoice, and be exceeding glad: for great *is* your reward in heaven: for so persecuted they the prophets which were before you.

THE three chapters which begin with these verses deserve the special attention of all readers of the Bible.

They contain what is commonly called the "Sermon on the Mount."

Every word of the Lord Jesus ought to be most precious to professing Christians. It is the voice of the Chief Shepherd; it is the charge of the great Bishop and Head of the Church; it is the Master speaking; it is the word of Him who "spake as never man spake," and by whom we shall all be judged at the last day.

Would we know what kind of people Christians ought to be? Would we know the character at which Christians ought to aim? Would we know the outward walk and inward habit of mind which become a follower of Christ? Then let us often study the Sermon on the Mount. Let us often ponder each sentence, and prove ourselves by it. Not least, let us often consider who they are that are called "blessed" at the beginning of the Sermon. Those whom the great High Priest blesses are blessed indeed!

The Lord Jesus calls those "blessed" who are *poor in spirit.* He means the humble, and lowly-minded, and self-abased; He means those who are deeply convinced of their own sinfulness in God's sight: these are they who are not "wise in their own eyes and prudent in their own sight." They are not "rich and increased with goods:" they do not fancy they "need nothing;" they regard themselves as "wretched, and miserable, and poor, and blind, and naked." Blessed are all such! Humility is the very first letter in the alphabet of Christianity. We must begin low, if we would build high. (Is. vi. 21; Rev. iii. 17.)

The Lord Jesus calls those "blessed" who *mourn.* He means those who sorrow for sin, and grieve daily over their own short-comings. These are they who trouble themselves more about sin than about anything on earth: the remembrance of it is grievous to them; the burden of it is intolerable. Blessed are all such! "The sacrifices of God are a broken spirit" and a contrite heart. (Ps. li. 17.) One day they shall weep no more: "they shall be comforted."

The Lord Jesus calls those "blessed" who are *meek* He means those who are of a patient and contented spirit. They are willing to put up with little honour here below; they can bear injuries without resentment: they are not ready to take offence. Like Lazarus in the parable, they are content to wait for their good things. Blessed are all such! They are never losers in the long run. One day they shall "reign on the earth." (Rev. v. 10.)

The Lord Jesus calls those "blessed" who *hunger and thirst after righteousness.* He means those who desire above all things to be entirely conformed to the mind of God. They long not so much to be rich, or wealthy, or learned, as to be holy. Blessed are all such! They shall have enough one day. They shall "awake up after God's likeness and be satisfied." (Psalm xvii. 15.)

The Lord Jesus calls those "blessed" who are *merciful* He means those who are full of compassion towards others. They pity all who are suffering either from sin or sorrow, and are tenderly desirous to make their sufferings less; they are "full of good works," and endeavours to do good. (Acts ix. 36.) Blessed are all such! Both in this life and in that which is to come they shall reap a rich reward.

The Lord Jesus calls those "blessed" who are *pure in heart.* He means those who do not aim merely at outward correctness, but at inward holiness. They are not satisfied with a mere external show of religion: they strive to have always a conscience void of offence, and to serve God with the spirit and the inner man. Blessed are all such! The heart is the man. "Man looketh on the outward appearance, but the Lord looketh on the heart." (1 Sam. xvi. 7.) He that is most spiritually-minded will have most communion with God.

The Lord Jesus call those "blessed" who are *peace-makers.* He means those who use all their influence to promote peace and charity on earth, in private and in public, at home and abroad. He means those who strive to make all men love one another, by teaching that Gospel which says, "Love is the fulfilling of the law." (Rom. xiii. 10.) Blessed are all such! They are doing the very work which the Son of God began when He came to earth the first time, and which He will finish when He returnes the second time.

Lastly, the Lord Jesus calls those "blessed" who are *persecuted for righteousness' sake.* He means those who are laughed at, mocked, despised, and ill used, because they endeavour to live as true Christians. Blessed are all such! They drink of the same cup which their Master drank. They are now confessing Him before men, and He will confess them before His Father and the angels at the last day. "Great is their reward."

Such are the eight foundation-stones which the Lord lays down at the beginning of the Sermon on the Mount. Eight great testing truths are placed before us. May we mark well each one of them, and learn wisdom.

Let us learn how entirely contrary are the principles of Christ to the principles of the world. It is vain to deny it: they are almost diametrically opposed. The very characters which the Lord Jesus praises the world despises; the very pride, and thoughtlessness, and high tempers, and worldliness, and selfishness, and formality, and unlovingness, which abound everywhere, the Lord Jesus condemns.

Let us learn how unhappily different is the teaching of Christ from the practice of many professing Christians. Where shall we find men and women among those who go to churches and chapels, who are striving to live up to the pattern we have read of to-day? There is too much reason to fear that many baptized persons are utterly ignorant of what the New Testament commands.

Above all, let us learn how holy and spiritually-minded all believers should be. They should never aim at any standard lower than that of the Sermon on the Mount. Christianity is emiently a practical religion: sound doctrine is its root and foundation, but holy living should always be its fruit; and if we would know what holy living is, let us often bethink ourselves who they are that Jesus calls "blessed."

MATTHEW V. 13—20.

13 Ye are the salt of the earth: but if the salt have lost his savour, wherewith shall it be salted? it is thenceforth good for nothing, but to be cast out, and to be trodden under foot of men.

14 Ye are the light of the world. A city that is set on an hill cannot be hid.

15 Neither do men light a candle, and put it under a bushel, but on a candlestick; and it giveth light unto all that are in the house.

16 Let your light so shine before men, that they may see your good works, and glorify your Father which is in heaven.

17 Think not that I am come to destroy the law, or the prophets: I am not come to destroy, but to fulfil.

18 For verily I say unto you, Till heaven and earth pass, one jot or one tittle shall in no wise pass from the law, till all be fulfilled.

19 Whosoever therefore shall break one of these least commandments, and shall teach men so, he shall be called the least in the kingdom of heaven: but whosoever shall do and teach *them*, the same shall be called great in the kingdom of heaven.

20 For I say unto you, That except your righteousness shall exceed *the righteousness* of the scribes and Pharisees, ye shall in no case enter into the kingdom of heaven.

THESE verses teach us, in the first place, *the character which true Christians must support and maintain in the world.*

The Lord Jesus tells us that true Christians are to be in the world like "salt." "Ye are the salt of the earth." Now salt has a peculiar taste of its own, utterly unlike anything else. When mingled with other substances it preserves them from corruption; it imparts a portion of its taste to everything it is mixed with. It is useful so long as it preserves its savour, but no longer. Are we true Christians? Then let us see here our office and our duties!

The Lord Jesus tells us that true Christians are to be in the world like light. "Ye are the light of the world." Now it is the property of light to be utterly distinct from darkness. The least spark in a dark room can be seen at once. Of all things created, light is the most useful: it fertilizes; it guides; it cheers. It was the first thing called into being. (Gen. i. 3.) Without it the world would be a gloomy blank. Are we true Christians? Then behold again our position and its responsibility!

Surely, if words mean anything, we are meant to learn from these two figures that there must be something marked, distinct, and peculiar about our character, if we are true Christians. It will never do to idle through life, thinking and living like others, if we mean to be owned by Christ as His people. Have we grace? Then it must be *seen.*—Have we the Spirit? Then there must be *fruit.*—Have we any saving religion? Then there must be a difference of habits, tastes, and turn of mind, between us and those who think only of the world.—It is perfectly clear that true Christianity is something more than being baptized and going to church. "Salt" and "light" evidently imply *peculiarity* both of heart and life, of faith and practice. We must dare to be singular and unlike the world, if we mean to be saved.

These verses teach us, in the second place, *the relation between Christ's teaching and that of the Old Testament.*

This is a point of great importance, and one about which great errors prevail. Our Lord clears up the point in one striking sentence: He says, "Think not that I am come to destroy the law, or the prophets: I am not come to destroy, but to fulfil." These are remarkable words. They were deeply important when spoken, as satisfying the natural anxiety of the Jews on the point; they will be deeply important as long as the world stands, as a testimony that the religion of the Old and New Testaments is one harmonious whole.

The Lord Jesus came to fulfil the predictions of the prophets, who had long foretold that a Saviour would one day appear.—He came to fulfil the ceremonial law, by becoming the great Sacrifice for sin, to which all the Mosaic offerings had ever pointed: He came to fulfil the moral law, by yielding to it a perfect obedience, which we could never have yielded,—and by paying the penalty for our breach of it with His atoning blood, which we could never have paid. In all these ways He exalted the law of God, and made its importance more evident even than it had been before. In a word, "He magnified the law and made it honourable." (Isaiah xlii. 21.)

There are deep lessons of wisdom to be learned from these words of our Lord about "the law and the prophets." Let us consider them well, and lay them up in our hearts.

For one thing, let us beware of despising the Old Testament, under any pretence whatever. Let us never listen to those who bid us throw it aside as an obsolete, antiquated, useless book. The religion of the Old Testament is the germ of Christianity. The Old Testament is the Gospel in the bud; the New Testament is the Gospel in full flower.—The Old Testament is the Gospel in the blade; the New Testament is the Gospel in full ear.—The saints in the Old Testament saw many things through a glass darkly; but they all looked by faith to the same Saviour, and were led by the same Spirit as ourselves. These are no light matters. Much infidelity begins with an ignorant contempt of the Old Testament.

For another thing, let us beware of despising the law of the Ten Commandments. Let us not suppose for a moment that it is set aside by the Gospel, or that Christians have nothing to do with it. The coming of Christ did not alter the position of the Ten Commandments one hair's breadth. If anything, it exalted and raised their authority. (Rom. iii. 31.) The law of the Ten Commandments is God's eternal measure of right and wrong. By it is the knowledge of sin; by it the Spirit shows men their need of Christ, and drives them to Him: to it Christ refers His people as their rule and guide for holy living. In its right place it is just as important as "the glorious Gospel."—It cannot save us: we cannot be justified by it; but never, never let us despise it. It is a symptom of an ignorant ministry, and an unhealthy state of religion, when the law is lightly esteemed. The true Christian "delights in the law of God." (Rom. vii. 22.)

In the last place, let us beware of supposing that the

Gospel has lowered the standard of personal holiness, and that the Christian is not intended to be as strict and particular about his daily life as the Jew. This is an immense mistake, but one that is unhappily very common. So far from this being the case, the sanctification of the New Testament saint ought to exceed that of him who has nothing but the Old Testament for his guide. The more light we have, the more we ought to love God: the more clearly we see our own complete and full forgiveness in Christ, the more heartily ought we to work for His glory. We know what it cost to redeem us far better than the Old Testament saints did. We have read what happened in Gethsemane and on Calvary, and they only saw it dimly and indistinctly as a thing yet to come. May we never forget our obligations! The Christian who is content with a low standard of personal holiness has got much to learn.

MATTHEW V. 21—37.

21 Ye have heard that it was said by them of old time, Thou shalt not kill; and whosoever shall kill shall be in danger of the judgment:

22 But I say unto you, That whosoever is angry with his brother without a cause shall be in danger of the judgment: and whosoever shall say to his brother, Raca, shall be in danger of the council: but whosoever shall say, Thou fool, shall be in danger of hell fire.

23 Therefore if thou bring thy gift to the altar, and there rememberest that thy brother hath ought against thee;

24 Leave there thy gift before the altar, and go thy way; first be reconciled to thy brother, and then come and offer thy gift.

25 Agree with thine adversary quickly, whiles thou art in the way with him; lest at any time the adversary deliver thee to the judge, and the judge deliver thee to the officer, and thou be cast into prison.

26 Verily I say unto thee, Thou shalt by no means come out thence, till thou hast paid the uttermost farthing.

27 Ye have heard that it was said by them of old time, Thou shalt not commit adultery:

28 But I say unto you, That whosoever looketh on a woman to lust after her hath committed adultery with her already in his heart.

29 And if thy right eye offend thee, pluck it out, and cast *it* from thee: for it is profitable for thee that one of thy members should perish, and not *that* thy whole body should be cast into hell.

30 And if thy right hand offend thee, cut it off, and cast *it* from thee: for it is profitable for thee that one of thy members should perish, and not *that* thy whole body should be cast into hell.

31 It hath been said, Whosoever

shall put away his wife, let him give her a writing of divorcement:
32 But I say unto you, That whosoever shall put away his wife, saving for the cause of fornication, causeth her to commit adultery: and whosoever shall marry her that is divorced committeth adultery.
33 Again, ye have heard that it hath been said by them of old time, Thou shalt not forswear thyself, but shalt perform unto the Lord thine oaths:
34 But I say unto you, Swear not at all; neither by heaven; for it is God's throne:
35 Nor by the earth; for it is his footstool: neither by Jerusalem; for it is the city of the great King.
36 Neither shalt thou swear by thy head, because thou canst not make one hair white or black.
37 But let your communication be, Yea, yea; Nay, nay: for whatsoever is more than these cometh of evil.

THESE verses deserve the closest attention of all readers of the Bible. A right understanding of the doctrines they contain lies at the very root of Christianity. The Lord Jesus here explains more fully the meaning of His words, "I came not to destroy the law, but to fulfil." He teaches us that His Gospel magnifies the Law, and exalts its authority: He shows us that the Law, as expounded by Him, was a far more spiritual and heart-searching rule than most of the Jews supposed; and He proves this by selecting three commandments out of the ten as examples of what He means.

He expounds *the sixth commandment.* Many thought that they kept this part of God's law so long as they did not commit actual murder. The Lord Jesus shows that its requirements go much further than this. It condemns all angry and passionate language, and especially when used without a cause. Let us mark this well. We may be perfectly innocent of taking life away, and yet be guilty of breaking the sixth commandment!

He expounds *the seventh commandment.* Many supposed that they kept this part of God's law if they did not actually commit adultery. The Lord Jesus teaches that we may break it in our thoughts, hearts, and imaginations, even when our outward conduct is moral and correct. The God with whom we have to do looks far beyond actions. With Him even a glance of the eye may be a sin!

He expounds *the third commandment.* Many fancied that they kept this part of God's law so long as they did not swear falsely, and performed their oaths. The Lord Jesus forbids all vain and light swearing altogether. All swearing by created things, even when God's name is not brought forward,—all calling upon God to witness, excepting on the most solemn occasions, is a great sin.

Now all this is very in structive. It ought to raise very serious reflections in our minds: it calls us loudly to use great searching of heart. And what does it teach?

It teaches us *the exceeding holiness of God.* He is a most pure and perfect Being, who sees faults and imperfections where man's eyes often see none. He reads our inward motives; He notes our words and thoughts, as well as our actions: "He desires truths in the inward parts." (Psa. li. 6.) It would be well if men would consider this part of God's character more than they do! There would be no room for pride, and self-righteousness, and carelessness, if men only saw God "as He is." (1 John iii. 2.)

It teaches us *the exceeding ignorance of man in spiritual things.* There are thousands and tens of thousands of professing Christians, it may be feared, who know no more of the requirements of God's law than the most ignorant Jews; they know the letter of the ten Commandments well enough; they fancy, like the young ruler, "all these have I kept from my youth up" (Matt. xix. 20): they never dream that it is possible to break the sixth and seventh commandments if they do not break them by outward acts or deeds. And so they live on satisfied with themselves, and quite content with their little bit of religion. Happy indeed are they who really understand God's law!

It teaches us *our exceeding need of the Lord Jesus Christ's atoning blood to save us.* What man or woman upon earth can ever stand before such a God as this, and plead "not guilty"? Who is there that has ever grown to years of discretion, and not broken the commandments thousands of times? "There is none righteous, no, not one." (Rom. iii. 10.) Without a mighty Mediator we should every one be condemned in the judgment day. Ignorance of the real meaning of the Law is one plain reason why so many do not value the Gospel, and content themselves with a little formal Christianity. They do not see the strictness and holiness of God's ten Commandments: if they did, they would never rest till they were safe in Christ.

In the last place, this passage teaches us *the exceeding importance of avoiding all occasions of sin.* If we really desire to be holy, we must "take heed to our ways, that we sin not with our tongues." (Psa. xxxix. 1.) We must be ready to make up quarrels and disagreements, lest they gradually lead on to greater evils. "The beginning of strife is as when one letteth out water." (Prov. xvii. 14.) We must labour to crucify our flesh and mortify our members, to make any sacrifice and endure any bodily inconvenience rather than sin: we must keep our lips as it were with a bridle, and exercise an hourly strictness over our words. Let men call us precise, if they will, for so doing: let them say, if they please, that we are "too particular." We need not be moved. We are merely doing as our Lord Jesus Christ bids us, and, if this is the case, we have no cause to be ashamed.

MATTHEW V. 38—48.

38 Ye have heard that it hath been said, An eye for an eye, and a tooth for a tooth:

39 But I say unto you, That ye resist not evil: but whosoever shall smite thee on thy right cheek, turn to him the other also.

40 And if any man will sue thee at the law, and take away thy coat, let him have *thy* cloak also.

41 And whosoever shall compel thee to go a mile, go with him twain.

42 Give to him that asketh thee, and from him that would borrow of thee turn not thou away.

43 Ye have heard that it hath been said, Thou shalt love thy neighbour, and hate thine enemy.

44 But I say unto you, Love your enemies, bless them that curse you, do good to them that hate you, and pray for them which despitefully use you, and persecute you;

45 That ye may be the children of your Father which is in heaven: for he maketh his sun to rise on the evil and on the good, and sendeth rain on the just and on the unjust.

46 For if ye love them which love you, what reward have ye? do not even the publicans the same?

47 And if ye salute your brethren only, what do ye more *than others?* do not even the publicans so?

48 Be ye therefore perfect even as your Father which is in heaven is perfect.

WE have here our Lord Jesus Christ's rules for our conduct one towards another. He that would know how he ought to feel and act towards his fellow-men, should often study these verses. They deserve to be written in letters of gold: they have extorted praise even from the enemies of Christianity. Let us mark well what they contain.

The Lord Jesus *forbids everything like an unforgiving and revengeful spirit.* "I say unto you, That ye resist not evil." A readiness to resent injuries, a quickness in taking offence, a quarrelsome and contentious disposition, a keenness in asserting our rights,—all, all are contrary to the mind of Christ. The world may see no harm in these habits of mind; but they do not become the character of the Christian. Our Master says, "Resist not evil."

The Lord Jesus *enjoins on us a spirit of universal love and charity.* "I say unto you, Love your enemies."

We ought to put away all malice: we ought to return good for evil, and blessing for cursing. Moreover we are not to love in word only, but in deed; we are to deny ourselves, and take trouble, in order to be kind and courteous: if any man "compel thee to go a mile, go with him twain." We are to put up with much and bear much, rather than hurt another, or give offence. In all things we are to be unselfish. Our thought must never be, "How do others behave to me?" but "What would Christ have me to do?"

A standard of conduct like this may seem, at first sight, extravagantly high. But we must never content ourselves with aiming at one lower. We must observe the two weighty arguments by which our Lord backs up this part of His instruction. They deserve serious attention.

For one thing, if we do not aim at the spirit and temper which are here recommended, *we are not yet children of God.* What does our "Father which is in heaven" do? He is kind to all: He sends rain on good and on evil alike; He causes "His sun" to shine on all without distinction.—A child should be like his father: but where is our likeness to our Father in heaven if we cannot show mercy and kindness to everybody? Where is the evidence that we are new creatures if we lack charity? It is altogether wanting. We must yet be "born again." (John iii. 7.)

For another thing, if we do not aim at the spirit and temper here recommended, *we are manifestly yet of the world.* "What do ye more than others?" is our Lord's solemn question. Even those who have no religion can "love those who love them:" they can do good and show kindness when affection or interest moves them. But a

Christian ought to be influenced by higher principles than these.—Do we flinch from the test? Do we find it impossible to do good to our enemies? If that be the case we may be sure we have yet to be converted. As yet we have not "received the Spirit of God." (1 Cor. ii. 12.)

There is much in all this which calls loudly for solemn reflection. There are few passages of Scripture so calculated to raise in our minds humbling thoughts. We have here a lovely picture of the Christian as he ought to be. We cannot look at it without painful feelings: we must all allow that it differs widely from the Christian as he is. Let us carry away from it two general lessons.

In the first place, if the spirit of these ten verses were more continually remembered by true believers *they would recommend Christianity to the world far more than they do.* We must not allow ourselves to suppose that the least words in this passage are trifling and of small moment: they are not so. It is attention to the spirit of this passage which makes our religion beautiful: it is the neglect of the things which it contains by which our religion is deformed. Unfailing courtesy, kindness, tenderness, and consideration for others, are some of the greatest ornaments to the character of a child of God. The world can understand these things if it cannot understand doctrine. There is no religion in rudeness, roughness, bluntness, and incivility. The perfection of practical Christianity consists in attending to the little duties of holiness as well as to the great.

In the second place, if the spirit of these ten verses had more dominion and power in the world, *how much happier the world would be than it is.* Who does not know that quarrellings, strifes, selfishness, and unkindness, cause half the miseries by which mankind is visited? Who can fail to see that nothing would so much tend to increase happiness as the spread of Christian love, such as is here recommended by our Lord? Let us remember this. Those who fancy that true religion has any tendency to make men unhappy, are greatly mistaken: it is the absence of it that does this, and not the presence. True religion has the directly contrary effect: it tends to promote peace, and charity, and kindness, and goodwill among men. The more men are brought under the teaching of the Holy Spirit, the more they will love one another, and the more happy they will be.

MATTHEW VI. 1—8.

1 Take heed that ye do not your alms before men, to be seen of them: otherwise ye have no reward of your Father which is in heaven.

2 Therefore when thou doest *thine* alms, do not sound a trumpet before thee, as the hypocrites do in the synagogues and in the streets, that they may have glory of men. Verily I say unto you, They have their reward.

3 But when thou doest alms, let not thy left hand know what thy right hand doeth:

4 That thine alms may be in secret: and thy Father which seeth in secret himself shall reward thee openly.

5 And when thou prayest, thou shall not be as the hypocrites *are*: for they love to pray standing in the synagogues and in the corners of the streets, that they may be seen of men. Verily I say unto you, They have their reward.

6 But thou, when thou prayest, enter into thy closet, and when thou hast shut thy door, pray to thy Father which is in secret: and thy Father which seeth in secret shall reward thee openly.

7 But when ye pray, use not vain repetitions, as the heathen *do*: for they think that they shall be heard for their much speaking.

8 Be not ye therefore like unto them: for your Father knoweth what things ye have need of, before ye ask him.

In this part of the Sermon on the Mount the Lord Jesus gives us instruction on two subjects: one is that of giving alms; the other is that of prayer. Both were subjects to which the Jews attached great importance: both in themselves deserve the serious attention of all professing Christians.

Let us observe that our Lord takes it for granted *that all who call themselves His disciples will give alms.* He assumes as a matter of course that they will think it a solemn duty to give, according to their means, to relieve the wants of others; the only point He handles is the manner in which the duty should be done. This is a weighty lesson: it condemns the selfish stinginess of many in the matter of giving money. How many are "rich towards themselves," but poor towards God! How many never give a farthing to do good to the bodies and souls of men! And have such persons any right to be called Christians in their present state of mind? It may well be doubted. A giving Saviour should have giving disciples.

Let us observe, again, that our Lord takes it for granted *that all who call themselves His disciples will pray.* He assumes this also as a matter of course: He only gives directions as to the best way of praying. This is another lesson which deserves to be continually remembered: it teaches plainly that prayerless people are not genuine Christians. It is not enough to join in the prayers of the congregation on Sundays, or attend the prayers of a family on week days: there must be private prayer also. Without this we may be outward members of Christ's Church, but we are not living members of Christ.

But what are the rules laid down for our guidance about almsgiving and praying? They are few and simple; but they contain much matter for thought.

In giving, *everything like ostentation is to be abhorred and avoided.* "When thou doest thine alms, do not sound a trumpet before thee." We are not to give as if we wished everybody to see how liberal and charitable we are, and desire the praise of our fellow-men. We are to shun everything like display: we are to give quietly, and make as little noise as possible about our charities; we are to aim at the spirit of the proverbial saying, "Let not thy left hand know what thy right hand doeth."

In praying, *the principal object to be sought is to be alone with God.* "When thou prayest, enter into thy closet." We should endeavour to find some place where no mortal eye sees us, and where we can pour out our hearts with the feeling that no one is looking at us but God.—This is a rule which many find it very difficult to follow; the poor man and the servant often find it almost impossible to be really alone; but it is a rule which we must make great efforts to obey. Necessity, in such cases, is often the mother of invention. When a person has a real will to find some place where he can be in secret with his God, he will generally find a way.

In all our duties, whether giving or praying, the great thing to be kept in mind is, *that we have to do with a heart-searching and all-knowing God.* "Our Father seeth in secret." Everything like formality, affectation, or mere bodily service, is abominable and worthless in God's sight. He takes no account of the quantity of money we give, or the quantity of words we use: the one thing at which His all-seeing eye looks is the nature of our motives and the state of our hearts.

May we all remember these things. Here lies a rock, on which many are continually making spiritual shipwreck. They flatter themselves that all must be right with their souls, if they only perform a certain amount of "religious duties:" they forget that God does not regard the quantity, but the quality of our service. His favour is not to be bought, as many seem to suppose, by the formal repetition of a number of words, or by the self-righteous payment of a sum of money to a charitable institution. Where are our hearts?—Are we doing all, whether we give or pray, "as to the Lord, and not to men?"—Do we realize the eye of God?—Do we simply and solely desire to please Him, who "seeth in secret," and by whom "actions are weighed"? (1 Sam. ii. 3.)—Are we sincere?—These are the sort of questions with which we should often ply our souls.

MATTHEW VI. 9—15.

9 After this manner therefore pray ye: Our Father which art in heaven, Hallowed be thy name.
10 Thy kingdom come. Thy will be done in earth, as *it is* in heaven.
11 Give us this day our daily bread.
12 And forgive us our debts, as we forgive our debtors.
13 And lead us not into temptation; but deliver us from evil: For thine is the kingdom, and the power, and the glory, for ever. Amen.
14 For if ye forgive men their trespasses, your heavenly Father will also forgive you:
15 But if ye forgive not men their trespasses, neither will your Father forgive your trespasses.

THESE verses are few in number, and soon read, but they are of immense importance. They contain that wonderful pattern of prayer with which the Lord Jesus has supplied His people, commonly called "The Lord's Prayer."

Perhaps no part of Scripture is so well known as this: its words are familiar, wherever Christianity is found; thousands and tens of thousands, who never saw a Bible, or heard the pure Gospel, are acquainted with "Our Father," or "Paternoster." Happy would it be for the world if this prayer was as well known in the spirit as it is in the letter.

No part of Scripture is so full, and so simple at the same time as this: it is the first prayer which we learn to offer up, when we are little children: here is its simplicity. It contains the germ of everything which the most advanced saint can desire: here is its fulness. The more we ponder every word it contains the more we shall feel "this prayer is of God."

The Lord's Prayer consists of ten parts or sentences. There is one declaration of the Being to whom we pray; there are three prayers respecting His name, His kingdom, and His will; there are four prayers respecting our daily wants, our sins, or weakness, and our dangers; there is one profession of our feeling towards others; there is one concluding ascription of praise.—In all these parts we are taught to say "we," and "our." We are to remember others, as well as ourselves.—On each of these parts a volume might be written. We must content ourselves at present with taking up sentence after sentence, and marking out the lessons which each sentence contains.

The first sentence declares *to whom we are to pray:* "Our Father which art in heaven." We are not to pray to saints and angels, but to the everlasting Father, the Father of spirits, the Lord of heaven and earth. We call Him Father in the lowest sense, as our Creator: as St. Paul told the Athenians, "in Him we live, and move, and have our being,—we are also His offspring." (Acts xvii. 28.) We call Him Father in the highest sense, as the Father of our Lord Jesus Christ, reconciling us to Himself through the death of His Son. (Coloss. i. 20—22.) We profess that which the old Testament saints only saw dimly and afar off,—we profess to be His children by faith in Christ, and to have "the Spirit of adoption, whereby we cry, Abba, Father." (Rom. viii. 15.) This, we must never forget, is the sonship that we must desire, if we would be saved. Without faith in Christ's blood and union with Him, it is useless to talk of trusting in the "Fatherhood" of God.

The second sentence is *a petition respecting God's name:* "Hallowed be Thy name." By the "Name" of God we mean all those attributes under which He is revealed to us,—His power, wisdom, holiness, justice, mercy, and truth. By asking that they may be "hallowed," we mean that they may be made known and glorified. The glory of God is the first thing that God's children should desire. It is the object of one of our Lord's own prayers: "Father, glorify Thy name." (John xii. 28.) It is the purpose for which the world was created; it is the end for which the saints are called and converted: it is the chief thing we should seek,—that "God in all things may be glorified." (1 Peter iv. 11.)

The third sentence is *a petition concerning God's kingdom:* "Thy kingdom come." By His kingdom we mean, first, the kingdom of grace which God sets up and maintains in the hearts of all living members of Christ, by His Spirit and Word. But we mean chiefly, the kingdom of glory which shall one day be set up, when Jesus shall come the second time, and "all shall know Him from the least to the greatest." (Heb. viii. 11.) This is the time when sin, and sorrow, and Satan shall be cast out of the world. It is the time when the Jews shall be converted, and the fulness of the Gentiles shall come in (Rom. xi. 25), and a time that is above all things to be desired. It therefore fills a foremost place in the Lord's Prayer. We ask that which is expressed in the words of the Burial Service: "that it may please God to hasten His kingdom."

The fourth sentence is *a petition concerning God's will:* "Thy will be done in earth, as it is in heaven." We here pray that God's laws may be obeyed by men as perfectly, readily, and unceasingly as they are by angels in heaven. We ask that those who now obey not His laws may be taught to obey them, and that those who do obey them may obey them better. Our truest happiness is perfect submission to God's will, and it is the highest charity to pray that all mankind may know it, obey it, and submit to it.

The fifth sentence is *a petition respecting our own daily wants:* "Give us this day our daily bread." We are here taught to acknowledge our entire dependence on God for the supply of our daily necessities. As Israel required daily manna, so we require daily "bread." We confess that we are poor, weak, wanting creatures, and beseech Him who is our Maker to take care of us. We ask for "bread," as the simplest of our wants, and in that word we include all that our bodies require.

The sixth sentence is *a petition respecting our sins:* "Forgive us our debts." We confess that we are sinners, and need daily grants of pardon and forgiveness. This is a part of the Lord's Prayer which deserves especially to be remembered. It condemns all self-righteousness and self-justifying. We are instructed here to keep up a continual habit of confession at the throne of grace, and a continual habit of seeking mercy and remission. Let this never be forgotten. We need daily to "wash our feet." (John xiii. 10.)

The seventh sentence is *a profession respecting our own feelings towards others:* we ask our Father to "Forgive us our debts, as we forgive our debtors." This is the only profession in the whole prayer, and the only part on which our Lord comments and dwells, when He has concluded the prayer. The object of it is to remind us that we must not expect our prayers for forgiveness to be heard if we pray with malice and spite in our hearts towards others. To pray in such a frame of mind is mere formality and hypocrisy: it is even worse than hypocrisy; it is as much as saying, "Do not forgive me at all." Our prayers are nothing without charity. We must not expect to be forgiven, if we cannot forgive.

The eighth sentence is *a petition respectiug our weakness:* "Lead us not into temptation." It teaches us that we are liable, at all times, to be led astray and to fall: it instructs us to confess our infirmity, and beseech God to hold us up, and not allow us to run into sin. We ask Him, who orders all things in heaven and earth, to restrain us from going into that which would injure our souls, and never to suffer us to be "tempted above that which we are able to bear." (1 Cor. x. 13.)

The ninth sentence is *a petition respecting our dangers:* "Deliver us from evil." We are here taught to ask God to deliver us from the evil that is in the world, the evil that is within our own hearts, and not least from that evil one, the devil. We confess that, so long as we are in the body, we are constantly seeing, hearing, and feeling the presence of evil. It is about us, and within us, and around us on every side; and we entreat Him, who alone can preserve us, to be continually delivering us from its power. (John xvii. 15.)

The last sentence is *an ascription of praise:* "Thine is the kingdom, and the power, and the glory." We declare in these words our belief that the kingdoms of this world are the rightful property of our Father; that to Him alone belongs all "power;" and that He alone deserves to receive all "glory." And we conclude by offering to Him the profession of our hearts, that we give Him all honour and praise, and rejoice that He is King of kings, and Lord of lords.

And now let us examine ourselves, and see whether we really desire to have the things which we are taught to ask for in the Lord's Prayer. Thousands, it may be feared, repeat these words daily as a form, but never consider what they are saying. They care nothing for the "glory," the "kingdom," or the "will" of God: they have no sense of dependence, sinfulness, weakness, or danger; they have no love or charity towards their enemies: and yet they repeat the Lord's Prayer! These things ought not to be so. May we resolve that, by God's help, our hearts shall always go together with our lips! Happy is he who can really call God his "Father" through Jesus Christ his Saviour, and can therefore say a heartfelt "Amen" to all that the Lord's Prayer contains.

MATTHEW VI. 16—24.

16 Moreover when ye fast, be not, as the hypocrites, of a sad countenance: for they disfigure their faces, that they may appear unto men to fast. Verily I say unto you, They have their reward.
17 But thou, when thou fastest, anoint thine head, and wash thy face:
18 That thou appear not unto men to fast, but unto thy Father which is in secret: and thy Father, which seeth in secret, shall reward thee openly.
19 Lay not up for yourselves treasures upon earth, where moth and rust doth corrupt, and where thieves break through and steal:
20 But lay up for yourselves treasures in heaven, where neither moth nor rust doth corrupt, and where thieves do not break through nor steal:
21 For where your treasure is, there will your heart be also.
22 The light of the body is the eye: if therefore thine eye be single, thy whole body shall be full of light,
23 But if thine eye be evil, thy whole body shall be full of darkness. If therefore the light that is in thee be darkness, how great *is* that darkness!
24 No man can serve two masters: for either he will hate the one, and love the other, or else he will hold to the one, and despise the other. Ye cannot serve God and mammon.

THERE are three subjects brought before us in this part of our Lord's Sermon on the Mount. These three are fasting, worldliness, and singleness of purpose in religion.

Fasting, or occasional abstinence from food, in order to bring the body into subjection to the spirit, is a practice frequently mentioned in the Bible, and generally in connection with prayer. David fasted when his child was sick; Daniel fasted when he sought special light from God; Paul and Barnabas fasted when they appointed elders; Esther fasted before going in to Ahasuerus.—It is a subject about which we find no direct command in the New Testament. It seems to be left to every one's discretion, whether he will fast or not.—In this absence of direct command, we may see great wisdom. Many a poor man never has enough to eat, and it would be an insult to tell him to fast: many a sickly person can hardly be kept well with the closest attention to diet, and could not fast without bringing on illness.—It is a matter in which every one must be persuaded in his own mind, and not rashly condemn others who do not agree with him.—One thing only must never be forgotten: those who fast should do it quietly, secretly, and without ostentation. Let them not "appear to men" to fast. Let them not fast to man, but to God.

Worldliness is one of the greatest dangers that beset man's soul. It is no wonder that we find our Lord speaking strongly about it: it is an insidious, specious, plausible enemy; it seems so innocent to pay close attention to our business! It seems so harmless to seek our happiness in this world, so long as we keep clear of open sins!—Yet here is a rock on which many make shipwreck to all eternity. They "lay up treasure on earth," and forget to "lay up treasure in heaven." May we all remember this! Where are our hearts? What do we love best? Are our chiefest affections on things in earth, or things in heaven? Life or death depends on the answer we can give to these questions. If our treasure is earthly, our hearts will be earthly also. "Where your treasure is, there will your heart be."

Singleness of purpose is one great secret of spiritual prosperity. If our eyes do not see distinctly, we cannot walk without stumbling and falling. If we attempt to work for two different masters, we are sure to give satisfaction to neither. It is just the same with respect to our souls. We cannot serve Christ and the world at the same time: it is vain to attempt it. The thing cannot be done: the ark and Dagon will never stand together. God must be king over our hearts: His law, His will His precepts, must receive our first attention; then, and not till then, everything in our inward man will fall into its right place. Unless our hearts are so ordered, everything will be in confusion. "Thy whole body shall be full of darkness."

Let us learn from our Lord's instructions about fasting, *the great importance of cheerfulness* in our religion. Those words, "anoint thy head, and wash thy face," are full of deep meaning. They should teach us to aim at letting men see that Christianity makes us happy. Never let us forget that there is no religion in looking melancholy and gloomy. Are we dissatisfied with Christ's wages, and Christ's service? Surely not! Then let us not look as if we were.

Let us learn from our Lord's caution about worldliness, *what need we have to watch and pray against an earthly spirit.* What are the vast majority of professing Christians round us doing? "They are laying up treasure on earth:" there can be no mistake about it; their tastes, their ways, their habits, tell a fearful tale. They are not "laying up treasure in heaven." Let us beware that we do not sink into hell by paying excessive attention to lawful things. Open transgression of God's law slays its thousands, but worldliness its tens of thousands.

Let us learn from our Lord's words about the "single eye," *the true secret of the failures* which so many Christians seem to make in their religion. There are failures, in all quarters. There are thousands in our churches uncomfortable, ill at ease, and dissatisfied with themselves; and they hardly know why. The reason is revealed here: they are trying to keep in with both sides; they are endeavouring to please God and please man, to serve Christ and serve the world at the same time.

Let us not commit this mistake. Let us be decided, thorough-going, uncompromising followers of Christ. Let our motto be that of Paul: "One thing I do." (Phil. iii. 13.) Then we shall be happy Christians: we shall feel the sun shining on our faces; heart, head, and conscience will all be full of light. Decision is the secret of happiness in religion. Be decided for Christ, and "thy whole body shall be full of light."

MATTHEW VI. 25—34.

25 Therefore I say unto you, Take no thought for your life, what ye shall eat, or what ye shall drink; nor yet for your body, what ye shall put on. Is not the life more than meat, and the body than raiment?

26 Behold the fowls of the air: for they sow not, neither do they reap, nor gather into barns; yet your heavenly Father feedeth them. Are ye not much better than they?

27 Which of you by taking thought can add one cubit unto his stature?

28 And why take ye thought for raiment? Consider the lilies of the field, how they grow; they toil not, neither do they spin:

29 And yet I say unto you, That even Solomon in all his glory was not arrayed like one of these.

30 Wherefore, if God so clothe the grass of the field, which to-day is, and to-morrow is cast into the oven, *shall* he not much more *clothe* you, O ye of little faith?

31 Therefore take no thought saying, What shall we eat? or What shall we drink? or Wherewithal shall we be clothed?

32 (For after all these things do the Gentiles seek:) for your heavenly Father knoweth that ye have need of all these things.

33 But seek ye first the kingdom of God, and his righteousness; and all these things shall be added unto you.

34 Take therefore no thought for the morrow: for the morrow shall take thought for the things of itself. Sufficient unto the day *is* the evil thereof.

THESE verses are a striking example of the combined wisdom and compassion of our Lord Jesus Christ's teaching. He knows the heart of a man: He knows that we are always ready to turn off warnings against worldliness, by the argument that we cannot help being anxions about the things of this life. "Have we not our families to provide for? Must not our bodily wants be supplied? How can we possibly get through life if we think first of our souls?" The Lord Jesus foresaw such thoughts, and furnished an answer.

He forbids us *to keep up an anxious spirit* about the things of this world. Four times over He says, "Take no thought." About life,—about food,—about clothing,—about the morrow, "take no thought." Be not over-careful: be not over-anxious. Prudent provision for the future is right: wearing, corroding, self-tormenting anxiety is wrong.

He reminds us of *the providential care that God continually takes of everything that He has created.* Has He given us "life"? Then He will surely not let us want anything necessary for its maintenance.—Has He given us a "body"? Then He will surely not let us die for want of clothing. He that calls us into being will doubtless find meat to feed us.

He points out *the uselessness of over-anxiety.* Our life is certainly in God's hand; all the care in the world will not make us continue a minute beyond the time which God has appointed. We cannot add one hour to our lives: we shall not die till our work is done.

He sends us *to the birds of the air* for instruction. They make no provision for the future: "they sow not, neither do they reap;" they lay up no stores against time yet to come; they do not "gather into barns:" they literally live from day to day on what they can pick up, by using the instinct God has put in them. They ought to teach us that no man doing his duty in the station to which God has called him, shall ever be allowed to come to poverty.

He bids us observe *the flowers of the field.* Year after year they are decked with the gayest colours, without the slightest labour or exertion on their part: "they toil not, neither do they spin." God, by His almighty power, clothes them with beauty every season. The same God is the Father of all believers: why should they doubt that He is able to provide them with raiment, as well as the "lilies of the field"? He who takes thought for perishable flowers, will surely not neglect the bodies in which dwell immortal souls.

He suggests to us that over-carefulness about the things of this world is *most unworthy of a Christian.* One great feature of heathenism is living for the present. Let the heathen, if he will, be anxious: he knows nothing of a Father in heaven; but let the Christian, who has clearer light and knowledge, give proof of it by his faith and contentment. When bereaved of those whom we love, we are not to "sorrow as others who have no hope." (1 Thess. iv. 13.) When tried by anxieties about this life, we are not to be over-careful, as if we had no God, and no Christ.

He offers us *a gracious promise* as a remedy against an anxious spirit. He assures us that if we "seek first" and foremost to have a place in the kingdom of grace and glory, everything that we really want in this world shall be given to us: it shall be "added," over and above our heavenly inheritance. "All things shall work together for good to them that love God." "No good thing will He withhold from them that walk uprightly." (Rom. viii. 28; Psalm lxxxiv. 11.)

Last of all, He seals up all His instruction on this subject by laying down *one of the wisest maxims.* "The morrow shall take thought for the things of itself. Sufficient unto the day is the evil thereof." We are not to carry cares before they come: we are to attend to to-day's business, and leave to-morrow's anxieties till to-morrow dawns. We may die before to-morrow: we know not what may happen on the morrow; this only we may be assured of,—that if to-morrow brings a cross, He who sends it can and will send grace to bear it.

In all this passage there is a treasury of golden lessons. Let us seek to use them in our daily life: let us not only read them, but turn them to practical account; let us watch and pray against an anxious and over-careful spirit. It deeply concerns our happiness to do so. Half our miseries are caused by fancying things that we think are coming upon us: half the things that we expect to come upon us never come at all. Where is our faith? Where is our confidence in our Saviour's words? We may well take shame to ourselves, when we read these verses, and then look into our hearts. We may be sure that David's words are true: "I have been young, and now am old; yet have I not seen the righteous forsaken, nor his seed begging bread." (Psalm xxxvii. 25.)

MATTHEW VII. 1—11.

1 Judge not, that ye be not judged.
2 For with what judgment ye judge, ye shall be judged: and with what measure ye mete, it shall be measured to you again.
3 And why beholdest thou the mote that is in thy brother's eye, but considerest not the beam that is in thine own eye?
4 Or how wilt thou say to thy brother, Let me pull out the mote out of thine eye: and, behold, a beam *is* in thine own eye?
5 Thou hypocrite, first cast out the beam out of thine own eye; and then shalt thou see clearly to cast out the mote out of thy brother's eye.
6 Give not that which is holy unto the dogs, neither cast ye your pearls before swine, lest they trample them under their feet, and turn again and rend you.
7 Ask, and it shall be given you: seek, and ye shall find; knock, and it shall be opened unto you:
8 For every one that asketh receiveth; and he that seeketh findeth; and to him that knocketh it shall be opened.

9 Or what man is there of you, whom if his son ask bread, will he give him a stone?
10 Or if he ask a fish, will he give him a serpent?
11 If ye then, being evil, know how to give good gifts unto your children, how much more shall your Father which is in heaven give good things to them that ask him?

THE first portion of these verses is one of those passages of Scripture which we must be careful not to strain beyond its proper meaning. It is frequently abused and misapplied by the enemies of true religion. It is possible to press the words of the Bible so far that they yield not medicine, but poison.

When our Lord says, "Judge not," He does not mean that it is wrong, under any circumstances, to pass an unfavourable judgment on the conduct and opinions of others. We ought to have decided opinions: we are to "prove all things;" we are to "try the spirits." (1 Thess. v. 21; 1 John iv. 1.)—Nor yet does He mean that it is wrong to reprove the sins and faults of others until we are perfect and faultless ourselves. Such an interpretation would contradict other parts of Scripture: it would make it impossible to condemn error and false doctrine; it would debar any one from attempting the office of a minister or a judge. The earth would be "given into the hands of the wicked" (Job ix. 24): heresy would flourish: wrong-doing would abound.

What our Lord means to condemn is a *censorious and fault-finding spirit.* A readiness to blame others for trifling offences or matters of indifference, a habit of passing rash and hasty judgments, a disposition to magnify the errors and infirmities of our neighbours, and make the worst of them,—this is what our Lord forbids. It was common among the Pharisees: it has always been common from their day down to the present time. We must watch against it. We should "believe all things," and "hope all things" about others, and be very slow to find fault. This is Christian charity. (1 Cor. xiii. 7.)

The second portion of these verses teaches us *the importance of exercising discretion as to the persons with whom we speak on the subject of religion.* Everything is beautiful in its place and season. Our zeal is to be tempered by a prudent consideration of times, places, and persons. "Reprove not a scorner," says Solomon, "lest he hate thee." (Prov. ix. 8.) It is not everybody to whom it is wise to open our minds on spiritual matters. There are many, who from violent tempers, or openly profligate habits, are utterly incapable of valuing the things of the Gospel: they will even fly into a passion, and run into greater excesses of sin, if we try to do good to their souls; to name the name of Christ to such people is truly to "cast pearls before swine." It does them not good, but harm: it rouses all their corruption, and makes them angry; in short, they are like the Jews at Corinth (Acts xviii. 6), or like Nabal, of whom it is written, that he was "such a son of Belial, that a man could not speak unto him." (1 Sam. xxv. 17.)

The lesson before us is one which it is peculiarly difficult to use in the proper way. The right application of it needs great wisdom. We are most of us far more likely to err on the side of over-caution than of over-zeal: we are generally far more disposed to remember the "time to be silent," than the "time to speak." It is lesson, however, which ought to stir up a spirit of self inquiry in all our hearts. Do we ourselves never check our friends from giving us good advice, by our moroseness and irritability of temper? Have we never obliged others to hold their peace and say nothing, by our pride and impatient contempt of counsel? Have we never turned against our kind advisers, and silenced them by our violence and passion? We may well fear that we have often erred in this matter.

The last portion of these verses teaches us *the duty of prayer, and the rich encouragements there are to pray.* There is a beautiful connection between this lesson and that which goes before it. Would we know when to be "silent," and when to "speak,"—when to bring forward "holy things," and produce our "pearls"? We must pray.—This is a subject to which the Lord Jesus evidently attaches great importance: the language that He uses is a plain proof of this. He employs three different words to express the idea of prayer: "Ask,"—"Seek,"—"Knock." He holds out the broadest, fullest promise to those who pray: "Every one that asketh receiveth." He illustrates God's readiness to hear our prayers by an argument drawn from the well-known practice of parents on earth: "evil" and selfish as they are by nature, they do not neglect the wants of their children according to the flesh; much more will a God of love and mercy attend to the cries of those who are His children by grace!

Let us take special notice of these words of our Lord about prayer. Few of His sayings, perhaps, are so well known and so often repeated as this. The poorest and most unlearned can generally tell us, that "if we do not seek we shall not find." But what is the good of knowing it, if we do not use it? Knowledge, not improved and well employed, will only increase our condemnation at the last day.

Do we know anything of this "asking, seeking, and knocking"? Why should we not? There is nothing so simple and plain as praying, if a man really has a will to pray. There is nothing unhappily, which men are so slow to do: they will use many of the forms of religion, attend many ordinances, do many things that are right, before they will do this; and yet without this, no soul can be saved!

Do we ever really pray? If not, we shall at last be without excuse before God, except we repent. We shall not be condemned for not doing what we could not have done, or not knowing what we could not have known; but we shall find that one main reason why we are lost is this,—that we never "asked" that we might be saved.

Do we indeed pray? Then let us pray on, and not faint. It is not lost labour; it is not useless: it will bear fruit after many days. Those words have never yet failed, "Every one that asketh receiveth."

MATTHEW VII. 12—20.

12 Therefore all things whatsoever ye would that men should do to you, do ye even so to them: for this is the law and the prophets.

13 Enter ye in at the strait gate: for wide is the gate, and broad is the way, that leadeth to destruction, and many there be which go in thereat:

14 Because strait is the gate, and narrow is the way, which leadeth unto life, and few there be that find it.

15 Beware of false prophets, which come to you in sheep's clothing, but inwardly they are ravening wolves.

16 Ye shall know them by their fruits. Do men gather grapes of thorns, or figs of thistles?

17 Even so every good tree bringeth forth good fruit; but a corrupt tree bringeth forth evil fruit.
18 A good tree cannot bring forth evil fruit, neither can a corrupt tree bring forth good fruit.
19 Every tree that bringeth not forth good fruit is hewn down, and cast into the fire.
20 Wherefore by their fruits ye shall know them.

In this part of the Sermon on the Mount our Lord begins to draw His discourse to a conclusion. The lessons He here enforces on our notice, are broad, general, and full of the deepest wisdom. Let us mark them in succession.

He lays down *a general principle for our guidance* in all doubtful questions between man and man. We are "to do to others as we would have others do to us." We are not to deal with others as others deal with us: this is mere selfishness and heathenism. We are to deal with others as we would like others to deal with us: this is real Christianity.

This is a golden rule indeed! It does not merely forbid all petty malice and revenge, all cheating and overreaching: it does much more. It settles a hundred difficult points, which in a world like this are continually arising between man and man; it prevents the necessity of laying down endless little rules for our conduct in specific cases; it sweeps the whole debateable ground with one mighty principle; it shows us a balance and measure, by which every one may see at once what is his duty.—Is there a thing we would not like our neighbour to do to us? Then let us always remember that this is the thing we ought not to do to him. Is there a thing we would like him to do to us? Then this is the very thing we ought to do to him.—How many intricate questions would be decided at once if this rule were honestly used!

In the second place, our Lord gives us a *general caution against the way of the many in religion.* It is not enough to think as others think, and do as others do. It must not satisfy us to follow the fashion, and swim with the stream of those among whom we live. He tells us that the way that leads to everlasting life is "narrow," and "few" travel in it; He tells us that the way that leads to everlasting destruction is "broad," and full of travellers: "Many there be that go in thereat."

These are fearful truths! They ought to raise great searchings of heart in the minds of all who hear them. —"Which way am I going? By what road am I travelling?"—In one or other of the two ways here described, every one of us may be found. May God give us an honest, self-inquiring spirit, and show us what we are!

We may well tremble and be afraid, if our religion is that of the multitude. If we can say no more than this that "we go where others go, and worship where others worship, and hope we shall do as well as others at last," we are literally pronouncing our own condemnation. What is this but being in the "broad way"? What is this but being in the road whose end is "destruction"? Our religion at present is not saving religion.

We have no reason to be discouraged and cast down if the religion we profess is not popular and few agree with us. We must remember the words of our Lord Jesus Christ in this passage: "The gate is strait." Repentance, and faith in Christ, and holiness of life, have never been fashionable. The true flock of Christ has always been small. It must not move us to find that we are reckoned singular, and peculiar, and bigoted, and narrow minded. This is "the narrow way." Surely it is better to enter into life eternal with a few, than to go to "destruction" with a great company.

In the last place, the Lord Jesus gives us *a general warning against false teachers in the Church.* We are to "beware of false prophets." The connection between this passage and the preceding one is striking. Would we keep clear of this "broad way"? We must beware of false prophets. They will arise: they began in the days of the apostles; even then the seeds of error were sown. They have appeared continually ever since. We must be prepared for them, and be on our guard.

This is a warning which is much needed. There are thousands who seem ready to believe anything in religion, if they hear it from an ordained minister. They forget that clergymen may err as much as laymen: they are not infallible. Their teaching must be weighed in the balance of Holy Scripture: they are to be followed and believed, so long as their doctrine agrees with the Bible, but not a minute longer. We are to try them "by their fruits." Sound doctrine and holy living are the marks of true prophets.—Let us remember this. Our minister's mistakes will not excuse our own. "If the blind lead the blind, both shall fall into the ditch." (Matt. xv. 14.)

What is the best safe-guard against false teaching? Beyond all doubt the regular study of the Word of God, with prayer for the teaching of the Holy Spirit. The Bible was given to be a lamp to our feet and a light to our path. (Psa. cxix. 105.) The man who reads it aright will never be allowed greatly to err. It is neglect of the Bible which makes so many a prey to the first false teacher whom they hear. They would fain have us believe that "they are not learned, and do not pretend to have decided opinions:" the plain truth is that they are lazy and idle about reading the Bible, and do not like the trouble of thinking for themselves. Nothing supplies false prophets with followers so much as spiritual sloth under a cloak of humility.

May we all bear in mind our Lord's warning! The world, the devil, and the flesh, are not the only dangers in the way of the Christian; there remains another yet, and that is the "false prophet:" the wolf in sheep's clothing. Happy is he who prays over his Bible, and knows the difference between truth and error in religion! There is a difference, and we are meant to know it, and to use our knowledge.

MATTHEW VII. 21—29.

21 Not every one that saith unto me, Lord, Lord, shall enter into the kingdom of heaven; but he that doeth the will of my Father which is in heaven.

22 Many will say to me in that day, Lord, Lord, have we not prophesied in thy name? and in thy name have cast out devils? and in thy name done many wonderful works?

23 And then will I profess unto them, I never knew you: depart from me, ye that work iniquity.

24 Therefore whosoever heareth these sayings of mine, and doeth them, I will liken him unto a wise man, which built his house upon a rock:

25 And the rain descended, and the floods came, and the winds blew, and beat upon that house; and it fell not: for it was founded upon a rock.

26 And every one that heareth these sayings of mine, and doeth them not, shall be likened unto a foolish man, which built his house upon the sand:

27 And the rain descended, and the floods came, and the winds blew, and beat upon that house; and it fell: and great was the fall of it.

28 And it came to pass, when Jesus had ended these sayings, the people were astonished at his doctrine:

29 For he taught them as *one* having authority, and not as the scribes.

THE Lord Jesus winds up the Sermon on the Mount by a passage of heart-piercing application. He turns from false prophets to false professors, from unsound teachers to unsound hearers. Here is a word for all. May we have grace to apply it to our own hearts!

The first lesson here is *the uselessness of a mere outward profession of Christianity.* Not every one that saith "Lord, Lord," shall enter the kingdom of heaven. Not all that profess and call themselves Christians shall be saved.

Let us take notice of this. It requires far more than most people seem to think necessary, to save a soul. We may be baptized in the name of Christ, and boast confidently of our ecclesiastical privileges; we may possess head knowledge, and be quite satisfied with our own state; we may even be preachers, and teachers of others, and do "many wonderful works" in connection with our Church: but all this time are we practically doing the will of our Father in heaven? Do we truly repent, truly believe on Christ, and live holy and humble lives? If not, in spite of all our privileges and profession, we shall miss heaven at last, and be for ever cast away. We shall hear those awful words, "I never knew you: depart from Me."

The day of judgment will reveal strange things. The hopes of many, who were thought great Christians while they lived, will be utterly confounded. The rottenness of their religion will be exposed and put to shame before the whole world. It will then be proved that to be saved means something more than "making a profession." We must make a "practice" of our Christianity as well as a "profession." Let us often think of that great day: let us often "judge ourselves, that we be not judged," and condemned by the Lord. Whatever else we are, let us aim at being real, true, and sincere.

The second lesson here is a *striking picture of two classes of Christian hearers.* Those who hear and do nothing,—and those who hear and do as well as hear,—are both placed before us, and their histories traced to their respective ends.

The man who hears Christian teaching, and practises what he hears, is like "a wise man who builds his house upon a rock." He does not content himself with listening to exhortations to repent, believe in Christ, and live a holy life. He actually repents: he actually believes. He actually ceases to do evil, learns to do well, abhors that which is sinful, and cleaves to that which is good. He is a doer as well as a hearer. (James i. 22.)

And what is the result? In the time of trial his religion does not fail him; the floods of sickness, sorrow, poverty, disappointments, bereavements beat upon him in vain. His soul stands unmoved; his faith does not give way: his comforts do not utterly forsake him. His religion may have cost him trouble in time past; his foundation may have been obtained with much labour and many tears: to discover his own interest in Christ may have required many a day of earnest seeking, and many an hour of wrestling in prayer. But his labour has not been thrown away: he now reaps a rich reward. The religion that can stand trial is the true religion.

The man who hears Christian teaching, and never gets beyond hearing, is like "a foolish man who builds his house upon the sand." He satisfies himself with listening and approving, but he goes no further. He flatters himself, perhaps, that all is right with his soul, because he has feelings, and convictions, and desires, of a spiritual kind. In these he rests. He never really breaks off from sin, and casts aside the spirit of the world; he never really lays hold on Christ; he never really takes up the cross: he is a hearer of truth, but nothing more.

And what is the end of this man's religion? It breaks down entirely under the first flood of tribulation; it fails him completely, like a summer-dried fountain, when his need is the sorest. It leaves its possessor high and dry, like a wreck on a sand-bank, a scandal to the Church, a by-word to the infidel, and a misery to himself. Most true is it that what costs little is worth little! A religion which costs us nothing, and consists in nothing but hearing sermons, will always prove at last to be a useless thing.

So ends the Sermon on the Mount. Such a sermon never was preached before: such a sermon perhaps has never been preached since. Let us see that it has a lasting influence on our own souls. It is addressed to us as well as to those who first heard it; we are they who shall have to give account of its heart-searching lessons. It is no light matter what we think of them. The word that Jesus has spoken, "the same shall judge us in the last day." (John xii. 48.)

MATTHEW VIII. 1—15.

1 When he was come down from the mountain, great multitudes followed him.

2 And, behold, there came a leper and worshipped him, saying, Lord, if thou wilt, thou canst make me clean.

3 And Jesus put forth *his* hand, and touched him, saying, I will; be thou clean. And immediately his leprosy was cleansed.

4 And Jesus saith unto him, See thou tell no man; but go thy way, shew thyself to the priest, and offer the gift that Moses commanded, for a testimony unto them.

5 And when Jesus was entered into Capernaum, there came unto him a centurion, beseeching him,

6 And saying, Lord, my servant

lieth at home sick of the palsy, grievously tormented.
7 And Jesus saith unto him, I will come and heal him.
8 The centurion answered and said, Lord, I am not worthy that thou shouldest come under my roof: but speak the word only, and my servant shall be healed.
9 For I am a man under authority, having soldiers under me: and I say to this *man*, Go, and he goeth; and to another, Come, and he cometh; and to my servant, Do this, and he doeth *it*.
10 When Jesus heard *it*, he marvelled, and said to them that followed, Verily I say unto you, I have not found so great faith, no, not in Israel.
11 And I say unto you, That many shall come from the east and west, and shall sit down with Abraham, and Isaac, and Jacob, in the kingdom of heaven.
12 But the children of the kingdom shall be cast out into outer darkness: there shall be weeping and gnashing of teeth.
13 And Jesus said unto the centurion, Go thy way; and as thou hast believed, *so* be it done unto thee. And his servant was healed in the selfsame hour.
14 And when Jesus was come into Peter's house, he saw his wife's mother laid, and sick of a fever.
15 And he touched her hand, and the fever left her: and she arose, and ministered unto them.

THE eighth chapter of St. Matthew's Gospel is full of our Lord's miracles: no less than five are specially recorded. There is a beautiful fitness in this. It was fitting that the greatest sermon ever preached should be immediately followed by mighty proofs that the preacher was the Son of God. Those who heard the Sermon on the Mount would be obliged to confess, that, as none "spake such words as this man," so also none did such works.

The verses we have now read contain three great miracles: a leper is healed with a touch; a palsied person is made well by a word; a woman sick with a fever is restored in a moment to health and strength. On the face of these three miracles we may read three striking lessons. Let us examine them, and lay them to heart.

Let us learn, for one thing, *how great is the power of our Lord Jesus Christ.* Leprosy is the most fearful disease by which man's body can be afflicted. He that has it is like one dead while he lives; it is a complaint regarded by physicians as incurable. (2 Kings v. 7.) Yet Jesus says "Be thou clean: and immediately the leprosy was cleansed."—To heal a person of the palsy without even seeing him, by only speaking a word, is to do that which our minds cannot even conceive: yet Jesus commands, and at once it is done. To give a woman prostrate with a fever, not merely relief, but strength to do work in an instant, would baffle the skill of all the physicians on earth: yet Jesus "touched" Peter's wife's mother, and "she arose, and ministered unto them."—These are the doings of One that is Almighty. There is no escape from the conclusion. This was "the finger of God." (Exod. viii. 19.)

Behold here a broad foundation for the faith of a Christian! We are told in the Gospel to come to Jesus, to believe on Jesus, to live the life of faith in Jesus; we are encouraged to lean on Him, to cast all our care on Him, to repose all the weight of our souls on Him. We may do so without fear: He can bear all; He is a strong rock: He is Almighty. It was a fine saying of an old saint, "My faith can sleep sound on no other pillow than Christ's omnipotence." He can give life to the dead; He can give power to the weak; He can "increase strength to them that have no might." Let us trust Him and not be afraid. The world is full of snares: our hearts are weak. But with Jesus nothing is impossible.

Let us learn, for another thing, the *mercifulness and compassion of our Lord Jesus Christ.* The circumstances of the three cases we are now considering were all different. He heard the leper's pitiful cry, "Lord, if

Thou wilt, Thou canst make me clean;" He was told of the centurion's servant, but He never saw him; He saw Peter's wife's mother, "laid, and sick of a fever," and we are not told that He spoke a word: yet in each case the heart of the Lord Jesus was one and the same. In each case He was quick to show mercy, and ready to heal. Each poor sufferer was tenderly pitied, and each effectually relieved.

Behold here another strong foundation for our faith! Our great High Priest is very gracious: He can be "touched with the feeling of our infirmities;" He is never tired of doing us good. He knows that we are a weak and feeble people, in the midst of a weary and troublous world: He is as ready to bear with us, and help us, as He was 1800 years ago. It is as true of Him now as it was then, "He despiseth not any." (Job xxxvi. 5.) No heart can feel for us so much as the heart of Christ.

Let us learn, in the last place, *what a precious thing is the grace of faith.* We know little about the centurion described in these verses; his name, his nation, his past history, are all hidden from us: but one thing we know, and that is, that he believed. "Lord," he says, "I am not worthy that Thou shouldest come under my roof. Speak the word only, and my servant shall be healed." He believed, let us remember, when scribes and Pharisees were unbelievers; he believed, though a Gentile born, when Israel was blinded: and our Lord pronounced upon him the commendation, which has been read all over the world from that time to this: "I have not found so great faith, no, not in Israel."

Let us lay firm hold on this lesson. It deserves to be

remembered. To believe Christ's power and willingness to help, and to make a practical use of our belief, is a rare and precious gift: let us ever be thankful if we have it. To be willing to come to Jesus as helpless, lost sinners, and commit our souls into His hands is a mighty privilege: let us ever bless God if this willingness is our's, for it is His gift. Such faith is better than all other gifts and knowledge in the world. Many a poor converted heathen, who knows nothing but that he is sick of sin, and trusts in Jesus, shall sit down in heaven, while many learned English scholars are rejected for evermore. Blessed indeed are they that believe!

What do we each know of this faith? This is the great question. Our learning may be small: but do we believe?—Our opportunities of giving and working for Christ's cause may be few: but do we believe?—We may neither be able to preach, nor write, nor argue for the Gospel: but do we believe?—May we never rest till we can answer this inquiry! Faith in Christ appears a small and simple thing to the children of this world. They see in it nothing great or grand. But faith in Christ is most precious in God's sight, and, like most precious things, is rare. By it true Christians live; by it they stand; by it they overcome the world. Without this faith no one can be saved.

MATTHEW VIII. 16—27.

16 When the even was come, they brought unto him many that were possessed with devils: and he cast out the spirits with *his* word, and healed all that were sick:

17 That it might be fulfilled which was spoken by Esaias the prophet, saying, Himself took our infirmities, and bare our *sicknesses*.

18 Now when Jesus saw great

multitudes about him, he gave commandment to depart unto the other side.

19 And a certain scribe came, and said unto him, Master, I will follow thee whithersoever thou goest.

20 And Jesus saith unto him, The foxes have holes, and the birds of the air *have* nests; but the Son of man hath not where to lay *his* head.

21 And another of his disciples said unto him, Lord, suffer me first to go and bury my father.

22 But Jesus said unto him, Follow me: and let the dead bury their dead.

23 And when he was entered into a ship, his disciples followed him.

24 And behold there arose a great tempest in the sea, insomuch that the ship was covered with the waves: but he was asleep.

25 And his disciples came to *him*, and awoke him, saying, Lord save us: we perish.

26 And he saith unto them, Why are ye fearful, O ye of little faith? Then he arose, and rebuked the winds and the sea; and there was a great calm.

27 But the men marvelled, saying, What manner of man is this, that even the winds and the sea obey him!

IN the first part of these verses we see a striking example of *our Lord's wisdom in dealing with those who professed a willingness to be His disciples.* The passage throws so much light on a subject frequently misunderstood in these days, that it deserves more than ordinary attention.

A certain Scribe offers to follow our Lord whithersoever He goes. It was a remarkable offer, when we consider the class to which the man belonged, and the time at which it was made. But the offer receives a remarkable answer. It is not directly accepted, nor yet flatly rejected. Our Lord only makes the solemn reply, "The foxes have holes, and the birds of the air have nests; but the Son of man hath not where to lay His head."

Another follower of our Lord next comes forward, and asks to be allowed to "bury his father," before going any further in the path of a disciple. The request seems, at first sight, a natural and lawful one. But it draws from our Lord's lips a reply no less solemn than that already referred to: "Follow Me, and let the dead bury their dead."

There is something deeply impressive in both these

sayings. They ought to be well weighed by all professing Christians. They teach us plainly, that people who show a desire to come forward and profess themselves true disciples of Christ, should be warned plainly to "count the cost," before they begin.—Are they prepared to endure hardship? Are they ready to carry the cross? If not, they are not yet fit to begin.—They teach us plainly that there are times when a Christian must literally give up all for Christ's sake, and when even such duties as attending to a parent's funeral must be left to be performed by others. Such duties some will always be ready to attend to; and at no time can they be put in comparison with the greater duty of preaching the Gospel, and doing Christ's work in the world.

It would be well for the Churches of Christ if these sayings of our Lord were more remembered than they are. It may be feared that the lesson they contain is too often overlooked by the ministers of the Gospel, and that thousands are admitted to full communion who are never warned to "count the cost." Nothing, in fact, has done more harm to Christianity than the practice of filling the ranks of Christ's army with every volunteer who is willing to make a little profession, and to talk fluently of his "experience." It has been painfully forgotten that numbers alone do not make strength, and that there may be a great quantity of mere outward religion, while there is very little real grace. Let us remember this. Let us keep back nothing from young professors and inquirers after Christ: let us not enlist them on false pretences. Let us tell them plainly that there is a crown of glory at the end; but let us tell them no less plainly, that there is a daily cross in the way.

In the latter part of these verses we learn *that true saving faith is often mingled with much weakness and infirmity.* It is a humbling lesson, but a very wholesome one.

We are told of our Lord and His disciples crossing the sea of Galilee in a boat; a storm arises, and the boat is in danger of being filled with water, by the waves that beat over it. Meanwhile our Lord is asleep. The frightened disciples awake Him, and cry to Him for help. He hears their cry and stills the waters with a word, so that there is "a great calm." At the same time He gently reproves the anxiety of His disciples: "Why are ye fearful, O ye of little faith?"

What a vivid and instructive picture we have here of the hearts of thousands of believers! How many have faith and love enough to forsake all for Christ's sake, and to follow Him whithersoever He goes, and yet are full of fears in the hour of trial! How many have grace enough to turn to Jesus in every trouble, crying, "Lord save us," and yet not grace enough to lie still, and believe in the darkest hour that all is well!

Let the prayer, "Lord, increase our faith," always form part of our daily petitions. We never perhaps know the weakness of our faith, until we are placed in the furnace of trial and anxiety. Blessed and happy is that person who finds by experience that his faith can stand the fire, and that he can say with Job, "though He slay me, yet will I trust in Him." (Job xiii. 15.)

We have great reason to thank God that Jesus, our

great High-priest, is very compassionate and tender-hearted. He knows our frame: He considers our infirmities. He does not cast off His people because of defects: He pities even those whom He reproves. The prayer even of "little faith" is heard, and gets an answer.

MATTHEW VIII. 28—34.

28 And when he was come to the other side into the country of the Gergesenes, there met him two possessed with devils, coming out of the tombs, exceeding fierce, so that no man might pass by that way.

29 And, behold, they cried out, saying, What have we to do with thee, Jesus, thou Son of God? art thou come hither to torment us before the time?

30 And there was a good way off from them an herd of many swine feeding.

31 So the devils besought him, saying, If thou cast us out, suffer us to go away into the herd of swine.

32 And he said unto them, Go. And when they were come out, they went into the herd of swine: and, behold, the whole herd of swine ran violently down a steep place into the sea, and perished in the waters.

33 And they that kept them fled, and went their ways into the city, and told every thing, and what was befallen to the possessed of the devils.

34 And, behold, the whole city came out to meet Jesus: and when they saw him, they besought him that he would depart out of their coasts.

THE subject of these seven verses is deep and mysterious. The casting out of a devil is here described with special fulness. It is one of those passages which throw strong light on a dark and difficult point.

Let us settle it firmly in our minds *that there is such a being as the devil.* It is an awful truth, and one too much overlooked. There is an unseen spirit ever near us, of mighty power, and full of endless malice against our souls. From the beginning of creation he has laboured to injure man; until the Lord comes the second time and binds him, he will never cease to tempt, and practise mischief. In the days when our Lord was upon earth, it is clear that He had a peculiar power over the bodies of certain men and women, as well as over their souls. Even in our own times there may be more of this bodily possession than some suppose, though confessedly in a far less degree than when Christ came in the flesh. But that the devil is ever near us, and ever ready to ply our hearts with temptations, ought never to be forgotten.

Let us, in the next place, settle it firmly in our minds *that the power of the devil is limited.* Mighty as he is, there is One mightier still. Keenly as his will is set on doing harm in the world, he can only work by permission. These verses show us that the evil spirits know they can only go to and fro, and ravage the earth until the time allowed them by the Lord of lords. "Art thou come to torment us," they say "before the time?" Their very petition shows us that they could not even hurt one of the swine of the Gergesenes, unless Jesus the Son of God suffered them. "Suffer us," they say, "to go into the herd of swine."

Let us, in the next place, settle it in our minds *that our Lord Jesus Christ is man's great deliverer from the power of the devil.* He can redeem us not only "from all iniquity," and "this present evil world," but from the devil. It was prophesied of old that He should bruise the serpent's head. He began to bruise that head when He was born of the Virgin Mary; He triumphed over that head when He died upon the cross; He showed His complete dominion over Satan by "healing all that were oppressed of the devil," when He was upon earth. (Acts x. 38.) Our great remedy, in all the assaults of the devil is to cry to the Lord Jesus, and to seek His help. He can break the chains that Satan casts round us, and set us free. He can cast out every devil that plagues our hearts, as surely as in the days of old. It would be miserable indeed to know that there is a devil ever near us, if we did not also know that Christ is "able to save to the uttermost, because He ever liveth to make intercession for us." (Heb. vii. 25.)

Let us not leave this passage without observing *the painful worldliness of the Gergesenes*, among whom this miracle of casting out a devil was wrought. They besought the Lord Jesus to "depart out of their coasts:" they had no heart to feel for anything but the loss of their swine; they cared not that two fellow-creatures, two immortal souls, were freed from Satan's bondage; they cared not that there stood among them a greater than the devil, Jesus the Son of God. They cared for nothing but that their swine were drowned, and the "hope of their gains was gone." (Acts xvi. 19.) They ignorantly regarded Jesus as one who stood between them and their profits, and they only wished to be rid of Him.

There are only too many like these Gergesenes. There are thousands who care not one jot for Christ, or Satan, so long as they can make a little more money, and have a little more of the good things of this world. From this spirit may we be delivered! Against this spirit may we ever watch and pray! It is very common: it is awfully infectious. Let us recollect every morning that we have souls to be saved, and that we shall one day die, and after that be judged. Let us beware of loving the world more than Christ.

MATTHEW IX. 1–13.

1 And he entered into a ship, and passed over, and came into his own city.

2 And, behold, they brought to him a man sick of the palsy, lying on a bed: and Jesus seeing their faith said unto the sick of the palsy, Son, be of good cheer: thy sins be forgiven thee.

3 And, behold, certain of the scribes said within themselves, This *man* blasphemeth.

4 And Jesus knowing their thoughts said, Wherefore think ye evil in your hearts?

5 For whether is easier, to say, *Thy* sins be forgiven thee; or to say, Arise, and walk?

6 But that ye may know that the Son of man hath power on earth to forgive sins, (then saith he to the sick of the palsy,) Arise, take up thy bed, and go unto thine house.

7 And he arose, and departed to his house.

8 But when the multitudes saw *it* they marvelled, and glorified God, which had given such power unto men.

9 And as Jesus passed forth from thence, he saw a man named Matthew, sitting at the receipt of custom: and he saith unto him, Follow me. And he arose, and followed him.

10 And it came to pass, as Jesus sat at meat in the house, behold, many publicans and sinners came and sat down with him and his disciples.

11 And when the Pharisees saw *it*, they said unto his disciples, Why eateth your Master with publicans and sinners?

12 But when Jesus heard *that*, he said unto them, They that be whole need not a physician, but they that are sick.

13 But go ye and learn what *that* meaneth, I will have mercy, and not sacrifice: for I am not come to call the righteous, but sinners to repentance.

LET us notice, in the first part of this passage, *our Lord's knowledge of men's thoughts.*

There were certain of the scribes who found fault with the words which Jesus spoke to a man sick of the palsy: they said secretly among themselves, "This man blasphemeth." They probably supposed that no one knew what was going on in their minds: they had yet to learn that the Son of God could read hearts, and discern spirits. Their malicious thought was publicly exposed: they were put to an open shame. Jesus "knew their thoughts."

There is an important lesson for us here. "All things are naked and open unto the eyes of Him with whom we have to do." (Heb. iv. 13.) Nothing can be concealed from Christ. What do we think of, in private, when no man sees us? What do we think of, in church, when we seem grave and serious? What are we thinking of at this moment, while these words pass under our eyes? Jesus knows. Jesus sees. Jesus records. Jesus will one day summon us to give account. It is written, that "God shall judge the secrets of men by Jesus Christ according to my Gospel." (Rom. ii. 16.) Surely we ought to be very humble when we consider these things: we ought to thank God daily that the blood of Christ can cleanse from all sin; we ought often to cry, "Let the words of my mouth, and the meditation of my heart be acceptable in Thy sight." (Psalm xix. 14.)

Let us notice, in the second place, *the wonderful call of the apostle Matthew to be Christ's disciple.*

We find the man, who afterwards was the first to write a Gospel, sitting at the receipt of custom: we see him absorbed in his worldly calling, and possibly thinking of nothing but money and gain; but suddenly the Lord Jesus calls on him to follow Him, and become His disciple. At once Matthew obeys: he "makes haste, and delays not" to keep Christ's commandments. (Psal. cxix. 60.) He arises and follows Him.

We should learn, from Matthew's case, that with Christ nothing is impossible. He can take a tax-gatherer, and make him an apostle: He can change any heart, and make all things new. Let us never despair of any one's salvation. Let us pray on, and speak on, and work on, in order to do good to souls, even to the souls of the worst. "The voice of the Lord is mighty in operation." (Psalm xxix. 4.) When He says by the power of the Spirit, "follow Me." He can make the hardest and most sinful obey.

We should observe Matthew's decision. He waited for nothing: he did not tarry for "a convenient season" (Acts xxiv. 25); and he reaped in consequence a great reward. He wrote a book which is known all over the earth; be became a blessing to others as well as blessed in his own soul; he left a name behind him which is better known than the names of princes and kings. The richest man of the world is soon forgotten when he dies; but as long as the world stands millions will know the name of Matthew the publican.

Let us notice, in the last place, our Lord's *precious declaration about His own mission.*

The Pharisees found fault with Him, because He allowed publicans and sinners to be in His company. In their proud blindness they fancied that a teacher sent from heaven ought to have no dealings with such people. They were wholly ignorant of the grand design for which the Messiah was to come into the world, to be a Saviour, a Physician, a healer of sin-sick souls; and they drew from our Lord's lips a severe rebuke, accompanied by the blessed words, "I am not come to call the righteous, but sinners to repentance."

Let us make sure that we thoroughly understand the doctrine that these words contain. The first thing needful, in order to have an interest in Christ, is to feel deeply our own corruption, and to be willing to come to Him for deliverance. We are not to keep away from Christ, as many ignorantly do, because we feel bad, and wicked, and unworthy; we are to remember that sinners are those He came into the world to save, and that if we feel ourselves such, it is well. Happy is he who really comprehends that one principal qualification for coming to Christ is a deep sense of sin!

Finally, if by the grace of God we really understand the glorious truth that sinners are those whom Christ came to call, let us take heed that we *never forget it.* Let us not dream that true Christians can ever attain such a state of perfection in this world, as not to need the mediation and intercession of Jesus. Sinners we are in the day we first come to Christ. Poor needy sinners we continue to be so long as we live, drawing all the grace we have every hour out of Christ's fulness. Sinners we shall find ourselves in the hour of our death, and shall die as much indebted to Christ's blood, as in the day when we first believed.

MATTHEW IX. 14—26.

14 Then came to him the disciples of John, saying, Why do we and the Pharisees fast oft, but thy disciples fast not?

15 And Jesus said unto them, Can the children of the bridechamber mourn, as long as the bridegroom is with them? but the days will come, when the bridegroom shall be taken from them, and then shall they fast.

16 No man putteth a piece of new cloth unto an old garment, for that which is put in to fill it up taketh from the garment, and the rent is made worse.

17 Neither do men put new wine into old bottles: else the bottles break, and the wine runneth out, and the bottles perish; but they put new wine into new bottles, and both are preserved.

18 While he spake these things unto them, behold, there came a certain ruler, and worshipped him saying, My daughter is even now dead; but come and lay thy hand upon her, and she shall live.

19 And Jesus arose, and followed him, and so *did* his disciples.

20 And, behold, a woman, which was diseased with an issue of blood twelve years, came behind him, and touched the hem of his garment:

21 For she said within herself, If I may but touch his garment, I shall be whole.

22 But Jesus turned him about, and when he saw her, he said, Daughter, be of good comfort; thy faith hath made thee whole. And the woman was made whole from that hour.

23 And when Jesus came into the ruler's house, and saw the minstrels and the people making a noise,

24 He said unto them, Give

place: for the maid is not dead, but sleepeth. And they laughed him to scorn.
25 But when the people were put forth, he went in, and took her by the hand, and the maid arose.
26 And the fame hereof went abroad into all that land.

LET us mark, in this passage, the gracious name by which the Lord Jesus speaks of Himself. He calls Himself "*the Bridegroom.*"

What the bridegroom is to the bride, the Lord Jesus is to the souls of all who believe in Him. He loves them with a deep and everlasting love; He takes them into union with Himself: they are "one with Christ and Christ in them." He pays all their debts to God; He supplies all their daily need; He sympathizes with them in all their troubles; He bears with all their infirmities, and does not reject them for a few weaknesses. He regards them as part of Himself: those that persecute and injure them are persecuting Him. The glory that He has received from His Father they will one day share with Him, and where He is, there shall they be. Such are the privileges of all true Christians. They are the Lamb's wife. (Rev. xix. 7.) Such is the portion to which faith admits us. By it God joins our poor sinful souls to one precious Husband; and those whom God thus joins together shall never be put asunder. Blessed indeed are they that believe!

Let us mark, in the next place, *what a wise principle the Lord Jesus lays down for the treatment of young disciples.*

There were some who found fault with our Lord's followers because they did not fast as John the Baptist's disciples did. Our Lord defends His disciples with an argument full of deep wisdom. He shows that there would be want of fitness in their fasting, so long as He, their Bridegroom, was with them: but He does not stop there. He goes on to show, by two parables, that young beginners in the school of Christianity must be dealt with gently. They must be taught as they are able to bear: they must not be expected to receive everything at once. To neglect this rule would be as unwise as to "put new wine into old bottles," or to put "a piece of new cloth to an old garment."

There is a mine of deep wisdom in this principle, which all would do well to remember in the spiritual teaching of those who are young in experience. We must be careful not to attach an excessive importance to the lesser things of religion; we must not be in a hurry to require a minute conformity to one rigid rule in things indifferent, until the first principles of repentance and faith have been thoroughly learned. To guide us in this matter, we have great need to pray for grace, and Christian common sense. Tact in dealing with young disciples is a rare gift, but a very useful one. To know what to insist upon as absolutely necessary from the first,—and what to reserve, as a lesson to be learned when the learner has come to more perfect knowledge,—is one of the highest attainments of a teacher of souls.

Let us mark, in the next place, *what encouragement our Lord gives to the humblest faith.*

We read in this passage, that a woman sorely afflicted with disease, came behind our Lord in the crowd, and "touched the hem" of His garment, in the hope that by so doing she should be healed. She said not a word to obtain help: she made no public confession of faith; but she had confidence that if she could only "touch His garment" she would be made well. And so it was. There lay hid in that act of her's a seed of precious faith, which obtained our Lord's commendation. She was made whole at once, and returned home in peace. To use the words of a good old writer, "she came trembling, and went back triumphing."

Let us store up in our minds this history; it may perhaps help us mightily in some hour of need. Our faith may be feeble; our courage may be small; our grasp of the Gospel, and its promises, may be weak and trembling,—but, after all, the grand question is, Do we really trust only in Christ? Do we look to Jesus, and only to Jesus, for pardon and peace? If this be so, it is well. If we may not touch His garment, we can touch His heart. Such faith saves the soul. Weak faith is less comfortable than strong faith: weak faith will carry us to heaven with far less joy than full assurance; but weak faith gives an interest in Christ as surely as strong faith. He that only touches the hem of Christ's garment shall never perish.

In the last place, let us mark in this passage, *our Lord's almighty power.* He restores to life one that was dead.

How wonderful that sight must have been! Who that has ever seen the dead can forget the stillness, the silence, the coldness, when the breath has left the body? Who can forget the awful feeling that a mighty change has taken place, and a mighty gulf been placed between ourselves and the departed? But behold! our Lord goes to the chamber where the dead lies, and calls the spirit back to its earthly tabernacle. The pulse once more beats; the eyes once more see; the breath once more comes and goes. The ruler's daughter is once more alive, and restored to her father and mother. This was omnipotence indeed! None could have done this but He who first created man, and has all power in heaven and earth.

This is the kind of truth we never can know too well. The more clearly we see Christ's power, the more likely we are to realize Gospel peace. Our position may be trying; our hearts may be weak; the world may be difficult to journey through; our faith may seem too small to carry us home; but let us take courage, when we think on Jesus, and let us not be cast down. Greater is He that is for us, then all they that are against us. Our Saviour can raise the dead: our Saviour is almighty.

MATTHEW IX. 27—38.

27 And when Jesus departed thence, two blind men followed him, crying, and saying, *Thou* Son of David, have mercy on us.

28 And when he was come into the house, the blind men came to him: and Jesus saith unto them, Believe ye that I am able to do this? They said unto him, Yea, Lord.

29 Then touched he their eyes, saying, According to your faith be it unto you.

30 And their eyes were opened; and Jesus straitly charged them, saying, See *that* no man know *it*.

31 But they, when they were departed, spread abroad his fame in all that country.

32 As they went out, behold, they brought to him a dumb man possessed with a devil.

33 And when the devil was cast out, the dumb spake: and the multitudes marvelled, saying, It was never so seen in Israel.

34 But the Pharisees said, He casteth out devils through the prince of the devils.

35 And Jesus went about all the cities and villages, teaching in their synagogues, and preaching the Gospel of the kingdom, and healing every sickness and every disease among the people.

36 But when he saw the multitudes, he was moved with compassion on them, because they fainted, and were scattered abroad, as sheep having no shepherd.

37 Then saith he unto his disciples, The harvest truly is plenteous, but the labourers *are* few;

38 Pray ye therefore the Lord of the harvest, that he will send forth labourers into his harvest.

THERE are four lessons in this passage which deserve close attention. Let us mark them each in succession.

Let us mark, in the first place, that *strong faith in Christ may sometimes be found where it might least have been expected.* Who would have thought that two blind men would have called our Lord the "Son of David"? They could not, of course, have seen the miracles that He did: they could only know Him by common report. But the eyes of their understanding were enlightened, if their bodily eyes were dark; they saw the truth which scribes and Pharisees could not see; they saw that Jesus of Nazareth was the Messiah. They believed that He was able to heal them.

An example like this shows us that we must never despair of any one's salvation merely because he lives in a position unfavourable to his soul. Grace is stronger than circumstances: the life of religion does not depend merely upon outward advantages. The Holy Ghost can give faith, and keep faith in active exercise, without book-learning, without money, and with scanty means of grace. Without the Holy Ghost a man may know all mysteries, and live in the full blaze of the Gospel, and yet be lost. We shall see many strange sights at the last day. Poor cottagers will be found to have believed in the Son of David, while rich men, full of university learning, will prove to have lived and died, like the Pharisees, in hardened unbelief. Many that are last will be first, and the first last. (Matt. xx. 16.)

Let us mark, in the next place, that our Lord Jesus Christ *has had great experience of disease and sickness.* He "went about all the cities and villages" doing good: He was an eye-witness of all the ills that flesh is heir to; He saw ailments of every kind, sort, and description; He was brought in contact with every form of bodily suffering. None were too loathsome for Him to attend to: none were too frightful for Him to cure. He was a healer of "every sickness and every disease."

There is much comfort to be drawn from this fact. We are each dwelling in a poor frail body: we never know how much suffering we may have to watch, as we sit by the bedsides of beloved relatives and friends; we never know what racking complaint we ourselves may have to submit to, before we lie down and die. But let us arm ourselves betimes with the precious thought that Jesus is specially fitted to be the sick man's friend. The great High-priest to whom we must apply for pardon and peace with God, is eminently qualified to sympathise with an aching body, as well as to heal an ailing conscience. The eyes of Him who is King of kings used often to look with pity on the diseased. The world cares little for the sick, and often keeps aloof from them; but the Lord Jesus cares especially for the sick: He is the first to visit them, and say, "I stand at the door and knock." Happy are they who hear His voice, and open the door! (Rev. iii. 20.)

Let us mark, in the next place, our Lord's *tender concern for neglected souls.* "He saw multitudes" of people, when he was on earth, scattered about "like sheep having no shepherd," and He was moved with compassion. He saw them neglected by those who for the time ought to have been teachers. He saw them ignorant, hopeless, helpless, dying, and unfit to die. The sight moved Him to deep pity. That loving heart could not see such things, and not feel.

Now what are our feelings, when we see such a sight? This is the question that should arise in our minds. There are many such to be seen on every side. There are millions of idolaters and heathen on earth,—millions of deluded Mahometans,—millions of superstitious Roman Catholics; there are thousands of ignorant and unconverted Protestants near our own doors: do we feel tenderly concerned about their souls? Do we deeply pity their spiritual destitution? Do we long to see that destitution relieved? These are serious inquiries, and ought to be answered. It is easy to sneer at missions to the heathen, and those who work for them; but the man who does not feel for the souls of all unconverted persons can surely not have "the mind of Christ." (1 Cor. ii. 16.)

Let us mark, in the last place, that *there is a solemn duty incumbent on all Christians* who would do good to the unconverted part of the world. They are to pray for more men to be raised up to work for the conversion of souls. It seems as if it was to be a daily part of our prayers. "Pray ye the Lord of the harvest that He would send forth labourers into His harvest."

If we know anything of prayer, let us make it a point of conscience never to forget this solemn charge of our Lord's. Let us settle it in our minds that it is one of the surest ways of doing good and stemming evil. Personal working for souls is good; giving money is good; but praying is best of all. By prayer we reach Him, without whom work and money are alike in vain:

we obtain the aid of the Holy Ghost.—Money can pay agents; universities can give learning; bishops may ordain; congregations may elect: but the Holy Ghost alone can make ministers of the Gospel, and raise up lay workmen in the spiritual harvest, who need not be ashamed. Never, never may we forget that if we would do good to the world, our first duty is to pray!

MATTHEW X. 1—15.

1 And when he had called unto *him* his twelve disciples, he gave them power *against* unclean spirits, to cast them out, and to heal all manner of sickness and all manner of disease.
2 Now the names of the twelve apostles are these; the first, Simon, who is called Peter, and Andrew his brother; James *the son* of Zebedee, and John his brother;
3 Philip, and Bartholomew; Thomas, and Matthew the publican; James *the son* of Alphæus. and Lebbæus, whose surname was Thaddæus;
4 Simon the Canaanite, and Judas Iscariot, who also betrayed him.
5 These twelve Jesus sent forth, and commanded them, saying, Go not into the way of the Gentiles, and into *any* city of the Samaritans enter ye not:
6 But go rather to the lost sheep of the house of Israel.
7 And as ye go, preach, saying, The kingdom of heaven is at hand.
8 Heal the sick, cleanse the lepers, raise the dead, cast out devils: freely ye have received, freely give.
9 Provide neither gold, nor silver, nor brass in your purses,
10 Nor scrip for *your* journey, neither two coats, neither shoes, nor yet staves: for the workman is worthy of his meat.
11 And into whatsoever city or town ye shall enter, enquire who in it is worthy; and there abide till ye go thence.
12 And when ye come into an house, salute it.
13 And if the house be worthy, let your peace come upon it: but if it be not worthy, let your peace return to you.
14 And whosoever shall not receive you, nor hear your words, when ye depart out of that house or city, shake off the dust of your feet.
15 Verily, I say unto you, It shall be more tolerable for the land of Sodom and Gomorrha in the day of judgment, than for that city.

THIS chapter is one of peculiar solemnity. Here is the record of the first ordination which ever took place in the Church of Christ. The Lord Jesus chooses and sends forth the twelve apostles.—Here is an account of the first charge ever delivered to newly ordained Christian ministers. The Lord Jesus Himself delivers it. Never was there so important an ordination! Never was there so solemn a charge!

There are three lessons which stand out prominently on the face of the first fifteen verses of this chapter. Let us take them in order.

We are taught, in the first place, *that all ministers are not necessarily good men.* We see our Lord choosing a Judas Iscariot to be one of His apostles. We cannot doubt that He who knew all hearts, knew well the characters of the men whom He chose; and He includes in the list of His apostles one who was a traitor!

We shall do well to bear in mind this fact. Orders do not confer the saving grace of the Holy Ghost: ordained men are not necessarily converted. We are not to regard them as infallible, either in doctrine or in practice; we are not to make Popes or idols of them, and insensibly to put them in Christ's place. We are to regard them as "men of like passions" with ourselves, liable to the same infirmities, and daily requiring the same grace; we are not to think it impossible for them to do very bad things, or to expect them to be above the reach of harm from flattery, covetousness, and the world. We are to prove their teaching by the Word of God, and to follow them so far as they follow Christ, but no further. Above all, we ought to pray for them, that they may be successors, not of Judas Iscariot, but of James and John. It is a serious responsibility to be a minister of the Gospel! Ministers need many prayers.

We are taught, in the next place, that *the great work of a minister of Christ is to do good.* He is sent to seek "lost sheep,"—to proclaim glad tidings,—to relieve those who are suffering,—to diminish sorrow,—and to increase joy. His life is meant to be one of "giving," rather than receiving.

This is a high standard, and a very peculiar one. Let it be well weighed, and carefully examined. It is plain, for one thing, that the life of a faithful minister of Christ cannot be one of ease. He must be ready to spend body and mind, time and strength, in the work of his calling: laziness and frivolity are bad enough in any profession, but worst of all in that of a watchman for souls.—It is plain, for another thing, that the position of the ministers of Christ is not that which ignorant people sometimes assign to them, and which they unhappily sometimes claim for themselves. They are not so much ordained to rule as to serve; they are not so much intended to have dominion over the Church, as to supply its wants, and to wait upon its members. (2 Cor. i. 24.) Happy would it be for the cause of true religion if these things were better understood! Half the diseases of Christianity have arisen from mistaken notions about the minister's office.

We are taught, in the last place, that *it is a most dangerous thing to neglect the offers of the Gospel.* It shall prove "more tolerable for the land of Sodom and Gomorrha," in the judgment day, than for those who have heard Christ's truth, and not received it.

This is a doctrine fearfully overlooked, and one that deserves serious consideration. Men are apt to forget that it does not require great open sins to be sinned in order to ruin a soul for ever. They have only to go on hearing without believing, listening without repenting, going to church without going to Christ, and by and by they will find themselves in hell! We shall all be judged according to our light; we shall have to give account of our use of religious privileges: to hear of the "great salvation," and yet neglect it, is one of the worst sins man can commit. (John xvi. 9; Heb. ii. 3.)

What are we doing ourselves with the Gospel? This is the question which everyone who reads this passage should put to his conscience. Let us assume that we are decent and respectable in our lives, correct and moral in all the relations of life, regular in our formal attendance on the means of grace: it is all well, so far as it goes; but is this all that can be said of us? Are we really receiving the love of the truth? Is Christ dwelling in our hearts by faith? If not, we are in fearful danger: we are far more guilty than the men of Sodom, who never heard the Gospel at all; we may awake to find that in spite of our regularity, and morality, and correctness, we have lost our souls to all eternity. It will not save us to have lived in the full sunshine of Christian privileges; and to have heard the Gospel faithfully preached every week: there must be experimental acquaintance with Christ; there must be personal reception of His truth; there must be vital union with Him: we must become His servants and disciples. Without this, the preaching of the Gospel only adds to our responsibility, increases our guilt, and will at length sink us more deeply into hell. These are hard sayings! But the words of Scripture, which we have read, are plain and unmistakable. They are all true.

MATTHEW X. 16—23.

16 Behold, I send you forth as sheep in the midst of wolves: be ye therefore wise as serpents, and harmless as doves.

17 But beware of men: for they will deliver you up to the councils, and they will scourge you in their synagogues;

18 And ye shall be brought before governors and kings for my sake, for a testimony against them and the Gentiles.

19 But when they deliver you up, take no thought how or what ye shall speak: for it shall be given you in that same hour what ye shall speak.

20 For it is not ye that speak, but the Spirit of your Father which speaketh in you.

21 And the brother shall deliver up the brother to death, and the father the child: and the children shall rise up against *their* parents, and cause them to be put to death.

22 And ye shall be hated of all *men* for my name's sake; but he that endureth to the end shall be saved.

23 But when they persecute you in this city, flee ye into another: for verily I say unto you, Ye shall not have gone over the cities of Israel, till the Son of man be come.

THE truths contained in these verses should be pondered by all who try to do good in the world. To the selfish man who cares for nothing but his own ease or comfort, there may seem to be little in them: to the minister of the Gospel, and to every one who seeks to save souls, these verses ought to be full of interest. No doubt there is much in them which applies especially to the days of the apostles; but there is much also which applies to all times.

We see, for one thing, *that those who would do good to souls, must be moderate in their expectations.* They must not think that universal success will attend their labours: they must reckon on meeting with much opposition; they must make up their minds to be "hated," persecuted, and ill-used, and that too by their nearest relations. They will often find themselves like "sheep in the midst of wolves."

Let us bear this in mind continually. Whether we preach, or teach, or visit from house to house,—whether we write or give counsel, or whatever we do, let it be a settled principle with us not to expect more than Scripture and experience warrant. Human nature is far more wicked and corrupt than we think: the power of evil is far greater than we suppose. It is vain to imagine that everbody will see what is good for them, and believe what we tell them: it is expecting what we shall not find, and will only end in disappointment. Happy is that labourer for Christ who knows these things at his first starting, and has not to learn them by bitter experience! Here lies the secret cause why many have turned back, who once seemed full of zeal to do good. They began with extravagant expectations; they did not "count the cost:" they fell into the mistake of the great German Reformer, who confessed he forget at one time that "old Adam was too strong for young Melancthon."

We see, for another thing, *that those who would do good have need to pray for wisdom, good sense, and a sound mind.* Our Lord tells His disciples to be "wise as serpents, and harmless as doves." He tells them that when they are persecuted in one place, they may lawfully "flee to another."

There are few of our Lord's instructions which it is so difficult to use rightly as this. There is a line marked out for us between two extremes, but a line that it requires great judgment to define. To avoid persecution, by holding our tongues and keeping our religion entirely to ourselves, is one extreme: we are not to err in that direction.—To court persecution, and thrust our religion upon every one we meet, without regard to place, time, or circumstances, is another extreme: in this direction also we are warned not to err, any more than in the other.—Truly we may say, "Who is sufficient for these things?" We have need to cry to "the only wise God" for wisdom.

The extreme into which most men are liable to fall in the present day is that of silence, cowardice, and letting others alone. Our so-called prudence is apt to degenerate into a compromising line of conduct, or downright unfaithfulness. We are only too ready to suppose that it is of no use trying to do good to certain people: we excuse ourselves from efforts to benefit their souls by saying it would be indiscreet, or inexpedient, or would give needless offence, or would even do positive harm. Let us all watch and be on our guard against this spirit; laziness and the devil are often the true explanation of it. To give way to it is pleasant to flesh and blood, no doubt, and saves us much trouble: but those who give way to it often throw away great opportunities of usefulness.

On the other hand, it is impossible to deny that there is such a thing as a righteous and holy zeal, which is "not according to knowledge." It is quite possible to create much needless offence, commit great blunders, and stir up much opposition, which might have been avoided by a little prudence, wise management, and exercise of judgment: let us all take heed that we are not guilty in this respect. We may be sure there is such a thing as Christian wisdom, which is quite distinct from Jesuitical subtlety, or carnal policy: this wisdom let us seek. Our Lord Jesus does not require us to throw aside our common sense, when we undertake to work for Him. There will be offence enough connected with our religion, do what we will; but let us not increase it without cause.

Let us strive to "walk circumspectly, not as fools but as wise." (Ephes. v. 15.)

It is to be feared that believers in the Lord Jesus do no sufficiently pray for the Spirit of knowledge, judgment, and a sound mind. They are apt to fancy that if they have grace, they have all they need: they forget that a gracious heart should pray that it may be full of wisdom, as well as of the Holy Ghost. (Acts vi. 3.) Let us all remember this. Great grace and common sense are perhaps one of the rarest combinations: that they may go together, the life of David and the ministry of the Apostle Paul are striking proofs. In this however, as in every other respect, our Lord Jesus Christ Himself is our most perfect example: none were ever so faithful as He; but none were ever so truly wise. Let us make Him our pattern and walk in His steps.

MATTHEW X. 24—23.

24 The disciple is not above *his* master, nor the servant above his lord.

25 It is enough for the disciple that he be as his master, and the servant as his lord. If they have called the master of the house Beelzebub, how much more *shall they call* them of his household?

26 Fear them not therefore: for there is nothing covered, that shall not be revealed; and hid, that shall not be known.

27 What I tell you in darkness, *that* speak ye in light; and what ye hear in the ear, *that* preach ye upon the housetops.

28 And fear not them which kill the body, but are not able to kill the soul: but rather fear him which is able to destroy both soul and body in hell.

29 Are not two sparrows sold for a farthing? and one of them shall not fall on the ground without your Father.

30 But the very hairs of your head are all numbered.

31 Fear ye not therefore, ye are of more value than many sparrows.

32 Whosoever therefore shall confess me before men, him will I confess also before my Father which is in heaven.

33 But whosoever shall deny me before men, him will I also deny before my Father which is in heaven.

To do good to souls in this world is very hard. All who try it find this out by experience: it needs a large stock of courage, faith, patience, and perseverance. Satan will fight vigorously to maintain his kingdom; human nature is desperately wicked: to do harm is easy; to do good is hard.

The Lord Jesus knew this well, when He sent forth His disciples to preach the Gospel for the first time. He knew what was before them, if they did not. He took care to supply them with a list of encouragements, in order to cheer them when they felt cast down. Weary missionaries abroad, or fainting ministers at home,—disheartened teachers of schools, and desponding visitors of districts, would do well to study often the nine verses we have just read. Let us mark what they contain.

For one thing, those who try to do good to souls *must not expect to fare better than their great Master.* "The disciple is not above his Master, nor the servant above his Lord." The Lord Jesus was slandered and rejected by those whom He came to benefit. There was no error in His teaching; there was no defect in His method of imparting instruction: yet many hated Him, and "called Him Beelzebub." Few believed Him, and cared for what He said. Surely we have no right to be surprised if we, whose best efforts are mingled with much imperfection, are treated in the same way as Christ. If we let the world alone, it will probably let us alone; but if we try to do it spiritual good, it will hate us as it did our Master.

For another thing, those who try to do good *must look forward with patience to the day of judgment.* "There is nothing covered that shall not be revealed, and hid that shall not be known." They must be content in this present world to be misunderstood, misrepresented, vilified, slandered, and abused. They must not cease to work because their motives are mistaken, and their characters fiercely assailed. They must remember continually that all will be set right at the last day: the secrets of all hearts shall then be revealed. "He shall bring forth thy righteousness as the light, and thy judgment as the noon-day." (Psal. xxxvii. 6.) The purity of their intentions, the wisdom of their labours, and the rightfulness of their cause, shall at length be made manifest to all the world. Let us work on steadily and quietly: men may not understand us, and may vehemently oppose us; but the day of judgment draws nigh: we shall be righted at last. The Lord, when He comes again, "will bring to light the hidden things of darkness, and will make manifest the counsels of the heart: and then shall every man have praise of God." (1 Cor. iv. 5.)

For another thing, those who try to do good *must fear God more than man.* Man can hurt the body, but there his enmity must stop: he can go no further. God "is able to destroy both soul and body in hell." We may be threatened with the loss of character, property, and all that makes life enjoyable, if we go on in the path of religious duty: we must not heed such threats, when our course is plain. Like Daniel and the three children we must submit to anything rather than displease God, and wound our consciences. The anger of man may be hard to bear, but the anger of God is much harder; the fear of man does indeed bring a snare, but we must make it give way to the expulsive power of a stronger principle, even the fear of God. It was a fine saying of good Colonel Gardiner, "I fear God, and therefore there is none else that I need fear."

For another thing, those who try to do good *must keep before their minds the providential care of God over them.* Nothing can happen in this world without His permission: there is no such thing in reality as chance, accident, or luck. "The very hairs of their heads are all numbered." The path of duty may sometimes lead them into great danger; health and life may seem to be perilled, if they go forward: let them take comfort in the thought that all around them is in God's hand. Their bodies, their souls, their characters are all in His safe keeping: no disease can seize them,—no hand can hurt them, unless He allows. They may say boldly to every fearful thing they meet with, "Thou couldest have no power at all against me, except it were given thee from above."

In the last place, those who try to do good *should continually remember the day when they will meet their Lord to receive their final portion.* If they would have Him own them, and confess them before His Father's throne, they must not be ashamed to own and "confess Him" before the men of this world. To do it may cost us much. It may bring on us laughter, mockery, persecution, and scorn; but let us not be laughed out of heaven: let us recollect the great and dreadful day of account, and let us not be afraid to show men that we love Christ, and want them to know and love Him also.

Let these encouragements be treasured up in the hearts of all who labour in Christ's cause, whatever their position may be. The Lord knows their trials, and has spoken these things for their comfort. He cares for all

His believing people, but for none so much as those who work for His cause, and try to do good. May we seek to be of that number! Every believer may do something if he tries. There is always something for every one to do. May we each have an eye to see it, and a will to do it!

MATTHEW X. 34—42.

34 Think not that I am come to send peace on earth: I came not to send peace, but a sword.

35 For I am come to set a man at variance against his father, and the daughter against her mother, and the daughter in law against her mother in law.

36 And a man's foes *shall be* they of his own household.

37 He that loveth father or mother more than me is not worthy of me: and he that loveth son or daughter more than me is not worthy of me.

38 And he that taketh not his cross, and followeth after me, is not worthy of me.

39 He that findeth his life shall lose it: and he that loseth his life for my sake shall find it.

40 He that receiveth you receiveth me, and he that receiveth me receiveth him that sent me.

41 He that receiveth a prophet in the name of a prophet shall receive a prophet's reward; and he that receiveth a righteous man in the name of a righteous man shall receive a righteous man's reward.

42 And whosoever shall give to drink unto one of these little ones a cup of cold *water* only in the name of a disciple, verily I say unto you, he shall in no wise lose his reward.

In these verses the great Head of the Church winds up His first charge to those whom He sends forth to make known His Gospel. He declares three great truths, which form a fitting conclusion to the whole discourse.

In the first place, He bids us remember *that His Gospel will not cause peace and agreement wherever it comes.* "I came not to send peace, but a sword." The object of His first coming on earth was not to set up a millennial kingdom in which all would be of one mind, but to bring in the Gospel, which would lead to strifes and divisions. We have no right to be surprised if we see this continually fulfilled: we are not to think it strange if the Gospel rends asunder families, and causes estrangement between the nearest relations. It is sure to do so in many cases, because of the deep corruption of man's heart. So long as one man believes, and another remains unbelieving, so long as one is resolved to keep his sins, and another is desirous to give them up, the result of the preaching of the Gospel must needs be division. For this the Gospel is not to blame, but the heart of man.

There is deep truth in all this, which is constantly forgotten and overlooked. Many talk vaguely about "unity," and "harmony," and "peace" in the Church of Christ, as if they were things that we ought always to expect, and for the sake of which everything ought to be sacrificed! Such persons would do well to remember the words of our Lord. No doubt unity and peace are mighty blessings; we ought to seek them, pray for them, and give up everything in order to obtain them, *excepting* truth and a good conscience: but it is an idle dream to suppose that the Churches of Christ will enjoy much of unity and peace before the millennium comes.

In the second place, our Lord tells us *that true Christians must make up their minds to trouble in this world.* Whether we are ministers or hearers, whether we teach or are taught, it makes little difference: we must carry "a cross." We must be content to lose even life itself for Christ's sake. We must submit to the loss of man's favour, we must endure hardships, we must deny ourselves in many things, or we shall never reach heaven at last. So long as the world, the devil, and our own hearts, are what they are, these things must be so.

We shall find it most useful to remember this lesson ourselves, and to impress it upon others. Few things do so much harm in religion as exaggerated expectations.

People look for a degree of worldly comfort in Christ's service, which they have no right to expect; and not finding what they looked for, are tempted to give up religion in disgust. Happy is he who thoroughly understands, that though Christianity holds out a crown in the end, it brings also a cross in the way.

In the last place, our Lord cheers us by saying, *that the least service done to those who work in His cause is observed and rewarded of God.* He that gives a believer so little as "a cup of cold water only in the name of a disciple shall in no wise lose his reward."

There is something very beautiful in this promise. It teaches us that the eyes of the great Master are ever upon those who labour for Him, and try to do good. They seem perhaps to work on unnoticed and unregarded; the proceedings of preachers, and missionaries, and teachers and visitors of the poor, may appear very trifling and insignificant, compared to the movements of kings and of parliaments, of armies and of statesmen: but they are not insignificant in the eyes of God. He takes notice who opposes His servants, and who helps them; He observes who is kind to them, as Lydia was to Paul; and who throws difficulties in their way, as Diotrephes did in the way of John. (Acts xvi. 15; 3 John 9.) All their daily experience is recorded, as they labour on in His harvest: all is written down in the great book of His remembrance, and will be brought to light at the last day. The chief butler forgot Joseph, when he was restored to his place; but the Lord Jesus never forgets any of His people. He will say to many who little expect it, in the resurrection morning, "I was an hungered, and ye gave Me meat: I was thirsty, and ye gave Me drink." (Matt. xxv. 35.)

Let us ask ourselves, as we close the chapter, in what light we regard Christ's work and Christ's cause in the world? Are we helpers of it or hinderers? Do we in any wise aid the Lord's "prophets," and "righteous men"? Do we assist His "little ones"? Do we impede His labourers, or do we cheer them on?—These are serious questions. They do well and wisely who give the "cup of cold water," whenever they have opportunity: they do better still who work actively in the Lord's vineyard. May we all strive to leave the world a better world than it was when we were born! This is to have the mind of Christ. This is to find out the value of the lessons this wonderful chapter contains.

MATTHEW XI. 1—15.

1 And it came to pass, when Jesus had made an end of commanding his twelve disciples, he departed thence to teach and to preach in their cities.

2 Now when John had heard in the prison the works of Christ, he sent two of his disciples,

3 And said unto him, Art thou he that should come, or do we look for another?

4 Jesus answered and said unto them, Go and show John again those things which ye do hear and see:

5 The blind receive their sight, and the lame walk, the lepers are cleansed, and the deaf hear, the dead are raised up, and the poor have the gospel preached to them.

6 And blessed is *he*, whosoever shall not be offended in me.

7 And as they departed, Jesus began to say unto the multitudes concerning John, What went ye out into the wilderness to see? A reed shaken with the wind?

8 But what went ye out for to see? A man clothed in soft raiment? behold, they that wear soft *clothing* are in king's houses.

9 But what went ye out for to see? A prophet? yea, I say unto you, and more than a prophet.

10 For this is *he*, of whom it is written, Behold, I send my messenger before thy face, which shall prepare thy way before thee.

11 Verily I say unto you, Among them that are born of women there hath not risen a greater than John the Baptist: notwithstanding he that is least in the kingdom of heaven is greater than he.

12 And from the days of John the Baptist until now the kingdom of heaven suffereth violence, and the violent take it by force.

13 For all the prophets and the law prophesied until John.

14 And if ye will receive *it*, this is Elias, which was for to come.

15 He that hath ears to hear, let him hear.

THE first thing that demands our attention in this passage *is the message which John the Baptist sends to our Lord Jesus Christ.* He "sent two of his disciples, and said unto Him, Art thou He that should come, or do we look for another?"

This question did not arise from doubt or unbelief on the part of John. We do that holy man injustice if we interpret it in such a way. It was asked for the benefit of his disciples: it was meant to give them an opportunity of hearing from Christ's own lips the evidence of His divine mission. No doubt John the Baptist felt that his own ministry was ended; something within him told him that he would never come forth from Herod's prison-house, but would surely die. He remembered the ignorant jealousies that had already been shown by his disciples towards the disciples of Christ. He took the most likely course to dispel those jealousies for ever: he sent his followers to "hear and see" for themselves.

The conduct of John the Baptist in this matter affords a striking example to ministers, teachers, and parents, when they draw near the end of their course. Their chief concern should be about the souls of those they are going to leave behind them; their great desire should be to persuade them to cleave to Christ. The death of those who have guided and instructed us on earth ought always to have this effect. It should make us lay hold more firmly on Him who dieth no more, "continueth ever," and "hath an unchangeable priesthood." (Heb. vii. 24.)

The second thing that demands our notice in this passage, is *the high testimony which our Lord bears to the character of John the Baptist.* No mortal man ever received such commendation as Jesus here bestows on His imprisoned friend. "Among them that are born of women there hath not risen a greater than John the Baptist." In time past John had boldly confessed Jesus before men, as the Lamb of God: now Jesus openly declares John to be more than a prophet.

There were some, no doubt, who were disposed to think lightly of John the Baptist, partly from ignorance of the nature of his ministry, partly from misunderstanding the question he had sent to ask. Our Lord Jesus silences such cavillers by the declaration He here makes: He tells them not to suppose that John was a timid, vacillating, unstable man, "a reed shaken by the wind;" if they thought so, they were utterly mistaken: he was a bold, unflinching witness to the truth.—He tells them not to suppose that John was at heart a worldly man, fond of King's courts, and delicate living; if they thought so, they greatly erred: he was a self-denying preacher of repentance, who would risk the anger of a King, rather than not reprove his sins.—In short, he would have them know that John was "more than a prophet." He was one to whom God had given more honour than to all the Old Thstament prophets: they indeed prophesied of Christ, but died without seeing Him; John not only prophesied of Him, but saw Him face to face. —they foretold that the days of the Son of man would certainly come, and the Messiah appear; John was an actual eye-witness of those days, and an honoured instrument in preparing men for them.—To them it was given to predict that Messiah would be "brought as a lamb to the slaughter," and "cut off" (Isai. liii. 7: Dan. x. 26); to John it was given to point to Him, and say, "Behold the Lamb of God, which taketh away the sin of the world." (John i. 29.)

There is something very beautiful and comforting to true Christians in this testimony which our Lord bears to John the Baptist. It shows us the tender interest which our great Head feels in the lives and characters of all His members; it shows us what honour He is ready to put on the work and labour that they go through in His cause. It is a sweet foretaste of the confession which He will make of them before the assembled world, when He presents them faultless at the last day before His Father's throne.

Do we know what it is to work for Christ? Have we ever felt cast down and dispirited, as if we were doing no good, and no one cared for us? Are we ever tempted to feel, when laid aside by sickness, or withdrawn by providence, "I have laboured in vain, and spent my strength for naught"?—Let us meet such thoughts by the recollection of this passage. Let us remember, there is One who daily records all we do for Him, and sees more beauty in His servants' work than His servants do themselves. The same tongue which bore testimony to John in prison, will bear testimony to all His people at the last day: He will say, "Come, ye blessed of my Father, inherit the kingdom prepared for you from the foundation of the world." (Matt. xxv 34.) And then shall His faithful witnesses discover, to their wonder and surprise, that there never was a word spoken on their Master's behalf, which does not receive a reward.

MATTHEW XI. 16—24.

16 But whereunto shall I liken this generation? It is like unto children sitting in the markets, and calling unto their fellows,

17 And saying, We have piped unto you, and ye have not danced; we have mourned unto you, and ye have not lamented.

18 For John came neither eating nor drinking, and they say, He hath a devil.

19 The Son of man came eating and drinking, and they say, Behold, a man gluttonous, and a winebibber, a friend of publicans and sinners. But wisdom is justified of her children.

20 Then began he to upbraid the cities wherein most of his mighty works were done, because they repented not:

21 Woe unto thee, Chorazin! woe unto thee, Bethsaida! for if the mighty works, which were done in you, had been done in Tyre and Sidon, they would have repented long ago in sackcloth and ashes.

22 But I say unto you, It shall be more tolerable for Tyre and Sidon at the day of judgment, than for you.

23 And thou, Capernaum, which art exalted unto heaven, shalt be brought down to hell: for if the mighty works, which have been done in thee, had been done in Sodom, it would have remained until this day.

24 But I say unto you, That it shall be more tolerable for the land of Sodom in the day of judgment, than for thee.

THESE sayings of the Lord Jesus were called forth by the state of the Jewish nation when He was upon earth. But they speak loudly to us also, as well as to the Jews: they throw great light on some parts of the natural man's character; they teach us the perilous state of many immortal souls in the present day.

The first part of these verses shows us the *unreasonableness of many unconverted men in the things of religion.* The Jews, in our Lord's time, found fault with every teacher whom God sent among them. First came John the Baptist, preaching repentance: an austere man, a man who withdrew himself from society, and lived an ascetic life. Did this satisfy the Jews? No! They found fault and said, "He hath a devil."—Then came Jesus the Son of God, preaching the Gospel: living as other men lived, and practising none of John the Baptist's peculiar austerities. And did this satisfy the Jews? No! They found fault again, and said, "Behold a man gluttonous and a wine-bibber, a friend of publicans and sinners." In short, they were as perverse and hard to please as wayward children.

It is a mournful fact, that there are always thousands of professing Christians just as unreasonable as these Jews. They are equally perverse, and equally hard to please: whatever we teach and preach, they find fault; whatever be our manner of life, they are dissatisfied. Do we tell them of salvation by grace, and justification by faith? At once they cry out against our doctrine as licentious and Antinomian.—Do we tell them of the holiness which the Gospel requires? At once they exclaim that we are too strict, and precise, and righteous overmuch.—Are we cheerful? They accuse us of levity. —Are we grave? They call us gloomy and sour.—Do we keep aloof from balls, and races, and plays? They denounce us as puritanical, exclusive, and narrow-minded—Do we eat, and drink, and dress like other people, and attend to our worldly callings, and go into society? They sneeringly insinuate that they see no difference between us and those who make no religious profession at all; and that we are not better than other men.—What is all this but the conduct of the Jews over again? "We have piped unto you, and ye have not danced: we have mourned unto you, and ye have not lamented." He who spake these words knew the hearts of men!

The plain truth is, that true believers must not expect unconverted men to be satisfied, either with their faith or their practice. If they do, they expect what they will not find. They must make up their minds to hear objections, cavils, and excuses, however holy their own lives may be. Well says Quesnel, "Whatever measures good men take, they will never escape the censures of the world. The best way is not to be concerned at them." After all, what saith the Scripture? "The carnal mind is enmity against God." "The natural man receiveth not the things of the Spirit of God." (Rom. viii. 7; 1 Cor. ii. 14.) This is the explanation of the whole matter.

The second part of these verses shows us *the exceeding wickedness of wilful impenitence.* Our Lord declares that it shall be "more tolerable for Tyre, Sidon, and Sodom, in the day of judgment," than for those towns where people had heard His sermons, and seen His miracles, but had not repented.

There is something very solemn in this saying. Let us look at it well: let us think for a moment what dark, idolatrous, immoral, profligate places Tyre and Sidon must have been; let us call to mind the unspeakable wickedness of Sodom; let us remember that the cities named by our Lord—Chorazin, Bethsaida, and Capernaum—were probably no worse than other Jewish towns; and, at all events, were far better and more moral than Tyre, Sidon, and Sodom. And then let us observe that the people of Chorazin, Bethsaida, and Capernaum, are to be in the lowest hell, because they heard the Gospel, and yet did not repent,—because they had great religious advantages, and did not use them. How awful this sounds!

Surely these words ought to make the ears of every one tingle, who hears the Gospel regularly, and yet remains unconverted. How great is the guilt of such a man before God! How great is the danger in which he daily stands! Moral, and decent, and respectable as his life may be, he is actually more guilty than an idolatrous Tyrian or Sidonian, or a miserable inhabitant of Sodom! They had no spiritual light: he has, and neglects it.—They heard no Gospel: he hears, but does not obey it.—Their hearts might have been softened, if they had enjoyed his privileges: Tyre and Sidon "would have repented:" Sodom "would have remained until this day." His heart under the full blaze of the Gospel remains hard and unmoved.—There is but one painful conclusion to be drawn: his guilt will be found greater than their's at the last day. Most true is the remark of an English Bishop, "Among all the aggravations of our sins, there is none more heinous than the frequent hearing of our duty."

May we all think often about Chorazin, Bethsaida, and Capernaum! Let us settle it in our minds that it will never do to be content with merely hearing and liking the Gospel: we must go further than this: we must actually "repent and be converted." (Acts iii. 19.) We must actually lay hold on Christ, and become one with Him: till then we are in awful danger. It will prove more tolerable to have lived in Tyre, Sidon, and Sodom, than to have heard the Gospel in England, and at last die unconverted.

MATTHEW XI. 25—30.

25 At that time Jesus answered and said, I thank thee, O Father, Lord of heaven and earth, because thou hast hid these things from the wise and prudent, and hast revealed them unto babes.

26 Even so, Father: for so it seemed good in thy sight.

27 All things are delivered unto me of my Father: and no man knoweth the Son, but the Father; neither knoweth any man the

Father, save the Son, and *he* to whomsoever the Son will reveal *him*.
28 Come unto me, all ye that labour and are heavy laden, and I will give you rest.
29 Take my yoke upon you, and learn of me: for I am meek and lowly in heart; and ye shall find rest unto your souls.
30 For my yoke *is* easy, and my burden is light.

THERE are few passages in the four Gospels more important than this.—There are few which contain in so short a compass, so many precious truths. May God give us an eye to see, and a heart to feel their value!

Let us learn, in the first place, *the excellence of a child-like and teachable frame of mind.* Our Lord says to His Father, "Thou hast hid these things from the wise and prudent, and revealed them unto babes."

It is not for us to attempt to explain why some receive and believe the Gospel, while others do not. The sovereignty of God in this matter is a deep mystery: we cannot fathom it. But one thing, at all events, stands out in Scripture, as a great practical truth to be had in everlasting remembrance: those from whom the Gospel is hidden are generally "the wise in their own eyes, and prudent in their own sight;" those to whom the Gospel is revealed are generally humble, simple-minded, and willing to learn. The words of the Virgin Mary are continually being fulfilled: "He hath filled the hungry with good things, and the rich He hath sent empty away." (Luke i. 53.)

Let us watch against pride in every shape,—pride of intellect, pride of wealth, pride in our own goodness, pride in our own deserts. Nothing is so likely to keep a man out of heaven, and prevent him seeing Christ, as pride: so long as we think we are something we shall never be saved. Let us pray for and cultivate humility;

let us seek to know ourselves aright, and to find out our place in the sight of a holy God. The beginning of the way to heaven, is to feel that we are in the way to hell, and to be willing to be taught of the Spirit. One of the first steps in saving Christianity, is to be able to say with Saul, "Lord what wilt Thou have me to do?" (Acts ix. 6.) There is hardly a sentence of our Lord's so frequently repeated as this, "He that humbleth himself shall be exalted." (Luke xviii. 14.)

Let us learn, in the second place, from these verses, *the greatness and majesty of our Lord Jesus Christ.*

The language of our Lord on this subject is deep and wonderful. He says "All things are delivered unto Me of my Father: and no man knoweth the Son save the Father, neither knoweth any man the Father save the Son, and he to whom the Son shall reveal Him." We may truly say, as we read these words, "Such knowledge is too wonderful for me; it is high: I cannot attain to it." (Psalm cxxxix. 6.) We see something of the perfect union which exists between the first and second Persons of the Trinity; we see something of the immeasurable superiority of the Lord Jesus to all who are nothing more than men: but still, when we have said all this, we must confess that there are heights and depths in this verse, which are beyond our feeble comprehension. We can only admire them in the spirit of little children: but the half of them, we must feel, remains untold.

Let us, however, draw from these words the great practical truth, that all power over everything that concerns our soul's interests is placed in our Lord Jesus Christ's hands. "All things are delivered unto Him."—

He bears the keys: to Him we must go for admission into heaven.—He is the door: through Him we must enter.—He is the Shepherd: we must hear His voice, and follow Him, if we would nor perish in the wilderness.—He is the Physician: we must apply to Him, if we would be healed of the plague of sin.—He is the bread of life: we must feed on Him, if we would have our souls satisfied.—He is the light: we must walk after Him if we would not wander in darkness.—He is the fountain: we must wash in His blood, if we would be cleansed, and made ready for the great day of account. Blessed and glorious are these truths! If we have Christ, we have all things. (1 Cor. iii. 22.)

Let us learn, in the last place, from this passage, *the breadth and fulness of the invitations of Christ's Gospel.*

The three last verses of the chapter, which contain this lesson, are indeed precious. They meet the trembling sinner who asks, "Will Christ reveal His Father's love to such an one as me?" with the most gracious encouragement. They are verses which deserve to be read with special attention. For eighteen hundred years they have been a blessing to the world, and have done good to myriads of souls. There is not a sentence in them which does not contain a mine of thought.

We should mark who they are that Jesus invites. He does not address those who feel themselves righteous and worthy: He addresses "all that labour and are heavy laden."—It is a wide description: it comprises multitudes in this weary world. All who feel a load on their heart, of which they would fain get free, a load of sin or a load of sorrow, a load of anxiety or a load of remorse,

—all, whosoever they may be, and whatsoever their past lives,—all such are invited to come to Christ.

We should mark what a gracious offer Jesus makes: "I will give you rest.—Ye shall find rest to your souls." How cheering and comfortable are these words! Unrest is one great characteristic of the world: hurry, vexation, failure, disappointment, stare us in the face on every side. But here is hope: there is an ark of refuge for the weary, as truly as there was for Noah's dove. There is rest in Christ, rest of conscience, and rest of heart, rest built on pardon of all sin, rest flowing from peace with God.

We should mark what a simple request Jesus makes to the labouring and heavy-laden ones. "Come unto Me:—Take my yoke upon you, learn of Me." He interposes no hard conditions; He speaks nothing of work to be done first, and deservingness of His gifts to be established: He only asks us to come to Him just as we are, with all our sins, and to submit ourselves like little children to His teaching. "Go not," He seems to say, "to man for relief. Wait not for help to arise from any other quarter. Just as you are, this very day, come to Me."

We should mark what an encouraging account Jesus gives of Himself. He says, "I am meek and lowly of heart." How true that is, the experience of all the saints of God has often proved. Mary and Martha at Bethany, Peter after his fall, the disciples after the resurrection, Thomas after his cold unbelief, all tasted the "meekness and gentleness of Christ." It is the only place in Scripture where the "heart" of Christ is actually named. It is a saying never to be forgotten.

We should mark, lastly, the encouraging account that Jesus gives of His service. He says, "My yoke is easy, and my burden is light." No doubt there is a cross to be carried, if we follow Christ; no doubt there are trials to be endured, and battles to be fought: but the comforts of the Gospel far outweigh the cross. Compared to the service of the world and sin, compared to the yoke of Jewish ceremonies, and the bondage of human superstition, Christ's service is in the highest sense easy and light. His yoke is no more a burden than the feathers are to a bird; His commandments are not grievous; His ways are ways of pleasantness, and all His paths are peace. (1 John v. 3; Prov. iii. 17.)

And now comes the solemn inquiry, "Have we accepted this invitation for ourselves? Have we no sins to be forgiven, no griefs to be removed, no wounds of conscience to be healed?" Let us hear Christ's voice: He speaks to us as well as to the Jews. He says, "Come unto Me."—Here is the key to true happiness; here is the secret of having a light heart. All turns and hinges on an acceptance of this offer of Christ.

May we never be satisfied till we know and feel that we have come to Christ by faith for rest, and do still come to Him for fresh supplies of grace every day! If we have come to Him already, let us learn to cleave to Him more closely. If we have never come to Him yet, let us begin to come to-day. His word shall never be broken: "Him that cometh unto Me, I will in no wise cast out." (John vi. 37.)

MATTHEW XII. 1—13.

1 At that time Jesus went on
the sabbath day through the corn;
and his disciples were an hungred,
and began to pluck the ears of corn,
and to eat.
2 But when the Pharisees saw
it, they said unto him, Behold, thy
disciples do that which is not lawful to do upon the sabbath day.
3 But he said unto them, Have
ye not read what David did, when
he was an hungred, and they that
were with him;
4 How he entered into the house
of God, and did eat the shewbread,
which was not lawful for him to
eat, neither for them which were
with him, but only for the priests?
5 Or have ye not read in the law,
how that on the sabbath days the
priests in the temple profane the
sabbath, and are blameless?
6 But I say unto you, That in
this place is *one* greater than the
temple.
7 But if ye had known what *this*
meaneth, I will have mercy, and
not sacrifice, ye would not have
condemned the guiltless.
8 For the Son of man is Lord
even of the sabbath day.
9 And when he was departed
thence, he went into their synagogue:
10 And, behold, there was a man
which had *his* hand withered. And
they asked him, saying, Is it lawful
to heal on the sabbath days? that
they might accuse him.
11 And he said unto them, What
man shall there be among you,
that shall have one sheep, and if
it fall into a pit on the sabbath
day, will he not lay hold on it, and
lift *it* out?
12 How much then is a man better
than a sheep? Wherefore it is lawful to do well on the sabbath days.
13 Then saith he to the man,
Stretch forth thine hand. And he
stretched *it* forth; and it was restored whole, like as the other.

THE one great subject which stands out prominently in this passage of Scripture, is the Sabbath day. It is a subject on which strange opinions prevailed among the Jews in our Lord's time. The Pharisees had added to the teaching of Scripture about it, and overlaid the true character of the day with the traditions of men. It is a subject on which divers opinions have often been held in the Churches of Christ, and wide differences exist among men at the present time. Let us see what we may learn about it from our Lord's teaching in these verses.

Let us learn, in the first place, from this passage, that *our Lord Jesus Christ does not do away with the observance of a weekly Sabbath day.* He neither does so here nor elsewhere in the four Gospels. We often find His opinion expressed about Jewish errors on the subject of the Sabbath; but we do not find a word to teach us that His disciples were not to keep a Sabbath at all.

It is of much importance to observe this. The mistakes that have arisen from a superficial consideration of our Lord's sayings on the Sabbath question, are neither few nor small; thousands have rushed to the hasty conclusion that Christians have nothing to do with the fourth commandment, and that it is no more binding on us than the Mosaic law about sacrifices: there is nothing in the New Testament to justify any such conclusion.

The plain truth is that our Lord did not abolish the law of the weekly Sabbath: He only freed it from incorrect interpretations, and purified it from man-made additions. He did not tear out of the decalogue the fourth commandment: He only stripped off the miserable traditions with which the Pharisees had incrusted the day, and by which they had made it, not a blessing, but a burden. He left the fourth commandment where He found it,—a part of the eternal law of God, of which no jot or tittle was ever to pass away. May we never forget this!

Let us learn, in the second place, from this passage, that *our Lord Jesus Christ allows all works of real necessity and mercy to be done on the Sabbath day.*

This is a principle which is abundantly established in the passage of Scripture we are now considering. We find our Lord justifying His disciples for plucking the ears of corn on a Sabbath: it was an act permitted in Scripture. (Deut. xxiii. 25.) They "were an hungred," and in need of food: therefore they were not to blame. —We find Him maintaining the lawfulness of healing a sick man on the Sabbath day. The man was suffering from disease and pain: in such a case it was no breach of God's commandment to afford relief. We ought never to rest from doing good.

The arguments by which our Lord supports the lawfulness of any work of necessity and mercy on the Sabbath, are striking and unanswerable. He reminds the Pharisees, who charge Him and His disciples with breaking the law, how David and his men, for want of other food, had eaten the holy shew-bread out of the tabernacle.—He reminds them how the priests in the temple are obliged to do work on the Sabbath, by slaying animals and offering sacrifices.—He reminds them how even a sheep would be helped out of a pit on the Sabbath, rather than allowed to suffer and die, by any one of themselves.—Above all, He lays down the great principle that no ordinance of God is to be pressed so far as to make us neglect the plain duties of charity. "I will have mercy, and not sacrifice." The first table of the law is not to be so interpreted as to make us break the second: the fourth commandment is not to be so explained as to make us unkind and unmerciful to our neighbour. There is deep wisdom in all this. We are reminded of the saying, "Never man spake like this man."

In leaving the subject, let us beware that we are never tempted to take low views of the sanctity of the Christian Sabbath. Let us take care that we do not make our gracious Lord's teaching an excuse for Sabbath profanation. Let us not abuse the liberty which He has so clearly marked out for us, and pretend that we do things on the Sabbath from "necessity and mercy," which in reality we do for our own selfish gratification.

There is great reason for warning people on this point. The mistakes of the Pharisee about the Sabbath were in one direction; the mistakes of the Christian are in another. The Pharisee pretended to add to the holiness of the day; the Christian is too often disposed to take away from that holiness, and to keep the day in an idle, profane, irreverent manner. May we all watch our own conduct on this subject! Saving Christianity is closely bound up with Sabbath observance. May we never forget that our great aim should be to "keep the Sabbath *holy!*" Works of necessity may be done: "It is lawful to do well," and show mercy; but to give the Sabbath to idleness, pleasure-seeking, or the world, is utterly unlawful. It is contrary to the example of Christ, and a sin against a plain commandment of God.

MATTHEW XII. 14—21.

14 Then the Pharisees went out, and held a council against him, how they might destroy him.

15 But when Jesus knew it, he withdrew himself from thence: and great multitudes followed him, and he healed them all;

16 And charged them that they should not make him known:

17 That it might be fulfilled which was spoken by Esaias the prophet, saying,

18 Behold my servant, whom I have chosen: my beloved, in whom my soul is well pleased: I will put my spirit upon him, and he shall shew judgment to the Gentiles.

19 He shall not strive, nor cry; neither shall any man hear his voice in the streets.

20 A bruised reed shall he not break, and smoking flax shall he not quench, till he send forth judgment unto victory.

21 And in his name shall the Gentiles trust.

THE first thing which demands our notice in this passage, is *the desperate wickedness of the human heart*, which it exemplifies. Silenced and defeated by our Lord's arguments, the Pharisees plunged deeper and deeper into sin. They "went out and held a council against Him how they might destroy Him."

What evil had our Lord done, that He should be so treated? None, none at all: no charge could be brought against His life. He was holy, harmless, undefiled, and separate from sinners; His days were spent in doing good.—No charge could be brought against His teaching: He had proved it to be agreeable to Scripture and reason, and no reply had been made to His proofs. But it mattered little how perfectly He lived or taught: He was hated.

This is human nature appearing in its true colours! The unconverted heart hates God, and will show its hatred whenever it dares, and has a favourable opportunity. It will persecute God's witnesses; it will dislike all who have anything of God's mind, and are renewed after His image. Why were so many of the prophets killed? Why were the names of the apostles cast out as evil by the Jews? Why were the early martyrs slain? Why were John Huss, and Jerome of Prague, and Ridley, and Latimer burned at the stake? Not for any sins that they had sinned,—not for any wickedness they had committed. They all suffered because they were godly men. And human nature, unconverted, hates godly men, because it hates God.

It must never surprise true Christians if they meet with the same treatment that the Lord Jesus met with. "Marvel not if the world hates you." (1 John iii. 13.) It is not the utmost consistency, or the closest walk with God, that will exempt them from the enmity of the natural man. They need not torture their consciences by fancying that if they were only more faultless and consistent, everybody would surely love them: it is all a mistake. They should remember, that there was never but one perfect man on earth, and that He was not loved, but hated. It is not the infirmities of a believer that the world dislikes, but his godliness; it is not the remains of the old nature that call forth the world's enmity, but the exhibition of the new. Let us remember these things, and be patient. The world hated Christ, and the world will hate Christians.

The second thing which demands our notice in this passage, is *the encouraging description of our Lord Jesus Christ's character*, which St. Matthew draws from the prophet Isaiah. "A bruised reed shall He not break, and smoking flax shall He not quench."

What are we to understand by the bruised reed, and smoking flax? The language of the prophet no doubt is figurative. What is it that these two expressions mean? The simplest explanation seems to be, that the Holy Ghost is here describing persons whose grace is at present weak, whose repentence is feeble, and whose faith is small. Towards such persons the Lord Jesus Christ will be very tender and compassionate. Weak as the bruised reed is, it shall not be broken; small as the spark of fire may be within the smoking flax, it shall not be quenched. It is a standing truth in the kingdom of grace, that weak grace, weak faith, and weak repentance, are all precious in our Lord's sight. Mighty as He is, "He despiseth not any." (Job xxxvi. 5.)

The doctrine here laid down is full of comfort and consolation. There are thousands in every Church of Christ to whom it ought to speak peace and hope. There are some in every congregation that hears the Gospel, who are ready to despair of their own salvation, because their strength seems so small; they are full of fears and despondency, because their knowledge, and faith, and hope, and love, appear so dwarfish snd diminutive. Let them drink comfort out of this text; let them know that weak faith gives a man as real and true an interest in Christ as strong faith, though it may not give him the same joy. There is life in an infant as truly as in a grown-up man; there is fire in a spark as truly as in a burning flame. The least degree of grace is an everlasting possession. It comes down from heaven; it is precious in our Lord's eyes: it shall never be overthrown.

Does Satan make light of the beginnings of repentance towards God, and faith towards our Lord Jesus Christ? No: indeed, he does not! He has great wrath, because he sees his time is short.—Do the angels of God think lightly of the first signs of penitence and feeling after God in Christ? No: indeed, "there is joy" among them, when they behold the sight! Does the Lord Jesus regard no faith and repentance with interest, unless they are strong and mighty? "No: indeed! As soon as that "bruised reed," Saul of Tarsus, begins to cry to Him, He sends Ananias to him, saying, "Behold he prayeth." (Acts ix. 11.) We err greatly if we do not encourage the very first movements of a soul towards Christ. Let the ignorant world scoff and mock, if it will; we may be sure that "bruised reeds" and "smoking flax" are very precious in our Lord's eyes.

May we all lay these things to heart, and use them in time of need, both for ourselves and others! It should be a standing maxim in our religion,—that a spark is better than utter darkness; and little faith better than no faith at all. "Who hath despised the day of small things?" (Zech. iv. 10.) It is not despised by Christ. It ought not to be despised by Christians.

MATTHEW XII. 22—37.

22 Then was brought unto him one possessed with a devil, blind, and dumb: and he healed him, insomuch that the blind and dumb both spake and saw.

23 And all the people were amazed, and said, Is not this the Son of David?

24 But when the Pharisees heard *it*, they said, This *fellow* doth not cast out devils, but by Beelzebub the prince of the devils.

25 And Jesus knew their thoughts, and said unto them, Every kingdom divided against itself is brought to desolation; and every city or house divided against itself shall not stand:

26 And if Satan cast out Satan, he is divided against himself; how shall then his kingdom stand?

27 And if I by Beelzebub cast out devils, by whom do your children cast *them* out? therefore they shall be your judges.

28 But if I cast out devils by the Spirit of God, then the kingdom of God is come unto you.

29 Or else how can one enter into a strong man's house, and spoil his goods, except he first bind the strong man? and then he will spoil his house.

30 He that is not with me is against me; and he that gathereth not with me scattereth abroad.

31 Wherefore I say unto you, All manner of sin and blasphemy shall be forgiven unto men: but the blasphemy *against* the *Holy Ghost* shall not be forgiven unto men.

32 And whosoever speaketh a word against the Son of man, it shall be forgiven him: but whosoever speaketh against the Holy Ghost, it shall not be forgiven him, neither in this world, neither in the *world* to come.

33 Either make the tree good, and his fruit good; or else make the tree corrupt, and his fruit corrupt: for the tree is known by *his* fruit.

34 O generation of vipers, how can ye, being evil, speak good things? for out of the abundance of the heart the mouth speaketh.

35 A good man out of the good treasure of the heart bringeth forth good things: and an evil man out of the evil treasure bringeth forth evil things.

36 But I say unto you, That every idle word that men shall speak, they shall give account thereof in the day of Judgment.

37 For by thy words thou shalt be justified, and by thy words thou shalt be condemned.

THIS passage of Scripture contains "things hard to be understood." The sin against the Holy Ghost in particular has never been fully explained by the most learned divines. It is not difficult to show from Scripture what the sin is not: it is difficult to show clearly what it is. We must not be surprised. The Bible would not be the book of God, if it had not deep places here and there, which man has no line to fathom. Let us rather thank God that there are lessons of wisdom to be gathered, even out of these verses, which the unlearned may easily understand.

Let us gather from them, in the first place, that there is *nothing too blasphemous for hardened and prejudiced men to say against religion.* Our Lord casts out a devil; and at once the Pharisees declare that He does it "by the prince of the devils."

This was an absurd charge. Our Lord shows that it was unreasonable to suppose that the devil would help to pull down his own kingdom, and "Satan cast out Satan." But there is nothing too absurd and unreasonable for men to say, when they are thoroughly set against religion. The Pharisees are not the only people who have lost sight of logic, good sense, and temper, when they have attacked the Gospel of Christ.

Strange as this charge may sound, it is one that has often been made against the servants of God. Their enemies have been obliged to confess that they are doing a work, and producing an effect on the world. The results of Christian labour stare them in the face: they cannot deny them. What then shall they say? They say the very thing that the Pharisees said of our Lord, "It is the devil." The early heretics used language of this kind about Athanasius; the Roman Catholics spread reports of this sort about Martin Luther. Such things will be said as long as the world stands.

We must never be surprised to hear of dreadful charges being made against the best of men, without cause. "If they called the Master of the house Beelzebub, how much more shall they call them of His household?"—It is an old device. When the Christian's arguments cannot be answered, and the Christian's works cannot be denied, the last resource of the wicked is to try to blacken the Christian's character. If this be our lot, let us bear it patiently: having Christ and a good conscience, we may be content; false charges will not keep us out of heaven. Our character will be cleared at the last day.

In the second place, let us gather from these verses *the impossibility of neutrality in religion.* "He that is not with Christ is against Him, and he that gathereth not with Him, scattereth abroad."

There are many persons in every age of the Church, who need to have this lesson pressed upon them. They endeavour to steer a middle course in religion: they are not so bad as many sinners, but still they are not saints. They feel the truth of Christ's Gospel, when it is brought before them; but they are afraid to confess what they feel. Because they have these feelings, they flatter themselves they are not so bad as others; and yet they shrink from the standard of faith and practice which the Lord Jesus sets up. They are not boldly fighting on Christ's side, and yet they are not openly against Him. Our Lord warns all such that they are in a dangerous position. There are only two parties in religious matters: there are only two camps: there are only two sides. Are we with Christ, and working in His cause?

If not, we are against Him. Are we doing good in the world? If not, we are doing harm.

The principal here laid down is one which it concerns us all to remember. Let us settle it in our minds that we shall never have peace and do good to others unless we are thorough-going and decided in our Christianity. The way of Gamaliel never yet brought happiness and usefulness to any one, and never will.

In the third place, let us gather from these verses *the exceeding sinfulness of sins against knowledge.*

This is a practical conclusion which appears to flow naturally from our Lord's words about the blasphemy against the Holy Ghost. Difficult as these words undoubtedly are, they seem fairly to prove that there are degrees in sin. Offences arising from ignorance of the true mission of the Son of man, will not be punished so heavily as offences committed against the noontide light of the dispensation of the Holy Ghost. The brighter the light, the greater the guilt of him who rejects it; the clearer a man's knowledge of the nature of the Gospel, the greater his sin, if he wilfully refuses to repent and believe.

The doctrine here taught is one that does not stand alone in Scripture. St. Paul says to the Hebrews, "It is impossible for those who were once enlightened, if they shall fall away, to renew them again unto repentance;" "If we sin wilfully, after that we have received the knowledge of the truth, there remaineth no more sacrifice for sins, but a fearful looking for of judgment." (Heb. vi. 4—6; x. 26, 27.) It is a doctrine of which we find mournful proofs in every quarter. The unconverted children of godly parents, the unconverted servants of godly families, and the unconverted members of evangelical congregations, are the hardest people on earth to impress. They seem past feeling. The same fire which melts the wax hardens the clay.—It is a doctrine, moreover, which receives awful confirmation from the histories of some whose last ends were eminently hopeless. Pharoah, and Saul, and Ahab, and Judas Iscariot, and Julian, and Francis Spira, are fearful illustrations of our Lord's meaning. In each of these cases there was a combination of clear knowledge and deliberate rejection of Christ. In each there was light in the head, but hatred of truth in the heart. And the end of each seems to have been "blackness of darkness for ever."

May God give us a will to use our knowledge, whether it be little or great! May we beware of neglecting our opportunities, and leaving our privileges unimproved! Have we light? Then let us live fully up to our light. Do we know the truth? Then let us walk in the truth. This is the best safeguard against the unpardonable sin.

In the last place, let us gather from these verses *the immense importance of carefulness about our daily words.* Our Lord tells us, that "for every idle word that men shall speak, they shall give account in the day of judgment." And He adds, "By thy words thou shalt be justified, and by thy words thou shalt be condemned."

There are few of our Lord's sayings which are so heart-searching as this. There is nothing, perhaps, to which most men pay less attention than their words. They go through their daily work, speaking and talking without thought or reflection, and seem to fancy that if they *do* what is right, it matters but little what they *say*.

But is it so? Are our words so utterly trifling and unimportant? We dare not say so, with such a passage of Scripture as this before our eyes. Our words are the evidence of the state of our hearts, as surely as the taste of the water is an evidence of the state of the spring. "Out of the abundance of the heart the mouth speaketh." The lips only utter what the mind conceives. Our words will form one subject of inquiry at the day of judgment: we shall have to give account of our sayings, as well as of our doings. Truly these are very solemn considerations. If there were no other text in the Bible, this passage ought to convince us, that we are all "guilty before God," and need a righteousness better than our own, even the righteousness of Christ. (Phil. iii. 9.)

Let us be humble as we read this passage, in the recollection of time past. How many idle, foolish, vain, light, frivolous, sinful, and unprofitable things we have all said! How many words we have used which, like thistle-down, have flown far and wide, and sown mischief in the hearts of others, that will never die! How often when we have met our friends, "our conversation," to use an old saint's expression, "has only made work for repentance." There is deep truth in the remark of Burkitt, "A profane scoff or atheistical jest may stick in the minds of those who hear it, after the tongue that spake it is dead. A word spoken is physically transient, but morally permanent." "Death and life," says Solomon, "are in the power of the tongue." (Prov. xviii. 21.)

Let us be watchful as we read this passage about words,

when we look forward to our days yet to come; let us resolve, by God's grace, to be more careful over our tongues, and more particular about our use of them; let us pray daily that our "Speech may be always with grace." (Coloss. iv. 6.) Let us say every morning with holy David, "I will take heed to my ways, that I sin not with my tongue;" let us cry with him to the Strong One for strength, and say, "Set a watch before my mouth, and keep the door of my lips." Well indeed might St. James say, "If any man offend not in word, the same is a perfect man." (Psal. xxxix. 1; cxli. 3; James iii. 2.)

MATTHEW XII. 38—50.

38 Then certain of the scribes and of the Pharisees answered, saying, Master, we would see a sign from thee.

39 But he answered and said unto them, An evil and adulterous generation seeketh after a sign; and there shall no sign be given to it, but the sign of the prophet Jonas:

40 For as Jonas was three days and three nights in the whale's belly: so shall the son of man be three days and three nights in the heart of the earth.

41 The men of Nineveh shall rise in judgment with this generation, and shall condemn it: because they repented at the preaching of Jonas: and, behold, a greater than Jonas *is* here.

42 The queen of the south shall rise up in the judgment with this generation, and shall condemn it: for she came from the uttermost parts of the earth to hear the wisdom of Solomon: and, behold, a greater than Solomon *is* here.

43 When the unclean spirit is gone out of a man, he walketh through dry places, seeking rest, and findeth none.

44 Then he saith, I will return into my house from whence I came out; and when he is come, he findeth *it* empty, swept, and garnished.

45 Then goeth he, and taketh with himself seven other spirits more wicked than himself, and they enter in and dwell there: and the last *state* of that man is worse than the first. Even so shall it be also unto this wicked generation.

46 While he yet talked to the people, behold, *his* mother and his brethren stood without, desiring to speak with him.

47 Then one said unto him, Behold, thy mother and thy brethren stand without, desiring to speak with thee.

48 But he answered and said unto him that told him, Who is my mother, and who are my brethren?

49 And he stretched forth his hand toward his disciples, and said, Behold my mother and my brethren!

50 For whosoever shall do the will of my Father which is in heaven, the same is my brother, and sister, and mother.

THE beginning of this passage is one of those places

which strikingly illustrate the truth of Old Testament History. Our Lord speaks of the Queen of the South, as a real true person, who had lived and died. He refers to the story of Jonah, and his miraculous preservation in the whale's belly, as undeniable matters of fact. Let us remember this if we hear men professing to believe the writers of the New Testament, and yet sneering at the things recorded in the Old Testament, as if they were fables: such men forget that in so doing they pour contempt upon Christ Himself. The authority of the Old Testament and the authority of the New stand or fall together; the same Spirit inspired men to write of Solomon and Jonah, who inspired the Evangelists to write of Christ. These are not unimportant points in this day: let them be well fixed in our minds.

The first practical lesson which demands our attention in these verses, is *the amazing power of unbelief.*

We should mark how the scribes and Pharisees call upon our Lord to show them more miracles. "Master, we would see a sign from Thee." They pretended that they only wanted more evidence in order to be convinced and become disciples: they shut their eyes to the many wonderful works which Jesus had already done. It was not enough for them that He had healed the sick, and cleansed the lepers, raised the dead, and cast out devils: they were not yet persuaded; they yet demanded more proof. They would not see what our Lord plainly pointed at in His reply,—that they had no real *will* to believe. There was evidence enough to convince them, but they had no wish to be convinced.

There are many in the Church of Christ who are

exactly in the state of these scribes and Pharisees: they flatter themselves that they only require a little more proof to become decided Christians; they fancy that if their reason and intellect could only be met with some additional arguments, they would at once give up all for Christ's sake, take up the cross, and follow Him. But in the mean time they wait. Alas, for their blindness! They will not see that there is abundance of evidence on every side of them. The truth is that they do not want to be convinced.

May we all be on our guard against the spirit of unbelief: it is a growing evil in these latter days. Want of simple childlike faith is an increasing feature of the times, in every rank of society. The true explanation of a hundred strange things that startle us in the conduct of leading men in Churches and States, is downright want of faith. Men who do not believe all that God says in the Bible, must necessarily take a vacillating and undecided line on moral and religious questions. "If ye will not believe, surely ye shall not be established." (Isaiah vii. 9.)

The second practical lesson which meets us in these verses is *the immense danger of a partial and imperfect religious reformation.*

We should mark what an awful picture our Lord draws of the man to whom the unclean spirit returns, after having once left him. How fearful are those words: "I will return into my house from whence I came out!" How vivid that description: "He findeth it empty, swept, and garnished!" How tremendous the conclusion: "He taketh with him seven other spirits more wicked than himself,—and the last state of that man is worse than the first!" It is a picture most painfully full of meaning. Let us scan it closely, and learn wisdom.

It is certain that we have in this picture *the history of the Jewish church and nation* at the time of our Lord's coming. Called as they were at first out of Egypt to be God's peculiar people, they never seem to have wholly lost the tendency to worship idols. Redeemed as they afterwards were from the captivity of Babylon, they never seem to have rendered to God a due return for His goodness. Aroused as they had been by John the Baptist's preaching, their repentance appears to have been only skin-deep. At the time when our Lord spoke they had become, as a nation, hardy and more perverse than ever; the grossness of idol-worship had given place to the deadness of mere formality: "Seven other spirits worse than the first" had taken possession of them. Their last state was rapidly becoming worse than the first: yet forty years, and their iniquity came to the full. They madly plunged into a war with Rome; Judæa became a very Babel of confusion; Jerusalem was taken; the temple was destroyed: the Jews were scattered over the face of the earth.

Again it is highly probable that we have in this picture *the history of the whole body of Christian Churches.* Delivered as they were from heathen darkness by the preaching of the Gospel, they have never really lived up to their light; revived as many of them were at the time of the Protestant Reformation, they have none of them made a right use of their privileges, or "gone on to perfection:" they have all more or less stopped short and settled on their lees. They have all been too ready to be satisfied with mere external amendments. And now there are painful symptoms in many quarters that the "evil spirit has returned to his house," and is preparing an outbreak of infidelity and false doctrine, such as the Churches have never yet seen. Between unbelief in some quarters, and formal superstition in others, everything seems ripe for some fearful manifestation of anti-christ. It may well be feared that "the last state" of the professing Christian Churches will prove "worse than the first."

Saddest and worst of all, we have in this picture *the history of many an individual's soul.* There are men who seemed at one time of their lives to be under the influence of strong religious feelings: they reformed their ways; they laid aside many things that were bad; they took up many things that were good: but they stopped there, and went no further, and by and by gave up religion altogether. The evil spirit returned to their hearts, and found them "empty, swept, and garnished:" they are now worse than they ever were before. Their consciences seem seared; their sense of religious things appears entirely destroyed: they are like men given over to a reprobate mind. One would say it was "impossible to renew them to repentance." None prove so hopelessly wicked as those who after experiencing strong religious convictions have gone back again to sin and the world.

If we love life, let us pray that these lessons may be deeply impressed on our minds. Let us never be content with a partial reformation of life, without thorough conversion to God, and mortification of the whole body of sin. It is a good thing to strive to cast sin out of our hearts; but let us take care that we also receive the grace of God in its place. Let us make sure that we not only get rid of the old tenant, the devil, but have also got dwelling in us the Holy Ghost.

The last practical lesson which meets us in these verses is *the tender affection with which the Lord Jesus regards His true disciples.*

We should mark how He speaks of every one who does the will of His Father in heaven. He says, "the same is My brother, and sister, and mother." What gracious words these are! Who can conceive the depth of our dear Lord's love towards His relatives according to the flesh? It was a pure, unselfish love. It must have been a mighty love, a love that passes man's understanding. Yet here we see that all His believing people are counted as His relatives: He loves them, feels for them, cares for them, as members of His family, bone of His bone, and flesh of His flesh.

There is a solemn warning here to all who mock and persecute true Christians on account of their religion. They consider not what they are doing; they are persecuting the near relatives of the King of kings. They will find at the last day that they have mocked those whom the Judge of all regards as "His brother, and sister, and mother."

There is rich encouragement here for all believers. They are far more precious in their Lord's eyes than they are in their own. Their faith may be feeble, their repentance weak, their strength small: they may be poor and needy in this world; but there is a glorious "whosoever" in the last verse of this chapter which ought to cheer them. "Whosoever" believes is a near relative of Christ: the Elder Brother will provide for him in time and eternity, and never let him be cast away. There is not one "little sister" in the family of the redeemed, whom Jesus does not remember. (Cant. viii. 8.) Joseph provided richly for all his relatives, and the Lord Jesus will provide for His.

MATTHEW XIII. 1—23.

1 The same day went Jesus out of the house, and sat by the sea side.

2 And great multitudes were gathered together unto him, so that he went into a ship, and sat; and the whole multitude stood on the shore.

3 And he spake many things unto them in parables, saying, Behold, a sower went forth to sow;

4 And when he sowed, some *seeds* fell by the way side, and the fowls came and devoured them up:

5 Some fell upon stony places, where they had not much earth: and forthwith they sprung up, because they had no deepness of earth:

6 And when the sun was up, they were scorched; and because they had no root, they withered away.

7 And some fell among thorns; and the thorns sprung up, and choked them:

8 But other fell into good ground, and brought forth fruit, some an hundredfold, some sixtyfold, some thirtyfold.

9 Who hath ears to hear, let him hear.

10 And the disciples came, and said unto him, Why speakest thou unto them in parables?

11 He answered and said unto them, Because it is given unto you to know the mysteries of the kingdom of heaven, but to them it is not given.

12 For whosoever hath, to him shall be given, and he shall have more abundance: but whosoever hath not, from him shall be taken away even that he hath.

13 Therefore speak I to them in parables: because they seeing see not; and hearing they hear not, neither do they understand.

14 And in them is fulfilled the prophecy of Esaias, which saith, By hearing ye shall hear, and shall not understand; and seeing ye shall see, and shall not perceive:

15 For this people's heart is waxed gross, and *their* ears are dull of hearing, and their eyes they have closed; lest at any time they should see with *their* eyes, and hear with *their* ears, and should understand with *their* heart, and should be converted, and I should heal them.

16 But blessed *are* your eyes, for they see; and your ears, for they hear.

17 For verily I say unto you, That many prophets and righteous *men* have desired to see *those things* which ye see, and have not seen *them;* and to hear *those things* which ye hear, and have not heard *them.*

18 Hear ye therefore the parable of the sower.

19 When any one heareth the word of the kingdom, and understandeth *it* not, then cometh the wicked *one,* and catcheth away that

which was sown in his heart. This is he which received seed by the way side.
20 But he that received the seed into stony places, the same is he that heareth the word, and anon with joy receiveth it;
21 Yet hath he not root in himself, but dureth for a while: for when tribulation or persecution ariseth because of the word, by and by he is offended.
22 He also that received seed among the thorns is he that heareth the word; and the care of this world, and the deceitfulness of riches, choke the word, and he becometh unfruitful.
23 But he that received seed into the good ground is he that heareth the word, and understandeth *it;* which also beareth fruit, and bringeth forth, some an hundredfold, some sixty, some thirty.

THE chapter which these verses begin is remarkable for the number of parables which it contains. Seven striking illustrations of spiritual truth are here drawn by the great Head of the Church from the book of nature. By so doing He shows us that religious teaching may draw helps from everything in creation. Those that would "find out acceptable words," should not forget this. (Ec. xii. 10.)

The parable of the Sower, which begins this chapter, is one of those parables which admit of a very wide application. It is being continually verified under our own eyes. Wherever the Word of God is preached or expounded, and people are assembled to hear it, the sayings of our Lord in this parable are found to be true. It describes what goes on, as a general rule, in all congregations.

Let us learn, in the first place, from this parable, that *the work of the preacher resembles that of the sower.*

Like the sower, the preacher must sow good seed, if he wants to see fruit. He must sow the pure Word of God, and not the traditions of the Church, or the doctrines of men. Without this, his labour will be vain. He may go to and fro, and seem to say much, and to work much in his weekly round of ministerial duty; but there will be no harvest of souls for heaven, no living results, and no conversions.

Like the sower, the preacher must be diligent. He must spare no pains; he must use every possible means to make his work prosper; he must patiently "sow beside all waters," and "sow in hope;" he must be "instant in season and out of season;" he must not be deterred by difficulties and discouragements: "he that observeth the wind shall not sow." No doubt his success does not entirely depend upon his labour and diligence; but without labour and diligence success will not be obtained. (Isa. xxxii. 20; 2 Tim. iv. 2; Eccles. xi. 4.)

Like the sower, the preacher cannot give life. He can scatter the seed committed to his charge, but he cannot command it to grow: he may offer the word of truth to a people, but he cannot make them receive it and bear fruit. To give life is God's solemn prerogative: "It is the Spirit that quickeneth." God alone can "give the increase." (John vi. 63; 1 Cor. iii. 7.)

Let these things sink down into our hearts. It is no light thing to be a real minister of God's Word. To be an idle, formal workman in the Church is an easy business: to be a faithful sower is very hard. Preachers ought to be specially remembered in our prayers.

In the next place, let us learn from this passage that *there are various ways of hearing the Word of God without benefit.*

We may listen to a sermon with a heart like the hard "way side:" careless, thoughtless, and unconcerned. Christ crucified may be affectionately set before us, and we may hear of His sufferings with utter indifference, as a subject in which we have no interest. Fast as the words fall on our ears, the devil may pluck them away, and we may go home as if we had not heard a sermon at all. Alas, there are many such hearers! It is as true of them as of the idols of old, "eyes have they, but they see not; they have ears, but they hear not." (Psa. cxxxv. 16, 17.) Truth seems to have no more effect on their hearts than water on a stone.

We may listen to a sermon with pleasure, while the impression produced on us is only temporary and short-lived. Our hearts, like the "stony ground," may yield a plentiful crop of warm feelings and good resolutions; but all this time there may be no deeply-rooted work in our souls, and the first cold blast of opposition or temptation may cause our seeming religion to wither away. Alas, there are many such hearers! The mere love of sermons is no sign of grace. Thousands of baptized people are like the Jews of Ezekiel's day: "Thou art unto them as a very lovely song of one that hath a pleasant voice, and can play well on an instrument; for they hear thy words, but they do them not." (Ezek. xxxiii. 32.)

We may listen to a sermon, and approve of every word it contains, and yet get no good from it, in consequence of the absorbing influence of this world. Our hearts, like the "thorny ground," may be choked with a rank crop of cares, pleasures, and worldly plans. We may really like the Gospel, and wish to obey it, and yet insensibly give it no chance of bearing fruit, by allowing other things to fill a place in our affections, until they occupy our whole hearts. Alas, there are many such hearers! They know the truth well: they hope one day to be decided Christians; but they never come to the point of giving up all for Christ's sake. They never make up their minds to "seek first the kingdom of God,"—and so die in their sins.

These are points that we ought to weigh well. We should never forget that there are more ways than one of hearing the Word without profit. It is not enough that we come to hear: we may come, and be careless. It is not enough that we are not careless hearers: our impressions may be only temporary, and ready to perish. It is not enough that our impressions are not merely temporary; but they may be continually yielding no result, in consequence of our obstinate cleaving to the world.—Truly "the heart is deceitful above all things, and desperately wicked: who can know it?" (Jeremiah xvii. 9.)

In the last place, let us learn from this parable that *there is only one evidence of hearing the Word rightly.* That evidence is to bear "fruit."

The fruit here spoken of is the fruit of the Spirit. Repentance towards God, faith towards the Lord Jesus Christ, holiness of life and character, prayerfulness, humility, charity, spiritual mindedness,—these are the only satisfactory proofs that the seed of God's Word is doing its proper work in our souls. Without such proofs our religion is vain, however high our profession: it is no better than sounding brass and a tinkling cymbal. Christ has said, "I have chosen you, and ordained you, that ye should go and bring forth *fruit.*" (John xv. 16.)

There is no part of the whole parable more important than this. We must never be content with a barren orthodoxy, and a cold maintenance of correct theological views; we must not be satisfied with clear knowledge, warm feelings, and a decent profession; we must see to it that the Gospel we profess to love, produces positive "fruit" in our hearts and lives. This is real Christianity. These words of St. James should often ring in our ears: "Be ye doers of the Word, and not hearers only, deceiving your own selves." (James i. 22.)

Let us not leave these verses without putting to ourselves the important question, "How do we hear?" We live in a Christian country; we probably go to a place of worship Sunday after Sunday, and hear sermons: in what spirit do we hear them? What effect have they upon our characters? Can we point to anything that deserves the name of "fruit"?

We may rest assured, that to reach heaven at last it needs something more than to go to church regularly on Sundays and listen to preachers. The Word of God must be received into our hearts, and become the mainspring of our conduct: it must produce practical impressions on our inward man, that shall appear in our outward behaviour. If it does not do this, it will only add to our condemnation in the day of judgment.

MATTHEW XIII. 24—43.

24 Another parable put he forth unto them, saying, The kingdom of heaven is likened unto a man which sowed good seed in his field:
25 But while men slept, his enemy came and sowed tares among the wheat, and went his way.
26 But when the blade was sprung up, and brought forth fruit, then appeared the tares also.
27 So the servants of the householder came and said unto him, Sir, didst not thou sow good seed in thy field? from whence then hath it tares?
28 He said unto them, An enemy hath done this. The servants said unto him, Wilt thou then that we go and gather them up?
29 But he said, Nay; lest while ye gather up the tares, ye root up also the wheat with them.

30 Let both grow together until the harvest: and in the time of harvest I will say to the reapers, Gather ye together first the tares, and bind them in bundles to burn them: but gather the wheat into my barn.

31 Another parable put he forth unto them, saying, The kingdom of heaven is like to a grain of mustard seed, which a man took, and sowed in his field:

32 Which indeed is the least of all seeds: but when it is grown, it is the greatest among herbs, and becometh a tree, so that the birds of the air come and lodge in the branches thereof.

33 Another parable spake he unto them; The kingdom of heaven is like unto leaven, which a woman took, and hid in three measures of meal, till the whole was leavened.

34 All these things spake Jesus unto the multitude in parables; and without a parable spake he not unto them:

35 That it might be fulfilled which was spoken by the prophet, saying, I will open my mouth in parables; I will utter things which have been kept secret from the foundation of the world.

36 Then Jesus sent the multitude away, and went into the house: and his disciples came unto him, saying, Declare unto us the parable of the tares of the field.

37 He answered and said unto them, He that soweth the good seed is the Son of man;

38 The field is the world; the good seed are the children of the kingdom; but the tares are the children of the wicked *one*.

39 The enemy that sowed them is the devil; the harvest is the end of the world; and the reapers are the angels.

40 As therefore the tares are gathered and burned in the fire; so shall it be in the end of this world.

41 The Son of man shall send forth his angels, and they shall gather out of his kingdom all things that offend, and them which do iniquity;

42 And shall cast them into a furnace of fire: there shall be wailing and gnashing of teeth.

43 Then shall the righteous shine forth as the sun in the kingdom of their Father. Who hath ears to hear, let him hear.

THE parable of the "wheat and tares," which occupies the chief part of these verses, is one of peculiar importance in the present day.* It is eminently calculated to correct the extravagant expectations in which many Christians indulge, as to the effect of missions abroad, and of preaching the Gospel at home. May we give it the attention which it deserves!

In the first place, this parable teaches us *that good and evil will always be found together in the professing Church, until the end of the world.*

The visible Church is set before us as a mixed body:

* The consideration of the parables of the "mustard seed" and the "leaven" is purposely deferred to a future part of the "Expository Thoughts on the Gospels."

it is a vast "field" in which "wheat and tares" grow side by side. We must expect to find believers and unbelievers, converted and unconverted, "the children of the kingdom and the children of the wicked one," all mingled together in every congregation of baptized people.

The purest preaching of the Gospel will not prevent this. In every age of the Church the same state of things has existed: it was the experience of the early Fathers; it was the experience of the Reformers; it is the experience of the best ministers at the present hour. There has never been a visible Church or a religious assembly of which the members have been all "wheat." The devil, that great enemy of souls, has always taken care to sow "tares."

The most strict and prudent discipline will not prevent this: Episcopalians, Presbyterians, and Independents, all alike find it to be so. Do what we will to purify a Church, we shall never succeed in obtaining a perfectly pure communion: tares will be found among the wheat; hypocrites and deceivers will creep in; and, worst of all, if we are extreme in our efforts to obtain purity, we do more harm than good: we run the risk of encouraging many a Judas Iscariot, and breaking many a bruised reed. In our zeal to "gather up the tares," we are in danger of "rooting up the wheat with them:" such zeal is not according to knowledge, and has often done much harm. Those who care not what happens to the wheat, provided they can root up the tares, show little of the mind of Christ: and after all, there is deep truth in the charitable saying of Augustine, "Those who are tares to-day, may be wheat to-morrow."

Are we inclined to look for the conversion of the whole world by the labours of missionaries and ministers? Let us place this parable before us, and beware of such an idea. We shall never see all the inhabitants of earth "the wheat" of God, in the present order of things: the tares and wheat will "grow together till the harvest." The kingdoms of this world will never become the kingdom of Christ, and the millennium will never begin, until the King Himself returns.

Are we ever tried by the scoffing argument of the infidel, that Christianity cannot be a true religion, because there are so many false Christians? Let us call to mind this parable, and remain unmoved. Let us tell the infidel that the state of things he scoffs at does not surprise us at all: our Master prepared us for it eighteen hundred years ago. He foresaw and foretold that His Church would be a field, containing not only "wheat," but "tares."

Are we ever tempted to leave one Protestant Church for another, because we see many of its members unconverted? Let us remember this parable, and take heed what we do. We shall never find a perfect Church. We may spend our lives in migrating from communion to communion, and pass our days in perpetual disappointment: go where we will, and worship where we may, we shall always find "tares."

In the second place, the parable teaches us *that there is to be a day of separation between the godly and the ungodly members of the visible Church, at the end of the world.*

The present mixed state of things is not to be for ever: the wheat and the tares are to be divided at last. The Lord Jesus shall "send forth His angels" in the day of

His second advent, and gather all professing Christians into two great companies. Those mighty reapers shall make no mistake: they shall discern with unerring judgment between the righteous and the wicked, and place every one in his own lot. The saints and faithful servants of Christ shall receive glory, honour, and eternal life; the worldly, the ungodly, the careless, and the unconverted, shall be "cast into a furnace of fire."

There is something peculiarly solemn in this part of the parable. The meaning of it admits of no mistake: our Lord Himself explains it in words of singular clearness, as if He would impress it deeply on our minds. Well may He say at the conclusion, "Who hath ears to hear, let him hear."

Let the ungodly man tremble when he reads this parable; let him see in its fearful language his own certain doom, unless he repents and is converted; let him know that he is sowing misery for himself, if he goes on still in his neglect of God; let him reflect that his end will be to be gathered among the "bundles of tares," and be burned. Surely such a prospect ought to make a man think! As Baxter truly says, "We must not misinterpret God's patience with the ungodly."

Let the believer in Christ take comfort when he reads this parable; let him see that there is happiness and safety prepared for him in the great and dreadful day of the Lord. The voice of the archangel and the trump of God will proclaim no terror for him: they will summon him to join what he has long desired to see,—a perfect Church and a perfect communion of saints. How beautiful will the whole body of believers appear when finally separated from the wicked! How pure will the wheat look in the garner of God when the tares are at length taken away! How brightly will grace shine when no longer dimmed by incessant contact with the worldly and unconverted! The righteous are little known in the present day: the world sees no beauty in them, even as it saw none in their Master. "The world knoweth us not, because it knew Him not." (1 John iii. 1.) But the righteous shall one day "shine forth as the sun in the kingdom of their Father." To use the words of Matthew Henry, "their sanctification will be perfected, and their justification will be published." "When Christ who is our life shall appear, then shall ye also appear with Him in glory." (Col. iii. 4.)

MATTHEW XIII. 44—50.

44 Again, the kingdom of heaven is like unto treasure hid in a field; the which when a man hath found, he hideth, and for joy thereof goeth and selleth all that he hath, and buyeth that field.

45 Again, the kingdom of heaven is like unto a merchant man, seeking goodly pearls:

46 Who, when he had found one pearl of great price, went and sold all that he had, and bought it.

47 Again, the kingdom of heaven is like unto a net, that was cast into the sea, and gathered of every kind:

48 Which, when it was full, they drew to shore, and sat down, and gathered the good into vessels, but cast the bad away.

49 So shall it be at the end of the world: the angels shall come forth, and sever the wicked from among the just,

50 And shall cast them into the furnace of fire: there shall be wailing and gnashing of teeth.

THE parables of the "treasure hid in a field," and the "merchant man seeking goodly pearls," appear intended to convey one and the same lesson. They vary, no doubt, in one striking particular: the "treasure" was found of one who does not seem to have sought it; the "pearl" was found of one who was actually seeking pearls. But the conduct of the finders, in both cases, was precisely alike: both "sold all" to make the thing found their own property; and it is exactly at this point that the instruction of both parables agrees.

These two parables are meant to teach us *that men really convinced of the importance of salvation will give up everything to win Christ and eternal life.*

What was the conduct of the two men our Lord describes? The one was persuaded that there was a "treasure hid in a field," which would amply repay him, if he bought the field, however great the price that he might give.—The other was persuaded that the "pearl" he had found was so immensely valuable, that it would answer to him to purchase it at any cost.—Both were convinced that they had found a thing of great value: both were satisfied that it was worth a great present sacrifice to make this thing their own. Others might wonder at them; others might think them foolish for paying such a sum of money for the "field" and "pearl:" but they knew what they were about. They were sure that they were making a good bargain.

We see, in this simple picture, the conduct of a true Christian explained. He is what he is, and does what he does in his religion, because he is *thoroughly persuaded* that it is worth while. He comes out from the world; he puts off the old man; he forsakes the vain companions of his past life. Like Matthew, he gives up everything, and, like Paul, he "counts all things loss" for Christ's sake. And why? Because he is convinced that Christ will make amends to him for all he gives up. He sees in Christ an endless "treasure;" he sees in Christ a precious "pearl:" to win Christ he will make any sacrifice. This is true faith: this is the stamp of a genuine work of the Holy Ghost.

We see in these two parables the real clue to the conduct of many unconverted people. They are what they are in religion, because they are *not fully persuaded* that it is worth while to be different. They flinch from decision; they shrink from taking up the cross; they halt between two opinions; they will not commit themselves: they will not come forward boldly on the Lord's side.—And why? Because they are not convinced that it will answer: they have not faith. They are not sure that "the treasure" is before them; they are not satisfied that "the pearl" is worth so great a price: they cannot yet make up their minds to "sell all," that they may win Christ. And so too often they perish everlastingly! When a man will venture nothing for Christ's sake, we must draw the sorrowful conclusion that he has not got the grace of God.

The parable of the net let down into the sea, has some points in common with that of the wheat and the tares. It is intended to instruct us on a most important subject: *the true nature of the visible Church of Christ.*

The preaching of the Gospel was the letting down of a large net into the midst of the sea of this world: the professing Church which it was to gather together, was to be a mixed body. Within the folds of the net there were to be fish of every kind, both good and bad: within the pale of the Church there were to be Christians of various sorts, unconverted as well as converted, false as well as true. The separation of good and bad was sure to come at last, but not before the end of the world. Such was the account which the great Master gave to His disciples of the Churches which they were to found.

It is of the utmost importance to have the lessons of this parable deeply graven on our minds. There is hardly any point in Christianity on which greater mistakes exist, than *the nature of the visible Church.* There is none, perhaps, on which mistakes are so perilous to the soul.

Let us learn, from this parable, that all congregations of professed Christians ought to be regarded as *mixed bodies:* they are all assemblies containing "good fish and bad," converted and unconverted, children of God and children of the world, and ought to be described and addressed as such. To tell all baptized people that they are born again, and have the Spirit, and are members of Christ, and are holy, in the face of such a parable as this, is utterly unwarrantable. Such a mode of address may flatter and please: it is not likely to profit or save. It is painfully calculated to promote self-righteousness, and lull sinners to sleep: it overthrows the plain teaching of Christ, and is ruinous to souls. Do we ever hear such doctrine? If we do, let us remember "the net."

Finally, let it be a settled principle with us never to be satisfied with mere *outward Church-membership.* We may be inside the net, and yet not be in Christ. The waters of baptism are poured on myriads who are never washed in the water of life; the bread and wine are eaten and drunk by thousands at the Lord's table, who never feed on Christ by faith. Are we converted? Are we among the "good fish"? This is the grand question! It is one which must be answered at last. The net will soon be "drawn to shore;" the true character of every man's religion will at length be exposed. There will be an eternal separation between the good fish and the bad: there will be a "furnace of fire" for the wicked. Surely, as Baxter says, "these plain words more need belief and consideration than exposition."

MATTHEW XIII. 51—58.

51 Jesus saith unto them, Have ye understood all these things? They say unto him, Yea, Lord.

52 Then said he unto them, Therefore every Scribe *which is* instructed unto the kingdom of heaven is like unto a man *that is* an householder, which bringeth forth out of his treasure *things* new and old.

53 And it came to pass, *that* when Jesus had finished these parables, he departed thence.

54 And when he was come into his own country, he taught them in their synagogue, insomuch that they were astonished, and said, Whence hath this *man* this wisdom, and *these* mighty works?

55 Is not this the carpenter's son? is not his mother called Mary? and his brethren, James, and Joses, and Simon, and Judas?

56 And his sisters, are they not all with us? Whence then hath this *man* all these things?

57 And they were offended in him. But Jesus said unto them, A prophet is not without honour, save in his own country, and in his own house.

58 And he did not many mighty works there because of their unbelief.

THE first thing which we ought to notice in these verses is *the striking question* with which our Lord winds up the seven wonderful parables of this chapter. He said, "Have ye understood all these things?"

Personal application has been called the "soul" of preaching. A sermon without application is like a letter posted without a direction: it may be well written, rightly dated, and duly signed; but it is useless, because it never reaches its destination. Our Lord's inquiry is an admirable example of real heart-searching application: "Have ye understood?"

The mere form of hearing a sermon can profit no man, unless he comprehends what it means: he might just as well listen to the blowing of a trumpet, or the beating of a drum; he might just as well attend a Roman Catholic service in Latin. His intellect must be set in motion, and his heart impressed: ideas must be received into his mind; he must carry off the seeds of new thoughts. Without this he hears in vain.

It is of great importance to see this point clearly: there is a vast amount of ignorance about it. There are thousands who go regularly to places of worship, and think they have done their religious duty, but never carry away an idea, or receive an impression. Ask them, when they return home on a Sunday evening, what they have learned, and they cannot tell you a word. Examine them at the end of a year, as to the religious knowledge they have attained, and you will find them as ignorant as the heathen.

Let us watch our souls in this matter. Let us take with us to church, not only our bodies, but our minds, our reason, our hearts, and our consciences. Let us often ask ourselves, "What have I got from this sermon? what have I learned? what truths have been impressed on my mind?"—Intellect, no doubt, is not everything in religion; but it does not therefore follow that it is nothing at all.—The heart is unquestionably the main point: but we must never forget that the Holy Ghost generally reaches the heart through the mind. Sleepy, idle, inattentive hearers are never likely to be converted.

The second thing which we ought to notice in these

verses is *the strange treatment which our Lord received in His own country.*

He came to the town of Nazareth, where He had been brought up, and "taught in their synagogue." His teaching, no doubt, was the same as it always was: "Never man spake like this man." But it had no effect on the people of Nazareth. They were "astonished," but their hearts were unmoved. They said, "Is not this the carpenter's son? Is not his mother called Mary?" They despised Him, because they were so familiar with Him. "They were offended in Him." And they drew from our Lord the solemn remark, "A prophet is not without honour, save in his own country, and in his own house."

Let us see, in this history, a melancholy page of human nature unfolded to our view. We are all apt to despise mercies, if we are accustomed to them, and have them cheap. The Bibles and religious books, which are so plentiful in England, the means of grace, of which we have so abundant a supply, the preaching of the Gospel, which we hear every week,—all, all are liable to be undervalued. It is mournfully true, that in religion, more than anything else, "familiarity breeds contempt." Men forget that truth is truth, however old and hackneyed it may sound,—and despise it because it is old. Alas, by so doing, they provoke God to take it away!

Do we wonder that the relatives, servants, and neighbours of godly people are not always converted? Do we wonder that the parishioners of eminent ministers of the Gospel are often their hardest and most impenitent hearers? Let us wonder no more. Let us mark the experience of our Lord at Nazareth, and learn wisdom.

Do we ever fancy that if we had only seen and heard Jesus Christ we should have been His faithful disciples? Do we think that if we had only lived near Him, and been eye-witnesses of His ways, we should not have been undecided, wavering, and half-hearted about religion? If we do, let us think so no longer. Let us observe the people of Nazareth, and learn wisdom.

The last thing which we ought to notice in these verses is *the ruinous nature of unbelief.* The chapter ends with the fearful words, "He did not many works there because of their unbelief."

We see in this single word the secret of the everlasting ruin of multitudes of souls! They perish for ever, because they *will not* believe. There is nothing beside in earth or heaven that prevents their salvation: their sins, however many, might all be forgiven; the Father's love is ready to receive them; the blood of Christ is ready to cleanse them; the power of the Spirit is ready to renew them. But a great barrier interposes: they will not believe. "Ye will not come to Me," says Jesus, "that ye might have life." (John v. 40.)

May we all be on our guard against this accursed sin! It is the old root-sin which caused the fall of man. Cut down in the true child of God by the power of the Spirit, it is ever ready to bud and sprout again. There are three great enemies against which God's children should daily pray: pride, worldliness, and unbelief. Of these three none is greater than unbelief.

MATTHEW XIV. 1—12.

1 At that time Herod the tetrarch heard of the fame of Jesus,
2 And said unto his servants, This is John the Baptist; he is risen from the dead; and therefore mighty works do shew forth themselves in him.
3 For Herod had laid hold on John, and bound him, and put *him* in prison for Herodias' sake, his brother Philip's wife.
4 For John said unto him, It is not lawful for thee to have her.
5 And when he would have put him to death, he feared the multitude, because they counted him as a prophet.
6 But when Herod's birthday was kept, the daughter of Herodias danced before them, and pleased Herod.
7 Whereupon he promised with an oath to give her whatsoever she would ask.
8 And she, being before instructed of her mother, said, Give me here John Baptist's head in a charger.
9 And the king was sorry: nevertheless for the oath's sake, and them which sat with him at meat, he commanded *it* to be given *her*.
10 And he sent, and beheaded John in the prison.
11 And his head was brought in a charger, and given to the damsel: and she brought *it* to her mother.
12 And his disciples came, and took up the body, and buried it, and went and told Jesus.

We have in this passage a page out of God's book of martyrs: the history of the death of John the Baptist. The wickedness of King Herod, the bold reproof which John gave him, the consequent imprisonment of the faithful reprover, and the disgraceful circumstances of his death, are all written for our learning. "Precious in the sight of the Lord is the death of His saints." (Psalm cxvi. 15.)

The story of John the Baptist's death is told more fully by St. Mark than by St. Matthew. For the present it seems sufficient to draw two general lessons from St. Matthew's narrative, and to fasten our attention exclusively upon them.

Let us learn, in the first place, from these verses, *the great power of conscience.*

King Herod hears of "the fame of Jesus," and says to his servants, "This is John the Baptist: he is risen from the dead." He remembered his own wicked dealings with that holy man, and his heart failed within him. His heart told him that he had despised his godly counsel, and committed a foul and abominable murder; and his heart told him, that though he had killed John, there would yet be a reckoning day. He and John the Baptist would yet meet again. Well says Bishop Hall, "A wicked man needs no other tormentor, especially for sins of blood, than his own heart."

There is a conscience in all men by nature. Let this never be forgotten. Fallen, lost, desperately wicked as we are all born into the world, God has taken care to leave Himself a witness in our bosoms. It is a poor blind guide, without the Holy Ghost: it can save no one; it leads no one to Christ: it may be "seared" and trampled under foot. But there is such a thing as conscience in every man, accusing or excusing him; and Scripture and experience alike declare it. (Rom. ii. 15.)

Conscience can make even kings miserable, when they have wilfully rejected its advice; it can fill the princes of this world with fear and trembling, as it did Felix, when Paul preached. They find it easier to imprison and behead the preacher, than to bind his sermon, and silence the voice of his reproof in their own hearts. God's witnesses may be put out of the way, but their testimony often lives and works on long after they are dead. God's prophets live not for ever, but their words often survive them. (2 Tim. ii. 9; Zech. i. 5.)

Let the thoughtless and ungodly remember this, and not sin against their consciences. Let them know that their sins will "surely find them out." They may laugh, and jest, and mock at religion for a little time. They may cry, "Who is afraid? Where is the mighty harm of our ways?" They may depend upon it they are sowing misery for themselves, and will reap a bitter crop sooner or later. Their wickedness will overtake them one day: they will find, like Herod, that it is "an evil thing and bitter to sin against God." (Jerem. ii. 19.)

Let ministers and teachers remember that there is a conscience in men, and let them work on boldly. Instruction is not always thrown away, because it seems to bear no fruit at the time it is given; teaching is not always in vain, though we fancy that it is unheeded, wasted, and forgotten. There is a conscience in the hearers of sermons; there is a conscience in the children at our schools. Many a sermon and lesson will yet rise again, when he who preached or taught it is lying, like John the Baptist, in the grave. Thousands know that we are right, and, like Herod, dare not confess it.

Let us learn, in the second place, *that God's children must not look for their reward in this world.*

If ever there was a case of godliness unrewarded in this life, it was that of John the Baptist. Let us think for a moment what a remarkable man he was during his short career, and then think to what end he came. Behold him that was the "Prophet of the Highest," and "greater than any born of woman," imprisoned like a malefactor!—Behold him cut off by a violent death, before the age of thirty-four: the "burning light" quenched, the faithful preacher murdered for doing his duty,—and this to gratify the hatred of an adulterous woman, and at the command of a capricious tyrant! Truly there was an event here, if there ever was one in the world, which might make an ignorant man say, "What profit is it to serve God?"

But these are the sort of things which show us that there will one day be a judgment. The God of the spirits of all flesh shall at last set up an assize, and reward every one according to his works. The blood of John the Baptist, and James the Apostle, and Stephen, —the blood of Polycarp, and Huss, and Ridley, and Latimer, shall yet be required. It is all written in God's Book. "The earth also shall disclose her blood, and shall no more cover her slain." (Isaiah xxvi. 21.) The world shall yet know that there is a God that judgeth the earth. "If thou seest the oppression of the poor, and violent perverting of judgment and justice in a province, marvel not at the matter, for He that is higher than the highest regardeth: and there be higher than they." (Eccl. v. 8.)

Let all true Christians remember that their best things are yet to come. Let us count it no strange thing if we have sufferings in this present time. It is a season of probation: we are yet at school. We are learning patience, longsuffering, gentleness, and meekness, which we could hardly learn if we had our good things now. But there is an eternal holiday yet to begin; for this let us wait quietly: it will make amends for all. "Our light affliction, which is but for a moment, worketh for us a far more exceeding and eternal weight of glory." (2 Cor. iv. 17.)

MATTHEW XIV. 13—21.

13 When Jesus heard *of it*, he departed thence by ship into a desert place apart: and when the people had heard *thereof*, they followed him on foot out of the cities.

14 And Jesus went forth, and saw a great multitude, and was moved with compassion toward them, and he healed their sick,

15 And when it was evening, his disciples came to him, saying, This is a desert place, and the time is now past; send the multitude away, that they may go into the villages, and buy themselves victuals.

16 But Jesus said unto them, They need not depart: give ye them to eat.
17 And they say unto him, We have here but five loaves, and two fishes.
18 He said, Bring them hither to me.
19 And he commanded the multitude to sit down on the grass, and took the five loaves, and the two fishes, and looking up to heaven, he blessed, and brake, and gave the loaves to *his* disciples, and the disciples to the multitude.
20 And they did all eat, and were filled: and they took up of the fragments that remained twelve baskets full.
21 And they that had eaten were about five thousand men, beside women and children.

THESE verses contain one of our Lord Jesus Christ's greatest miracles: the feeding of "five thousand men, beside women and children," with five loaves and two fishes. Of all the miracles worked by our Lord, not one is so often mentioned in the New Testament as this. Matthew, Mark, Luke, and John, all dwell upon it. It is plain that this event in our Lord's history is intended to receive special attention. Let us give it that attention, and see what we may learn.

In the first place, this miracle is *an unanswerable proof of our Lord's Divine power.*

To satisfy the hunger of more than five thousand people with so small a portion of food as five loaves and two fishes, would be manifestly impossible without a supernatural multiplication of the food. It was a thing that no magician, impostor, or false prophet would ever have attempted. Such a person might possibly pretend to cure a single sick person, or to raise a single dead body, and by jugglery and trickery might persuade weak people that he succeeded; but such a person would never attempt such a mighty work as that which is here recorded. He would know well that he could not persuade ten thousand men, women, and children that they were full when they were hungry: he would be exposed as a cheat and impostor on the spot.

Yet this is the mighty work which our Lord actually performed, and by performing it gave a conclusive proof that He was God. He called that into being which did not before exist: He provided visible, tangible, material food for more than five thousand people, out of a supply which in itself would not have satisfied fifty. Surely we must be blind if we do not see in this the hand of Him who "giveth food to all flesh" (Psalm cxxxvi. 25), and made the world and all that therein is. To *create* is the peculiar prerogative of God.

We ought to lay firm hold on such passages as this. We should treasure up in our minds every evidence of our Lord's divine power. The cold, orthodox, unconverted man may see little in the story: the true believer should store it in his memory. Let him think of the world, the devil, and his own heart, and learn to thank God that his Saviour, the Lord Jesus Christ, is almighty.

In the second place, this miracle is a *striking example of our Lord's compassion toward men.*

Jesus "saw a great multitude" in a desert place, ready to faint for hunger. He knew that many in that multitude had no true faith and love towards Himself: they followed Him for fashion's sake, or from curiosity, or some equally low motive. (John vi. 26.) But our Lord had pity upon all: all were relieved; all partook of the food miraculously provided. All were "filled," and none went hungry away.

Let us see in this the heart of our Lord Jesus Christ towards sinners. He is ever the same. He is now as He was of old, "the Lord, the Lord God, merciful and gracious, longsuffering, and abundant in goodness and truth." (Exod. xxxiv. 6.) He does not deal with men according to their sins, or reward them according to their iniquities. He loads even His enemies with benefits. None will be so excuseless as those who are found impenitent at last: the Lord's goodness leads them to repentance. (Rom. ii. 4.) In all His dealings with men on earth, He showed Himself one that "delighteth in mercy." (Micah vii. 18.) Let us strive to be like Him. "We ought," says an old writer, "to have abundance of pity and compassion on diseased souls."

In the last place, this miracle is a *lively emblem of the sufficiency of the Gospel to meet the soul-wants of all mankind.*

There can be little doubt that all our Lord's miracles have a deep figurative meaning, and teach great spiritual truths. They must be handled reverently and discreetly. Care must be taken that we do not, like many of the Fathers, see allegories where the Holy Spirit meant none to be seen. But, perhaps, if there is any miracle worked by Christ which has a manifest figurative meaning, in addition to the plain lessons which may be drawn from its surface, it is that which is now before us.

What does this hungry multitude in a desert place represent to us? It is an emblem of *all mankind.* The children of men are a large assembly of perishing sinners, famishing in the midst of a wilderness world,—helpless, hopeless, and on the way to ruin. We have all gone astray like lost sheep (Isaiah liii. 6); we are by nature far away from God. Our eyes may not be opened to the full extent of our danger: but in reality we are "wretched, and miserable, and poor, and blind, and naked." (Rev. iii. 17.) There is but a step between us and everlasting death."

What do these loaves and fishes represent, apparently so inadequate to meet the necessities of the case, but by miracle made sufficient to feed ten thousand people? They are an emblem of *the doctrine of Christ crucified for sinners,* as their vicarious Substitute, and making atonement by His death for the sin of the world. That doctrine seems to the natural man weakness itself. Christ crucified was "to the Jews a stumbling-block, and to the Greeks foolishness." (1 Cor. i. 23.) And yet Christ crucified has proved the "bread of God which cometh down from heaven, and giveth life to the world." (John vi. 33.) The story of the cross has amply met the spiritual wants of mankind wherever it has been preached. Thousands of every rank, age, and nation, are witnesses that it is "the wisdom of God, and the power of God." They have eaten of it and been "filled:" they have found it "meat indeed and drink indeed."

Let us ponder these things well. There are great depths in all our Lord Jesus Christ's recorded dealings upon earth, which no one has ever fully fathomed. There are mines of rich instruction in all His words and ways, which no one has thoroughly explored. Many a passage of the Gospels is like the cloud which Elijah's servant saw. (1 Kings xviii. 44.) The more we look at it the greater it will appear. There is an inexhaustible fulness in Scripture. Other writings seem comparatively poor and threadbare, when we become familiar with them; but the more we read the Bible the richer we shall find it.

MATTHEW XIV. 22—36.

22 And straightway Jesus constrained his disciples to get into a ship, and to go before him unto the other side, while he sent the multitudes away.
23 And when he had sent the multitudes away, he went up into a mountain apart to pray: and when the evening was come, he was there alone.
24 But the ship was now in the midst of the sea, tossed with waves: for the wind was contrary.
25 And in the fourth watch of the night Jesus went unto them, walking on the sea.
26 And when the disciples saw him walking on the sea, they were troubled, saying, It is a spirit; and they cried out for fear.
27 But straightway Jesus spake unto them, saying, Be of good cheer; it is I; be not afraid.
28 And Peter answered him and said, Lord, if it be thou, bid me come unto thee on the water.
29 And he said, Come. And when Peter was come down out of the ship, he walked on the water, to go to Jesus.
30 But when he saw the wind boisterous, he was afraid; and beginning to sink, he cried, saying Lord, save me.
31 And immediately Jesus stretched forth *his* hand, and caught him, and said unto him, O thou of little faith, wherefore didst thou doubt?
32 And when they were come into the ship, the wind ceased.
33 Then they that were in the ship came and worshipped him, saying, Of a truth thou art the Son of God.
34 And when they were gone over, they came into the land of Gennesaret.
35 And when the men of that place had knowledge of him, they sent out into all that country round about, and brought unto him all that were diseased;
36 And besought him that they might only touch the hem of his garment: and as many as touched were made perfectly whole.

THE history contained in these verses is one of singular interest. The miracle here recorded brings out in strong light the character both of Christ and His people. The power and mercy of the Lord Jesus, and the mixture of faith and unbelief in His best disciples, are beautifully illustrated.

We learn, in the first place, from this miracle, *what absolute dominion our Saviour has over all created things.* We see Him "walking on the sea," as if it was dry land. Those angry waves which tossed the ship of His disciples to and fro, obey the Son of God, and become a solid floor under His feet. That liquid surface, which was agitated by the least breath of wind, bears up the feet of our Redeemer, like a rock. To our poor, weak, minds, the whole event is utterly incomprehensible. The picture of two feet walking on the sea, is said by Doddridge to have been the Egyptian emblem of an impossible thing; the man of science will tell us, that for material flesh and blood to walk on water is a physical impossibility: enough for us to know that it was done. Enough for us to remember, that to Him who created the seas at the beginning, it must have been perfectly easy to walk over their waves when He pleased.

There is encouragement here for all true Christians. Let them know that there is nothing created which is not under Christ's control: "All things serve Him." He may allow His people to be tried for a season, and to be tossed to and fro by storms of trouble; He may be later than they wish in coming to their aid, and not draw near till the "fourth watch of the night:" but never let them forget that winds, and waves, and storms are all Christ's servants. They cannot move without Christ's permission. "The Lord on high is mightier than the voice of many waters, yea than the mighty waves of the sea." (Psalm xciii. 4.) Are we ever tempted to cry with Jonah, "The floods compass me about: all Thy billows and Thy waves pass over me"? (Jonah ii. 3.) Let us remember they are "His" billows. Let us wait patiently. We may yet see Jesus coming to us, and "walking on the sea."

We learn, in the second place, from this miracle, *what power Jesus can bestow on them that believe on Him.* We see Simon Peter coming down out of the ship and walking on the water, like his Lord. What a wonderful proof was this of our Lord's divinity! To walk on the sea Himself was a mighty miracle; but to enable a poor weak disciple to do the same, was a mightier miracle still.

There is a deep meaning in this part of the history: it shows us what great things our Lord can do for those that hear His voice, and follow Him. He can enable them to do things which at one time they would have thought impossible: He can carry them through difficulties and trials, which without Him they would never have dared to face; He can give them strength to walk through fire and water unharmed, and to get the better of every foe. Moses in Egypt, Daniel in Babylon, the saints in Nero's household, are all examples of His mighty power. Let us fear nothing, if we are in the path of duty. The waters may seem deep; but if Jesus says, "Come," we have no cause to be afraid. "He that believeth on Me, the works that I do shall he do also, and greater works than these shall he do." (John xiv. 12.)

Let us learn, in the third place, from this miracle, *how much trouble disciples bring upon themselves by unbelief.* We see Peter walking boldly on the water for a little way; but by and by, when he sees "the wind boisterous" he is afraid, and begins to sink. The weak flesh gets the better of the willing spirit: he forgets the wonderful proofs of his Lord's goodness and power, which he had just received; he considered not that the same Saviour who had enabled him to walk one step, must be able to hold him up for ever; he did not reflect that he was nearer to Christ when once on the water, than he was when he first left the ship. Fear took away his memory: alarm confused his reason. He thought of nothing but the winds and waves, and his immediate danger, and his faith gave way. "Lord," he cried, "save me."

What a lively picture we have here of the experience of many a believer! How many there are who have faith enough to take the first step in following Christ, but not faith enough to go on as they began. They take fright at the trials and dangers which seem to be in their way. They look at the enemies that surround them, and the difficulties that seem likely to beset their path: they look at them more than at Jesus, and at once their feet begin to sink; their hearts faint within them; their hope vanishes away: their comforts disappear.—And why is all this? Christ is not altered: their enemies are not greater than they were.—It is just because, like Peter, they have ceased to look to Jesus, and have given way to unbelief. They are taken up with thinking about their enemies, instead of thinking about Christ. May we lay this to heart, and learn wisdom!

Let us learn, in the last place, from this miracle, *how merciful our Lord Jesus Christ is to weak believers.* We see Him stretching forth His hand immediately to save Peter, as soon as Peter cried to Him. He does not leave him to reap the fruit of his own unbelief, and to sink in the deep waters: He only seems to consider his trouble, and to think of nothing so much as delivering him from it. The only word He utters is the gentle reproof, "O thou of little faith, wherefore didst thou doubt?"

We should mark, in this concluding part of the miracle, the exceeding "gentleness of Christ." He can bear with much, and forgive much, when He sees true grace in a man's heart. As a mother deals gently with her infant, and does not cast it away because of its waywardness and frowardness, so does the Lord Jesus deal gently with His people. He loved and pitied them before conversion, and after conversion He loves and pities them still more. He knows their feebleness, and bears long with them. He would have us know that doubting does not prove that a man has no faith, but only that his faith is small; and even when our faith is small, the Lord is ready to help us. "When I said, My foot slippeth; Thy mercy, O Lord, held me up." (Psalm xciv. 18.)

How much there is in all this to encourage men to serve Christ! Where is the man that ought to be afraid to begin running the Christian race, with such a Saviour as Jesus? If we fall, He will raise us again. If we err, He will bring us back. But His mercy shall never be altogether taken from us. He has said, "I will never leave thee, nor forsake thee," and He will keep His word. (Heb. xiii. 5.) May we only remember that while we do not despise little faith we must not sit down content with it. Our prayer must ever be, "Lord, increase our faith."

MATTHEW XV. 1—9.

1 Then came to Jesus scribes and Pharisees, which were of Jerusalem, saying,

2 Why do thy disciples transgress the tradition of the elders? for they wash not their hands when they eat bread.

3 But he answered and said unto them, Why do ye also transgress the commandment of God by your tradition?

4 For God commanded, saying, Honour thy father and mother: and, He that curseth father or mother, let him die the death.

5 But ye say, Whosoever shall say to *his* father or *his* mother, *It is* a gift, by whatsoever thou mightest be profited by me:

6 And honour not his father or his mother, *he shall be free.* Thus have ye made the commandment

of God of none effect by your tradition.
7 *Ye* hypocrites, well did Esaias prophesy of you, saying,
8 This people draweth nigh unto me with their mouth, and honoureth me with *their* lips; but their heart is far from me.
9 But in vain they do worship me, teaching *for* doctrines the commandments of men.

We have in these verses a conversation between our Lord Jesus Christ and certain scribes and Pharisees. The subject of it may seem, at first sight, of little interest in modern days; but it is not so in reality: the principles of the Pharisees are principles that never die. There are truths laid down here, which are of deep importance.

We learn, for one thing, *that hypocrites generally attach great importance to mere outward things in religion.*

The complaint of the scribes and Pharisees in this place, is a striking case in point. They brought an accusation to our Lord against His disciples: but what was its nature? It was not that they were covetous or self-righteous; it was not that they were untruthful or uncharitable; it was not that they had broken any part of the law of God: but they "transgressed the traditions of the elders.—They did not wash their hands when they ate bread;" they did not observe a rule of merely human authority, which some old Jew had invented! This was the head and front of their offence!

Do we see nothing of the spirit of the Pharisees in the present day? Unhappily we see only too much. There are thousands of professing Christians, who seem to care nothing about the religion of their neighbours, provided that it agrees in outward matters with their own. Does their neighbour worship according to their particular form? Can he repeat their shibboleth, and talk a little about their favourite doctrines? If he can, they are satisfied, though there is no evidence that he is converted; if he cannot, they are always finding fault, and cannot speak peaceably of him, though he may be serving Christ better than themselves. Let us beware of this spirit: it is the very essence of hypocrisy. Let our principle be, "The kingdom of God is not meat and drink, but righteousness and peace, and joy in the Holy Ghost." (Rom. xiv. 17.)

We learn, for another thing, from these verses, *the great danger of attempting to add anything to the Word of God.* Whenever a man takes upon him to make additions to the Scriptures, he is likely to end with valuing his own additions above Scripture itself.

We see this point brought out most strikingly in our Lord's answer to the charge of the Pharisees against His disciples. He says, "Why do ye also transgress the commandment of God by your traditions?" He strikes boldly at the whole system of *adding* anything, as needful to salvation, to God's perfect Word. He exposes the mischievous tendency of the system by an example: He shows how the vaunted traditions of the Pharisees were actually destroying the authority of the fifth commandment. In short, He establishes the great truth, which ought never to be forgotten,—that there is an inherent tendency in all traditions to "make the Word of God of none effect." The authors of these traditions may have meant no such thing; their intentions may have been pure: but that there is a tendency in all religious institutions of mere human authority to usurp the authority of God's Word, is evidently the doctrine of Christ. It is a solemn remark of Bucer's, that "a man is rarely to be found who pays an excessive attention to human inventions in religion who does not put more trust in them than in the grace of God."

And have we not seen melancholy proof of this truth in the history of the Church of Christ? Unhappily we have seen only too much. As Baxter says, "Men think God's laws too many and too strict, and yet make more of their own, and are precise for keeping them." Have we never read how some have exalted canons, rubrics, and ecclesiastical laws above the Word of God, and have punished disobedience to them with far greater severity than open sins, like drunkenness and swearing? Have we never heard of the extravagant importance which the Church of Rome attaches to monastic vows, and vows of celibacy, and keeping feasts and fasts, insomnch that she seems to place them far above family duties, and the ten commandments?—Have we never heard of men who make more ado about eating flesh in Lent, than about gross impurity of life, or murder?—Have we never observed in our own land, how many seem to make adherence to Episcopacy the weightiest matter in Christianity, and to regard "Churchmanship," as they call it, as far outweighing repentance, faith, holiness, and the graces of the Spirit? These are questions which can only receive one sorrowful answer. The spirit of the Pharisees still lives, after eighteen hundred years: the disposition to "make the Word of God of none effect by traditions," is to be found among Christians, as well as among Jews: the tendency practically to exalt man's inventions above God's Word, is still fearfully prevalent. May we watch against it and be on our guard! May we remember that no tradition or man-made institition in religion can ever excuse the neglect of relative duties, or justify disobedience to any plain commandment of God's Word.

We learn, in the last place, from these verses, that *the religious worship which God desires, is the worship of the heart.* We find our Lord establishing this by a quotation from Isaiah: "This people draweth near to Me with their lips, but their heart is far from Me."

The heart is the principal thing in the relation of husband and wife, of friend and friend, of parent and child. The heart must be the principal point to which we attend in all the relations between God and our souls. What is the first thing we need, in order to be Christians? A new heart.—What is the sacrifice God asks us to bring to Him? A broken and a contrite heart.—What is the true circumcision? The circumcision of the heart.—What is genuine obedience? To obey from the heart.—What is saving faith? To believe with the heart.—Where ought Christ to dwell? To dwell in our hearts by faith.—What is the chief request that Wisdom makes to every one? "My son, give me thine heart."

Let us leave the passage with honest self-inquiry as to the state of our own hearts. Let us settle it in our minds, that all formal worship of God, whether in public or private, is utterly in vain, so long as our "hearts are far from Him." The bended knee, the bowed head, the loud Amen, the daily chapter, the regular attendance at the Lord's table, are all useless and unprofitable, so long as our affections are nailed to sin, or pleasure, or money, or the world. The question of our Lord must yet be answered satisfactorily, before we can be saved. He says to every one, "Lovest thou Me?" (John xxi. 17.)

MATTHEW XV. 10—20.

10 And he called the multitude, and said unto them, Hear, und understand.
11 Not that which goeth into the mouth defileth a man: but that which cometh out of the mouth, this defileth a man.
12 Then came his disciples, and said unto him, Knowest thou that the Pharisees were offended, after they heard this saying?
13 But he answered and said, Every plant, which my heavenly Father hath not planted, shall be rooted up.
14 Let them alone: they be blind leaders of the blind. And if the blind lead the blind, both shall fall into the ditch.
15 Then answered Peter and said unto him, Declare unto us this parable.
16 And Jesus said, Are ye also yet without understanding?
17 Do not ye yet understand, that whatsoever entereth in at the mouth goeth into the belly, and is cast out into the draught?
18 But those things which proceed out of the mouth come forth from the heart; and they defile the man.
19 For out of the heart proceed evil thoughts, murders, adulteries, fornications, thefts, false witness, blasphemies.
20 These are *the things* which defile a man: but to eat with unwashen hands defileth not a man.

THERE are two striking sayings of the Lord Jesus in this passage. One respects false doctrine: the other respects the human heart. Both of them deserve the closest attention.

Respecting false doctrine, our Lord declares *that it is a duty to oppose it; that its final destruction is sure; and that its teachers ought to be forsaken.* He says, "Every plant that my heavenly Father hath not planted, shall be rooted up. Let them alone."

It is clear, from examination of the passage, that the disciples were surprised at our Lord's strong language about the Pharisees and their traditions. They had probably been accustomed from their youth to regard the Pharisees as the wisest and best of men. They were startled to hear their Master denouncing them as hypocrites, and charging them with transgressing the commandment of God. "Knowest thou," they said, "that the Pharisees were offended?" To this question we are indebted for our Lord's explanatory declaration, —a declaration which perhaps has never received the notice it deserves.

The plain meaning of our Lord's words is, that false doctrine, like that of the Pharisees, was a plant to which no mercy should be shown. It was a "plant which His heavenly Father had not planted," and a plant which it was a duty to "root up," whatever offence it might cause. To spare it was no charity, because it was injurious to the souls of men.—It mattered nothing that those who planted it were high in office, or learned: if it contradicted the Word of God it ought to be opposed, refuted, and rejected. His disciples must therefore understand that it was right to resist all teaching that was unscriptural, and to "let alone" and forsake all instructors who persisted in it.—Sooner or later they would find that all false doctrine will be completely overthrown and put to shame, and that nothing shall stand but that which is built on the Word of God.

There are lessons of deep wisdom in this saying of our Lord, which serve to throw light on the duty of many a professing Christian. Let us mark them well, and see what they are. It was practical obedience to this saying which produced the blessed Protestant Reformation. Its lessons deserve close attention.

Do we not see here the duty of boldness in resisting false teaching? Beyond doubt we do. No fear of giving offence, no dread of ecclesiastical censure, should make us hold our peace, when God's truth is in peril. If we are true followers of our Lord, we ought to be outspeaking, unflinching witnesses against error. "Truth," says Musculus, "must not be suppressed because men are wicked and blind."

Do we not see again the duty of forsaking false teachers, if they will not give up their delusions? Beyond doubt we do. No false delicacy, no mock humility should make us shrink from leaving the ministrations of any minister who contradicts God's Word. It is at our peril if we submit to unscriptural teaching: our blood will be on our own heads. To use the words of Whitby, "It never can be right to follow the blind into the ditch."

Do we not see, in the last place, the duty of patience, when we see false teaching abound? Beyond doubt we do. We may take comfort in the thought that it will not stand long: God Himself will defend the cause of His own truth; sooner or later every heresy "shall be rooted up." We are not to fight with carnal weapons, but wait, and preach, and protest, and pray. Sooner or later, as Wycliffe said, "the truth shall prevail."

Respecting the heart of man our Lord declares in these verses *that it is the true source of all sin and defilement.* The Pharisees taught that holiness depended on meats and drinks; on bodily washings and purifications. They held that all who observed their traditions on these matters were pure and clean in God's sight; and that all who neglected them were impure and unclean.—Our Lord overthrew this miserable doctrine, by showing His disciples that the real fountain of all defilement was not without a man, but within. "Out of the heart," He says, "proceed evil thoughts, murders, adulteries, fornications, thefts, false witnesses, blasphemies: these are the things which defile a man."—He that would serve God aright, needs something far more important than bodily washings. He must seek to have a "clean heart."

What an awful picture we have here of human nature, and drawn too by One who "knew what was in man!" What a fearful catalogue is this of the contents of our own bosoms! What a melancholy list of seeds of evil our Lord has exposed, lying deep down within every one of us, and ready at any time to start into active life! What can the proud and self-righteous say, when they read such a passage as this? This is no sketch of the heart of a robber or murderer: it is the true and faithful account of the hearts of all mankind. May God grant that we may ponder it well, and learn wisdom!

Let it be a settled resolution with us that in all our religion the state of our hearts shall be the main thing. Let it not content us to go to church, and observe the forms of religion: let us look far deeper than this, and desire to have a "heart right in the sight of God." (Acts viii. 21.) The right heart is a heart sprinkled with the blood of Christ, and renewed by the Holy Ghost, and purified by faith. Never let us rest till we find within the witness of the Spirit, that God has created in us a clean heart, and made all things new. (Psalm li. 10; 2 Cor. v. 17.)

Finally, let it be a settled resolution with us to "keep our hearts with all diligence," all the days of our lives. (Prov. iv. 23.) Even after renewal they are weak: even after putting on the new man they are deceitful. Let us never forget that our chief danger is from within. The world and the devil combined, cannot do us so much harm as our own hearts will, if we do not watch and pray. Happy is he who daily remembers the words of Solomon: "He that trusteth in his own heart is a fool." (Prov. xxviii. 26.)

MATTHEW XV. 21—28.

21 Then Jesus went thence, and departed into the coasts of Tyre and Sidon.

22 And, behold, a woman of Canaan came out of the same coasts, and cried unto him, saying, Have mercy on me, O Lord, *thou* son of David; my daughter is grievously vexed with a devil.

23 But he answered her not a word. And his disciples came and besought him, saying, Send her away; for she crieth after us.

24 But he answered and said, I am not sent but unto the lost sheep of the house of Israel.

25 Then came she and worshipped him, saying, Lord, help me.

26 But he answered and said, It is not meet to take the children's bread, and to cast *it* to dogs.

27 And she said, Truth, Lord: yet the dogs eat of the crumbs which fall from their masters' table

28 Then Jesus answered and said unto her, O woman, great *is* thy faith: be it unto thee even as thou wilt. And her daughter was made whole from that very hour.

Another of our Lord's miracles is recorded in these verses: the circumstances which attend it are peculiarly full of interest; let us take them up in order, and see what they are. Every word in these narratives is rich in instruction.

We see, in the first place, *that true faith may sometimes be found where it might have been least expected.*

A Canaanitish woman cries to our Lord for help, on behalf of her daughter. "Have mercy on me," she says, "O Lord, thou son of David." Such a prayer would have showed great faith had she lived in Bethany or Jerusalem; but when we find that she came from the "coasts of Tyre and Sidon," such a prayer may well fill us with surprise. It ought to teach us, that it is grace, not place, which makes people believers. We may live in a prophet's family, like Gehazi, the servant of Elisha, and yet continue impenitent, unbelieving, and fond of the world. We may dwell in the midst of superstition and dark idolatry, like the little maid in Naaman's house, and yet be faithful witnesses for God and His Christ. Let us not despair of any one's soul, merely because his lot is cast in an unfavourable position. It is possible to dwell in the coasts of Tyre and Sidon, and yet sit down in the kingdom of God.

We see, in the second place, *that affliction sometimes proves a blessing to a person's soul.*

The Canaanitish mother, no doubt, had been sorely tried. She had seen her darling child vexed with a devil, and been unable to relieve her; but yet that trouble brought her to Christ, and taught her to pray. Without it she might have lived and died in careless ignorance, and never seen Jesus at all: surely it was good for her that she was afflicted. (Psalm cxix. 71.)

Let us mark this well. There is nothing which shows our ignorance so much as our impatience under trouble. We forget that every cross is a messsage from God, and intended to do us good in the end. Trials are intended to make us think,—to wean us from the world,—to send us to the Bible,—to drive us to our knees. Health is a good thing; but sickness is far better, if it leads us to God. Prosperity is a great mercy; but adversity is a greater one, if it brings us to Christ. Anything, anything is better than living in carelessness, and dying in sin Better a thousand times be afflicted, like the Canaanitish mother, and like her flee to Christ, than live at ease, like the rich "fool," and die at last without Christ and without hope. (Luke xii. 20.)

We see, in the third place, *that Christ's people are often less gracious and compassionate than Christ Himself.*

The woman about whom we are reading found small favour with our Lord's disciples. Perhaps they regarded an inhabitant of the coasts of Tyre and Sidon as unworthy of their Master's help. At any rate they said, "Send her away."

There is only too much of this spirit among many who profess and call themselves believers. They are apt to discourage inquirers after Christ, instead of helping them forward. They are too ready to doubt the reality of a beginner's grace, because it is small, and to treat him as Saul was treated when he first came to Jerusalem after his conversion: "They believed not that he was a disciple." (Acts ix. 26.) Let us beware of giving way to this spirit: let us seek to have more of the mind that was in Christ. Like Him, let us be gentle, and kind, and encouraging in all our treatment of those who are seeking to be saved: above all, let us tell men continnally that they must not judge of Christ by Christians. Let us assure them that there is far more in that gracious Master than there is in the best of His servants. Peter, and James, and John, may say to the afflicted soul, "Send her away:" but such a word never came from the lips of Christ. He may sometimes keep us long waiting, as He did this woman; but He will never send us empty away.

We see, in the last place, *what encouragement there is to presevere in prayer, both for ourselves and others.*

It is hard to conceive a more striking illustration of

this truth, than we have in this passage. The prayer of this afflicted mother at first seemed entirely unnoticed: Jesus "answered her not a word." Yet she prayed on. —The saying which by and by fell from our Lord's lips sounded discouraging: "I am not sent but unto the lost sheep of the house of Israel." Yet she prayed on: "Lord, help me."—The second saying of our Lord was even less encouraging than the first: "It is not meet to take the children's bread, and cast it to dogs." Yet "hope deferred" did not make her heart sick." (Prov. xiii. 12.) Even then she was not silenced: even then she finds a plea for some "crumbs" of mercy to be granted to her. And her importunity obtained at length a gracious reward: "O woman, great is thy faith: be it unto thee even as thou wilt." That promise never yet was broken: "Seek, and ye shall find." (Matt. vii. 7.)

Let us remember this history, *when we pray for ourselves.* We are sometimes tempted to think that we get no good by our prayers, and that we may as well give them up altogether. Let us resist the temptation: it comes from the devil. Let us believe, and pray on. Against our besetting sins, against the spirit of the world, against the wiles of the devil, let us pray on, and not faint.—For strength to do duty, for grace to bear our trials, for comfort in every trouble, let us "continue in prayer." Let us be sure that no time is so well spent in every day as that which we spend upon our knees. Jesus hears us, and in His own good time will give an answer.

Let us remember this history *when we intercede for others.* Have we children whose conversion we desire?

Have we relations and friends about whose salvation we are anxious? Let us follow the example of this Canaanitish woman, and lay the state of their souls before Christ. Let us name their names before Him night and day, and never rest till we have an answer. We may have to wait many a long year: we may seem to pray in vain, and intercede without profit; but let us never give up, while life lasts. Let us believe that Jesus is not changed, and that He who heard the Canaanitish mother, and granted her request, will also hear us, and one day give us an answer of peace.

MATTHEW XV. 29—39.

29 And Jesus departed from thence, and came nigh unto the sea of Galilee; and went up into a mountain, and sat down there.

30 And great multitudes came unto him, having with them *those that were* lame, blind, dumb, maimed, and many others, and cast them down at Jesus' feet; and he healed them:

31 Insomuch that the multitude wondered, when they saw the dumb to speak, the maimed to be whole, the lame to walk, and the blind to see: and they glorified the God of Israel.

32 Then Jesus called his disciples *unto him*, and said, I have compassion on the multitude, because they continue with me now three days, and have nothing to eat: and I will not send them away fasting, lest they faint in the way.

33 And his disciples say unto him, Whence should we have so much bread in the wilderness, as to fill so great a multitude?

34 And Jesus saith unto them, How many loaves have ye? And they said, Seven, and a few little fishes.

35 And he commanded the multitude to sit down on the ground.

36 And he took the seven loaves and the fishes, and gave thanks, and break *them*, and gave to his disciples and the disciples to the multitude.

37 And they did all eat, and were filled: and they took up of the broken *meat* that was left seven baskets full.

38 And they that did eat were four thousand men, beside women and children.

39 And he sent away the multitude, and took ship, and came into the coasts of Magdala.

THE beginning of this passage contains three points which deserve our special attention. For the present let us dwell exclusively on them.

In the first place, let us remark *how much more pains people take about the relief of their bodily diseases than about their souls.* We read, that "great multitudes came to Jesus, having with them those that were lame, blind, dumb, maimed, and many others." Many of them, no doubt, had journeyed many miles, and gone through great fatigues. Nothing is so difficult and troublesome as to move sick people. But the hope of being healed was in sight: such hope is everything to a sick man.

We know little of human nature if we wonder at the conduct of these people. We need not wonder at all. They felt that health was the greatest of earthly blessings; they felt that pain was the hardest of all trials to bear. There is no arguing against sense. A man feels his strength failing; he sees his body wasting and his face becoming pale; he is sensible that his appetite is leaving him: he knows, in short, that he is ill, and needs a physician. Show him a physician within reach, who is said never to fail in working cures, and he will go to him without delay.

Let us however not forget that our souls are far more diseased than our bodies, and let us learn a lesson from the conduct of these people. Our souls are afflicted with a malady far more deep-seated, far more complicated, far more hard to cure than any ailment that flesh is heir to. They are in fact plague-stricken by sin. They must be healed, and healed effectually, or perish everlastingly. Do we really know this? Do we feel it? Are we alive to our spiritual disease? Alas, there is but one answer to these questions! The bulk of mankind do not feel it at all. Their eyes are blinded. They are utterly insensible to their danger. For bodily health they crowd the waiting-rooms of doctors; for bodily health they take long journeys to find purer air; but for their souls' health they take no thought at all. Happy indeed is that man or woman who has found out his soul's disease! Such an one will never rest till he has found Jesus. Troubles will seem nothing to him. Life, life, eternal life is at stake! He will "count all things loss that he may win Christ," and be healed. (Phil. iii. 8.)

In the second place, let us mark *the marvellous ease and power with which our Lord healed all who were brought to Him.* We read that "the multitude wondered when they saw the dumb to speak, the maimed to be whole, the lame to walk, and the blind to see; and they glorified the God of Israel."

Behold in these words a lively emblem of our Lord Jesus Christ's power to heal sin-diseased souls. There is no ailment of heart that He cannot cure. There is no form of spiritual complaint that He cannot overcome. The fever of lust, the palsy of the love of the world, the slow consumption of indolence and sloth, the heart-disease of unbelief,—all, all, give way when He sends forth His Spirit on any one of the children of men. He can put a new song in a sinner's mouth, and make him speak with love of that Gospel which he once ridiculed and blasphemed; He can open the eyes of a man's understanding and make him see the kingdom of God; He can open the ears of a man, and make him willing to hear His voice, and to follow Him wheresoever He goeth; He can give power to a man who once walked in the broad way that leadeth unto destruction, to walk in the way of life; He can make hands that were once instruments of sin, serve Him and do His will. The time of miracles is not yet passed. Every conversion is a miracle. Have we ever seen a real instance of conversion? Let us know that we saw in it the hand of Christ. We should have seen nothing really greater if we had seen our Lord making the dumb to speak and the lame to walk, when He was on earth.

Would we know what to do if we desire to be saved? Do we feel soul-sick and want a cure? We must just go to Christ by faith, and apply to Him for relief. He is not changed: eighteen hundred years have made no difference in Him. High at the right hand of God, He is still the great Physician. He still "receiveth sinners." (Luke xv. 2.) He is still mighty to heal.

In the third place, let us remark *the abundant compassion of our Lord Jesus Christ.* We read that "He called His disciples and said, I have compassion on the multitude." A great crowd of men and women is always a solemn sight. It should stir our hearts to feel that each is a dying sinner, and each has a soul to be saved. None ever seems to have felt so much when He saw a crowd, as Christ.

It is a curious and striking fact, that of all the feelings experienced by our Lord when upon earth, there is none so often mentioned as "compassion." His joy, His sorrow, His thankfulness, His anger, His wonder, His zeal, all are occasionally recorded. But none of these feelings are so frequently mentioned as "compassion." The Holy Spirit seems to point out to us that this was the distinguishing feature of His character, and the predominant feeling of His mind when He was among men. Nine times over,—to say nothing of expressions in parables,—nine times over the Spirit has caused that word "compassion" to be written in the Gospels.

There is something very touching and instructive in this circumstance. Nothing is written by chance in the Word of God: there is a special reason for the selection of every single expression. That word "compassion," no doubt, was specially chosen for our profit.

It ought to encourage all who are hesitating about beginning to walk in God's ways. Let them remember that their Saviour is full of "compassion." He will receive them graciously; He will forgive them freely; He will remember their former iniquities no more; He will supply all their need abundantly. Let them not be afraid. Christ's mercy is a deep well, of which no one ever found the bottom.

It ought to comfort the saints and servants of the Lord when they feel weary. Let them call to mind that Jesus is "full of compassion." He knows what a world it is in which they live; He knows the body of a man and all its frailties; He knows the devices of their enemy, the devil. And the Lord pities His people: let them not be cast down. They may feel that weakness, failure, and imperfection are stamped on all they do; but let them not forget that word which says, "His compassions fail not." (Lament. iii. 22.)

MATTHEW XVI. 1—12.

1 The Pharisees also with the Sadducees came, and tempting desired him that he would shew them a sign from heaven.

2 He answered and said unto them, When it is evening, ye say, *It will be* fair weather: for the sky is red.

3 And in the morning, *It will be* foul weather to-day: for the sky is red and lowring. O *ye* hypocrites, ye can discern the face of the sky;

but can ye not *discern* the signs of the times?
4 A wicked and adulterous generation seeketh after a sign; and there shall no sign be given unto it, but the sign of the prophet Jonas. And he left them, and departed.
5 And when his disciples were come to the other side, they had forgotten to take bread.
6 Then Jesus said unto them, Take heed and beware of the leaven of the Pharisees and of the Sadducees.
7 And they reasoned among themselves, saying, *It is* because we have taken no bread.
8 *Which* when Jesus perceived, he said unto them, O ye of little faith, why reason ye among yourselves, because ye have brought no bread?
9 Do ye not yet understand, neither remember the five loaves of the five thousand, and how many baskets ye took up?
10 Neither the seven loaves of the four thousand, and how many baskets ye took up?
11 How is it that ye do not understand that I spake *it* not to you concerning bread, that ye should beware of the leaven of the Pharisees and of the Sadducees?
12 Then understood they how that he bade *them* not beware of the leaven of bread, but of the doctrine of the Pharisees and of the Sadducees.

In these verses we find our Lord assailed by the untiring enmity of the Pharisees and Sadducees. As a general rule these two sects were at enmity between themselves: in persecuting Christ, however, they made common cause. Truly it was an unholy alliance! Yet how often we see the same thing in the present day. Men of the most opposite opinions and habits will agree in disliking the Gospel, and will work together to oppose its progress. "There is no new thing under the sun." (Eccles. i. 9.)

The first point in this passage which deserves special notice is *the repetition which our Lord makes of words used by Him on a former occasion.* He says, "a wicked and adulterous generation seeketh after a sign; and there shall no sign be given unto it, but the sign of the prophet Jonas." If we turn to the twelfth chapter of this Gospel and the 39th verse, we shall find that He had said the very same thing once before.

This repetition may seem a trifling and unimportant matter in the eyes of some. But it is not so in reality.

It throws light on a subject, which has perplexed the minds of many sincere lovers of the Bible, and ought therefore to be specially observed.

This repetition shows us that our Lord was in the habit of *saying the same things over again.* He did not content Himself with saying a thing once, and afterwards never repeating it. It is evident that it was His custom to bring forward certain truths again and again, and thus to impress them more deeply on the minds of His disciples. He knew the weakness of our memories on spiritual things; He knew that what we hear twice, we remember better than what we hear once. He therefore brought out of His treasury old things as well as new.

Now what does all this teach us? It teaches us that we need not be so anxious to *harmonize* the narratives we read in the four Gospels, as many are disposed to be. It does not follow that the sayings of our Lord, which we find the same in St. Matthew and St. Luke, were always used at the same time, or that the events with which they are connected must necessarily be the same. —St. Matthew may be describing one event in our Lord's life; St. Luke may be describing another: and yet the words of our Lord, on both occasions, may have been precisely alike.—To attempt to make out the two events to be one and the same, because of the sameness of the words used, has often led Bible students into great difficulties. It is far safer to hold the view here maintained,—that at different times our Lord often used the same words.

The second point which deserves special notice in these verses is *the solemn warning which our Lord takes occasion to give to His disciples.* His mind was evidently pained with the false doctrines which He saw among the Jews, and the pernicious influence which they exercised. He seizes the opportunity to utter a caution. "Take heed, and beware of the leaven of the Pharisees and of the Sadducees." Let us mark well what those words contain.

To whom was this warning addressed? To the twelve apostles,—to the first ministers of the Church of Christ, —to men who had forsaken all for the Gospel's sake! Even they are warned! The best of men are only men, and at any time may fall into temptation. "Let Him that thinketh he standeth take heed lest he fall." (1 Cor. x. 12.) If we love life, and would see good days, let us never think that we do not need that hint: "Take heed and beware."

Against what does our Lord warn His apostles? Against the "doctrine" of the Pharisees and of the Sadducees. The Pharisees, we are frequently told in the Gospels, were self-righteous formalists; the Sadducees were sceptics, freethinkers, and half infidels. Yet even Peter, James, and John must beware of their doctrines! Truly the best and holiest of believers may well be on his guard!

By what figure does our Lord describe the false doctrines against which He cautions His disciples? He calls them *leaven.* Like leaven, they might seem a small thing compared to the whole body of truth; like leaven, once admitted, they would work secretly and noiselessly; like leaven, they would gradually change the whole character of the religion with which they were mixed. How much is often contained in a single word! It was not merely the open danger of heresy, but "leaven," of which the apostles were to beware.

There is much in all this that calls loudly for the close attention of all professing Christians. The caution of our Lord in this passage has been shamefully neglected. It would have been well for the Church of Christ if the warnings of the Gospel had been as much studied as its promises.

Let us then remember that this saying of our Lord's about the "leaven of the Pharisees and Sadducees" was intended for all time. It was not meant only for the generation to which it was spoken: it was meant for the perpetual benefit of the Church of Christ. He who spoke it saw with prophetical eye the future history of Christianity. The Great Physician knew well that Pharisee-doctrines and Sadducee-doctrines would prove the two great wasting diseases of His Church, until the end of the world. He would have us know that there will always be Pharisees and Sadducees in the ranks of Christians: their succession shall never fail: their generation shall never become extinct. Their name may change, but their spirit will always remain. Therefore He cries to us, "Take heed, and beware."

Finally, let us make a personal use of this caution, by keeping up a holy jealousy over our own souls. Let us remember that we live in a world where Pharisaism and Sadduceeism are continually striving for the mastery in the Church of Christ. Some want to add to the Gospel, and some want to take away from it; some would bury it, and some would pare it down to nothing; some would stifle it by heaping on additions, and some would bleed it to death by subtraction from its truths. Both parties agree only in one respect: both would kill and destroy the life of Christianity, if they succeeded in having their own way. Against both errors let us watch and pray, and stand upon our guard. Let us not add to the Gospel, to please the Roman Catholic Pharisee; let us not subtract from the Gospel, to please the Neologian Sadducee. Let our principle be "the truth, the whole truth, and nothing but the truth:" nothing added to it, and nothing taken away.

MATTHEW XVI. 13—20.

13 When Jesus came into the coasts of Cæsarea Philippi, he asked his disciples, saying, Whom do men say that I the Son of man am?

14 And they said, Some *say that thou art* John the Baptist: some Elias; and others, Jeremias, or one of the prophets.

15 He saith unto them, But whom say ye that I am?

16 And Simon Peter answered and said, Thou art the Christ, the Son of the living God.

17 And Jesus answered and said unto him, Blessed art thou, Simon Bar-jona: for flesh and blood hath not revealed *it* unto thee, but my Father which is in heaven.

18 And I say also unto thee, That thou art Peter, and upon this rock I will build my church; and the gates of hell shall not prevail against it.

19 And I will give unto thee the keys of the kingdom of heaven: and whatsoever thou shalt bind on earth shall be bound in heaven: and whatsoever thou shalt loose on earth shall be loosed in heaven.

20 Then charged he his disciples that they should tell no man that he was Jesus the Christ.

THERE are words in this passage which have led to painful differences and divisions among Christians. Men have striven and contended about their meaning till they have lost sight of all charity, and yet have failed to carry conviction to one another's minds. Let it suffice us to glance briefly at the controverted words, and then pass on to more practical lessons.

What then are we to understand, when we read that remarkable saying of our Lord's, "Thou art Peter, and upon this rock I will build my church"? Does it mean that the Apostle Peter himself was to be the foundation on which Christ's Church was to be built? Such an interpretation, to say the least, appears exceedingly improbable. To speak of an erring, fallible child of Adam as the foundation of the spiritual temple, is very unlike the ordinary language of Scripture. Above all, no reason can be given why our Lord should not have said, "I will build my Church upon *thee*," if such had been His meaning, instead of saying, "I will build my Church upon *this rock*."

The true meaning of "the Rock," in this passage, appears to be the truth of our Lord's Messiahship and Divinity, which Peter had just confessed. It is as though our Lord had said, "Thou art rightly called by the name Peter, or stone, for thou hast confessed that mighty *truth*, on which, as on a rock, I will build my Church."*

But what are we to understand when we read the promise which our Lord makes to Peter: "I will give unto thee the keys of the kingdom of heaven"? Do these words mean that the right of admitting souls to heaven was to be placed in Peter's hands? The idea is preposterous. Such an office is the special prerogative

* There is nothing modern, or peculiarly Protestant, in the view here maintained. It was held by Chrysostom long ago. It was taught by Ferus, a famous Roman Catholic preacher, of the Franciscan Order, at Mayence, in the sixteenth century, in his Homilies on St. Matthew.

It may be well to remark, in this place, that it is a complete delusion to suppose that the Scriptures can be interpreted according to the "unanimous consent of the Fathers." *There is no such unanimous consent!* It is a mere high-sounding phrase, utterly destitute of any foundation in facts. The Fathers disagree as much in explaining Scripture, as Whitby and Gill, or Matthew Henry and D'Oyly and Mant.

of Christ Himself. (Rev. i. 18.) Do the words mean that Peter was to have any primacy or superiority over the rest of the Apostles? There is not the slightest proof that such a meaning was attached to the words in the New Testament times, or that Peter had any rank or dignity above the rest of the twelve.

The true meaning of the promise to Peter appears to be, that he was to have the special privilege of first opening the door of salvation, both to the Jews and Gentiles. This was fulfilled to the letter, when he preached on the day of Pentecost to the Jews, and visited the Gentile Cornelius at his own house. On each occasion he used "the keys," and threw open the door of faith. And of this he seems to have been sensible himself: "God," he says, "made choice among us, that by my mouth the Gentiles should hear the word of the Gospel, and believe." (Acts xv. 7.)

Finally, what are we to understand when we read the words, "Whatsoever thou shalt bind on earth shall be bound in heaven, and whatsoever thou shalt loose on earth shall be loosed in heaven"? Does this mean that the Apostle Peter was to have any power of forgiving sins, and absolving sinners? Such an idea is derogatory to Christ's special office, as our Great High Priest. It is a power which we never find Peter, or any of the Apostles, once exercising. They always refer men to Christ.

The true meaning of this promise appears to be, that Peter and his brethren, the apostles, were to be specially commissioned to teach with authority the way of salvation. As the Old Testament priest declared authoritatively whose leprosy was cleansed, so the apostles were appointed to "declare and pronounce" authoritatively, whose sins were forgiven. Beside this, they were to be specially inspired to lay down rules and regulations for the guidance of the Church on disputed questions. Some things they were to "bind" or forbid; others they were to "loose" or allow. The decision of the Council at Jerusalem, that the Gentiles need not be circumcised, was one example of the exercise of this power (Acts xvi. 19); but it was a commission specially confined to the apostles. In discharging it they had no successors. With them it began, and with them it expired.

We will leave these controverted words here: enough perhaps has been said upon them for our personal edification. Let us only remember that, in whatever sense men take them, they have nothing to do with the Church of Rome. Let us now turn our attention to points which more immediately concern our own souls.

In the first place, let us admire *the noble confession which the apostle Peter makes in this passage.* He says, in reply to our Lord's question, "Whom say ye that I am?"—"Thou art the Christ, the Son of the living God."

At first sight, a careless reader may see nothing very remarkable in these words of the apostle: he may think it extraordinary that they should call forth such strong commendation from our Lord: but such thoughts arise from ignorance and inconsideration. Men forget that it is a widely different thing to believe in Christ's divine mission when we dwell in the midst of professing Christians, and to believe in it when we dwell in the midst of hardened and unbelieving Jews. The glory of

Peter's confession lies in this,—that he made it when few were with Christ and many against Him. He made it when the rulers of his own nation, the Scribes, and Priests, and Pharisees, were all opposed to his Master; he made it when our Lord was in the "form of a servant," without wealth, without royal dignity, without any visible mark of a King. To make such a confession at such a time, required great faith and great decision of character. The confession itself, as Brentius says, "was an epitome of all Christianity, and a compendium of true doctrine about religion." Therefore it was that our Lord said, "Blessed art thou, Simon Bar-jona."

We shall do well to copy that hearty zeal and affection which Peter here displayed. We are perhaps too much disposed to underrate this holy man, because of his occasional instability, and his thrice-repeated denial of his Lord. This is a great mistake. With all his faults, Peter was a true-hearted, fervent, single-minded servant of Christ; with all his imperfections, he has given us a pattern that many Christians would do wisely to follow. Zeal like his may have its ebbs and flows, and sometimes lack steadiness of purpose; zeal like his may be ill-directed, and sometimes make sad mistakes: but zeal like his is not to be despised. It awakens the sleeping; it stirs the sluggish; it provokes others to exertion. Anything is better than sluggishness, lukewarmness, and torpor, in the Church of Christ. Happy would it have been for Christendom had there been more Christians like Simon Peter and Martin Luther.

In the next place, let us take care that *we understand what our Lord means when He speaks of His Church.*

The Church which Jesus promises to build upon a rock is the "blessed company of all faithful people." It is not the visible Church of any one nation, or country, or place: it is the whole body of believers of every age, and tongue, and people. It is a Church composed of all who are washed in Christ's blood, clothed in Christ's righteousness, renewed by Christ's Spirit, joined to Christ by faith, and epistles of Christ in life; it is a Church of which every member is baptized with the Holy Ghost, and is really and truly holy; it is a Church which is one body: all who belong to it are of one heart and one mind, hold the same truths, and believe the same doctrines as necessary to salvation. It is a Church which has only one Head: that Head is Jesus Christ Himself. "He is the Head of the body." (Col. i. 18.)

Let us beware of mistakes on this subject. Few words are so much misunderstood as the word "Church;" few mistakes have so much injured the cause of pure religion. Ignorance on this point has been a fertile source of bigotry, sectarianism, and persecution. Men have wrangled and contended about Episcopal, Presbyterian, and Independent Churches, as if it were needful to salvation to belong to some particular party, and as if, belonging to that party, we must of course belong to Christ. All this time they have lost sight of the one true Church, outside of which there is no salvation at all. It will matter nothing at the last day where we have worshipped, if we are not found members of the true Church of God's elect.

In the last place, let us mark *the glorious promises which our Lord makes to His Church:* He says, "The gates of hell shall not prevail against it."

The meaning of this promise is,—that the power of Satan shall never destroy the people of Christ. He that brought sin and death into the first creation by tempting Eve, shall never bring ruin on the new creation by overthrowing believers. The mystical body of Christ shall never perish or decay. Though often persecuted, afflicted, distressed, and brought low, it shall never come to an end: it shall outlive the wrath of Pharaohs and Roman Emperors. Visible churches, like Ephesus, may come to nothing; but the true Church never dies. Like the bush that Moses saw, it may burn, but shall not be consumed. *Every* member of it shall be brought safe to glory. In spite of falls, failures, and short-comings,—in spite of the world, the flesh, and the devil,—no member of the true Church shall ever be cast away. (John x. 28.)

MATTHEW XVI. 21—23.

21 From that time forth began Jesus to show unto his disciples, how that he must go unto Jerusalem, and suffer many things of the elders and chief priests and scribes, and be killed, and be raised again the third day.

22 Then Peter took him, and began to rebuke him, saying, Be it far from thee, Lord: this shall not be unto thee.

23 But he turned, and said unto Peter, Get thee behind me, Satan: thou art an offence unto me: for thou savourest not the things that be of God, but those that be of men.

In the beginning of these verses we find our Lord revealing to His disciples a great and startling truth. That truth was His approaching death upon the cross. For the first time He places before their minds the astounding announcement that "He must go to Jerusalem, and suffer,—and be killed." He had not come on earth to take a kingdom, but to die. He had not come to reign, and be ministered to; but to shed His blood as a sacrifice, and to give His life as a ransom for many.

It is almost impossible for us to conceive how strange and incomprehensible these tidings must have seemed to His disciples. Like most of the Jews, they could form no idea of a suffering Messiah. They did not understand that the fifty-third chapter of Isaiah must be literally fulfilled; they did not see that the sacrifices of the law were all meant to point them to the death of the true Lamb of God. They thought of nothing but the second glorious coming of Messiah, which is yet to take place at the end of the world. They thought so much of Messiah's crown, that they lost sight of His cross. We shall do well to remember this: a right understanding of this matter throws strong light on the lessons which this passage contains.

We learn, in the first place, from these verses, that *there may be much spiritual ignorance even in a true disciple of Christ.*

We cannot have a clearer proof of this than the conduct of the apostle Peter in this passage. He tries to dissuade our Lord from suffering on the cross. "Be it far from Thee," he says: "this shall not be unto Thee." He did not see the full purpose of our Lord's coming into the world. His eyes were blinded to the necessity of our Lord's death. He actually did what he could to prevent that death taking place at all! And yet we know that Peter was a converted man: he really believed that Jesus was the Messiah. His heart was right in the sight of God.

These things are meant to teach us that we must neither regard good men as infallible, because they are good men, nor yet suppose they have no grace, because their grace is weak and small. One brother may possess singular gifts, and be a bright and shining light in the Church of Christ; but let us not forget that he is a man, and as a man liable to commit great mistakes. Another brother's knowledge may be scanty: he may fail to judge rightly on many points of doctrine; he may err both in word and deed. But has he faith and love towards Christ? Does he hold the Head? If so, let us deal patiently with him. What he sees not now, he may see hereafter. Like Peter, he may now be in the dark, and yet, like Peter, enjoy one day the full light of the Gospel.

Let us learn, in the second place, from these verses, that *there is no doctrine of Scripture so deeply important as the doctrine of Christ's atoning death.*

We cannot have clearer proof of this than the language used by our Lord in rebuking Peter. He addresses him by the awful name of "Satan," as if he was an adversary, and doing the devil's work, in trying to prevent His death. He says to him, whom He had so lately called "blessed," "Get thee behind Me, thou art an offence unto Me." He tells the man whose noble confession He had just commended so highly, "Thou savourest not the things that be of God, but those that be of men." Stronger words than these never fell from our Lord's lips. The error that drew from such a loving Saviour such a stern rebuke to such a true disciple, must have been a mighty error indeed.

The truth is that our Lord would have us regard the crucifixion as the central truth of Christianity. Right views of His vicarious death, and the benefits resulting from it, lie at the very foundation of Bible-religion. Never let us forget this. On matters of church-government, and the form of worship, men may differ from us, and yet reach heaven in safety. On the matter of Christ's atoning death, as the way of peace, truth is only one. If we are wrong here, we are ruined for ever. Error on many points is only a skin disease; error about Christ's death is a disease at the heart. Here let us take our stand: let nothing move us from this ground. The sum of all our hopes must be, that "Christ has died for us." (1 Thess. v. 10.) Give up that doctrine, and we have no solid hope at all.

MATTHEW XVI. 24—28.

24 Then said Jesus unto his disciples, If any *man* will come after me, let him deny himself, and take up his cross, and follow me.

25 For whosoever will save his life shall lose it: and whosoever will lose his life for my sake shall find it.

26 For what is a man profited, if he shall gain the whole world, and lose his own soul? or what shall a man give in exchange for his soul?

27 For the Son of man shall come in the glory of his Father with his angels; and then he shall reward every man according to his works.

28 Verily I say unto you, There be some standing here, which shall not taste of death, till they see the Son of man coming in his kingdom.

In order to see the connection of these verses we must remember the mistaken impressions of our Lord's disciples as to the purpose of His coming into the world. Like Peter they could not bear the idea of the crucifixion: they thought that Jesus had come to set up an earthly kingdom; they did not see that He must needs suffer and die. They dreamed of worldly honours and temporal rewards in their Master's service; they did not understand that true Christians, like Christ, must be "made perfect through sufferings." Our Lord corrects these misapprehensions in words of peculiar solemnity, which we shall do well to lay up in our hearts.

Let us learn, in the first place, from these verses, *that men must make up their minds to trouble and self-denial, if they follow Christ.*

Our Lord dispels the fond dreams of His disciples, by telling them that His followers must "take up the cross." The glorious kingdom they were expecting was not about to be set up immediately. They must make up their minds to persecution and affliction, if they intended to be His servants: they must be content to "lose their lives," if they would have their souls saved.

It is good for us all to see this point clearly. We must not conceal from ourselves that true Christianity brings with it a daily cross in this life, while it offers us a crown of glory in the life to come. The flesh must be daily crucified; the devil must be daily resisted; the world must be daily overcome. There is a warfare to be waged, and a battle to be fought. All this is the inseparable accompaniment of true religion: heaven is not to be won without it. Never was there a truer word than the old saying, "No cross, no crown!" If we have never found this out by experience, our souls are in a poor condition.

Let us learn, in the second place, from these verses, *that there is nothing so precious as a man's soul.*

Our Lord teaches this lesson by asking one of the most solemn questions that the New Testament contains. It is a question so well known, and so often repeated, that people often lose sight of its searching character; but it is a question that ought to sound in our ears like a trumpet, whenever we are tempted to neglect our eternal interests: "What shall it profit a man if he gain the whole world and lose his own soul?"

There can only be one answer to this question. There is nothing on earth, or under the earth, that can make amends to us for the loss of our souls: there is nothing that money can buy, or man can give, to be named in comparison with our souls. The world and all that it contains, is temporal: it is all fading, perishing, and passing away. The soul is *eternal:* that one single word is the key to the whole question. Let it sink down deeply into our hearts. Are we wavering in our religion? Do we fear the cross? Does the way seem too narrow? Let our Master's words ring in our ears: "What shall it profit a man?" and let us doubt no more.

Let us learn, in the last place, *that the second coming of Christ is the time when His people shall receive their rewards.* "The Son of Man shall come in the glory of His Father, and then shall He reward every man according to his works."

There is deep wisdom in this saying of our Lord's, when viewed in connection with the preceding verses. He knows the heart of a man: He knows how soon we are ready to be cast down, and, like Israel of old, to be "discouraged because of the way." (Num. xxi. 4.) He therefore holds out to us a gracious promise. He reminds us that He has yet to come a second time, as surely as He came the first time: He tells us that this is the time when His disciples shall receive their good things. There will be glory, honour, and reward in abundance one day for all who have served and loved Jesus; but it is to be in the dispensation of the second advent, and not of the first. The bitter must come before the sweet, the cross before the crown. The first advent is the dispensation of the crucifixion; the second advent is the dispensation of the kingdom. We must submit to take part with our Lord in His humiliation, if we desire to share in His glory.

And now let us not leave these verses without serious self-inquiry as to the matters which they contain. We have heard of the necessity of taking up the cross, and denying ourselves: have we taken it up, and are we carrying it daily? We have heard of the value of the soul: do we live as if we believed it? We have heard of Christ's second advent: do we look forward to it with hope and joy?—Happy is that man who can give a satisfactory answer to these questions!

MATTHEW XVII. 1—13.

1 And after six days Jesus taketh Peter, James, and John his brother, and bringeth them up into an high mountain apart,

2 And was transfigured before them: and his face did shine as the sun, and his raiment was white as the light.

3 And, behold, there appeared unto them Moses and Elias talking with him.

4 Then answered Peter, and said unto Jesus, Lord, it is good for us to be here: if thou wilt, let us make here three tabernacles; one for thee, and one for Moses, and one for Elias.

5 While he yet spake, behold, a bright cloud overshadowed them: and behold a voice out of the cloud, which said, This is my beloved Son, in whom I am well pleased; hear ye him.

6 And when the disciples heard *it*, they fell on their face, and were sore afraid.

7 And Jesus came and touched them, and said, Arise, and be not afraid.

8 And when they had lifted up their eyes, they saw no man, save Jesus only.

9 And as they came down from the mountain, Jesus charged them, saying, Tell the vision to no man, until the Son of man be risen again from the dead.

10 And his disciples asked him, saying, Why then say the scribes that Elias must first come?

11 And Jesus answered and said unto them, Elias truly shall first come, and restore all things.

12 But I say unto you, That Elias is come already, and they knew him not, but have done unto him whatsoever they listed. Likewise shall also the Son of man suffer of them.

13 Then the disciples understood that he spake unto them of John the Baptist.

THESE verses contain one of the most remarkable events in our Lord's earthly ministry,—the event commonly called the transfiguration. The order in which it is recorded is beautiful and instructive. The latter part of the last chapter showed us the cross: here we are graciously allowed to see something of the coming reward. The hearts which have just been saddened by a plain statement of Christ's sufferings, are at once gladdened by a vision of Christ's glory. Let us mark this. We often lose much by not tracing the connection between chapter and chapter in the Word of God.

There are some mysterious things, no doubt, in the vision here described. It must needs be so. We are yet in the body: our senses are conversant with gross and material things; our ideas and perceptions about glorified bodies and dead saints must necessarily be vague and imperfect. Let us content ourselves with endeavouring to mark out the practical lessons which the transfiguration is meant to teach us.

In the first place, we have in these verses *a striking pattern of the glory in which Christ and His people will appear when He comes the second time.*

There can be little question that this was one main object of this wonderful vision. It was meant to encourage the disciples, by giving them a glimpse of good things yet to come. That "face shining as the sun," and that "raiment white as the light," were intended to give the disciples some idea of the majesty in which Jesus will appear to the world, when He comes the second time, and all His saints with Him. The corner of the veil was lifted up, to show them their Master's true dignity. They were taught that if He did not yet appear to the world in the guise of a King, it was only because the time for putting on His royal apparel was not yet come. It is impossible to draw any other conclusion from St. Peter's language, when writing on the subject. He says, with distinct reference to the transfiguration, "We were eye witnesses of His majesty.' (2 Peter i. 16.)

It is good for us to have the coming glory of Christ and His people deeply impressed on our minds. We are sadly apt to forget it. There are few visible indications of it in the world: "We see not yet all things put under" our Lord's feet. (Heb. ii. 8.) Sin, unbelief, and superstition abound. Thousands are practically saying, "We will not have this man to reign over us."—It doth not yet appear what His people shall be: their crosses, their tribulations, their weaknesses, their conflicts, are all manifest enough; but there are few signs of their future reward. Let us beware of giving way to doubts in this matter: let us silence such doubts by reading over the history of the transfiguration. There is laid up for Jesus, and all that believe on Him, such glory as the heart of man never conceived. It is not only promised, but part of it has actually been seen by three competent witnesses. One of them says, "We beheld His glory, the glory as of the only begotten of the Father." (John i. 14.) Surely that which has been seen may well be believed.

In the second place, we have in these verses, *an unanswerable proof of the resurrection of the body, and the life after death* We are told that Moses and Elijah appeared visibly in glory with Christ: they were seen in a bodily form. They were heard talking with our Lord. Fourteen hundred and eighty years had rolled round, since Moses died and was buried; more than nine hundred years had passed away, since Elijah "went up by a whirlwind into heaven:" yet here they are seen alive by Peter, James, and John!

Let us lay firm hold on this part of the vision. It deserves close attention. We must all feel, if we ever think at all, that the state of the dead is a wonderful and mysterious subject. One after another we bury them out of our sight: we lay them in their narrow beds, and see them no more, and their bodies become dust. But will they really live again? Shall we really see them any more? Will the grave really give back the dead at the last day? These are questions that will occasionally come across the minds of some, in spite of all the plainest statements in the Word of God.

Now we have in the transfiguration the clearest evidence that the dead will rise again. We find two men appearing on earth, in their bodies, who had long been separate from the land of the living,—and in them we have a pledge of the resurrection of all. All that have ever lived upon earth will again be called to life, and render up their account: not one will be found missing. There is no such thing as annihilation. All that have ever fallen asleep in Christ will be found in safe keeping,—patriarchs, prophets, apostles, martyrs,—down to the humblest servant of God in our own day. "Though unseen to us they all live to God." "He is not a God of the dead, but of the living." (Luke xx. 38.) Their spirits live as surely as we live ourselves, and will appear hereafter in glorified bodies, as surely as Moses and Elijah in the mount. These are indeed solemn thoughts! There is a resurrection, and men like Felix may well tremble. There is a resurrection, and men like Paul may well rejoice.

In the last place, we have in these verses *a remarkable testimony to Christ's infinite superiority over all that are born of woman.*

This is a point which is brought out strongly by the voice from heaven, which the disciples heard. Peter, bewildered by the heavenly vision, and not knowing what to say, proposed to build three tabernacles, one for Christ, one for Moses, and one for Elijah. He seemed, in fact, to place the law-giver and the prophet side by side with his divine Master, as if all three were equal. At once, we are told, the proposal was rebuked in a marked manner.—A cloud covered Moses and Elijah, and they were no more seen. A voice at the same time came forth from the cloud, repeating the solemn words, made use of at our Lord's baptism, "This is My beloved Son, in whom I am well pleased: hear ye Him." That voice was meant to teach Peter that there was One there far greater than Moses or Elijah. Moses was a faithful servant of God; Elijah was a bold witness for the truth: but Christ was far above either one or the other. He was the Saviour to whom law and prophets were continually pointing; He was the true Prophet, whom all were commanded to hear. (Deut. xviii. 15.) Moses and Elijah were great men in their day; but Peter and his companions were to remember that in nature, dignity, and office, they were far below Christ.—He was the true sun: they were the stars depending daily on His light. He was the root: they were the branches. He was the

Master: they were the servants. Their goodness was all derived: His was original and His own.—Let them honour Moses and the prophets, as holy men; but if they would be saved they must take Christ alone for their Master, and glory only in Him. "Hear ye Him."

Let us see, in these words, a striking lesson to the whole Church of Christ. There is a constant tendency in human nature to "hear man." Bishops, priests, deacons, popes, cardinals, councils, presbyterian preachers, and independent ministers, are continually exalted to a place which God never intended them to fill, and made practically to usurp the honour of Christ. Against this tendency let us all watch, and be on our guard. Let these solemn words of the vision ever ring in our ears: "Hear ye Christ."

The best of men are only men at their very best. Patriarchs, prophets, and apostles,—martyrs, fathers, reformers, puritans,—all, all are sinners, who need a Saviour: holy, useful, honourable in their place,—but sinners after all. They must never be allowed to stand between us and Christ. He alone is "the Son, in whom the Father is well pleased;" He alone is sealed and appointed to give the bread of life; He alone has the keys in His hands: "God over all, blessed for ever." (Rom. ix. 5.) Let us take heed that we hear His voice, and follow Him; let us value all religious teaching just in proportion as it leads us to Jesus. The sum and substance of saving religion is to "hear Christ."

MATTHEW XVII. 14—21.

14 And when they were come to
the multitude, there came to him
a *certain* man, kneeling down to
him, and saying,
15 Lord have mercy on my son:
for he is lunatic, and sore vexed:
for ofttimes he falleth into the fire,
and oft into the water.
16 And I brought him to thy
disciples, and they could not cure
him.
17 Then Jesus answered and
said, O faithless and perverse generation, how long shall I be with
you? how long shall I suffer you?
bring him hither to me.
18 And Jesus rebuked the devil;
and he departed out of him: and
the child was cured from that very
hour.
19 Then came the disciples to
Jesus apart, and said, Why could
not we cast him out?
20 And Jesus said unto them,
Because of your unbelief: for verily
I say unto you, If ye have faith as
a grain of mustard seed, ye shall
say unto this mountain, Remove
hence to yonder place; and it shall
remove; and nothing shall be impossible unto you.
21 Howbeit this kind goeth not
out but by prayer and fasting.

We read in this passage another of our Lord's great miracles. He heals a young man lunatic and possessed with a devil.

The first thing we see in these verses is *a lively emblem of the awful influence sometimes exercised by Satan over the young.* We are told of a certain man's son, who was "lunatic and sore vexed." We are told of the evil spirit pressing him on to the destruction of body and soul: "Oft-times he falleth into the fire, and oft into the water." It was one of those cases of Satanic possession, which, however common in our Lord's times, in our own day is rarely seen; but we can easily imagine that, when they did occur, they must have been peculiarly distressing to the relations of the afflicted. It is painful enough to see the bodies of those we love racked by disease: how much more painful must it have been to see body and mind completely under the influence of the devil! "Out of hell," says Bishop Hall, "there could not be greater misery."

But we must not forget that there are many instances

of Satan's spiritual dominion over young people, which are quite as painful, in their way, as the case described in this passage. There are thousands of young men who seem to have wholly given themselves up to Satan's temptations, and to be led "captive at his will." (2 Tim. ii. 26.) They cast off all fear of God, and all respect for His commandments; they serve divers lusts and pleasures; they run wildly into every excess of riot; they refuse to listen to the advice of parents, teachers, or ministers; they fling aside all regard for health, character, or worldly respectability. They do all that lies in their power to ruin themselves, body and soul, for time and eternity: they are willing bond-slaves of Satan.—Who has not seen such young men? They are to be seen in town and in country; they are to be found among rich and among poor. Surely such young men give mournful proof that although Satan now-a-days seldom has possession of man's body, he still exercises a fearful dominion over some men's souls.

Yet even about such young men as these, be it remembered, we must never despair. We must call to mind the almighty power of our Lord Jesus Christ. Bad as this boy's case was, of whom we read in these verses, he was "cured from the very hour" that he was brought to Christ! Parents, and teachers, and ministers should go on praying for young men, even at their worst Hard as their hearts seem now, they may yet be softened: desperate as their wickedness now appears, they may yet be healed. They may yet repent, and be converted, like John Newton, and their last state prove better than their first. Who can tell? Let it be a settled principle with us, when we read our Lord's miracles, never to despair of the conversion of any soul.

In the second place, we see in these verses *a striking example of the weakening effect of unbelief.* The disciples anxiously inquired of our Lord, when they saw the devil yielding to His power, "Why could not we cast him out?" They received an answer full of the deepest instruction: "Because of your unbelief." Would they know the secret of their own sad failure in the hour of need? It was want of faith.

Let us ponder this point well, and learn wisdom. Faith is the key to success in the Christian warfare: unbelief is the sure road to defeat. Once let our faith languish and decay, and all our graces will languish with it. Courage, patience, long-suffering, and hope, will soon wither and dwindle away: faith is the root on which they all depend. The same Israelites who at one time went through the Red Sea in triumph, at another time shrunk from danger like cowards, when they reached the borders of the promised land. Their God was the same who had brought them out of the land of Egypt; their leader was that same Moses who had wrought so many wonders before their eyes: but their faith was not the same. They gave way to shameful doubts of God's love and power. "They could not enter in because of unbelief." (Heb. iii. 19.)

In the last place, we see in these verses, *that Satan's kingdom is not to be pulled down without diligence and pains.* This seems to be the lesson of the verse which concludes the passage we are now considering: "This kind goeth not out but by prayer and fasting." A gentle rebuke to the disciples appears to be implied in the words. Perhaps they had been too much lifted up by past successes; perhaps they had been less careful in the use of means in their Master's absence, than they were under their Master's eye. At any rate they receive a plain hint from our Lord, that the warfare against Satan must never be lightly carried on. They are warned that no victories are to be won easily over the prince of this world: without fervent prayer, and diligent self-mortification, they would often meet with failure and defeat.

The lesson here laid down is one of deep importance. "I would," says Bullinger, "that this part of the Gospel pleased us as much as those parts which concede liberty." We are all apt to contract a habit of doing religious acts in a thoughtless, perfunctory way. Like Israel, puffed up with the fall of Jericho, we are ready to say to ourselves, "The men of Ai are but few" (Josh. vii. 3); "there is no need to put forth all our strength." Like Israel, we often learn by bitter experience, that spiritual battles are not to be won without hard fighting. The ark of the Lord must never be handled irreverently: God's work must never be carelessly done.

May we all bear in mind our Lord's words to His disciples, and make a practical use of them. In the pulpit and on the platform, in the Sunday school and in the district, in our use of family prayers and in reading our own Bibles, let us diligently watch our own spirit. Whatever we do, let us "do it with our might." (Eccles. ix. 10.) It is a fatal mistake to underrate our foes. Greater is He that is for us than he that is against us; but, for all that, he that is against us is not to be despised. He is the "prince of this world:" he is a "strong man" armed, keeping his house, who will not "go out," and part with his goods without a struggle. "We wrestle not against flesh and blood, but against principalities and powers." (Ephes. vi. 12.) We have need to take the whole armour of God, and not only to take it, but to use it too. We may be very sure that those who win most victories over the world, the flesh, and the devil, are those who pray most in private, and "keep under their bodies, and bring them into subjection." (1 Cor. ix. 27.)

MATTHEW XVII. 22—27.

22 And while they abode in Galilee, Jesus said unto them, The Son of man shall be betrayed into the hands of men:

23 And they shall kill him, and the third day he shall be raised again. And they were exceeding sorry.

24 And when they were come to Capernaum, they that received tribute *money* came to Peter, and said, Doth not your master pay tribute?

25 He saith, Yes. And when he was come into the house, Jesus prevented him, saying, What thinkest thou, Simon? of whom do the kings of the earth take custom or tribute? of their own children, or of strangers?

26 Peter saith unto him, Of strangers. Jesus saith unto him, Then are the children free.

27 Notwithstanding, lest we should offend them, go thou to the sea, and cast an hook, and take up the fish that first cometh up; and when thou hast opened his mouth, thou shalt find a piece of money: that take, and give unto them for me and thee.

THESE verses contain a circumstance in our Lord's history which is not recorded by any of the Evangelists excepting St. Matthew. A remarkable miracle is worked in order to provide payment of the tribute-money required for the service of the temple. There are three striking points in the narrative, which deserve attentive observation.

Let us observe, in the first place, *our Lord's perfect knowledge of everything that is said and done in this world.* We are told that those who "received tribute-money came to Peter, and said, Doth not your Master pay tribute? He saith, Yes." It is evident that our Lord was not present, when the question was asked and the answer given; and yet no sooner did Peter come into the house than our Lord asked him, "What thinkest thou, Simon? of whom do the kings of the earth take custom or tribute?" He showed that He was as well acquainted with the conversation as if he had been listening or standing by.

There is something unspeakably solemn in the thought that the Lord Jesus knows all things. There is an eye that sees all our daily conduct; there is an ear that hears all our daily words. All things are naked and opened unto the eyes of Him with whom we have to do. Concealment is impossible: hypocrisy is useless. We may deceive ministers; we may impose upon our relations and neighbours: but the Lord sees us through and through. We cannot deceive Christ.

We ought to endeavour to make practical use of this truth. We should strive to live as in the Lord's sight, and, like Abraham, to "walk before Him." (Gen. xvii. 1.) Let it be our daily aim to say nothing we would not like Christ to hear, and to do nothing we would not like Christ to see. Let us measure every difficult question as to right and wrong by one simple test: "How would I behave if Jesus was standing by my side?" Such a standard is not extravagant and absurd. It is a standard that interferes with no duty or relation of life: it interferes with nothing but sin. Happy is he that tries to realize his Lord's presence, and to do all and say all as unto Christ.

Let us observe, in the next place, *our Lord's almighty*

power over all creation. He makes a fish his pay-master: He makes a dumb creature bring the tribute-money to meet the collector's demand. Well says Jerome, "I know not which to admire most here, our Lord's foreknowledge or His greatness."

We see here a literal fulfilment of the Psalmist's words: "Thou madest Him to have dominion over the works of Thy hands; Thou hast put all things under His feet:—the fowl of the air, and the fish of the sea, and whatsoever passeth through the paths of the seas." (Psalm viii. 6—8.)

Here is one among many proofs of the majesty and greatness of our Lord Jesus Christ. He only who first created could at His will command the obedience of all His creatures. "By Him were all things created.—By Him all things consist." (Col. i. 16—18.) The believer who goes forth to do Christ's work among the heathen may safely commit himself to his Master's keeping: he serves One who has all power, even over the beasts of the earth. How wonderful the thought, that such an Almighty Lord should condescend to be crucified for our salvation! How comfortable the thought, that when He comes again the second time He will gloriously manifest His power over all created things to the whole world: "the wolf and the lamb shall feed together, and the lion shall eat straw like the bullock: and dust shall be the serpent's meat." (Isaiah lxv. 25.)

In the last place, let us observe in these verses, *our Lord's willingness to make concessions, rather than give offence.* He might justly have claimed exemption from the payment of this tribute-money. He, who was Son of God, might fairly have been excused from paying for the maintenance of His Father's house; He who was "greater than the temple," might have shown good cause for declining to contribute to the support of the temple: but our Lord does not do so. He claims no exemption. He desires Peter to pay the money demanded. At the same time He declares His reasons: it was to be done, "lest we should offend them." "A miracle is worked," says Bishop Hall, "rather than offend even a tax-collector."

Our Lord's example in this case deserves attention of all who profess and call themselves Christians. There is deep wisdom in those five words, "lest we should offend them." They teach us plainly that there are matters in which Christ's people ought to sink their own opinions, and submit to requirements which they may not thoroughly approve, rather than give offence and "hinder the Gospel of Christ." God's rights undoubtedly we ought never to give up; but we may sometimes safely give up our own. It may sound very fine and seem very heroic to be always standing out tenaciously for our *rights!* But it may well be doubted, with such a passage as this, whether such tenacity is always wise, and shows the mind of Christ. There are occasions when it shows more grace in a Christian to submit than to resist.

Let us remember this passage as *citizens and subjects.* We may not like all the political measures of our rulers; we may disapprove of some of the taxes they impose: but the grand question after all is, Will it do any good to the cause of religion to resist the powers that be? Are their measures really injuring our souls? If not, let us hold our peace, "lest we should offend them." "A

Christian," says Bullinger, "never ought to disturb the public peace for things of mere temporary importance."

Let us remember this passage as *members of a Church.* We may not like every jot and tittle of the forms and ceremonies used in our communion; we may not think that those who rule us in spiritual matters are always wise: but after all, are the points on which we are dissatisfied really of vital importance? Is any great truth of the Gospel at stake? If not, let us be quiet, "lest we should offend them."

Let us remember this passage as *members of society.* There may be usages and customs in the circle where our lot is cast, which to us, as Christians, are tiresome, useless, and unprofitable: but are they matters of principle? Do they injure our souls? Will it do any good to the cause of religion, if we refuse to comply with them? If not, let us patiently submit, "lest we should offend them."

Well would it be for the Church and the world if these five words of our Lord had been more studied, pondered, and used! Who can tell the damage that has been done to the cause of the Gospel by morbid scrupulosity, and conscientiousness, falsely so called! May we all remember the example of the great Apostle of the Gentiles: "We suffer all things, lest we should hinder the Gospel of Christ." (1 Cor. ix. 12.)

MATTHEW XVIII. 1—14.

1 At the same time came the disciples unto Jesus, saying, Who is the greatest in the kingdom of heaven?

2 And Jesus called a little child unto him, and set him in the midst of them,

3 And said, Verily I say unto you, Except ye be converted, and become as little children, ye shall not enter into the kingdom of heaven.

4 Whosoever therefore shall humble himself as this little child,

the same is greatest in the kingdom of heaven.
5 And whoso shall receive one such little child in my name receiveth me.
6 But whoso shall offend one of these little ones which believe in me, it were better for him that a millstone were hanged about his neck, and *that* he were drowned in the depth of the sea.
7 Woe unto the world because of offences! for it must needs be that offences come; but woe to that man by whom the offence cometh!
8 Wherefore if thy hand or thy foot offend thee, cut them off, and cast *them* from thee: it is better for thee to enter into life halt or maimed, rather than having two hands or two feet to be cast into everlasting fire.
9 And if thine eye offend thee, pluck it out, and cast *it* from thee: it is better for thee to enter into life with one eye, rather than having two eyes to be cast into hell fire.
10 Take heed that ye despise not one of these little ones; for I say unto you, That in heaven their angels do always behold the face of my father which is in heaven.
11 For the Son of man is come to save that which was lost.
12 How think ye? if a man have an hundred sheep, and one of them be gone astray, doth he not leave the ninety and nine, and goeth into the mountains, and seeketh that which is gone astray.
13 And if so be that he find it, verily I say unto you, he rejoiceth more of that *sheep*, than of the ninety and nine which went not astray.
14 Even so it is not the will of your Father which is in heaven, that one of these little ones should perish.

THE first thing that we are taught in these verses is *the necessity of conversion, and of conversion manifested by childlike humility.* The disciples came to our Lord with the question, "Who is the greatest in the kingdom of heaven?" They spoke as men half-enlightened, and full of carnal expectations. They received an answer well calculated to awaken them from their day-dream, —an answer containing a truth which lies at the very foundation of Christianity: "Except ye be converted, and become as little children, ye shall not enter into the kingdom of heaven."

Let these words sink down deeply in our hearts. Without conversion there is no salvation. We all need an entire change of nature: of ourselves we have neither faith, nor fear, nor love towards God. We "must be born again." (John iii. 8.) Of ourselves we are utterly unfit for dwelling in God's presence. Heaven would be no heaven to us if we were not "converted." It is true of all ranks, classes, and orders of mankind: all are born in sin and children of wrath, and all, without exception, need to be born again and made new creatures. A new heart must be given to us, and a new spirit put within us; old things must pass away, and all things must become new. It is a good thing to be baptized into the Christian Church, and use Christian means of grace: but after all, "are we converted?"

Would we know whether we are really converted? Would we know the test by which we must try ourselves? The surest mark of true conversion is humility. If we have really received the Holy Ghost, we shall show it by a meek and childlike spirit. Like children, we shall think humbly of our own strength and wisdom, and be very dependent on our Father in heaven. Like children, we shall not seek great things in this world; but having food and raiment and a Father's love, we shall be content. Truly this is a heart-searching test! It exposes the unsoundness of many a so-called conversion. It is easy to be a convert from one party to another party, from one sect to another sect, from one set of opinions to another set of opinions: such conversions save no one's soul. What we all want is a conversion from pride to humility,—from high thoughts of ourselves to lowly thoughts of ourselves,—from self-conceit to self-abasement,—from the mind of the Pharisee to the mind of the Publican. A conversion of this kind we must experience, if we hope to be saved. These are the conversions that are wrought by the Holy Ghost.

The next thing that we are taught in these verses is

the great sin of putting stumbling-blocks in the way of believers. The words of the Lord Jesus on this subject are peculiarly solemn: "Woe unto the world because of offences!—Woe to that man by whom the offence cometh."

We put offences or stumbling-blocks in the way of men's souls whenever we do anything to keep them back from Christ,—or to turn them out of the way of salvation,—or to disgust them with true religion. We may do it directly, by persecuting, ridiculing, opposing, or dissuading them from decided service of Christ; we may do it indirectly, by living a life inconsistent with our religious profession, and by making Christianity loathsome and distasteful by our own conduct. Whenever we do anything of the kind, it is clear, from our Lord's words, that we commit a great sin.

There is something very fearful in the doctrine here laid down: it ought to stir up within us great searchings of heart. It is not enough that we wish to do good in this world: are we quite sure that we are not doing harm?—We may not openly persecute Christ's servants; but are there none that we are injuring by our ways and our example? It is awful to think of the amount of harm that can be done by one inconsistent professor of religion. He gives a handle to the infidel; he supplies the worldly man with an excuse for remaining undecided; he checks the inquirer after salvation; he discourages the saints. He is, in short, a living sermon on behalf of the devil. The last day alone will reveal the wholesale ruin of souls, that "offences" have occasioned in the Church of Christ. One of Nathan's charges against David was,

"Thou has given great occasion to the enemies of the Lord to blaspheme." (2 Sam. xii. 14.)

The next thing that we are taught in these verses is *the reality of future punishment after death.* Two strong expressions are used by our Lord on this point. He speaks of being "cast into everlasting fire:" He speaks of being "cast into hell fire."

The meaning of these words is clear and unmistakable. There is a place of unspeakable misery in the world to come, to which all who die impenitent and unbelieving, must ultimately be consigned. There is revealed in Scripture a "fiery indignation," which sooner or later will devour all God's adversaries. (Heb. x. 27.) The same sure Word which holds out a heaven to all who repent and are converted, declares plainly that there will be a hell for all the ungodly.

Let no man deceive us with vain words upon this awful subject. Men have arisen in these latter days who profess to deny the eternity of future punishment, and repeat the devil's old argument, that we "shall not surely die." (Gen. iii. 4.) Let none of their reasonings move us, however plausible they may sound. Let us stand fast in the old paths. The God of love and mercy is also a God of justice: He will surely requite. The flood in Noah's day, and the burning of Sodom, were meant to show us what He will one day do. No lips have ever spoken so clearly about hell as those of Christ Himself. Hardened sinners will find out, to their cost, that there is such a thing as the "wrath of the Lamb." (Rev. vi. 17.)

The last thing we are taught in these verses, is *the*

value that God sets on the least and lowest of believers. "It is not the will of your Father in heaven, that one of these little ones should perish."

These words are meant for the encouragement of all true Christians, and not for little children only. The connection in which they are found with the parable of the hundred sheep and one that went astray, seems to place this beyond doubt. They are meant to show us that our Lord Jesus is a Shepherd, who cares tenderly for every soul committed to His charge. The youngest, the weakest, the sickliest of His flock is as dear to Him as the strongest: they shall never perish: none shall ever pluck them out of His hand. He will lead them gently through the wilderness of this world: He will not overdrive them a single day, lest any die. (Gen. xxxiii. 13.) He will carry them through every difficulty; He will defend them against every enemy. The saying which He spoke shall be literally fulfilled: "Of them which Thou gavest me have I lost none." (John xviii. 9.) With such a Saviour, who need fear beginning to be a thorough Christian? With such a Shepherd, who having once begun, need fear being cast away?

MATTHEW XVIII. 15—20.

15 Moreover if thy brother shall trespass against thee, go and tell him his fault between thee and him alone: if he shall hear thee, thou hast gained thy brother.

16 But if he will not hear *thee*, *then* take with thee one or two more, that in the mouth of two or three witnesses every word may be established.

17 And if he shall neglect to hear them, tell *it* unto the church: but if he neglect to hear the church, let him be unto thee as a heathen man and a publican.

18 Verily I say unto you, Whatsoever ye shall bind on earth shall be bound in heaven: and whatsoever ye shall loose on earth shall be loosed in heaven.

19 Again I say unto you, That if two of you shall agree on earth as touching anything that they shall ask, it shall be done for them of my Father which is in heaven.
20 For where two or three are gathered together in my name, there am I in the midst of them.

THESE words of the Lord Jesus contain an expression which has often been misapplied. The command to "hear the Church," has been so interpreted as to contradict other passages of God's Word. It has been falsely applied to the authority of the whole visible Church in matters of doctrine, and so been made an excuse for the exercise of much ecclesiastical tyranny. But the abuse of Scripture truths must not tempt us to neglect the use of them. We must not turn away altogether from any text, because some have perverted it, and made it poison.

Let us notice, in the first place, *how admirable are the rules laid down by our Lord for the healing of differences among brethren.*

If we have unhappily received any injury from a fellow-member of Christ's Church, the first step to be taken is to visit him "alone," and tell him his fault. He may have injured us unintentionally, as Abimelech did Abraham (Gen. xxi. 26); his conduct may admit of explanation, like that of the tribes of Reuben, Gad, and Manasseh, when they built an altar as they returned to their own land (Joshua xxii. 24): at any rate, this friendly, faithful, straightforward way of dealing is the most likely course to win a brother, if he is to be won. "A soft tongue breaketh the bone." (Prov. xxv. 15.) Who can tell but he may say at once, "I was wrong,"—and make ample reparation?

If however this course of proceeding fails to produce any good effect, a second step is to be taken. We are to "take with us one or two" companions, and tell our brother of his fault in their presence and hearing. Who can tell but his conscience may be stricken, when he finds his misconduct made known, and he may be ashamed and repent? If not, we shall at all events have the testimony of witnesses, that we did all we could to bring our brother to a right mind, and that he deliberately refused, when appealed to, to make amends.

Finally, if this second course of proceeding prove useless, we are to refer the whole matter to the Christian *congregation* of which we are members: we are to "tell it to the Church." Who can tell but the heart which has been unmoved by private remonstrances, may be moved by the fear of public exposure? If not, there remains but one view to take of our brother's case: we must sorrowfully regard him as one who has shaken off all Christian principles, and will be guided by no higher motives than "a heathen man and a publican."

The passage is a beautiful instance of the mingled wisdom and tender consideration of our Lord's teaching. What a knowledge it shows of human nature! Nothing does so much harm to the cause of religion as the quarrels of Christians: no stone should be left unturned, no trouble spared, in order to prevent their being dragged before the public.—What a delicate thoughtfulness it shows for the sensitiveness of poor human nature! Many a scandalous breach would be prevented, if we were more ready to practice the rule of "between thee and him alone." Happy would it be for the Church and the world, if this portion of our Lord's teaching was more carefully studied and obeyed! Differences and divisions there will be, so long as the world stands; but many of them would be extinguished at once, if the course recommended in these verses was tried.

In the second place, let us observe *what a clear argument we have in these verses for the exercise of discipline in a Christian congregation.*

Our Lord commands disagreements between Christians, which cannot be otherwise settled, to be referred to the decision of the Church, or Christian assembly to which they belong. "Tell it," He says, "to the Church." It is evident, from this, that He intends every congregation of professing Christians to take cognizance of the moral conduct of its members, either by the action of the whole body collectively, or of heads and elders to whom its authority may be delegated. It is evident also that He intends every congregation to have the power of excluding disobedient and refractory members from participation in its ordinances. "If he refuse," He says, "to hear the Church, let him be to thee as a heathen man and a publican." He says not a word about temporal punishment and civil disabilities: spiritual penalties are the only penalty He permits the Church to inflict; and when rightly inflicted, they are not to be lightly regarded. "Whatsoever ye shall bind on earth shall be bound in heaven." Such appears to be the substance of our Lord's teaching about ecclesiastical discipline.

It is vain to deny that the whole subject is surrounded with difficulties. On no point has the influence of the world weighed so heavily on the action of Churches: on no point have Churches made so many mistakes,—sometimes on the side of sleepy remissness, sometimes on the side of blind severity. No doubt the power of excommunication has been fearfully abused and perverted, and, as Quesnel says, "we ought to be more afraid of our sins than of all the excommunications in the world." Still it is impossible to deny, with such a passage as this before us, that Church discipline is according to the mind of Christ, and, when wisely exercised, is calculated to promote a Church's health and well-being. It can never be right that all sorts of people, however wicked and ungodly, should be allowed to come to the table of the Lord, no man letting or forbidding: it is the bounden duty of every Christian to use his influence to prevent such a state of things. A perfect communion can never be attained in this world, but purity should be the mark at which we aim. An increasingly high standard of qualification for full church-membership, will always be found one of the best evidences of a prosperous Church.

Let us observe, in the last place, *what gracious encouragement Christ holds out to those who meet together in His name.* He says, "Where two or three are gathered together in my name, there am I in the midst of them." That saying is a striking proof of our Lord's divinity. God alone can be in more places than one at the same time.

There is comfort in these words for all who love to meet together for religious purposes. At every assembly for public worship, at every gathering for prayer and praise, at every missionary meeting, at every Bible reading, the King of kings is present, Christ Himself attends. We may be often disheartened by the small number who are present on such occasions, compared with the number of those who meet for worldly ends; we may sometimes find it hard to bear the taunts and ridicule of an illnatured world, which cries like the enemy of old, "What do these feeble people?" (Nehem. iv. 2.) But we have no reason for despondency: we may boldly fall back on these words of Jesus. At all such meetings we have the company of Christ Himself.

There is solemn rebuke in these words for all who neglect the public worship of God, and never attend meetings for any religious purpose. They turn their backs on the society of the Lord of lords; they miss the opportunity of meeting Christ Himself. It avails nothing to say that the proceedings of religious meetings are marked by weakness and infirmity, or that as much good is got by staying at home as going to church: the words of our Lord should silence such arguments at once. Surely men are not wise when they speak contemptuously of any gathering where Christ is present.

May we all ponder these things! If we have met together with God's people for spiritual purposes in times past, let us persevere, and not be ashamed. If we have hitherto despised such meetings, let us consider our ways, and learn wisdom.

MATTHEW XVIII. 21—35.

21 Then came Peter to him, and said, Lord, how oft shall my brother sin against me, and I forgive him? till seven times?

22 Jesus saith unto him, I say not unto thee, until seven times: but, Until seventy times seven.

23 Therefore is the kingdom of heaven likened unto a certain king, which would take account of his servants.

24 And when he had begun to reckon, one was brought unto him, which owed him ten thousand talents.

25 But forasmuch as he had not to pay, his lord commanded him to be sold, and his wife and children, and all that he had, and payment to be made.

26 The servant therefore fell down, and worshipped him, saying,

Lord, have patience with me, and I will pay thee all.
27 Then the Lord of that servant was moved with compassion, and loosed him, and forgave him the debt.
28 But the same servant went out, and found one of his fellow-servants, which owed him an hundred pence: and he laid hands on him, and took *him* by the throat, saying, Pay me that thou owest.
29 And his fellowservant fell down at his feet, and besought him, saying, Have patience with me, and I will pay thee all.
30 And he would not: but went and cast him into prison, till he should pay the debt.
31 So when his fellowservants saw what was done, they were very sorry, and came and told unto their Lord all that was done.
32 Then his lord, after that he had called him, said unto him, O thou wicked servant, I forgave thee all that debt, because thou desiredst me:
33 Shouldst not thou also have had compassion on thy fellowservant, even as I had pity on thee?
34 And his lord was wroth, and delivered him to the tormentors, till he should pay all that was due unto him.
35 So likewise shall my heavenly Father do also unto you, if ye from your hearts forgive not every one his brother their trespasses.

In these verses the Lord Jesus deals with a deeply important subject,—the forgiveness of injuries. We live in a wicked world, and it is vain to expect that we can escape ill-treatment, however carefully we may behave. To know how to conduct ourselves, when we are ill-treated, is of great moment to our souls.

In the first place, *the Lord Jesus lays it down as a general rule, that we ought to forgive others to the uttermost.* Peter put the question, "How oft shall my brother sin against me and I forgive him? till seven times?" He received for answer, "I say not unto thee till seven times, but until seventy times seven."

The rule here laid down must of course be interpreted with sober-minded qualification. Our Lord does not mean that offences against the law of the land and the good order of society, are to be passed over in silence; He does not mean that we are to allow people to commit thefts and assaults with impunity: all that He means is, that we are to study a general spirit of mercy and forgivingness towards our brethren. We are to bear much, and to put up with much, rather than quarrel; we are to look over much, and submit to much, rather than have any strife; we are to lay aside everything like malice, strife, revenge, and retaliation. Such feelings are only fit for heathens: they are utterly unworthy of a disciple of Christ.

What a happy world it would be if this rule of our Lord's was more known and better obeyed! How many of the miseries of mankind are occasioned by disputes, quarrels, lawsuits, and an obstinate tenacity about what men call "their rights!" How many of them might be altogether avoided, if men were more willing to forgive, and more desirous for peace! Let us never forget that a fire cannot go on burning without fuel: just in the same way it takes two to make a quarrel. Let us each resolve, by God's grace, that of these two we will never be one. Let us resolve to return good for evil, and blessing for cursing, and so to melt down enmity, and change our foes into friends. (Rom. xii. 20.) It was a fine feature in Archbishop Cranmer's character, that if you did him an injury he was sure to be your friend.

In the second place, our Lord supplies us with *two powerful motives for exercising a forgiving spirit.* He tells us a story of a man who owed an enormous sum to his master, and had "nothing to pay;" nevertheless at the time of reckoning his master had compassion on him, and "forgave him all." He tells us that this very man, after being forgiven himself, refused to forgive a fellow-servant a trifling debt of a few pence: he actually cast him into prison, and would not abate a jot of his demand. He tells us how punishment overtook this wicked and cruel man, who, after receiving mercy, ought surely to have shown mercy to others: and finally, he concludes the parable with the impressive words, "So likewise shall my heavenly Father do unto you, if ye from your hearts forgive not every one his brother their trespasses."

It is clear from this parable that one motive for forgiving others ought to be the recollection that we all need forgiveness at God's hands ourselves. Day after day we are coming short in many things, "leaving undone what we ought to do, and doing what we ought not to do:" day after day we require mercy and pardon. Our neighbours' offences against us are mere trifles, compared with our offences against God. Surely it ill becomes poor erring creatures like us to be extreme in marking what is done amiss by our brethren, or slow to forgive it.

Another motive for forgiving others ought to be the recollection of the day of judgment, and the standard by which we shall all be tried in that day. There will be no forgiveness in that day for unforgiving people. Such people would be unfit for heaven: they would not be able to value a dwelling-place to which "mercy" is the only title, and in which "mercy" is the eternal subject of song. Surely if we mean to stand at the right hand, when Jesus sits on the throne of His glory, we must learn, while we are on earth, to forgive.

Let these truths sink down deeply into our hearts. It is a melancholy fact that there are few Christian duties so little practised as that of forgiveness: it is sad to see how much bitterness, unmercifulness, spite, hardness, and unkindness there is among men. Yet there are few duties so strongly enforced in the New Testament Scriptures as this duty is, and few the neglect of which so clearly shuts a man out of the kingdom of God.

Would we give proof that we are at peace with God, washed in Christ's blood, born of the Spirit, and made God's children by adoption and grace? Let us remember this passage: like our father in heaven, let us be forgiving. Has any man injured us? Let us this day forgive him. As Leighton says, "We ought to forgive ourselves little, and others much."

Would we do good to the world? Would we have any influence on others, and make them see the beauty of true religion? Let us remember this passage. Men who care not for doctrines can understand a forgiving temper.

Would we grow in grace ourselves, and become more holy in all our ways, words, and works? Let us remember this passage.—Nothing so grieves the Holy Spirit, and brings spiritual darkness over the soul, as giving way to a quarrelsome and unforgiving temper. (Ephes. iv. 30—32.)

MATTHEW XIX. 1—15.

1 And it came to pass, *that* when Jesus had finished these sayings, he departed from Galilee, and came into the coasts of Judæa beyond Jordan;

2 And great multitudes followed him; and he healed them there.

3 The Pharisees also came unto him, tempting him, and saying unto him, Is it lawful for a man to put away his wife for every cause?

4 And he answered and said unto them, Have ye not read, that he which made *them* at the beginning made them male and female,

5 And said, For this cause shall a man leave father and mother, and shall cleave to his wife: and they twain shall be one flesh?

6 Wherefore they are no more twain, but one flesh. What therefore God hath joined together, let not man put asunder.

7 They say unto him, Why did Moses then command to give a writing of divorcement, and to put her away?

8 He saith unto them, Moses because of the hardness of your hearts suffered you to put away your wives: but from the beginning it was not so.

9 And I say unto you, Whosoever shall put away his wife, except *it be* for fornication, and shall marry another, committeth adultery: and whoso marrieth her which is put away doth commit adultery.
10 His disciples say unto him, If the case of the man be so with *his* wife, it is not good to marry.
11 But he said unto them, All *men* cannot receive this saying, save *they* to whom it is given.
12 For there are some eunuchs, which were so born from *their* mother's womb: and there are some eunuchs which were made eunuchs of men: and there be eunuchs, which have made themselves eunuchs for the kingdom of heaven's sake. He that is able to receive *it*, let him receive *it*.
13 Then were there brought unto him little children, that He should put *his* hands on them, and pray: and the disciples rebuked them.
14 But Jesus said, Suffer little children, and forbid them not, to come unto me: for of such is the kingdom of heaven.
15 And he laid *his* hands on them, and departed thence.

In these verses we have the mind of Christ declared on two subjects of great moment. One is the relation of husband and wife: the other is the light in which we should regard little children, in the matter of their souls.

It is difficult to overrate the importance of these two subjects: the well-being of nations, and the happiness of society, are closely connected with right views upon them. Nations are nothing but a collection of families. The good order of families depends entirely on keeping up the highest standard of respect for the marriage tie, and on the right training of children. We ought to be thankful, that on both these points, the great Head of the Church pronounced judgment so clearly.

With respect to marriage, our Lord teaches that *the union of husband and wife ought never to be broken off, except for the greatest of all causes, namely, actual unfaithfulness.*

In the days when our Lord was upon earth divorces were permitted among the Jews for the most trifling and frivolous causes. The practice, though tolerated by Moses, to prevent worse evils,—such as cruelty, or murder,—

had gradually become an enormous abuse, and no doubt led to much immorality. (Malachi ii. 14—16.) The remark made by our Lord's disciples shows the deplorably low state of public feeling on the subject: they said, "If the case of the man be so, it is not good to marry." They meant, of course, "if a man may not put away his wife for a slight cause at any time, he had better not marry at all." Such language from the mouths of apostles sounds strange indeed!

Our Lord brings forward a widely different standard for the guidance of His disciples. He first founds His judgment on the original institution of marriage: He quotes the words used in the beginning of Genesis, where the creation of man and the union of Adam and Eve are described, as a proof that no relation should be so highly regarded as that of husband and wife. The relation of parent and child may seem very close, but there is one closer still: "A man shall leave father and mother, and cleave to his wife."—He then backs up the quotation by His own solemn words, "What God hath joined together, let not man put asunder."—And finally He brings in the grave charge of breaking the seventh commandment, against marriage contracted after a divorce for light and frivolous causes: "Whosoever shall put away his wife, except it be for fornication, and shall marry another, committeth adultery."

It is clear, from the whole tenor of the passage, that the relation of marriage ought to be highly reverenced and honoured among Christians. It is a relation which was instituted in paradise, in the time of man's innocency, and is a chosen figure of the mystical union between

Christ and His Church: it is a relation which nothing but death ought to terminate. It is a relation which is sure to have the greatest influence on those whom it brings together, for happiness or for misery, for good or for evil. Such a relation ought never to be taken in hand unadvisedly, lightly, or wantonly, but soberly, discreetly, and with due consideration. It is only too true, that inconsiderate marriages are one of the most fertile causes of unhappiness, and too often it may be feared, of sin.

With respect to little children, we find our Lord instructing us in these verses, *both by word and deed, both by precept and example.* "Little children were brought to Him, that He should put his hands on them and pray." They were evidently tender infants, too young to receive instruction, but not too young to receive benefit by prayer. The disciples seem to have thought them beneath their Master's notice, and rebuked those that brought them. But this drew forth a solemn declaration from the great Head of the Church: "Jesus said, Suffer little children, and forbid them not, to come unto Me: for of such is the kingdom of heaven."

There is something deeply interesting both in the language and action of our Lord on this occasion. We know the weakness and feebleness, both in mind and body of a little infant: of all creatures born into the world none is so helpless and dependent. We know who it was who here took such notice of infants, and found time, in His busy ministry among grown-up men and women, to "put His hands on them and pray:" it was the eternal Son of God, the great High Priest, the

King of kings, by whom all things consist, "the brightness of the Father's glory, and the express image of His person." (Heb. i. 3.) What an instructive picture the whole transaction places before our eyes! No wonder that the great majority of the Church of Christ have always seen in this passage a strong through indirect argument in favour of infant baptism.

Let us learn, from these verses, that the Lord Jesus cares tenderly for the souls of little children. It is probable that Satan specially hates them: it is certain that Jesus specially loves them. Young as they are, they are not beneath His thoughts and attention. That mighty heart of His has room for the babe in its cradle, as well as for the king on his throne: He regards each infant as possessing within its little body an undying principle, that will outlive the pyramids of Egypt, and see sun and moon quenched at the last day. With such a passage as this before us we may surely hope well about the salvation of all who die in infancy. "Of such is the kingdom of heaven."

Finally, let us draw from these verses encouragement to attempt great things in the religious instruction of children. Let us begin from their very earliest years to deal with them as having souls to be lost or saved, and let us strive to bring them to Christ; let us make them acquainted with the Bible, as soon as they can understand anything; let us pray with them, and pray for them, and teach them to pray for themselves. We may rest assured that Jesus looks with pleasure on such endeavours, and is ready to bless them: we may rest assured that such endavours are not in vain. The seed sown in infancy, is often found after many days. Happy is that Church whose infant members are cared for as much as the oldest communicants! The blessing of Him that was crucified will surely be on that Church! He "put His hands" on little children: He prayed for them.

MATTHEW XIX. 16–22.

16 And, behold, one came and said unto him, Good Master, what good thing shall I do, that I may have eternal life?
17 And he said unto him, Why callest thou me good? *there is* none good but one, *that is*, God: but if thou wilt enter into life, keep the commandments.
18 He saith unto him, Which? Jesus said, Thou shalt do no murder, Thou shalt not commit adultery, Thou shalt not steal, Thou shalt not bear false witness,
19 Honour thy father and thy mother: and, Thou shalt love thy neighbour as thyself.
20 The young man saith unto him, All these things have I kept from my youth up: what lack I yet?
21 Jesus said unto him, If thou wilt be perfect, go *and* sell that thou hast, and give to the poor, and thou shalt have treasure in heaven: and come *and* follow me.
22 But when the young man heard that saying, he went away sorrowful: for he had great possessions.

THESE verses detail a conversation between our Lord Jesus Christ and a young man, who came to Him to inquire about the way to eternal life. Like every conversation recorded in the Gospels, between our Lord and an individual, it deserves special attention. Salvation is an individual business: every one who wishes to be saved, must have private personal dealings with Christ about his own soul.

We see, for one thing, from the case of this young man, *that a person may have desires after salvation, and yet not be saved.* Here is one who in a day of abounding unbelief comes of his own accord to Christ. He comes not to have a sickness healed; He comes not to plead about a child: he comes about his own soul. He opens the conference with the frank question, "Good Master, what good thing shall I do, that I may have eternal life?" Surely we might have thought, "This is a promising case: this is no prejudiced ruler or Pharisee: this is a hopeful inquirer." Yet by and by this very young man "goes away sorrowful;"—and we never read a word to show that he was converted!

We must never forget that good feelings alone in religion are not the grace of God. We may know the truth intellectually; we may often feel pricked in conscience; we may have religious affections awakened within us, have many anxieties about our souls, and shed many tears: but all this is not conversion. It is not the genuine saving work of the Holy Ghost.

Unhappily this is not all that must be said on this point. Not only are good feelings alone not grace, but they are even positively dangerous, if we content ourselves with them, and do not *act* as well as *feel*. It is a profound remark of that mighty master on moral questions, Bishop Butler,—that passive impressions, often repeated, gradually lose all their power; actions, often repeated, produce a habit in man's mind; feelings often indulged in, without leading to corresponding actions, will finally exercise no influence at all.

Let us apply this lesson to our own state. Perhaps we know what it is to feel religious fears, wishes, and desires. Let us beware that we do not rest in them. Let us never be satisfied till we have the witness of the Spirit in our hearts, that we are actually born again and new creatures; let us never rest till we know that we have really repented, and laid hold on the hope set before us in the

Gospel. It is good to feel; but it is far better to be converted.

We see, for another thing, from this young man's case, *that an unconverted person is often profoundly ignorant on spiritual subjects.* Our Lord refers this inquirer to the eternal standard of right and wrong, the moral law. Seeing that he speaks so boldly about "doing," He tries him by a command well calculated to draw out the real state of his heart: "If thou wilt enter into life, keep the commandments." He even repeats to him the second table of the law; and at once the young man confidently replies, "All these have I kept from my youth up: what lack I yet?" So utterly ignorant is he of the spirituality of God's statutes, that he never doubts that he has perfectly fulfilled them. He seems thoroughly unaware that the commandments apply to the thoughts and words, as well as to the deeds, and that if God were to enter into judgment with him, he could "not answer Him one of a thousand." (Job ix. 3.) How dark must his mind have been as to the nature of God's law! How low must his ideas have been as to the holiness which God requires!

It is a melancholy fact that ignorance like that of this young man is only too common in the Church of Christ. There are thousands of baptized people who know no more of the leading doctrines of Christianity than the veriest heathen; tens of thousands fill churches and chapels weekly, who are utterly in the dark as to the full extent of man's sinfulness. They cling obstinately to the old notion, that in some sort or other their own doings can save them; and when ministers visit them on their death-beds, they prove as blind as if they had never heard truth at all. So true is it, that the "natural man receiveth not the things of the Spirit of God, for they are foolishness to him." (1 Cor. ii. 14.)

We see, in the last place, from this young man's case, *that one idol cherished in the heart may ruin a soul for ever.* Our Lord, who knew what was in man, at last shows His inquirer his besetting sin. The same searching voice which said to the Samaritan woman, "Go, call thy husband" (John iv. 16), says to the young man, "Go sell that thou hast, and give to the poor." At once the weak point in his character is detected. It turns out that, with all his wishes and desires after eternal life, there was one thing he loved better than his soul, and that was his money. He cannot stand the test. He is weighed in the balance, and found wanting. And the history ends with the melancholy words, "He went away sorrowful, for he had great possessions."

We have in this history one more proof of the truth, "The love of money is the root of all evil." (1 Tim. vi. 10.) We must place this young man in our memories by the side of Judas, Ananias and Sapphira, and learn to beware of covetousness. Alas, it is a rock on which thousands are continually making shipwreck. There is hardly a minister of the Gospel who could not point to many in his congregation, who, humanly speaking, are "not far from the kingdom of God:" but they never seem to make progress. They wish; they feel; they mean; they hope: but there they stick fast! And why? Because they are fond of money.

Let us prove our own selves, as we leave the passage. Let us see how it touches our own souls. Are we honest and sincere in our professed desire to be true Christians? Have we cast away all our idols? Is there no secret sin that we are silently clinging to, and refusing to give up? Is there no thing or person that we are privately loving more than Christ and our souls? These are questions that ought to be answered. The true explanation of the unsatisfactory state of many hearers of the Gospel is spiritual idolatry. We need not wonder that St. John says, "Keep yourselves from idols." (1 John v. 21.)

MATTHEW XIX. 23—30.

23 Then said Jesus unto his disciples, Verily I say unto you, That a rich man shall hardly enter into the kingdom of heaven.

24 And again I say unto you, It is easier for a camel to go through the eye of a needle, than for a rich man to enter into the kingdom of God.

25 When his disciples heard *it*, they were exceedingly amazed, saying, Who then can be saved?

26 But Jesus beheld *them*, and said unto them, With men this is impossible; but with God all things are possible.

27 Then answered Peter and said unto him, Behold, we have forsaken all, and followed thee; what shall we have therefore?

28 And Jesus said unto them, Verily I say unto you, That ye which have followed me, in the regeneration when the Son of man shall sit in the throne of his glory, ye also shall sit upon twelve thrones, judging the twelve tribes of Israel?

29 And every one that hath forsaken houses, or brethren, or sisters, or father, or mother, or wife, or children, or lands, for my name's sake, shall receive an hundred-fold, and shall inherit everlasting life.

30 But many *that are* first shall be last; and the last *shall be* first.

THE first thing that we learn in these verses is *the immense danger which riches bring on the souls of those who possess them.* The Lord Jesus declares, that "a rich man shall hardly enter into the kingdom of heaven." He goes even further. He uses a proverbial saying to strengthen His assertion: "It is easier for a camel to go through the eye of a needle than for a rich man to enter into the kingdom of God."

Few of our Lord's sayings sound more startling than

this; few run more counter to the opinions and prejudices of mankind; few are so little believed: yet this saying is true, and worthy of all acceptation. Riches, which all desire to obtain,—riches, for which men labour and toil, and become gray before their time,—riches are the most perilous possession. They often inflict great injury on the soul; they lead men into many temptations; they engross men's thoughts and affections; they bind heavy burdens on the heart, and make the way to heaven even more difficult than it naturally is.

Let us beware of the love of money. It is possible to use it well, and do good with it; but for one who makes a right use of money, there are thousands who make a wrong use of it, and do harm both to themselves and others. Let the worldly man, if he will, make an idol of money, and count him happiest who has most of it; but let the Christian, who professes to have "treasure in heaven," set his face, like a flint, against the spirit of the world in this matter. Let him not worship gold. He is not the best man in God's eyes who has most money, but he who has most grace.

Let us pray daily for rich men's souls. They are not to be envied: they are deeply to be pitied. They carry heavy weights in the Christian course: they are of all men the least likely "so to run as to obtain." (1 Cor. ix. 24.) Their prosperity in this world is often their destruction in the world to come. Well may the Litany of the Church of England contain the words, "In all time of our wealth, good Lord, deliver us."

The second thing that we learn in this passage is *the almighty power of God's grace in the soul.* The disciples were amazed, when they heard our Lord's language about rich men. It was language so entirely contrary to all their notions about the advantages of wealth, that they cried out with surprise, "Who then can be saved?" They drew from our Lord a gracious answer: "With men this is impossible; but with God all things are possible." The Holy Ghost can incline even the richest of men to seek treasure in heaven. He can dispose even kings to cast their crowns at the feet of Jesus, and to count all things but loss for the sake of the kingdom of God. Proof upon proof of this is given to us in the Bible. Abraham was very rich, yet he was the Father of the faithful; Moses might have been a prince or king in Egypt, but he forsook all his brilliant prospects for the sake of Him who is invisible; Job was the wealthiest man in the East, yet he was a chosen servant of God; David, Jehoshaphat, Josiah, Hezekiah, were all wealthy monarchs, but they loved God's favour more than their earthly greatness. They all show us that "nothing is too hard for the Lord," and that faith can grow even in the most unlikely soil.

Let us hold fast this doctrine, and never let it go. No man's place or circumstances shut him out from the kingdom of God: let us never despair of any one's salvation. No doubt rich people require special grace, and are exposed to special temptations. But the Lord God of Abraham, and Moses, and Job, and David, is not changed: He who saved them in spite of their riches, can save others also. When He works, who shall let it? (Isaiah xliii. 13.)

The last thing that we learn in these verses is *the*

immense encouragement the Gospel offers to those who give up everything for Christ's sake. We are told that Peter asked our Lord what he and the other apostles, who had forsaken their little all for His sake, should receive in return. He obtained a most gracious reply. A full recompense shall be made to all who make sacrifices for Christ's sake: they "shall receive an hundred fold, and shall inherit everlasting life."

There is something very cheering in this promise. Few in the present day, excepting converts among the heathen, are ever required to forsake homes, relatives, and lands, on account of their religion; yet there are few true Christians who have not much to go through, in one way or another, if they are really faithful to their Lord. The offence of the cross is not yet ceased: laughter, ridicule, mockery, and family persecution, are often the portion of an English believer. The favour of the world is often forfeited, places and situations are often perilled, by a conscientious adherence to the demands of the Gospel of Christ. All who are exposed to trials of this kind may take comfort in the promise of these verses. Jesus foresaw their need, and intended these words to be their consolation.

We may rest assured that no man shall ever be a real loser by following Christ. The believer may seem to suffer loss for a time, when he first begins the life of a decided Christian; he may be much cast down by the afflictions that are brought upon him on account of his religion: but let him rest assured that he will never find himself a loser in the long run. Christ can raise up friends for us who shall more than compensate for those we lose;

Christ can open hearts and homes to us far more warm and hospitable than those that are closed against us; above all, Christ can give us peace of conscience, inward joy, bright hopes, and happy feelings, which shall far outweigh every pleasant earthly thing that we have cast away for His sake. He has pledged His royal word that it shall be so. None ever found that word fail: let us trust it and not be afraid.

MATTHEW XX. 1—16.

1 For the kingdom of heaven is like unto a man *that* is an householder, which went out early in the morning to hire labourers into his vineyard.

2 And when he had agreed with the labourers for a penny a day, he sent them into his vineyard.

3 And he went out about the third hour, and saw others standing idle in the market-place.

4 And said unto them, Go ye also into the vineyard, and whatsoever is right I will give you. And they went their way.

5 Again he went out about the sixth and ninth hour, and did likewise.

6 And about the eleventh hour he went out, and found others standing idle, and saith unto them, Why stand ye here all the day idle?

7 They say unto him, Because no man hath hired us. He saith unto them, Go ye also into the vineyard; and whatsoever is right, *that* shall ye receive.

8 So when even was come, the lord of the vineyard saith unto his steward, Call the labourers, and give them *their* hire, beginning from the last unto the first.

9 And when they came that *were hired* about the eleventh hour, they received every man a penny.

10 But when the first came, they supposed that they should have received more; and they likewise received every man a penny.

11 And when they had received *it*, they murmured against the good man of the house,

12 Saying, These last have wrought *but* one hour, and thou hast made them equal unto us, which have borne the burden and heat of the day.

13 But he answered one of them, and said, Friend, I do thee no wrong: didst not thou agree with me for a penny?

14 Take *that* thine is, and go thy way: I will give unto this last, even as unto thee.

15 Is it not lawful for me to do what I will with mine own? Is thine eye evil, because I am good?

16 So the last shall be first, and the first last: for many be called, but few chosen.

THERE are undeniable difficulties in the parable contained in these verses: the key to the right explanation of them must be sought in the passage which concludes the last chapter. *There* we find the apostle Peter asking our Lord a remarkable question: "We have forsaken all, and followed Thee; what shall we have therefore?" *There* we find Jesus giving a remarkable answer. He makes a special promise to Peter and his fellow-disciples: "They should one day sit on twelve thrones, judging the twelve tribes of Israel." He makes a general promise to all who suffer loss for His sake: "They should receive an hundred-fold, and inherit everlasting life."

Now we must bear in mind that Peter was a Jew: like most Jews he had probably been brought up in much ignorance as to God's purposes respecting the salvation of the Gentiles; in fact, we know from the Acts, that it required a vision from heaven to take that ignorance away. (Acts x. 28.) Furthermore we must bear in mind that Peter and his fellow-disciples were weak in faith and knowledge. They were probably apt to attach a great importance to their own sacrifices for Christ's sake, and inclined to self-righteousness and self-conceit.—Both these points our Lord knew well. He therefore speaks this parable for the special benefit of Peter and his companions. He read their hearts: He saw what spiritual medicine those hearts required, and supplied it without delay. In a word, He checked their rising pride, and taught them humility.

In expounding this parable, we need not inquire closely into the meaning of the "penny," the "market-place," the "steward," or the "hours:" such inquiries often darken counsel by words without knowledge. Well says a great divine, "the theology of parables is not argumentative." The hint of Chrysostom deserves notice. He says, "It is not right to search curiously, and word by word, into all things in a parable; but when we have learned the object for which it was composed, we are to reap this, and not to busy ourselves about anything further. Two main lessons appear to stand out on the face of the parable, and to embrace the general scope of its meaning. Let us content ourselves with these two.

We learn, in the first place, that *in the calling of nations to the professed knowledge of Himself, God exercises free, sovereign, and unconditional grace.* He calls the families of the earth into the visible Church at His own time, and in His own way.

We see this truth wonderfully brought out in the history of God's dealings with the world. We see the children of Israel called and chosen to be God's people in the very beginning of "the day;" we see some of the Gentiles called at a later period, by the preaching of the Apostles; we see others being called in the present age, by the labours of missionaries; we see others, like the millions of Chinese and Hindoos, still "standing idle, because no man hath hired them."—And why is all this? We cannot tell. We only know that God loves to hide pride from Churches, and to take away all occasion of boasting: He will never allow the older branches of His Church to look contemptuously on the younger. His Gospel holds out pardon and peace with God through Christ to the heathen of our own times, as fully as it did to St. Paul: the converted inhabitants of Tinnevelly and New Zealand shall be as fully admitted to heaven as the holiest patriarch who died 3500 years ago. The old wall between Jews and Gentiles is removed. There is nothing to prevent the believing heathen being "a fellow-heir and partaker of the same hope" with the believing

Israelite. The Gentiles, converted at "the eleventh hour" of the world, shall be as really and truly heirs of glory as the Jews; they shall sit down with Abraham, and Isaac, and Jacob, in the kingdom of heaven, while many of the children of the kingdom are for ever cast out. "The last shall indeed be first."

We learn, in the second place, that in *the saving of individuals, as well as in the calliny of nations, God acts as a sovereign, and gives no account of His matters.* "He has mercy on whom He will have mercy," and that too at His own time. (Rom. ix. 15.)

This is a truth which we see illustrated on every side in the Church of Christ, as a matter of experience. We see one man called to repentance and faith in the beginning of his days, like Timothy, and labouring in the Lord's vineyard for forty or fifty years; we see another man called "at the eleventh hour," like the thief on the cross, and plucked like a brand out of the fire,—one day a hardened impenitent sinner, and the next day in paradise: and yet the whole tenor of the Gospel leads us to believe that both these men are equally forgiven before God. Both are equally washed in Christ's blood, and clothed in Christ's righteousness; both are equally justified, both accepted, and both will be found at Christ's right hand at the last day.

There can be no doubt that this doctrine sounds strange to the ignorant and inexperienced Christian. It confounds the pride of human nature; it leaves the self-righteous no room to boast; it is a levelling, humbling, doctrine, and gives occasion to many a murmur: but it is impossible to reject it, unless we reject the whole

Bible. True faith in Christ, though it be but a day old, justifies a man before God as completely as the faith of him who has followed Christ for fifty years. The righteousness in which Timothy will stand at the day of judgment, is the same as that of the penitent thief: both will be saved by grace alone; both will owe all to Christ. We may not like this: but it is the doctrine of this parable, and not of this parable only, but of the whole New Testament. Happy is he who can receive the doctrine with humility! Well says Bishop Hall, "If some have cause to magnify God's bounty, none have cause to complain."

Before we leave this parable let us arm our minds with some necessary cautions. It is a portion of Scripture that is frequently perverted and misapplied. Men have often drawn from it, not milk, but poison.

Let us beware of supposing, from anything in this parable, that salvation is in the slightest degree to be obtained by works: to suppose this is to overthrow the whole teaching of the Bible. Whatever a believer receives in the next world, is a matter of grace, and not of debt: God is never a debtor to us, in any sense whatever; when we have done all, we are unprofitable servants. (Luke xvii. 10.)

Let us beware of supposing, from this parable, that the distinction between Jews and Gentiles is entirely done away by the Gospel: to suppose this is to contradict many plain prophecies, both of the Old Testament and New. In the matter of justification, there is no distinction between the believing Jew and the Greek; but in the matter of national privileges, Israel is still a special people, and not "numbered among the nations." God has many purposes concerning the Jews which are yet to be fulfilled.

Let us beware of supposing, from this parable, that all saved souls will have the same degree of glory: to suppose this is to contradict many plain texts of Scripture. The title of all believers no doubt is the same,—the righteousness of Christ. But all will not have the same place in heaven. "Every man shall receive his own reward, according to his own labour." (1 Cor. iii. 8.)

Finally, let us beware of supposing, from this parable, that it is safe for any one to put off repentance till the end of his days: to suppose this is a most dangerous delusion. The longer men refuse to obey Christ's voice, the less likely they are to be saved. "Now is the accepted time: now is the day of salvation." (2 Cor. vi. 2.) Few are ever saved on their death-beds. One thief on the cross was saved, that none should despair; but only one, that none should presume. A false confidence in those words, "the eleventh hour," has ruined thousands of souls.

MATTHEW XX. 17—23.

17 And Jesus going up to Jerusalem took the twelve disciples apart in the way, and said unto them,

18 Behold, we go up to Jerusalem; and the Son of man shall be betrayed unto the chief priests and unto the scribes, and they shall condemn him to death.

19 And shall deliver him to the Gentiles to mock, and to scourge, and to crucify *him*: and the third day he shall rise again.

20 Then came to him the mother of Zebedee's children, with her sons, worshipping *him*, and desiring a certain thing of him.

21 And he said unto her, What wilt thou? She saith unto him, Grant that these my two sons may sit, the one on thy right hand, and the other on the left, in thy kingdom.

22 But Jesus answered and said, Ye know not what ye ask. Are ye able to drink of the cup that I shall drink of, and to be baptized with the baptism that I am baptized with? They say unto him, We are able.

23 And he saith unto them, Ye shall drink indeed of my cup, and be baptized with the baptism that I am baptized with: but to sit on my right hand, and on my left, is not mine to give, but *it shall be given to them* for whom it is prepared of my Father.

THE first thing that we should notice in these verses is *the clear announcement which the Lord Jesus Christ makes of His own approaching death.* For the third time we find Him telling His disciples the astounding truth, that He, their wonder-working Master, must soon suffer and die.

The Lord Jesus knew from the beginning, all that was before Him. The treachery of Judas Iscariot, the fierce persecution of chief priests and scribes, the unjust judgment, the delivery to Pontius Pilate, the mocking, the scourging, the crown of thorns, the cross, the hanging between two malefactors, the nails, the spear,—all, all were spread before His mind like a picture.

How great an aggravation of suffering fore-knowledge is, those know well who have lived in the prospect of some fearful surgical operation! Yet none of these things moved our Lord. He says, "I was not rebellious, neither turned away back. I gave my back to the smiters, and my cheeks to them that plucked off the hair: I hid not my face from shame and spitting." (Isa. l. 5, 6.) He saw Calvary in the distance all His life through, and yet walked calmly up to it, without turning to the right hand or to the left. Surely there never was sorrow like unto His sorrow, or love like His love.

The Lord Jesus was a voluntary sufferer. When He died on the cross, it was not because He had not power to prevent it: He suffered intentionally, deliberately, and of His own free will. (John x. 18.) He knew that without shedding of His blood there could be no remission of man's sin; He knew that He was the Lamb of God, who must die to take away the sin of the world; He knew that His death was the appointed sacrifice, which must be offered up to make reconciliation for iniquity. Knowing all this, He went willingly to the cross: His heart was set on finishing the mighty work He came into the world to do. He was well aware that all hinged on His own death, and that, without that death, His miracles and preaching would have done comparatively nothing for the world. No wonder that He thrice pressed on the attention of His disciples that He "must needs" die. Blessed and happy are they who know the real meaning and importance of the sufferings of Christ!

The next thing that we should notice in these verses *is the mixture of ignorance and faith that may be found even in true hearted Christians.* We see the mother of James and John coming to our Lord with her two sons, and preferring on their behalf a strange petition. She asks that they "may sit, one on His right hand, and the other on His left, in His kingdom." She seems to have forgotten all He had just been saying about His suffering: her eager mind can think of nothing but His glory. His plain warnings about the crucifixion appear to have been thrown away on her sons: their thoughts were full of nothing but His throne, and the day of His power. There was much of faith in their request, but there was much more of infirmity. There was something to be commended, in that they could see in Jesus of Nazareth a coming king; but there was also much to blame, in that they did not remember that He was to be crucified before He could reign. Truly "the flesh lusteth against the spirit" in all God's children, and Luther well remarks, "the flesh ever seeks to be glorified before it is crucified."

There are many Christians who are very like this woman and her sons. They see in part, and know in part, the things of God; they have faith enough to follow Christ; they have knowledge enough to hate sin, and come out from the world: and yet there are many truths of Christianity of which they are deplorably ignorant. They talk ignorantly, they act ignorantly, and commit many sad mistakes. Their acquaintance with the Bible is very scanty: their insight into their own hearts is very small.—But we must learn from these verses to deal gently with such people, because the Lord has received them. We must not set them down as graceless and godless, because of their ignorance: we must remember that true faith may lay at the bottom of their hearts, though there is much rubbish at the top. We must reflect that the sons of Zebedee, whose knowledge was at one time so imperfect, became at a later period pillars of the Church of Christ: just so a believer may begin his course in much darkness, and yet prove finally a man mighty in the Scriptures, and a worthy follower of James and John.

The last thing that we should notice in these verses *is the solemn reproof which our Lord gives to the ignorant request of the mother of Zebedee's children and her two sons.* He says to them, "Ye know not what ye ask." They had asked to share in their Master's reward, but they had not considered that they must first be partakers in their Master's sufferings. (1 Pet. iv. 13.) They had forgotten that those who would stand with Christ in glory, must drink of His cup, and be baptized with His baptism; they did not see that those who carry the cross, and those alone, shall receive the crown. Well might our Lord say, "Ye know not what ye ask."

But do we never commit the same mistake that the sons of Zebedee committed? Do we never fall into their error, and make thoughtless, inconsiderate requests? Do we not often say things in prayer without "counting the cost," and ask for things to be granted to us, without reflecting how much our supplications involve? These are heart-searching questions: it may well be feared that many of us cannot give them a satisfactory answer.

We ask that our souls may be saved and go to heaven when we die. It is a good request indeed. But are we prepared to take up the cross, and follow Christ? Are we willing to give up the world for His sake? Are we ready to put off the old man and put on the new,—to fight, to labour, and to run so as to obtain? Are we ready to withstand a taunting world, and endure hardships for Christ's sake?—What shall we say? If we are not so ready, our Lord might say to us also, "Ye know not what ye ask."

We ask that God would make us holy and good. It is a good request indeed. But are we prepared to be sanctified by any process that God in His wisdom may call on us to pass through? Are we ready to be purified by affliction, weaned from the world by bereavements, drawn nearer to God by losses, sicknesses, and sorrow? Alas, these are hard questions! But if we are not, our Lord might well say to us, "Ye know not what ye ask."

Let us leave these verses with a solemn resolution to consider well what we are about, when we draw nigh to God in prayer. Let us beware of thoughtless, inconsiderate, and rash petitions. Well might Solomon say, "Be not rash with thy mouth, and let not thine heart be hasty to utter anything before God." (Eccles. v. 2.)

MATTHEW XX. 24—28.

24 And when the ten heard *it*, they were moved with indignation against the two brethren.
25 But Jesus called them *unto him*, and said, Ye know that the princes of the Gentiles exercise dominion over them, and they that are great exercise authority upon them.
26 But it shall not be so among you; but whosoever will be great among you, let him be your minister;
27 And whosoever will be chief among you, let him be your servant:
28 Even as the Son of man came not to be ministered unto, but to minister, and to give his life a ransom for many.

THESE verses are few in number, but they contain lessons of great importance to all professing Christians. Let us see what they are.

In the first place, we learn that *there may be pride, jealousy, and love of pre-eminence, even among true disciples of Christ.* What saith the Scripture? "When the ten heard" what James and John had asked, "they were moved with indignation against the two brethren."

Pride is one of the oldest and most mischievous of sins: by it the angels fell; for "they kept not their first estate." (Jude 6.) Through pride Adam and Eve were seduced into eating the forbidden fruit: they were not content with their lot, and thought they would "be as gods." From pride the saints of God receive their greatest injuries after their conversion. Well, says Hooker, "Pride is a vice which cleaveth so fast unto the hearts of men, that if we were to strip ourselves of all faults one by one, we should undoubtedly find it the very last and hardest to put off." It is a quaint but true saying of Bishop Hall, that "pride is the inmost coat, which we put off last, and which we put on first."

In the second place, we learn that a *life of self-denying kindness to others is the true secret of greatness in the kingdom of Christ.* What saith the Scripture? "Whosoever will be great among you, let him be your minister:—Whosoever will be chief among you, let him be your servant."

The standard of the world, and the standard of the Lord Jesus, are widely different. They are more than different: they are flatly contradictory one to the other. Among the children of this world he is thought the greatest man who has most land, most money, most servants, most rank, and most earthly power: among the children of God he is reckoned the greatest who does most to promote the spiritual and temporal happiness of his fellow-creatures. True greatness consists, not in receiving, but in giving,—not in selfish absorption of good things, but in imparting good to others,—not in being served, but in serving,—not in sitting still, and being ministered to, but in going about and ministering to others. The angels of God see far more beauty in the work of the missionary than in the work of the Australian digger for gold. They take far more interest in the labours of men like Howard and Judson than in the victories of Generals, the political speeches of Statesmen, or the council-chambers of Kings. Let us remember these things. Let us beware of seeking false greatness:

let us aim at that greatness which alone is true. There is a mine of profound wisdom in that saying of our Lord's, "It is more blessed to give than to receive." (Acts xx. 35.)

In the third place, we learn that *the Lord Jesus Christ is intended to be the example of all true Christians.* What saith the Scripture? We ought to serve one another, "even as the Son of man came not to be ministered unto, but to minister."

The Lord God has mercifully provided His people with everything necessary to their sanctification. He has given those who follow after holiness the clearest of precepts, the best of motives, and the most encouraging of promises: but this is not all. He has furthermore supplied them with the most perfect pattern and example,—even the life of His own Son. By that life He bids us frame our own; in the steps of that life He bids us walk. (1 Peter ii. 21.) It is the model after which we must strive to mould our tempers, our words, and our works, in this evil world.—"Would my Master have spoken in this manner? Would my Master have behaved in this way?" These are the questions by which we ought daily to try ourselves.

How humbling this truth is! What searchings of heart it ought to raise within us! What a loud call it is to "lay aside every weight, and the sin which most easily besets us!" (Heb. xii. 1.) What manner of persons ought they to be who profess to copy Christ! What poor unprofitable religion is that which makes a man content with talk and empty profession, while his life is unholy and unclean! Alas, those who know nothing of Christ as an example, will find at last that

He knows nothing of them as His saved people. "He that saith he abideth in Him ought himself also so to walk even as He walked." (1 John ii. 6.)

Finally, let us learn from these verses *that Christ's death was an atonement for sin.* What saith the Scripture? "The Son of man came to give His life a ransom for many."

This is the mightiest truth in the Bible. Let us take care that we grasp it firmly, and never let it go. Our Lord Jesus Christ did not die merely as a martyr, or as a splendid example of self-sacrifice and self-denial: those who can see no more than *that* in His death, fall infinitely short of the truth; they lose sight of the very foundation-stone of Christianity, and miss the whole comfort of the Gospel. Christ died as a sacrifice for man's sin; He died to make reconciliation for man's iniquity; He died to purge our sins by the offering of Himself; He died to redeem us from the curse which we all deserved, and to make satisfaction to the justice of God, which must otherwise have condemned us. Never let us forget this!

We are all by nature debtors. We owe to our holy Maker ten thousand talents, and are not able to pay. We cannot atone for our own transgressions, for we are weak and frail, and only adding to our debts every day. But, blessed be God, what we could not do, Christ came into the world to do for us; what we could not pay, He undertook to pay for us: to pay it, He died for us upon the cross. "He offered Himself to God." (Heb. ix. 14.) "He suffered for sin, the just for the unjust, that He might bring us to God." (1 Peter iii. 18.) Once more, never let us forget this!

Let us not leave these verses without asking ourselves, where is our humility? what is our idea of true greatness? what is our example? what is our hope?—Life, eternal life, depends on the answer we give to these questions. Happy is that man who is truly humble, strives to do good in his day, walks in the steps of Jesus, and rests all his hopes on the ransom paid for him by Christ's blood. Such a man is a true Christian!

MATTHEW XX. 29—34.

29 And as they departed from
Jericho, a great multitude followed
him.
30 And, behold, two blind men
sitting by the way side, when they
heard that Jesus passed by, cried
out, saying, Have mercy on us, O
Lord, *thou* Son of David.
31 And the multitude rebuked
them, because they should hold
their peace: but they cried the
more, saying, Have mercy on us,
O Lord, *thou* Son of David.
32 And Jesus stood still, and
called them, and said, What will
ye that I shall do unto you?
33 They say unto him, Lord,
that our eyes may be opened.
34 So Jesus had compassion *on*
them, and touched their eyes: and
immediately their eyes received
sight, and they followed him.

In these verses we have a touching picture of an event in our Lord's history. He heals two blind men sitting by the way-side, near Jericho. The circumstances of the event contain several deeply interesting lessons, which all professing Christians would do well to remember.

For one thing, let us mark *what strony faith may sometimes be found where it might least have been expected.* Blind as these two men were, they believed that Jesus was able to help them. They never saw any of our Lord's miracles: they knew Him only by hear-say, and not face to face; and yet, as soon as they heard that He was passing by, they "cried out, saying, Have mercy on us, O Lord, thou son of David."

Such faith may well put us to shame. With all our books of evidence, and lives of saints, and libraries of divinity, how few know anything of simple, child-like confidence in Christ's mercy and Christ's power; and even among those who are believers, the degree of faith is often strangely disproportionate to the privileges enjoyed. Many an unlearned man, who can only read his New Testament with difficulty, possesses the spirit of unhesitating trust in Christ's advocacy, while deeply-read divines are harassed by questionings and doubts. They who, humanly speaking, ought to be first, are often last, and the last first.

For another thing, let us mark *what wisdom there is in using every opportunity for getting good for our souls.* These blind men "sat by the way-side:" had they not done so, they might never have been healed. Jesus never returned to Jericho, and they might never have met with Him again.

Let us see, in this simple fact, the importance of diligence in the use of means of grace. Let us never neglect the house of God, never forsake the assembling of ourselves with God's people, never omit the reading of our Bibles, never let drop the practice of private prayer. These things, no doubt, will not save us without the grace of the Holy Ghost: thousands make use of them, and remain dead in trespasses and sins. But it is just in the use of these things that souls are converted and saved: they are the ways in which Jesus walks. It is they who "sit by the way-side" who are likely to be healed. Do we know the diseases of our souls? Do we feel any desire to see the great Physician? If we do, we must not wait in idleness, saying, "If I am to be saved, I shall be saved." We must arise and go to the road where Jesus walks: who can tell but He will soon pass by for the last time? Let us sit daily "by the wayside."

For another thing, let us mark *the value of pains and perseverance in seeking Christ.* These blind men were "rebuked" by the multitude that accompanied our Lord: men told them to "hold their peace." But they were not to be silenced in this way: they felt their need of help; they cared nothing for the check which they received. "They cried the more, saying, Have mercy on us, O Lord, Thou son of David."

We have in this part of their conduct, a most important example. We are not to be deterred by opposition or discouraged by difficulties, when we begin to seek the salvation of our souls. We must "pray always, and not faint" (Luke xviii. 1); we must remember the parable of the importunate widow, and of the friend who came to borrow bread at midnight: like them we must press our petitions at the throne of grace, and say, "I will not let Thee go, except Thou bless me." (Gen. xxxii. 26.) Friends, relatives, and neighbours may say unkind things, and reprove our earnestness; we may meet with coldness and want of sympathy, where we might have looked for help: but let none of these things move us. If we feel our diseases, and want to find Jesus, the great Physician, —if we know our sins, and desire to have them pardoned, —let us press on. "The violent take the kingdom by force." (Matt. xi. 12.)

Finally, let us mark *how gracious the Lord Jesus is to*

those who seek Him. "He stood still and called" the blind men; He kindly asked them what it was that they desired; He heard their petition, and did what they requested. He "had compassion on them, and touched their eyes: and immediately their eyes received sight."

We see here an illustration of that old truth, which we can never know too well,—the mercifulness of Christ's heart towards the sons of men. The Lord Jesus is not only a mighty Saviour, but merciful, kind, and gracious to a degree that our minds cannot conceive. Well might the Apostle Paul say, that "the love of Christ passeth knowledge." (Eph. iii. 19.) Like him, let us pray that we may "know" more of that love. We need it when we first begin our Christian course, poor trembling penitents, and babes in grace; we need it afterwards, as we travel along the narrow way, often erring, often stumbling, and often cast down; we shall need it in the evening of our days, when we "walk through the valley of the shadow of death." Let us then grasp the love of Christ firmly, and keep it daily before our minds. We shall never know, till we wake up in the next world, how much we are indebted to it.

MATTHEW XXI. 1—11.

1 And when they drew nigh unto Jerusalem, and were come to Bethphage, unto the mount of Olives, then sent Jesus two disciples,

2 Saying unto them, Go into the village over against you, and straightway ye shall find an ass tied, and a colt with her: loose *them*, and bring *them* unto me.

3 And if any *man* say ought unto you, ye shall say, The Lord hath need of them; and straightway he will send them.

4 All this was done, that it might be fulfilled which was spoken by the prophet, saying,

5 Tell ye the daughter of Sion, Behold, thy King cometh unto thee, meek, and sitting upon an ass, and a colt the foal of an ass.

6 And the disciples went, and did as Jesus commanded them,

7 And brought the ass, and the colt, and put on them their clothes, and they set *him* thereon.

8 And a very great multitude

spread their garments in the way; others cut down branches from the trees, and strawed *them* in the way.

9 And the multitudes that went before, and that followed, cried, saying, Hosanna to the Son of David: Blessed *is* he that cometh in the name of the Lord; Hosanna in the highest.

10 And when he was come into Jerusalem, all the city was moved, saying, Who is this?

11 And the multitude said, This is Jesus, the prophet of Nazareth of Galilee.

THESE verses contain a very remarkable passage in our Lord Jesus Christ's life. They describe His public entry into Jerusalem, when He came there for the last time, before He was crucified.

There is something peculiarly striking in this incident in our Lord's history. The narrative reads like the account of some royal conqueror's return to his own city: "A very great multitude" accompanies Him in a kind of triumphal procession; loud cries and expressions of praise are heard around Him: "All the city was moved." The whole transaction is singularly at variance with the past tenor of our Lord's life; it is curiously unlike the ways of Him who did not "cry, nor strive, nor let His voice be heard in the streets,"—who withdrew Himself from the multitude on other occasions, and sometimes said to those He healed, "See thou say nothing to any man." (Mark i. 44.) And yet the whole transaction admits of explanation. The reasons of this public entry are not hard to find out.—Let us see what they were.

The plain truth is that our Lord knew well that the time of His earthly ministry was drawing to a close; He knew that the hour was approaching when He must finish the mighty work He came to do, by dying for our sins upon the cross; He knew that His last journey had been accomplished, and that there remained nothing now in His earthly ministry, but to be offered as a sacrifice on Calvary. Knowing all this, He no longer, as in times past, sought secrecy; knowing all this, He thought it good to enter the place where He was to be delivered to death, with peculiar solemnity and publicity. It was not fitting that the Lamb of God should come to be slain on Calvary privately and silently: before the great sacrifice for the sin of the world was offered up, it was right that every eye should be fixed on the victim. It was suitable that the crowning act of our Lord's life should be done with as much notoriety as possible: therefore it was that He made this public entry; therefore it was that He attracted to Himself the eyes of the wondering multitude; therefore it was that "all Jerusalem was moved." The atoning blood of the Lamb of God was about to be shed: this deed was not to be "done in a corner." (Acts xxvi. 26.)

It is good to remember these things. The real meaning of our Lord's conduct at this period of His history is not sufficiently considered by many readers of this passage. It remains for us to consider the practical lessons which these verses appear to point out.

In the first place, let us notice in these verses *an example of our Lord Jesus Christ's perfect knowledge.* He sends His two disciples into a village; He tells them that they will there find the ass on which He was to ride; He provides them with an answer to the inquiry of those to whom the ass belonged; He tells them that on giving that answer the ass will be sent: and all happens exactly as He foretells.

There is nothing hid from the Lord's eyes: there are

no secrets with Him. Alone or in company, by night or by day, in private or in public, He is acquainted with all our ways. He that saw Nathanael under the fig-tree is unchanged. Go where we will, and retire from the world as we may, we are never out of sight of Christ.

This is a thought that ought to exercise a restraining and sanctifying effect on our souls. We all know the influence which the presence of the rulers of this world has upon their subjects: nature itself teaches us to put a check on our tongues, and demeanour, and behaviour, when we are under the eye of a King. The sense of our Lord's Jesus Christ's perfect knowledge of all our ways, ought to have the same effect upon our hearts. Let us do nothing we would not like Christ to see, and say nothing we would not like Christ to hear; let us seek to live and move and have our being under a continual recollection of Christ's presence; let us behave as we would have done had we walked beside Him, in the company of James and John, by the sea of Galilee. This is the way to be trained for heaven. In heaven, "we shall ever be *with the Lord*." (1 Thess. iv. 17.)

In the second place, let us notice in these verses *an example of the manner in which prophecies concerning our Lord's first coming were fulfilled.* We are told that His public entry fulfilled the words of Zachariah: "Thy King cometh unto thee, meek, and sitting upon an ass."

It appears that this prediction was literally and exactly fulfilled. The words which the prophet spake by the Holy Ghost received no figurative accomplishment: as he said, so it came to pass; as he foretold, so it was done. Five hundred and fifty years had passed away since the prediction was made,—and then, when the appointed time arrived, the long-promised Messiah did literally ride into Zion "on an ass." No doubt the vast majority of the inhabitants of Jerusalem saw nothing in the circumstance; the veil was upon their hearts: but we are not left in doubt as to the fulfilment of the prophecy. We are told plainly, "All this was done that it might be fulfilled."

From the fulfilment of God's word in time past, we are surely intended to gather something as to the manner of its fulfilment in time to come. We have a right to expect that prophecies respecting the *second* advent of Christ will be as literally fulfilled as those respecting His *first* advent. He came to this earth literally in person the first time; He will come to this earth literally in person the second time; He came in humiliation once literally to suffer; He will come again in glory literally to reign. Every prediction respecting things accompanying His first advent was literally accomplished: it will be just the same when He returns. All that is foretold about the restoration of the Jews,—the judgments on the ungodly, the unbelief of the world, the gathering of the elect,—shall be made good to the letter. Let us not forget this. In the study of unfulfilled prophecy, a fixed principle of interpretation is of the first importance.

Finally, let us notice in these verses a *striking example of the worthlessness of man's favour*. Of all the admiring crowds who thronged round our Lord as He entered Jerusalem, none stood by Him when He was delivered into the hands of wicked men. Many cried, "Hosannah," who four days after cried, "Away with Him, crucify Him."

But this is a faithful picture of human nature: this is a proof of the utter folly of thinking more of the praise of man than the praise of God. Nothing in truth is so fickle and uncertain as popularity: it is here to-day and gone to-morrow; it is a sandy foundation, and sure to fail those who build upon it. Let us not care for it. Let us seek the favour of Him who is "the same yesterday, and to-day and for ever." (Heb. xiii. 8.) Christ never changes: those whom He loves, He loves to the end. His favour endureth for ever.

MATTHEW XXI. 12—22.

12 And Jesus went into the temple of God, and cast out all them that sold and bought in the temple, and overthrew the tables of the money-changers, and the seats of them that sold doves,

13 And said unto them, It is written, My house shall be called the house of prayer; but ye have made it a den of thieves.

14 And the blind and the lame came to him in the temple; and he healed them.

15 And when the chief priests and scribes saw the wonderful things that he did, and the children crying in the temple, and saying, Hosanna to the Son of David; they were sore displeased,

16 And said unto him, Hearest thou what these say? And Jesus saith unto them, Yea; have ye never read, Out of the mouth of babes and sucklings thou hast perfected praise?

17 And he left them, and went out of the city into Bethany; and he lodged there.

18 Now in the morning as he returned into the city, he hungered.

19 And when he saw a fig tree in the way, he came to it, and found nothing thereon, but leaves only, and said unto it, Let no fruit grow on thee henceforward for ever. And presently the fig tree withered away.

20 And when the disciples saw *it*, they marvelled, saying, How soon is the fig tree withered away!

21 Jesus answered and said unto them, Verily I say unto you, If ye have faith, and doubt not, ye shall not only do this *which is done* to the fig tree, but also if ye shall say unto this mountain, Be thou removed, and be thou cast into the sea; it shall be done.

22 And all things whatsoever ye shall ask in prayer, believing, ye shall receive.

WE have in these verses an account of two remarkable events in our Lord's history. In both, there was something eminently figurative and typical: each was an emblem of spiritual things. Beneath the surface of each lie lessons of solemn instruction.

The first event that demands our attention is *our Lord's visit to the temple.* He found His Father's house in a state which too truly shadowed forth the general condition of the whole Jewish Church: everything out of order, and out of course. He found the courts of that holy building disgracefully profaned by worldly transactions. Trading, and buying, and selling, were actually going on within its walls; *there* stood dealers ready to supply the Jew who came from distant countries, with any sacrifice he wanted; *there* sat the money-changer, ready to change foreign money for the current coin of the land. Bullocks, and sheep, and goats, and pigeons, were there exposed for sale, as if the place had been a market: the jingling of money might there be heard, as if those holy courts had been a bank or an exchange. Such were the scenes that met our Lord's eyes. He saw it all with holy indignation. "He cast out all them that sold and bought;" He "overthrew the tables of the money-changers:" resistance there was none, for men knew that He was right; objection there was none, for all felt that He was only reforming a notorious abuse, which had been basely permitted for the sake of gain. Well might He sound in the ears of the astonished traders, as they fled from the temple, those solemn words of Isaiah, "It is written, My house shall be called the house of prayer; but ye have made it a den of thieves."

Let us see in our Lord's conduct on this occasion, a striking type of what He will do when He comes again the second time. He will purify His visible Church as He purified the temple; He will cleanse it from every thing that defiles and works iniquity, and cast every worldly professor out of its pale; He will allow no worshipper of money, or lover of gain to have a place in that glorious temple, which He will finally exhibit before the world. May we all strive to live in the daily expectation of that coming! May we judge ourselves that we be not condemned, and cast out in that searching and sifting day! We should often study those words of Malachi: "Who may abide the day of His coming? and who shall stand when He appeareth? for He is like a refiner's fire, and like fuller's soap." (Mal. iii. 2.)

The second event that demands our attention in these verses is *our Lord's curse upon the fruitless fig-tree.* We are told that being hungry, He came to a fig-tree in the way, and "found nothing thereon but leaves only, and said unto it, Let no fruit grow on thee henceforward for ever. And presently the fig-tree withered away." This is an instance almost without parallel in all our Lord's ministry: it is almost the only occasion on which we find Him making one of His creatures suffer, in order to teach a spiritual truth. There was a heart-searching lesson in that withered fig-tree: it preaches a sermon we shall do well to hear.

That fig-tree, full of leaves, but barren of fruit, was a striking emblem of the Jewish Church, when our Lord was upon earth. The Jewish Church had everything to make an outward show: it had the temple, the priesthood, the daily service, the yearly feasts, the Old Testament Scriptures, the courses of the Levites, the morning and evening sacrifice. But beneath these goodly leaves, the Jewish Church was utterly destitute of fruit. It had no grace, no faith, no love, no humility, no spirituality, no real holiness, no willingness to receive its Messiah (John i. 11.) And hence, like the fig-tree, the Jewish Church was soon to wither away. It was to be stripped of all its outward ornaments, and its members scattered over the face of the earth; Jerusalem was to be destroyed; the temple was to be burned; the daily sacrifice was to be taken away; the tree was to wither down to the very ground. And so it came to pass: never was there a type so literally fulfilled. In every wandering Jew we see a branch of the fig-tree that was cursed.

But we may not stop here. We may find even more instruction in the event we are now considering. These things were written for our sakes, as well as for the Jews.

Is not every fruitless branch of Christ's visible Church in awful danger of becoming a withered fig-tree? Beyond doubt it is. High ecclesiastical profession, without holiness among a people,—overweening confidence in councils, bishops, liturgies, and ceremonies, while repentance and faith have been neglected,—have ruined many a visible Church in time past, and may yet ruin many more. Where are the once famous Churches of Ephesus, and Sardis, and Carthage, and Hippo? They are all gone. They had leaves, but no fruit. Our Lord's curse came upon them: they became withered fig-trees. The decree went forth, "Hew them down." (Dan. iv. 23.) Let us remember this. Let us beware of church-pride: let us not be high-minded, but fear. (Rom. xi. 20.)

Finally, is not every fruitless professor of Christianity in awful danger of becoming a withered fig-tree? There can be no doubt of it. So long as a man is content with the mere *leaves* of religion,—with a name to live while he is dead, and a form of godliness without the power, —so long his soul is in great peril. So long as he is satisfied with going to church or chapel, or receiving the Lord's Supper, and being called a Christian, while his heart is not changed, and his sins not forsaken,—so long he is daily provoking God to cut him off without remedy. Fruit, fruit,—the fruit of the Spirit is the only sure proof that we are savingly united to Christ, and in the way to heaven. May this sink down into our hearts, and never be forgotten!

MATTHEW XXI. 23—32.

23 And when he was come into the temple, the chief priests and the elders of the people came unto him as he was teaching, and said, By what authority doest thou these things, and who gave thee this authority?

24 And Jesus answered and said unto them, I also will ask you one thing, which if ye tell me, I in like wise will tell you by what authority I do these things.

25 The baptism of John, whence was it? from heaven, or of men? And they reasoned with themselves, saying, If we shall say, From heaven; he will say unto us, Why did ye not then believe him?

26 But if we shall say, Of men; we fear the people; for all hold John as a prophet.

27 And they answered Jesus, and said, We cannot tell. And he said unto them, Neither tell I you by what authority I do these things.

28 But what think ye? A *certain* man had two sons; and he came to the first, and said, Son, go work to-day in my vineyard.

29 He answered and said, I will not: but afterward he repented, and went.

30 And he came to the second, and said likewise. And he answered and said, I *go*, sir: and went not.

31 Whether of them twain did the will of *his* father? They say unto him, The first. Jesus saith unto them, Verily I say unto you, That the publicans and the harlots go into the kingdom of God before you.

32 For John came unto you in the way of righteousness, and ye believed him not: but the publicans and the harlots believed him: and ye, when ye had seen *it*, repented not afterward, that ye might believe him.

THESE verses contain a conversation between our Lord Jesus Christ and the chief priests and elders of the people. Those bitter enemies of all righteousness saw the sensation which the public entry into Jerusalem, and the cleansing of the temple, had produced. At once they came about our Lord, like bees, and endeavoured to find occasion for an accusation against Him.

Let us observe, in the first place, *how ready the enemies of truth are to question the authority of all who do more good than themselves.* The chief priests have not a word to say about our Lord's teaching: they make no charge against the lives or conduct of Himself or His followers. The point on which they fasten is His commission: "By what authority doest Thou these things? And who gave Thee this authority?"

The same charge has often been made against the servants of God, when they have striven to check the progress of ecclesiastical corruption. It is the old engine by which the children of this world have often laboured to stop the progress of revivals and reformations; it is the weapon which was often brandished in the face of the Reformers, the Puritans, and the Methodists of the last century; it is the poisoned arrow which is often shot at city-missionaries and lay-agents in the present day. Too many care nothing for the manifest blessing of God on a man's work, so long as he is not sent forth by their own sect or party. It matters nothing to them, that some humble labourer in God's harvest can point to numerous conversions of souls through his instrumentality; they still cry, "By what authority doest Thou these things?" His success is nothing: they demand his commission. His cures are nothing: they want his diploma. Let us neither be surprised nor moved, when we hear such things. It is old charge which was brought against

Christ Himself. "There is no new thing under the sun." (Eccles. i. 9.)

Let us observe, in the second place, *the consummate wisdom with which our Lord replied to the question put to Him.* His enemies asked Him for His authority for doing what He did. They doubtless intended to make His answer a handle for accusing Him. He knew the drift of their inquiry, and said, "I also will ask you one thing, which if ye tell me, I in like wise will tell you by what authority I do these things. The baptism of John, whence was it? from heaven or of men?"

We must distinctly understand that in this answer of our Lord's there was no evasion: to suppose this is a great mistake. The counter-question which He asked was in reality an answer to His enemies' inquiry. He knew they dared not deny that John the Baptist was "a man sent from God;" He knew that, this being granted, He needed only to remind them of John's testimony to Himself.—Had not John declared Him to be "the Lamb of God that taketh away the sin of the world"? Had not John pronounced Him to be the Mighty One, who was to "baptize with the Holy Ghost"?—in short, our Lord's question was a home-thrust to the conscience of His enemies. If they once conceded the divine authority of John the Baptist's mission, they must also concede the divinity of His own; if they acknowledged that John came from heaven, they must acknowledge that He Himself was the Christ

Let us pray that in this difficult world, we may be supplied with the same kind of wisdom which was here displayed by our Lord. No doubt we ought to act on the injunction of St. Peter, "and be always ready to give a reason of the hope that is in us, with meekness and with fear." (1 Peter. iii. 15.) We ought to shrink from no inquiry into the principles of our holy religion, and to be ready at any time to defend and explain our practice; but for all this we must never forget that "wisdom is profitable to direct," and that we should strive to speak wisely in defence of a good cause. The words of Solomon deserve consideration: "Answer not a fool according to his folly, lest thou be like unto him." (Prov. xxvi. 4.)

In the last place, let us observe in these verses *what immense encouragement our Lord holds out to those who repent.* We see this strikingly brought out in the parable of the "two sons." Both were told to go and work in their father's vineyard: one son, like the profligate publicans, for some time flatly refused obedience, but "afterwards" repented and went; the other, like the formal Pharisees, pretended willingness to go, but after all went not. "Whether of them twain," says our Lord, "did the will of his father?" Even His enemies were obliged to reply, "The first."

Let it be a settled principle in our Christianity that the God and Father of our Lord Jesus Christ is infinitely willing to receive penitent sinners.—It matters nothing what a man has been in time past. Does he repent, and come to Christ? Then old things are passed away, and all things are become new.—It matters nothing how high and self-confident a man's profession of religion may be. Does he really give up his sins? If not, his profession is abominable in God's sight, and he himself is still under the curse.—Let us take courage ourselves, if we have been great sinners hitherto: only let us repent and believe in Christ, and there is hope. Let us encourage others to repent; let us hold the door wide open to the very chief of sinners. Never will that word fail, "If we confess our sins, He is faithful and just to forgive us our sins, and to cleanse us from all unrighteousness." (1 John i. 9.)

MATTHEW XXI. 33—46.

33 Hear another parable: There was a certain householder, which planted a vineyard, and hedged it round about, and digged a winepress in it, and built a tower, and let it out to husbandmen, and went into a far country:

34 And when the time of the fruit drew near, he sent his servants to the husbandmen, that they might receive the fruits of it.

35 And the husbandmen took his servants, and beat one, and killed another, and stoned another.

36 Again, he sent other servants more than the first: and they did unto them likewise.

37 But last of all he sent unto them his son, saying, They will reverence my son.

38 But when the husbandmen saw the son, they said among themselves, This is the heir; come, let us kill him, and let us seize on his inheritance.

39 And they caught him, and cast *him* out of the vineyard, and slew *him*.

40 When the lord therefore of the vineyard cometh, what will he do unto those husbandmen?

41 They say unto him, He will miserably destroy those wicked men, and will let out *his* vineyard unto other husbandmen, which shall render him the fruits in their seasons.

42 Jesus saith unto them, Did ye never read in the scriptures, The stone which the builders rejected, the same is become the head of the corner: this is the Lord's doing, and it is marvellous in our eyes?

43 Therefore say I unto you, The kingdom of God shall be taken from you, and given to a nation bringing forth the fruits thereof.

44 And whosoever shall fall on this stone shall be broken: but on whomsoever it shall fall, it will grind him to powder.

45 And when the chief priests and Pharisees had heard his parables, they perceived that he spake of them.

46 But when they sought to lay hands on him, they feared the multitude, because they took him for a prophet.

THE parable contained in these verses was spoken with special reference to the Jews. They are the husbandmen here described: their sins are set before us here as in a picture. Of this there can be no doubt: it is written, that "He spake of them."

But we must not flatter ourselves that this parable

contains nothing for the Gentiles. There are lessons laid down for us, as well as for the Jew. Let us see what they are.

We see, in the first place, *what distinguishing privileges God is pleased to bestow on some nations.*

He chose Israel to be a peculiar people to Himself. He separated them from the other nations of the earth, and bestowed on them countless blessings; He gave them revelations of Himself, while all the rest of the earth was in darkness; He gave them the law, and the covenants, and the oracles of God, while all the world beside was let alone. In short, God dealt with the Jews as a man deals with a piece of land which he fences out and cultivates, while all the country around is left untilled and waste. The vineyard of the Lord was the house of Israel. (Isai. v. 7.)

And have we no privileges? Beyond doubt we have many. We have the Bible, and liberty for every one to read it; we have the Gospel, and permission to every one to hear it; we have spiritual mercies in abundance, of which five hundred millions of our fellow-men know nothing at all. How thankful we ought to be! The poorest man in England may say every morning, "There are five hundred millions of immortal souls worse off than I am. Who am I, that I should differ? Bless the Lord, O my soul."

We see, in the next place, *what a bad use nations sometimes make of their privileges.*

When the Lord separated the Jews from other people, He had a right to expect that they would serve Him, and obey His laws. When a man has taken pains with a vineyard, he has a right to expect fruit. But Israel rendered not a due return for all God's mercies. They mingled with the heathen, and learned their works (Psalm cvi. 35): they hardened themselves in sin and unbelief; they turned aside after idols; they kept not God's ordinances; they despised God's temple; they refused to listen to His prophets; they ill-used those whom He sent to call them to repentance; and, finally, they brought their wickedness to a height, by killing the Son of God Himself, even Christ the Lord.

And what are we doing ourselves with our privileges? Truly this is a serious question, and one that ought to make us think. It may well be feared, that we are not, as a nation, living up to our light, or walking worthy of our many mercies. Must we not confess with shame, that millions amongst us seem utterly without God in the world? Must we not acknowledge, that in many a town, and in many a village, Christ seems hardly to have any disciple, and the Bible seems hardly to be believed? It is vain to shut our eyes to these facts. The fruit that the Lord receives from His vineyard in Great Britain, compared with what it ought to be, is disgracefully small. It may well be doubted whether we are not as provoking to Him as the Jews.

We see, in the next place, *what an awful reckoning God sometimes has with Nations and Churches which make a bad use of their privileges.*

A time came when the longsuffering of God towards the Jews had an end. Forty years after our Lord's death, the cup of their iniquity was at length full, and they received a heavy chastisement for their many sins. Their holy city, Jerusalem, was destroyed; their temple was burned: they themselves were scattered over the face of the earth. "The kingdom of God was taken from them, and given to a nation bringing forth the fruits thereof."

And will the same thing ever happen to us? Will the judgments of God ever come down on this nation of England because of her unfruitfulness under so many mercies? Who can tell? We may well cry with the prophet, "Lord God, Thou knowest." We only know that judgments have come on many a Church and Nation in the last eighteen hundred years. The kingdom of God has been taken from the African Churches: the Mahometan power has overwhelmed most of the Churches of the East. At all events it becomes all English believers to intercede much on behalf of their country. Nothing offends God so much as neglect of privileges. Much has been given to us, and much will be required.

We see, in the last place, *the power of conscience even in wicked men.*

The chief priests and elders at last discovered that our Lord's parable was specially meant for themselves: the point of its closing words was too sharp to be escaped. "They perceived that He spake of them."

There are many hearers of the Gospel in every congregation who are exactly in the condition of these unhappy men. They know that what they hear Sunday after Sunday is all true; they know that they are wrong themselves, and that every sermon condemns them: but they have neither will nor courage to acknowledge this. They are too proud or too fond of the world to confess their past mistakes, and to take up the cross and follow Christ. Let us all beware of this awful state of mind. The last day will prove that there was more going on in the consciences of hearers than was at all known to preachers. Thousands and ten thousands will be found, like the chief priests, to have been convicted by their own consciences, and yet to have died unconverted.

MATTHEW XXII. 1—14.

1 And Jesus answered and spake unto them again by parables, and said,

2 The kingdom of heaven is like unto a certain king, which made a marriage for his son,

3 And sent forth his servants to call them that were bidden to the wedding: and they would not come.

4 Again, he sent forth other servants, saying, Tell them which are bidden, Behold, I have prepared my dinner: my oxen and *my* fatlings *are* killed, and all things *are* ready: come unto the marriage.

5 But they made light of it, and went their ways, one to his farm, another to his merchandise:

6 And the remnant took his servants, and entreated *them* spitefully, and slew *them*.

7 But when the king heard *thereof*, he was wroth: and he sent forth his armies, and destroyed those murderers, and burned up their city.

8 Then saith he to his servants, The wedding is ready, but they which were bidden were not worthy.

9 Go ye therefore into the highways, and as many as ye shall find, bid to the marriage.

10 So those servants went out into the highways, and gathered together all as many as they found, both bad and good: and the wedding was furnished with guests.

11 And when the king came in to see the guests, he saw there a man which had not on a wedding garment:

12 And he saith unto him, Friend, how camest thou in hither not having a wedding garment? And he was speechless.

13 Then said the king to the servants, Bind him hand and foot, and take him away, and cast *him* into outer darkness; there shall be weeping and gnashing of teeth.

14 For many are called, but few *are* chosen.

THE parable related in these verses is one of very wide signification. In its first application it unquestionably points to the Jews.—But we may not confine it to them. It contains heart-searching lessons for all among whom the Gospel is preached: it is a spiritual picture which speaks to us this day, if we have an ear to hear. The remark of a learned divine is wise and true: "Parables are like many-sided precious stones, cut so as to cast lustre in more than one direction."

Let us observe, in the first place, that *the salvation of the Gospel is compared to a marriage feast.* The Lord Jesus tells us that a "certain King made a marriage for his son."

There is in the Gospel a complete provision for all the wants of man's soul: there is a supply of everything that can be required to relieve spiritual hunger and spiritual thirst. Pardon, peace with God, lively hope in this world, glory in the world to come,—are set before us in rich abundance. It is "a feast of fat things." All this provision is owing to the love of the Son of God, Jesus Christ our Lord. He offers to take us into union with Himself, to restore us to the family of God as dear children, to clothe us with His own righteousness, to give us a place in His kingdom, and to present us faultless before His Father's throne at the last day. The Gospel, in short, is an offer of food to the hungry, of joy to the mourner, of a home to the outcast, of a loving friend to the lost. It is glad tidings. God offers, through His dear Son, to be at one with sinful man. Let us not forget this. "Herein is love, not that we loved God, but that He loved us, and sent His Son to be the propitiation for our sins." (1 John iv. 10.)

Let us observe, in the second place, that *the invitations of the Gospel are wide, full, broad and unlimited.* The Lord Jesus tells us in the parable, that the King's servants said to those who were bidden, "All things are ready: come unto the marriage."

There is nothing wanting on God's part for the

salvation of sinners' souls: no one will ever be able to say at last that it was God's fault, if he is not saved. The Father is ready to love and receive; the Son is ready to pardon and cleanse guilt away; the Spirit is ready to sanctify and renew; angels are ready to rejoice over the returning sinner; grace is ready to assist him; the Bible is ready to instruct him; heaven is ready to be his everlasting home. One thing only is needful, and that is,—the sinner must be ready and willing himself. Let this also never be forgotten: let us not quibble and split hairs upon the point. God will be found clear of the blood of all lost souls. The Gospel always speaks of sinners as *responsible* and accountable beings; the Gospel places an open door before all mankind: no one is excluded from the range of its offers. Though efficient only to believers, those offers are sufficient for all the world: though few enter the strait gate, all are invited to come in.

Let us observe, in the third place, that *the salvation of the Gospel is rejected by many to whom it is offered.* The Lord Jesus tells us that those whom the King's servants bade to the wedding "made light of it, and went their way."

There are thousands of hearers of the Gospel who derive from it no benefit whatever. They listen to it Sunday after Sunday, and year after year, and do not believe to the saving of the soul. They feel no special need of the Gospel; they see no special beauty in it; they do not perhaps hate it, or oppose it, or scoff at it, but they do not receive it into their hearts. They like other things far better. Their money, their land, their business, or their pleasures, are all far more interesting subjects to them than their souls.—It is an awful state of mind to be in, but awfully common. Let us search our own hearts, and take heed that it is not cur own. Open sin may kill its thousands; but indifference and neglect of the Gospel kill their tens of thousands. Multitudes will find themselves in hell, not so much because they openly broke the ten commandments, as because they made light of the truth. Christ died for them on the cross, but they neglected Him.

Let us observe, in the last place, that *all false professors of religion will be detected, exposed, and eternally condemned at the last day.* The Lord Jesus tells us that when the wedding was at last furnished with guests, the King came in to see them, and "saw a man which had not on a wedding garment." He asked him how he came in there without one, and he received no reply; and he then commanded the servants to "bind him hand and foot, and take him away."

There will always be some false professors in the Church of Christ, as long as the world stands. "In this parable," it has been truly remarked, "one single castaway represents all the rest." It is impossible to read the hearts of men: deceivers and hypocrites will never be entirely excluded from the ranks of those who call themselves Christians. So long as a man professes subjection to the Gospel, and lives an outwardly correct life, we dare not say positively that he is not clothed in the righteousness of Christ. But there will be no deception at the last day: the unerring eye of God will discern who are His own people, and who are not.

Nothing but true faith shall abide the fire of His judgment; all spurious Christianity shall be weighed in the balance and found wanting: none but true believers shall sit down at the marriage supper of the Lamb. It shall avail the hypocrite nothing that he has been a loud talker about religion, and had the reputation of being an eminent Christian among men. His triumphing shall be but for a moment: he shall be stripped of his borrowed plumage, and stand naked and shivering before the bar of God, speechless, self-condemned, hopeless, and helpless. He shall be cast into outer darkness with shame, and reap according as he has sown. Well may our Lord say, "There shall be weeping and gnashing of teeth."

Let us learn wisdom from the solemn pictures of this parable, and give diligence to make our calling and election sure. We ourselves are among those to whom the word is spoken: "All things are ready, come to the marriage." Let us see that we refuse not Him that speaketh: let us not sleep as others do, but watch and be sober. Time hastens on. The King will soon come in to see the guests: have we or have we not got on the wedding garment? Have we put on Christ? That is the grand question that arises out of this parable. May we never rest till we can give a satisfactory answer! May those heart-searching words daily ring in our ears, "Many are called, but few are chosen!"

MATTHEW XXII. 15—22.

15 Then went the Pharisees, and took counsel how they might entangle him in *his* talk.
16 And they sent out unto him their disciples with the Herodians, saying, Master, we know that thou art true, and teachest the way of God in truth, neither carest thou

for any *man:* for thou regardest not the person of men.
17 Tell us therefore, What thinkest thou? Is it lawful to give tribute unto Cæsar, or not?
18 But Jesus perceived their wickedness, and said, Why tempt ye me, *ye* hypocrites?
19 Shew me the tribute money. And they brought unto him a penny.
20 And he saith unto them, Whose is this image and superscription?
21 They say unto him, Cæsar's. Then saith he unto them, Render therefore unto Cæsar the things which are Cæsar's; and unto God the things that are God's.
22 When they had heard *these words*, they marvelled, and left him, and went their way.

We see, in this passage, the first of a series of subtle attacks which were made on our Lord during the last days of His earthly ministry. His deadly foes, the Pharisees, saw the influence which He was obtaining, both by His miracles and by His preaching: they were determined by some means to silence Him, or put Him to death; they therefore endeavoured to "entangle Him in His talk." They sent forth "their disciples with the Herodians," to try Him with a hard question: they wished to entice him into saying something which might serve as a handle for an accusation against Him. Their scheme, we are told in these verses, entirely failed: they took nothing by their aggressive movement, and retreated in confusion.

The first thing which demands our attention in these verses is *the flattering language with which our Lord was accosted by His enemies.* "Master," they said, "we know that Thou are true, and teachest the way of God in truth, neither carest Thou for any man; for Thou regardest not the person of men."—How well these Pharisees and Herodians talked! What smooth and honeyed words were these! They thought no doubt, that by good words and fair speeches they would throw our Lord off His guard. It might truly be said of them, "The words of his mouth were smoother than butter, but war was in his heart: his words were softer than oil, yet were they drawn swords." (Psalm lv. 21.)

It becomes all professing Christians to be much on their guard against flattery. We mistake greatly if we suppose that persecution and hard usage are the only weapons in Satan's armoury: that crafty foe has other engines for doing us mischief, which he knows well how to work. He knows how to poison souls by the world's seductive kindness, when he cannot frighten them by the "fiery dart" or the sword. Let us not be ignorant of his devices. "By peace he destroys many."

We are only too apt to forget this truth: we overlook the many examples which God has given us in Scripture for our learning. What brought about the ruin of Samson? Not the armies of the Philistines, but the pretended love of a Philistine woman.—What led to Solomon's backsliding? Not the strength of outward enemies, but the blandishment of his numerous wives.—What was the cause of King Hezekiah's greatest mistake? Not the sword of Sennacherib, or the threats of Rab-shakeh, but the flattery of the Babylonian ambassadors.—Let us remember these things, and be on our guard. Peace often ruins nations more than war; sweet things occasion far more sickness than bitter; the sun makes the traveller cast off his protective garments far sooner than the north wind. Let us beware of the flatterer. Satan is never so dangerous as when he appears as an angel of light: the world is never so dangerous to the Christian as when it smiles. When Judas betrayed his Lord, it was with a kiss. The believer that is proof against the world's frown does well; but he that is proof against its flattery does better.

The second thing that demands our attention in these verses is the *marvellous wisdom of the reply which our Lord made to His enemies.* The Pharisees and Herodians asked whether it was lawful to give tribute to Cæsar or not. They doubtless thought that they had put a question which our Lord could not answer without giving them an advantage.—Had He simply replied that it was *lawful* to pay tribute, they would have denounced Him to the people as one who dishonoured the privileges of Israel, and considered the children of Abraham no longer free, but subjects to a foreign power.—Had He, on the other hand, replied that it was *not lawful* to pay tribute, they would have denounced Him to the Romans as a mover of sedition, and a rebel against Cæsar, who refused to pay his taxes.—But our Lord's conduct completely baffled them. He demanded to see the "tribute-money:" He asks them whose head is on that coin. They reply, "Cæsar's." They acknowledge that the Roman Emperor Cæsar has some authority over them, by using money bearing his image and superscription, since he that coins the current money is ruler of the land where that money is current. And at once they receive an irresistibly conclusive answer to their question: "Render to Cæsar the things which are Cæsar's, and unto God the things that are God's."

The principle laid down in these well-known words is one of deep importance. There is *one* obedience owing by every Christian to the civil government under which he lives, in all matters which are temporal, and not purely spiritual. He may not approve of every requirement of that civil government; but he must submit to the laws of the commonwealth, so long as those laws are unrepealed. He must "render unto Cæsar the things that are Cæsar's."—There is *another* obedience which the Christian owes to the God of the Bible in all matters which are purely spiritual. No temporal loss, no civil disability, no displeasure of the powers that be, must ever tempt him to do things which the Scripture plainly forbids. His position may be very trying; he may have to suffer much for his conscience sake: but he must never fly in the face of unmistakable requirements of Scripture. If Cæsar coins a new Gospel, he is not to be obeyed. We must "render to God the things that are God's."

The subject unquestionably is one of great difficulty and delicacy. It is certain that the Church must not swallow up the State; it is no less certain that the State must not swallow up the Church. On no point, perhaps, have conscientious men been so much tried; on no point have good men disagreed so much as in solving the problem, "where the things of Cæsar end, and where the things of God begin."—The *civil* power, on the one side, has often encroached terribly on the rights of conscience,—as the English Puritans found to their cost in the unhappy times of the Stuarts; the *spiritual* power, on the other side, has often pushed its claims to an extravagant extent, so as to take Cæsar's sceptre out of his hands,—as it did when the Church of Rome trampled on our own English King John. In order to have a right judgment in all questions of this kind, every true Christian should constantly pray for "wisdom from above." The man whose eye is single, and who daily seeks for grace and practical common sense, will never be allowed greatly to err.

MATTHEW XXII. 23—33.

23 The same day came to him the Sadducees, which say that there is no resurrection, and asked him,
24 Saying, Master, Moses said, If a man die, having no children, his brother shall marry his wife, and raise up seed unto his brother.
25 Now there were with us seven brethren: and the first, when he had married a wife, deceased, and, having no issue, left his wife unto his brother:
26 Likewise the second also, and the third, unto the seventh.
27 And last of all the woman died also.
28 Therefore in the resurrection whose wife shall she be of the seven? for they all had her.
29 Jesus answered and said unto them, Ye do err, not knowing the scriptures, nor the power of God.
30 For in the resurrection they neither marry, nor are given in marriage, but are as the angels of God in heaven.
31 But as touching the resurrection of the dead, have ye not read that which was spoken unto you by God, saying,
32 I am the God of Abraham, and the God of Isaac, and the God of Jacob? God is not the God of the dead, but of the living.
33 And when the multitude heard *this*, they were astonished at his doctrine.

THIS passage describes a conversation between our Lord Jesus Christ and the Sadducees. These unhappy men, who said that there was "no resurrection," attempted, like the Pharisees and Herodians, to perplex our Lord with hard questions. Like them, they hoped "to entangle Him in His talk," and to injure His reputation among the people: like them, they were completely baffled.

Let us observe, in the first place, that *absurd sceptical objections to Bible truths are ancient things.* The Sadducees wished to show the absurdity of the doctrine of the resurrection and the life to come; they therefore came to our Lord with a story which was probably invented for the occasion. They told Him that a certain woman had married seven brothers in succession, who had all died and left no children: they then asked, "whose wife" this woman would be in the next world, when all rose again?—The object of the question was plain and transparent. They meant, in reality, to bring the whole doctrine of a resurrection into contempt;

they meant to insinuate that there must needs be confusion and strife and unseemly disorder, if after death men and women were to live again.

It must never surprise us, if we meet with like objections against the doctrines of Scripture, and especially against those doctrines which concern another world. There never probably will be wanting "unreasonable men," who will "intrude" into things unseen, and make imaginary difficulties their excuse for unbelief. *Supposed cases* are one of the favourite strongholds in which an unbelieving mind loves to entrench itself: such a mind will often set up a shadow of its own imagining, and fight with it, as if it was a truth; such a mind will often refuse to look at the overwhelming mass of plain evidence by which Christianity is supported, and will fasten down on some one single difficulty, which it fancies is unanswerable. The talk and arguments of people of this character should never shake our faith for a moment. For one thing, we should remember that there must needs be deep and dark things in a religion which comes from God, and that a child may put questions which the greatest philosopher cannot answer; for another thing, we should remember that there are countless truths in the Bible which are clear and unmistakable. Let us first attend to them, believe them, and obey them: so doing, we need not doubt that many a thing now unintelligible to us will yet be made plain; so doing, we may be sure that "what we know not now we shall know hereafter."

Let us observe, in the second place, what a *remarkable text our Lord brings forward in proof of the reality of a life to come.* He places before the Sadducees the words which God spake to Moses in the bush: "I am the God of Abraham, and the God of Isaac, and the God of Jacob." (Exod. iii. 6.) He adds the comment, "God is not the God of the dead, but of the living." At the time when Moses heard these words, Abraham, Isaac, and Jacob had been dead and buried many years; two centuries had passed away since Jacob, the last of the three, was carried to his tomb: and yet God spoke of them as being still His people, and of Himself as being still their God. He said not, "I was their God," but "I *am*."

Perhaps we are not often tempted to doubt the truth of a resurrection, and a life to come; but unhappily, it is easy to hold truths theoretically, and yet not realize them practically. There are few of us who would not find it good to meditate on the mighty verity which our Lord here unfolds, and to give it a prominent place in our thoughts. Let us settle it in our minds that the dead are in one sense still alive. From our eyes they have passed away, and their place knows them no more: but in the eyes of God they live, and will one day come forth from their graves to receive an everlasting sentence. There is no such thing as annihilation: the idea is a miserable delusion. The sun, moon, and stars,—the solid mountains, and deep sea, will one day come to nothing; but the weakest babe of the poorest man shall live for evermore in another world. May we never forget this! Happy is he who can say from his heart the words of the Nicene Creed: "I look for the resurrection of the dead, and the life of the world to come."

Let us observe, in the last place, *the account which our*

Lord gives of the state of men and women after the resurrection. He silences the fancied objections of the Sadducees, by showing that they entirely mistook the true character of the resurrection state. They took it for granted that it must needs be a gross, carnal existence, like that of mankind upon earth: our Lord tells them that in the next world we may have a real material body, and yet a body of very different constitution, and different necessities, from that which we have now. He speaks only of the saved, be it remembered: He omits all mention of the lost. He says, "In the resurrection they neither marry nor are given in marriage, but are as the angels of God in heaven."

We know but little of the life to come in heaven. Perhaps our clearest ideas of it are drawn from considering what it will *not* be, rather than what it will be. It is a state in which we shall hunger no more, nor thirst any more; sickness, pain, and disease, will not be known: wasting old age, and death will have no place. Marriages, births, and a constant succession of inhabitants, will no more be needed: they who are once admitted into heaven shall dwell there for evermore.—And, to pass from negatives, to positives, one thing we are told plainly: we shall be "as the angels of God." Like them, we shall serve God perfectly, unhesitatingly, and unweariedly; like them, we shall ever be in God's presence; like them, we shall ever delight to do His will; like them, we shall give all glory to the Lamb. These are deep things: but they are all true.

Are we ready for this life? Should we enjoy it, if admitted to take part in it? Is the company of God, and the service of God pleasant to us now? Is the occupation of angels one in which we should delight? These are solemn questions. Our hearts must be heavenly on earth, while we live, if we hope to go to heaven when we rise again in another world. (Coloss. iii. 1—4.)

MATTHEW XXII. 34—46.

34 But when the Pharisees had heard that he had put the Sadducees to silence, they were gathered together.

35 Then one of them, *which was* a lawyer, asked *him a question*, tempting him, and saying,

36 Master, which *is* the great commandment in the law?

37 Jesus said unto him, Thou shalt love the Lord thy God with all thy heart, and with all thy soul, and with all thy mind.

38 This is the first and great commandment.

39 And the second *is* like unto it, Thou shalt love thy neighbour as thyself.

40 On these two commandments hang all the law and the prophets.

41 While the Pharisees were gathered together, Jesus asked them,

42 Saying, What think ye of Christ? Whose son is he? They say unto him, *The Son* of David.

43 He saith unto them, How then doth David in spirit call him Lord, saying,

44 The LORD said unto my Lord, Sit thou on my right hand, till I make thine enemies thy footstool?

45 If David then call him Lord, how is he his son?

46 And no man was able to answer him a word, neither durst any *man* from that day forth ask him any more *questions*.

IN the beginning of this passage we find our Lord replying to the question of a certain lawyer, who asked Him which was "the great commandment of the law?" That question was asked in no friendly spirit; but we have reason to be thankful that it was asked at all: it drew from our Lord an answer full of precious instruction. Thus we see how good may come out of evil.

Let us mark *what an admirable summary these verses contain of our duty towards God and our neighbour.* Jesus says, "Thou shalt love the Lord thy God with all thy heart, and with all thy soul, and with all thy mind:" He says again, "Thou shalt love thy neighbour as thyself;" and He adds, "On these two commandments hang all the law and the prophets."

How simple are these two rules, and yet how comprehensive! How soon the words are repeated, and yet how much they contain! How humbling and condemning they are! How much they prove our daily need of mercy and the precious blood of atonement! Happy would it be for the world if these rules were more known and more practised.

Love is the grand secret of true obedience to God. When we feel towards Him as children feel towards a dear father, we shall delight to do His will: we shall not find His commandments grievous, or work for Him like slaves under fear of the lash; we shall take pleasure in trying to keep His laws, and mourn when we transgress them. None work so well as they who work for love: the fear of punishment, or the desire of reward, are principles of far less power. They do the will of God best who do it from the heart. Would we train children right? Let us teach them to *love* God.

Love is the grand secret of right behaviour towards our fellow-men. He who loves his neighbour will scorn to do him any wilful injury, either in person, property, or character.—But he will not rest there: he will desire in every way to do him good; he will strive to promote his comfort and happiness in every way; he will endeavour to lighten his sorrows, and increase his joys. When a man loves us, we feel confidence in him: we know that he will never intentionally do us harm, and that in every time of need he will be our friend. Would we teach children to behave aright towards others? Let us teach them to "love everybody as themselves, and do to others as they would have others do to them."

But how shall we obtain this love towards God? It is no natural feeling. We are "born in sin," and as sinners, are afraid of Him: how then can we love Him? We can never really love Him till we are at peace with Him through Christ. When we feel our sins forgiven, and ourselves reconciled to our holy Maker, then, and not till then, we shall love Him and have the Spirit of adoption. Faith in Christ is the true spring of love to God: they love most who feel most forgiven. "We love Him because He first loved us." (1 John iv. 19.)

And how shall we obtain this love towards our neighbour? This also is no natural feeling. We are born selfish, hateful, and hating one another. (Titus iii. 3.) We shall never love our fellow-men aright till our hearts are changed by the Holy Ghost: we must be born again; we must put off the old man, and put on the new, and receive the mind that was in Christ Jesus. Then, and not till then, our cold hearts will know true God-like love towards all. "The fruit of the Spirit is love." (Gal. v. 22.)

Let these things sink down into our hearts. There is much vague talk in these latter days about "love" and "charity:" men profess to admire them and desire to see them increased, and yet hate the principles which alone can produce them. Let us stand fast in the old paths. We cannot have fruits and flowers without roots: we cannot have love to God and man without faith in Christ, and without regeneration. The way to spread true love in the world, is to teach the atonement of Christ, and the work of the Holy Ghost.

The concluding portion of the passage contains *a question put to the Pharisees by our Lord.* After answering with perfect wisdom the inquiries of His adversaries, He at last asks them, "What think ye of Christ? Whose Son is He?" They reply at once, "The Son of David." He then asks them to explain why David in the Book of Psalms calls Him Lord. (Psalm cx. 1.) "If David then call Him Lord, how is He his Son?" At once His enemies were put to silence: "No man was able to answer Him a word." The scribes and Pharisees no doubt were familiar with the Psalm He quoted, but they could not explain its application: it could only be explained by conceding the pre-existence and divinity of the Messiah. This the Pharisees would not concede: their only idea of Messiah was that He was to be a man like one of themselves: their ignorance of the Scriptures, of which they pretended to know more than others, and their low, carnal view of the true nature of Christ, were thus exposed at one and the same time. Well may Matthew say, by the Holy Ghost, "From that day forth durst no man ask Him any more questions."

Let us not leave these verses without making a practical use of our Lord's solemn question, "What think ye of Christ?" What do we think of His person, and His offices? What do we think of His life, and what of His death for us on the cross? What do we think of His resurrection, ascension, and intercession at the right hand of God? Have we tasted that He is gracious?

Have we laid hold on Him by faith? Have we found by experience that He is precious to our souls? Can we truly say, "He is my Redeemer and my Saviour, my Shepherd and my Friend"?

These are serious inquiries. May we never rest till we can give a satisfactory answer to them! It will not profit us to read about Christ, if we are not joined to Him by living faith. Once more then let us test our religion by this question: "What think we of Christ?"

MATTHEW XXIII. 1—12.

1 Then spake Jesus to the multitude, and to his disciples,
2 Saying, The scribes and the Pharisees sit in Moses' seat:
3 All therefore whatsoever they bid you observe, *that* observe and do; but do not ye after their works: for they say, and do not.
4 For they bind heavy burdens and grievous to be borne, and lay *them* on men's shoulders; but they *themselves* will not move them with one of their fingers.
5 But all their works they do for to be seen of men; they make broad their phylacteries, and enlarge the borders of their garments,
6 And love the uppermost rooms at feasts, and the chief seats in the synagogues,
7 And greetings in the markets, and to be called of men, Rabbi, Rabbi.
8 But be ye not called Rabbi: for one is your Master, *even* Christ; and all ye are brethren.
9 And call no *man* your father upon the earth: for one is your Father, which is in heaven.
10 Neither be ye called masters: for one is your master, *even* Christ.
11 But he that is greatest among you shall be your servant.
12 And whosoever shall exalt himself shall be abased: and he that shall humble himself shall be exalted.

We are now beginning a chapter which in one respect is the most remarkable in the four Gospels: it contains the last words which the Lord Jesus ever spoke within the walls of the temple. Those last words consist of a withering exposure of the scribes and Pharisees, and a sharp rebuke of their doctrines and practices. Knowing full well that His time on earth was drawing to a close, our Lord no longer keeps back His opinion of the leading teachers of the Jews. Knowing that He would soon leave His followers alone, like sheep among wolves, He warns them plainly against the false shepherds by whom they were surrounded.

The whole chapter is a signal example of boldness and faithfulness in denouncing error. It is a striking proof that it is possible for the most loving heart to use the language of stern reproof: above all, it is an awful evidence of the guilt of unfaithful teachers. So long as the world stands, this chapter ought to be a warning and a beacon to all ministers of religion: no sins are so sinful as their's in the sight of Christ.

In the twelve verses which begin the chapter, we see firstly, *the duty of distinguishing between the office of a false teacher and his example.* "The scribes and Pharisees sat in Moses' seat:" rightly or wrongly, they occupied the position of the chief public teachers of religion among the Jews; however unworthily they filled the place of authority, their office entitled them to respect. But while their office was respected, their bad lives were not to be copied: and although their teaching was to be adhered to, so long as it was Scriptural, it was not to be observed when it contradicted the Word of God. To use the words of a great divine, "They were to be heard when they taught what Moses taught," but no longer. That such was our Lord's meaning is evident from the whole tenor of the chapter we are reading: false doctrine is there denounced as well as false practice.

The duty here placed before us is one of great importance. There is a constant tendency in the human mind to run into extremes: if we do not regard the office of the minister with idolatrous veneration, we are apt to treat it with indecent contempt. Against both these extremes we have need to be on our guard. However much we may disapprove of a minister's practice, or dissent from his teaching, we must never forget to respect his office: we must show that we can honour the commission, whatever we may think of the officer that holds it. The example of St. Paul on a certain occasion is worthy of notice: "I wist not, brethren, that he was the high priest: for it is written, Thou shalt not speak evil of the ruler of thy people." (Acts xxiii. 5.)

We see, secondly, in these verses, *that inconsistency, ostentation, and love of pre-eminence, among professors of religion, are specially displeasing to Christ.* As to *inconsistency*, it is remarkable that the very first thing our Lord says of the Pharisees is, that "they say, and do not." They required from others what they did not practise themselves.—As to *ostentation*, our Lord declares, that they did all their works "to be seen of men:" they had their phylacteries, or strips of parchment with texts written on them, which many Jews wore on their clothes, made of an excessive size; they had the "borders," or fringes of their garments, which Moses bade Israelites to wear as a remembrance of God, made of an extravagant width (Num. xv. 38); and all this was done to attract notice, and to make people think how holy they were. —As to *love of pre-eminence*, our Lord tells us that the Pharisees loved to have "the chief seats" given them in public places, and to have flattering titles addressed to them. All these things our Lord holds up to reprobation:

against all He would have us watch and pray. They are soul-ruining sins: "How can ye believe which receive honour one of another?" (John v. 44.) Happy would it have been for the Church of Christ if this passage had been more deeply pondered and the spirit of it more implicitly obeyed. The Pharisees are not the only people who have imposed austerities on others, and affected a sanctity of apparel, and loved the praise of man. The annals of Church history show that only too many Christians have walked closely in their steps. May we remember this and be wise! It is perfectly possible for a baptized Englishman to be in spirit a thorough Pharisee.

We see, in the third place, from these verses, that *Christians must never give to any man the titles and honours which are due to God alone and to His Christ.* We are to "call no man Father on earth."

The rule here laid down must be interpreted with proper Scriptural qualification. We are not forbidden to esteem ministers very highly in love for their work's sake. (1 Thess. v. 13.) Even St. Paul, one of the humblest saints, called Titus "his own son in the faith," and says to the Corinthians, "I have begotten you through the Gospel." (1 Cor. iv. 15.) But still we must be very careful that we do not insensibly give to ministers a place and an honour which do not belong to them: we must never allow them to come between ourselves and Christ. The very best are not infallible. They are not priests who can atone for us; they are not mediators who can undertake to manage our soul's affairs with God: they are men of like passions with ourselves, needing the same cleansing blood, and the same renewing Spirit: set apart to a high and holy calling, but still after all only men. Let us never forget these things. Such cautions are always useful: human nature would always rather lean on a visible minister, than an invisible Christ.

We see, in the last place, that *there is no grace which should distinguish the Christian so much as humility.* He that would be great in the eyes of Christ, must aim at a totally different mark from that of the Pharisees: his aim must be, not so much to rule as to serve the Church. Well says Baxter, "Church *greatness* consisteth in being *greatly* serviceable." The desire of the Pharisee was to receive honour, and to be called "master;" the desire of the Christian must be to do good, and to give himself, and all that he has, to the service of others. Truly this is a high standard, but a lower one must never content us. The example of our blessed Lord, the direct command of the apostolic Epistles, both alike require us to be "clothed with humility." (1 Peter v. 5.) Let us seek that blessed grace day by day: none is so beautiful, however much despised by the world; none is such an evidence of saving faith and true conversion to God; none is so often commended by our Lord. Of all His sayings, hardly any is so often repeated as that which concludes the passage we have now read: "He that shall humble himself shall be exalted."

MATTHEW XXIII. 13—33.

13 But woe unto you, scribes and Pharisees, hypocrites! for ye shut up the kingdom of heaven against men: for ye neither go in *yourselves*, neither suffer ye them that are entering to go in.

14 Woe unto you, scribes and Pharisees, hypocrites! for ye devour widows' houses, and for a pretence make long prayer: therefore ye shall receive the greater damnation.

15 Woe unto you, scribes and Pharisees, hypocrites! for ye compass sea and land to make one proselyte, and when he is made, ye make him twofold more the child of hell than yourselves.

16 Woe unto you, *ye* blind guides, which say, Whosoever shall swear by the temple, it is nothing: but whosoever shall swear by the gold of the temple, he is a debtor!

17 *Ye* fools and blind: for whether is greater, the gold, or the temple that sanctifieth the gold?

18 And Whosoever shall swear by the altar, it is nothing; but whosoever sweareth by the gift that is upon it, he is guilty.

19 *Ye* fools and blind: for whether *is* greater, the gift, or the altar that sanctifieth the gift?

20 Whoso therefore shall swear by the altar, sweareth by it, and by all things thereon.

21 And whoso shall swear by the temple, sweareth by it, and by him that dwelleth therein.

22 And he that shall swear by heaven, sweareth by the throne of God, and by him that sitteth thereon.

23 Woe unto you, scribes and Pharisees, hypocrites! for ye pay tithe of mint and anise and cummin, and have omitted the weightier *matters* of the law, judgment, mercy, and faith: these ought ye to have done, and not to leave the other undone.

24 *Ye* blind guides, which strain at a gnat, and swallow a camel.

25 Woe unto you, scribes and Pharisees, hypocrites! for ye make clean the outside of the cup and of the platter, but within they are full of extortion and excess.

26 *Thou* blind Pharisee, cleanse first that *which* is within the cup and platter, that the outside of them may be clean also.

27 Woe unto you, scribes and Pharisees, hypocrites! for ye are like unto whited sepulchres, which indeed appear beautiful outward, but are within full of dead men's bones, and of all uncleanness.

28 Even so ye also outwardly appear righteous unto men, but within ye are full of hypocrisy and iniquity.

29 Woe unto you, scribes and Pharisees, hypocrites! because ye build the tombs of the prophets, and garnish the sepulchres of the righteous,

30 And say, If we had been in the days of our fathers, we would not have been partakers with them in the blood of the prophets.

31 Wherefore be ye witnesses unto yourselves, that ye are the children of them which killed the prophets.

32 Fill ye up then the measure of your fathers.

33 *Ye* serpents, *ye* generation of vipers, how can ye escape the damnation of hell?

WE have in these verses the charges of our Lord against the Jewish teachers, ranged under eight heads. Standing in the midst of the temple, with a listening crowd around Him, He publicly denounces the main errors of the scribes and Pharisees, in unsparing terms. Eight times He uses the solemn expression, "Woe unto you;" seven times He calls them "hypocrites;" twice He speaks of them as blind guides,—twice as "fools and blind,"—once as "serpents and a generation of vipers." Let us mark that language well. It teaches a solemn lesson. It shows how utterly abominable the spirit of the scribes and Pharisees is in God's sight, in whatever form it may be found.

Let us glance shortly at the eight charges which our Lord brings forward, and then seek to draw from the whole passage some general instruction.

The first "woe" in the list is directed against the systematic opposition of the scribes and Pharisees to the progress of the Gospel. They "shut up the kingdom of heaven:" they would neither go in themselves, nor suffer others to go in; they rejected the warning voice of John the Baptist; they refused to acknowledge Jesus, when He appeared among them as the Messiah; they tried to keep back Jewish inquirers. They would not believe the Gospel themselves, and they did all in their power to prevent others believing it: this was a great sin.

The second "woe" in the list is directed against the covetousness and self-aggrandizing spirit of the scribes and Pharisees. They "devoured widows' houses, and for a pretence made long prayer;" they imposed on the credulity of weak and unprotected women, by an affectation of great devoutness, until they were regarded as their spiritual directors. They scrupled not to abuse the influence, thus unrighteously obtained, to their own temporal advantage; and, in a word, to make money by their religion: this again was a great sin.

The third "woe" in the list is directed against the zeal of the scribes and Pharisees for making partizans. They "compassed sea and land to make one proselyte:" they laboured incessantly to make men join their party and adopt their opinions. They did this from no desire to benefit men's souls in the least, or to bring them to God; they only did it to swell the ranks of their sect, and to increase the number of their adherents, and their own importance. Their religious zeal arose from sectarianism, and not from the love of God: this also was a great sin.

The fourth "woe" in the list is directed against the doctrines of the scribes and Pharisees about oaths. They drew subtle distinctions between one kind of oath and another; they taught the Jesuitical tenet, that some oaths were binding on men, while others were not; they attached greater importance to oaths sworn "by the gold" offered to the temple, than to oaths sworn "by the temple" itself. By so doing they brought the third commandment into contempt,—and by making men overrate the value of alms and oblations, advanced their own interests: this again was a great sin.*

The fifth "woe" in the list is directed against the practice of the scribes and Pharisees to exalt trifles in religion above serious things; to put the last things first, and the first last. They made great ado about tithing "mint," and other garden herbs, as if they could not be too strict in their obedience to God's law; and yet at the same time they neglected great plain duties, such as justice, charity, and honesty: this again was a great sin.

* This practice of tampering with oaths was well known among the heathen as a feature in the Jewish character. It is a striklng fact that Martial, the Roman poet, specially refers to it.

"Ecce negas, jurasque mihi per templa Tonantis:
Non credo: Jura, verpe, per Anchialum."—MARTIAL ix. 94.

The sixth and seventh "woes" in the list possess too much in common to be divided. They are directed against a general characteristic of the religion of the scribes. They set outward purity and decency above inward sanctification and purity of heart; they made it a religious duty to cleanse the "outside" of their cups and platters, while they neglected their own inward man: they were like whitened sepulchres, clean and beautiful externally, but within full of all corruption. "Even so they outwardly appeared righteous, but within were full of hypocrisy and iniquity:" this also was a great sin.

The last "woe" in the list is directed against the affected veneration of the scribes and Pharisees for the memory of dead saints. They built the "tombs of the prophets," and garnished "the sepulchres of the righteous;" and yet their own lives proved that they were of one mind with those who "killed the prophets:" their own conduct was a daily evidence that they liked dead saints better than living ones. The very men that pretended to honour dead prophets, could see no beauty in a living Christ: this also was a great sin.*

Such is the melancholy picture which our Lord gives of Jewish teachers. Let us turn from the contemplation

* A passage from the Berlenberger Bible on this subject is sufficiently striking to deserve insertion.

"Ask in Moses's times who were the good people: they will be Abraham, Isaac, and Jacob, but not Moses,—he should be stoned. Ask in Samuel's times who were the good people: they will be Moses and Joshua, but not Samuel. Ask in the times of Christ who were such: they will be all the former prophets, with Samuel, but not Christ and His apostles."

The Latin proverbs "mortui non mordent," and "sit divus, dummodo non vivus," are both illustrative of the same truth.

of it with sorrow and humiliation. It is a fearful exhibition of the morbid anatomy of human nature: it is a picture which unhappily has been reproduced over and over again in the history of the Church of Christ. There is not a point in the character of the scribes and Pharisees in which it might not be easily shown that persons calling themselves Christians have often walked in their steps. *

Let us learn, from the whole passage, how deplorable was the condition of the Jewish nation when our Lord was upon earth. When such were the teachers, what must have been the miserable darkness of the taught! Truly the iniquity of Israel had come to the full. It was high time, indeed, for the Sun of Righteousness to arise, and for the Gospel to be preached.

Let us learn, from the whole passage, how abominable is hypocrisy in the sight of God. These scribes and Pharisees are not charged with being thieves or murderers, but with being hypocrites to the very core. Whatever we are in our religion, let us resolve never to wear a cloak: let us by all means be honest and real.

Let us learn, from the whole passage, how awfully dangerous is the position of an unfaithful minister. It is bad enough to be blind ourselves: it is a thousand times worse to be a blind guide. Of all men none is so

* I cannot resist the opportunity of here expressing my firm conviction that our Lord's sayings in this chapter were meant to bear a prophetical signification, and to apply to corruptions which He foresaw would spring up in His professing Church. Beyond doubt there is a most unhappy similarity between the doctrines and practices of the scribes and Pharisees, and many of the leading corruptions of the Church of Rome.

culpably wicked as an unconverted minister, and none will be judged so severely. It is a solemn saying about such an one, "He resembles an unskilful pilot: he does not perish alone."

Finally, let us beware of supposing from this passage that the safest course in religion is to make no profession at all. This is to run into a dangerous extreme. It does not follow that there is no such thing as true profession, because some men are hypocrites: it does not follow that all money is bad because there is much counterfeit coin. Let not hypocrisy prevent our confessing Christ, or move us from our steadfastness, if we have confessed Him. Let us press on, looking unto Jesus, and resting on Him, praying daily to be kept from error, and saying with David, "Let my heart be sound in Thy statutes." (Psalm cxix. 80.)

MATTHEW XXIII. 34–39.

34 Wherefore, behold I send unto you prophets, and wise men and scribes: and *some* of them ye shall kill and crucify: and *some* of them shall ye scourge in your synagogues, and persecute *them* from city to city.

35 That upon you may come all the righteous blood shed upon the earth, from the blood of righteous Abel unto the blood of Zacharias son of Barachias, whom ye slew between the temple and the altar.

36 Verily I say unto you, All these things shall come upon this generation.

37 O Jerusalem, Jerusalem, *thou* that killest the prophets, and stonest them which are sent unto thee, how often would I have gathered thy children together, even as a hen gathereth her chickens under *her* wings, and ye would not!

38 Behold your house is left unto you desolate.

39 For I say unto you, Ye shall not see me henceforth, till ye shall say, Blessed *is* he that cometh in the name of the Lord.

THESE verses form the conclusion of our Lord Jesus Christ's address on the subject of the scribes and Pharisees. They are the last words which He ever spoke, as a public teacher, in the hearing of the people. The characteristic tenderness and compassion of our Lord, shine forth in a striking manner at the close of His ministry. Though He left His enemies in unbelief, He shows that He loved and pitied them to the last.

We learn, in the first place, from these verses, that *God often takes great pains with ungodly men.* He sent the Jews "prophets, and wise men, and scribes." He gave them repeated warnings: He sent them message after message; He did not allow them to go on sinning without rebuke. They could never say they were not told when they did wrong.

This is the way in which God generally deals with unconverted Christians. He does not cut them off in their sins without a call to repentance: He knocks at the door of their hearts by sicknesses and afflictions; He assails their consciences by sermons, or by the advice of friends; He summons them to consider their ways by opening the grave under their eyes, and taking away from them their idols. They often know not what it all means; they are often blind and deaf to all His gracious messages: but they will see His hand at last, though perhaps too late. They will find that "God spake once, yea, twice, but they perceived it not." (Job xxxiii. 14.) They will discover that they too, like the Jews, had prophets, and wise men, and scribes, sent to them. There was a voice in every providence, "Turn ye, turn ye, why will ye die?" (Ezek. xxxiii. 11.)

We learn, in the second place, from these verses, that *God takes notice of the treatment which His messengers and ministers receive, and will one day reckon for it.* The

Jews, as a nation, had often given the servants of God most shameful usage: they had often dealt with them as enemies, because they told them the truth. Some they had persecuted, and some they had scourged, and some they had even killed. They thought, perhaps, that no account would be required of their conduct: but our Lord tells them they were mistaken. There was an eye that saw all their doings; there was a hand that registered all the innocent blood they shed, in books of everlasting remembrance. The dying words of Zacharias, who was "slain between the temple and the altar," would be found, after eight hundred and fifty years, not to have fallen to the ground.—He said, as he died, "The Lord look upon it and require it." (2 Chron. xxiv. 22.)* Yet a few years, and there would be such an inquisition for blood at Jerusalem as the world had never seen. The holy city would be destroyed. The nation which had murdered so many prophets would itself be wasted by famine, pestilence, and the sword; and even those that escaped would be scattered to the four winds, and become, like Cain the murderer, "fugitives and vagabonds upon earth." We all know how literally these sayings were fulfilled. Well might

* It is remarkable that the Zacharias here spoken of, is described in Chronicles as the son of Jehoiada. Our Lord speaks of him as the son of Barachias. This discrepancy has led some to suppose that the Zacharias here spoken of could not be the one who was murdered in the days of Joash, but an entirely different person. But there seems no sufficient reason for this supposition. By far the most satisfactory explanation appears to be, that the father of Zacharias had two names, Jehoiada and Barachias. It was not at all uncommon among the Jews to have two names. Matthew was called Levi; aud Jude, Thaddeus.

our Lord say, "Verily all these things shall come upon this generation."

It is good for us all to mark this lesson well. We are too apt to think that "bygones are bygones," and that things which to us are past, and done, and old, will never be raked up again. But we forget that with God "one day is as a thousand years," and that the events of a thousand years ago are as fresh in His sight as the events of this very hour. God "requireth that which is past" (Eccles. iii. 15), and above all, God will require an account of the treatment of His saints. The blood of the primitive Christians shed by the Roman Emperors; the blood of the Vallenses and Albigenses, and the sufferers at the massacre of St. Batholomew; the blood of the martyrs who were burned at the time of the Reformation, and of those who have been put to death by the Inquisition,—all, all will yet be accounted for. It is an old saying, that "the mill-stones of God's justice grind slowly, but they grind very fine." The world will yet see that "there is a God that judgeth in the earth." (Ps. lviii. 11.)

Let those who persecute God's people in the present day, take heed what they are doing. Let them know that all who injure, or ridicule, or mock, or slander others on account of their religion, commit a great sin. Let them know that Christ takes notice of every one who persecutes his neighbour because he is better than himself, or because he prays, reads his Bible, and thinks about his soul. He lives who said, "He that toucheth you, toucheth the apple of mine eye." (Zech. ii. 8.) The judgment-day will prove that the King of kings will reckon with all who insult His servants.

We learn, in the last place, from these verses, *that those who are lost for ever, are lost through their own fault.*

The words of our Lord Jesus Christ are very remarkable. He says, "I would have gathered thy children together,—and ye would not."

There is something peculiarly deserving of notice in this expression: it throws light on a mysterious subject, and one which is often darkened by human explanations. It shows that Christ has feelings of pity and mercy for many who are not saved, and that the grand secret of man's ruin is his want of will. Impotent as man is by nature,—unable to think a good thought of himself,—without power to turn himself to faith and calling upon God,—he still appears to have a mighty ability to ruin his own soul. Powerless as he is to good, he is still powerful to evil. We say rightly that a man can do nothing of himself, but we must always remember that the seat of impotence is his *will*. A will to repent and believe no man can give himself, but a will to reject Christ and have his own way, every man possesses by nature, and if not saved at last, that will shall prove to have been his destruction. "Ye *will* not come to Me," says Christ, "that ye might have life." (John v. 40.)

Let us leave the subject with the comfortable reflection that with Christ nothing is impossible. The hardest heart can be made willing in the day of His power. Grace beyond doubt is irresistible; but never let us forget that the Bible speaks of man as a *responsible* being, and that it says of some, "Ye do always resist the Holy Ghost." (Acts vii. 51.) Let us understand that the ruin of those who are lost, is not because Christ was not willing to save them,—nor yet because they wanted to be saved, but could not,—but because they would not come to Christ. Let the ground we take up be always that of the passage we are now considering: Christ would gather men, but they *will not* to be gathered; Christ would save men, but they *will not* to be saved. Let it be a settled principle in our religion, that man's salvation, if saved, is wholly of God; and that man's ruin, if lost, is wholly of himself. The evil that is in us is all our own: the good, if we have any, is all of God. The saved in the next world will give God all the glory: the lost in the next world will find that they have destroyed themselves. (Hosea xiii. 9.)

MATTHEW XXIV. 1—14.

1 And Jesus went out, and departed from the temple: and his disciples came to *him* for to shew him the buildings of the temple.

2 And Jesus said unto them, See ye not all these things? verily I say unto you, There shall not be left here one stone upon another, that shall not be thrown down.

3 And as he sat upon the mount of Olives, the disciples came unto him privately, saying, Tell us, when shall these things be? and what *shall be* the sign of thy coming, and of the end of the world?

4 And Jesus answered and said unto them, Take heed that no man deceive you.

5 For many shall come in my name saying, I am Christ; and shall deceive many.

6 And ye shall hear of wars and rumours of wars: see that ye be not troubled: for all *these things* must come to pass, but the end is not yet.

7 For nation shall rise against nation, and kingdom against kingdom: and there shall be famines and pestilences, and earthquakes, in divers places.

8 All these *are* the beginning of sorrows.

9 Then shall they deliver you up to be afflicted, and shall kill you: and ye shall be hated of all nations for my name's sake.

10 And then shall many be offended, and shall betray one another, and shall hate one another.

11 And many false prophets shall rise, and shall deceive many.

12 And because iniquity shall abound, the love of many shall wax cold.

13 But he that shall endure unto the end, the same shall be saved.

14 And this Gospel of the kingdom shall be preached in all the world for a witness unto all nations; and then shall the end come.

THESE verses begin a chapter full of prophecy: prophecy

of which a large portion is unfulfilled; prophecy which ought to be deeply interesting to all true Christians. It is a subject to which, the Holy Ghost says, we "do well to take heed." (2 Peter i. 19.)

All portions of Scripture like this ought to be approached with deep humility, and earnest prayer for the teaching of the Spirit. On no point have good men so entirely disagreed as on the interpretation of prophecy: on no point have the prejudices of one class, the dogmatism of a second, and the extravagance of a third, done so much to rob the Church of truths, which God intended to be a blessing. Well says a certain divine, "What does not man see, or fail to see, when it serves to establish his own favourite opinions?"

To understand the drift of the whole chapter we must carefully keep in view the question which gave rise to our Lord's discourse. On leaving the temple for the last time, the disciples, with the natural feeling of Jews, had called their Master's attention to the splendid buildings of which it was composed. To their surprise and amazement, He tells them that the whole was about to be destroyed. These words appear to have sunk deeply into the minds of the disciples. They came to Him, as He sat upon the Mount of Olives, and asked Him with evident anxiety, "Tell us when shall these things be? and what shall be the sign of Thy coming, and of the end of the world?"—In these words we see the clue to the subject of the prophecy now before us. It embraces three points: one, the destruction of Jerusalem; another, the second personal advent of Christ; and a third, the end of the world. These three points are undoubtedly in some parts of the chapter so entwined together that it is difficult to separate and disentangle them: but all these points appear distinctly in the chapter, and without them it cannot be fairly explained.

The first fourteen verses of the prophecy are taken up with general lessons of wide range and application. They seem to apply with equal force to the close of both Jewish and Christian dispensations, the one event being strikingly typical of the other. They certainly demand special notice from us, "on whom the ends of the world are come." (1 Cor. x. 11.) Let us now see what those lessons are.

The first general lesson before us is *a warning against deception.* The very first words of the discourse are, "Take heed that no man deceive you."

A more needful warning than this cannot be conceived. Satan knows well the value of prophecy, and has ever laboured to bring the subject into contempt. How many false Christs and false prophets arose before the destruction of Jerusalem, the works of Josephus abundantly prove. In how many ways the eyes of man are continually blinded in the present day, as to things to come, it might easily be shown. Irvingism and Mormonism have been only too successfully used as arguments for rejecting the whole doctrine of the second advent of Christ. Let us watch, and be on our guard.

Let no man deceive us as to the leading *facts* of unfulfilled prophecy, by telling us they are impossible,—or as to the *manner* in which they will be brought to pass, by telling us it is improbable, and contrary to past experience. Let no man deceive us as to the *time* when unfulfilled prophecies will be accomplished, either by fixing dates on the one hand, or bidding us wait for the conversion of the world on the other.—On all these points let the plain meaning of Scripture be our only guide, and not the traditional interpretations of men. Let us not be ashamed to say that we expect a literal fulfilment of unfulfilled prophecy: let us frankly allow that there are many things we do not understand, but still hold our ground tenaciously,—believe much, wait long,—and not doubt that all will one day be made clear: above all, let us remember that the first coming of Messiah to *suffer* was the most improbable event that could have been conceived, and let us not doubt that as He literally came in person to suffer, so He will literally come again in person to *reign.*

The second grand lesson before us is *a warning against over-sanguine and extravagant expectations as to things which are to happen before the end comes.* It is a warning as deeply important as the preceding one. Happy would it have been for the Church if it had not been so much neglected.

We are not to expect a reign of universal peace, happiness, and prosperity, before the end comes: if we do, we shall be greatly deceived. Our Lord bids us look for "wars, famines, pestilence," and persecution. It is vain to expect peace until the Prince of peace returns: then, and not till then, the swords shall be beaten into ploughshares, and nations learn war no more; then, and not till then, the earth shall bring forth her increase. (Isa. ii. 4; Ps. lxvii. 6.)

We are not to expect a time of universal purity of

doctrine and practice in the Church of Christ, before the end comes: if we do, we shall be greatly mistaken. Our Lord bids us look for the rising of "false prophets," the "abounding of iniquity," and the "waxing cold of the love of many." The truth will never be received by all professing Christians, and holiness will never be the rule among men, until the great Head of the Church returns, and Satan is bound: then, and not till then, there will be a glorious Church, without spot or blemish. (Ephes. v. 27.)

We are not to expect that all the world will be converted before the end comes: if we do, we shall be greatly mistaken. "The Gospel is to be *preached* in all the world for a witness unto all nations," but we must not think that we shall see it universally *believed.* It will "take out a people," wherever it is faithfully preached, as witnesses to Christ, but the full gathering of the nations shall never take place until Christ comes: then, and not till then, shall the earth be full of the knowledge of the Lord, as the waters cover the sea. (Acts xv. 14; Habak. ii. 14.)

Let us lay these things to heart, and remember them well. They are eminently truths for the present times. Let us learn to be moderate in our expectations from any existing machinery in the Church of Christ, and we shall be spared much disappointment: let us make haste to spread the Gospel in the world, for the time is *short, not long.*—The night cometh when no man can work. Troublous times are a-head. Heresies and persecutions may soon weaken and distract the Churches; a fierce war of principles may soon convulse the nations; the doors now open to do good may soon be shut for ever: our eyes may yet see the sun of Christianity go down like the sun of Judaism, in clouds and storm. Above all, let us long for our Lord's return. May we all have a heart to pray daily, "Come, Lord Jesus!" (Rev. xxii. 20.)

MATTHEW XXIV. 15—28.

15 When ye therefore shall see the abomination of desolation, spoken of by Daniel the prophet, stand in the holy place, (whoso readeth, let him understand:)

16 Then let them which be in Judæa flee into the mountains:

17 Let him which is on the housetop not come down to take any thing out of his house:

18 Neither let him which is in the field return back to take his clothes.

19 And woe unto them that are with child, and to them that give suck in those days!

20 But pray ye that your flight be not in the winter, neither on the sabbath day;

21 For then shall be great tribulation, such as was not since the beginning of the world to this time, no, nor ever shall be.

22 And except those days should be shortened, there should no flesh be saved: but for the elect's sake those days shall be shortened.

23 Then if any man shall say unto you, Lo, here *is* Christ, or there: believe *it* not.

24 For there shall arise false Christs, and false prophets, and shall shew great signs and wonders; insomuch that, if *it were* possible, they shall deceive the very elect.

25 Behold I have told you before.

26 Wherefore if they shall say unto you, Behold he is in the desert; go not forth: behold *he is* in the secret chambers; believe *it* not.

27 For as the lightning cometh out of the east, and shineth even unto the west; so shall also the coming of the Son of man be.

28 For wheresoever the carcase is, there will the eagles be gathered together.

ONE main subject of this part of our Lord's prophecy is the taking of Jerusalem by the Romans. That great event took place about forty years after the words we have now read were spoken. A full account of it is to be found in the writings of the historian Josephus: those writings are the best comment on our Lord's words; they are a striking proof of the accuracy of every tittle of His predictions.* The horrors and miseries which

* These are the words of Josephus. They are the more remarkable when we remember that he was not a Christian. "No

the Jews endured throughout the siege of their city exceed anything on record: it was truly a time of tribulation, such as was not since the beginning of the world."

It surprises some to find so much importance attached to the taking of Jerusalem: they would rather regard the whole chapter as unfulfilled. Such persons forget that Jerusalem and the temple were the heart of the old Jewish dispensation: when they were destroyed, the old Mosaic system came to an end. The daily sacrifice, the yearly feasts, the altar, the holy of holies, the priesthood, were all essential parts of revealed religion, till Christ came,—but no longer. When He died upon the cross, their work was done: they were dead, and it only remained that they should be buried.—But it was not fitting that this thing should be done quietly. The ending of a dispensation given with so much solemnity at mount Sinai, might well be expected to be marked with peculiar solemnity; the destruction of the holy temple, where so many old saints had seen "shadows of good things to come," might well be expected to form a subject of prophecy: and so it was. The Lord Jesus specially predicts the desolation of "the holy place." The great High Priest describes the end of the dispensation which had been a schoolmaster to bring men to Himself.

But we must not suppose that this part of our Lord's prophecy is exhausted by the first taking of Jerusalem. It is more than probable that our Lord's words have a

other city ever suffered such things. All the calamities which have ever happened to any from the beginning, seem not comparable to those which befel the Jews."

further and deeper application still. It is more than probable that they apply to a *second siege of Jerusalem*, which is yet to take place, when Israel has returned to their own land; and to a *second tribulation* on the inhabitants thereof, which shall only be stopped by the advent of our Lord Jesus Christ. Such a view of this passage may sound startling to some.* But those who doubt its correctness would do well to study the last chapter of the prophet Zechariah, and the last chapter of Daniel. These two chapters contain solemn things: they throw great light on these verses we are now reading, and their connection with the verses which immediately follow.

It now remains for us to consider the lessons which this passage contains for our own personal edification. These lessons are plain and unmistakable: in them at least there is no darkness at all.

For one thing, we see that *flight from danger may sometimes be the positive duty of a Christian.* Our Lord Himself commanded His people under certain circumstances "to flee."

The servant of Christ undoubtedly is not to be a coward. He is to confess his Master before men; he is to be willing to die, if needful, for the truth: but the servant of Christ is not required to run into danger, unless it comes in the line of duty. He is not to be

* I think it well to say that Irenœus and Hilary among the Fathers, and Ferus in the sixteenth century, all refer the fulfilment of this part of our Lord's prophecy to the end of the world, when a personal Antichrist shall appear. Hilary considers that the verse which speaks of "the abomination of desolation standing in the holy place," will be fulfilled by the rise of a mighty personal Antichrist who shall be worshipped by infidels. In connection with this verse, 2 Thess. ii. 4, deserves attentive study.

ashamed to use reasonable means to provide for his personal safety, when no good is to be done by dying at his post. There is deep wisdom in this lesson. The true martyrs are not always those who court death, and are in a hurry to be beheaded or burned. There are times when it shows more grace to be quiet, and wait, and pray, and watch for opportunities, than to defy our adversaries, and rush into the battle. May we have wisdom to know how to act in time of persecution! It is possible to be rash as well as to be a coward; and to stop our own usefulness by being over hot as well as by being over cold.

We see, for another thing, that *in delivering this prophecy our Lord makes special mention of the Sabbath.* "Pray ye," He says, "that your flight be not on the Sabbath day."

This is a fact that deserves special notice. We live in times when the obligation of the Sabbath upon Christians is frequently denied by good men. They tell us that it is no more binding on us than the ceremonial law. It is difficult to see how such a view can be reconciled with our Lord's words on this solemn occasion. He seems intentionally to mention the Sabbath, when He is foretelling the final destruction of the temple and the Mosaic ceremonies, as if to mark the day with honour. He seems to hint that although His people would be absolved from the yoke of sacrifices and ordinances, there would yet remain the keeping of a Sabbath for them. (Heb. iv. 9.) The friends of a holy Sunday ought carefully to remember this text. It is one which will bear much weight.

We see, for another thing, *that God's elect are always special objects of God's care.* Twice in this passage our Lord mentions them. "For the elect's sake the days of tribulation are to be shortened." It will not be possible to deceive the "elect."

Those whom God has chosen to salvation by Christ are those whom God specially loves in this world: they are the jewels among mankind. He cares more for them than for kings on their thrones, if kings are not converted; He hears their prayers; He orders all the events of nations, and the issues of wars, for their good and their sanctification; He keeps them by His Spirit; He allows neither man nor devil to pluck them out of His hand. Whatever tribulation comes on the world, God's elect are safe. May we never rest till we know that we are of this blessed number! There breathes not the man or woman who can prove that he is not one. The promises of the Gospel are open to all. May we give diligence to make our calling and election sure! God's elect are a people who cry unto Him night and day. When Paul saw the faith, and hope, and love of the Thessalonians, then he knew "their election of God." (1 Thess. i. 4; Luke xviii. 7.)

Finally, we see from these verses, that *whenever the second advent of Christ takes place it will be a very sudden event.* It will be "as the lightning coming out of the east, and shining even to the west."

This is a practical truth that we should ever keep before our minds. That our Lord Jesus will come again in person to this world, we know from Scripture; that He will come in a time of great tribulation, we also know:

but the precise period, the year, the month, the day, the hour, are all hidden things. We only know that it will be a very sudden event. Our plain duty then is to live always prepared for His return. Let us walk by faith, and not by sight; let us believe on Christ, serve Christ, follow Christ, and love Christ: so living, whenever Christ may return, we shall be ready to meet Him.

MATTHEW XXIV. 29—35.

29 Immediately after the tribulation of those days shall the sun be darkened, and the moon shall not give her light, and the stars shall fall from heaven, and the powers of the heavens shall be shaken:

30 And then shall appear the sign of the Son of man in heaven: and then shall all the tribes of the earth mourn, and they shall see the Son of man coming in the clouds of heaven with power and great glory.

31 And he shall send his angels with a great sound of a trumpet, and they shall gather together his elect from the four winds, from one end of heaven to the other.

32 Now learn a parable of the fig tree; When his branch is yet tender, and putteth forth leaves, ye know that summer *is* nigh:

33 So likewise ye, when ye shall see all these things, know that it is near, *even* at the doors.

34 Verily I say unto you, This generation shall not pass, till all these things be fulfilled.

35 Heaven and earth shall pass away, but my words shall not pass away.

In this part of our Lord's prophecy He describes His own second coming to judge the world. This, at all events, seems the natural meaning of the passage: to take any lower view appears to be a violent straining of Scripture language. If the solemn words here used mean nothing more than the coming of the Roman armies to Jerusalem, we may explain away anything in the Bible. The event here described is one of far greater moment than the march of an earthly army; it is nothing less than the closing act of the present dispensation,—the second personal advent of Jesus Christ.

These verses teach us, in the first place, *that when the*

Lord Jesus returns to this world He shall come with peculiar glory and majesty. He shall come "in the clouds of heaven with power and great glory." Before His presence the very sun, moon, and stars shall be darkened, and "the powers of heaven shall be shaken."

The second personal coming of Christ shall be as different as possible from the first. He came the first time as "a man of sorrows and acquainted with grief:" He was born in the manger of Bethlehem, in lowliness and humiliation; He took on Him the form of a servant, and was despised and rejected of men; He was betrayed into the hands of wicked men; condemned by an unjust judgment, mocked, scourged, crowned with thorns, and at last crucified between two thieves.—He shall come the second time as the King of all the earth, with royal majesty: the princes and great men of this world shall themselves stand before His throne to receive an eternal sentence: before Him every mouth shall be stopped, and every knee bow, and every tongue shall confess that Jesus Christ is Lord. May we all remember this! Whatever ungodly men may do now, there will be no scoffing, no jesting at Christ, no infidelity at the last day. The servants of Jesus may well wait patiently: their Master shall one day be acknowledged King of kings by all the world.

These verses teach us, in the second place, *that when Christ returns to this world He will first take care of His believing people.* He shall "send His angels," and "gather together His elect."

When Christ returns in glory and the judgment begins, true Christians shall be perfectly safe. Not a hair of their heads shall fall to the ground: not one bone of Christ's mystical body shall be broken. There was an ark for Noah, in the day of the flood; there was a Zoar for Lot, when Sodom was destroyed; there shall be a hiding-place for all believers in Jesus, when the wrath of God at last bursts on this wicked world. Those mighty angels who rejoiced in heaven when each sinner repented, shall gladly catch up the people of Christ to meet their Lord in the air. The day of Christ's second advent no doubt will be an awful day, but believers may look forward to it without fear.

When Christ returns in glory, true Christians shall at length be gathered together. The saints of every age and every tongue shall be assembled out of every land: all shall be there, from righteous Abel down to the last soul that is converted to God,—from the oldest patriarch down to the little infant that just breathed and died. Let us think what a happy gathering that will be, when all the family of God are at length together. If it has been pleasant to meet one or two saints occasionally on earth, how much more pleasant will it be to meet a "multitude that no man can number!" Surely we may be content to carry the cross, and to put up with partings for a few years. We travel on towards a day, when we shall meet to part no more.

These verses teach us, in the third place, that *until Christ returns to this earth the Jews will always remain a separate people.* Our Lord tells us, "This generation shall not pass till all these things be fulfilled." *

* I see no other interpretation of these much controverted words, "this generation," which is in the least satisfactory,

The continued existence of the Jews as a distinct nation is undeniably a great miracle: it is one of those evidences of the truth of the Bible which the Infidel can never overthrow. Without a land, without a king, without a government, scattered and dispersed over the world for eighteen hundred years, the Jews are never absorbed among the people of the countries where they live, like Frenchmen, Englishmen, and Germans,—but "dwell alone." (Numb. xxiii. 9.) Nothing can account for this but the finger of God. The Jewish nation stands before the world a crushing answer to infidelity, and a living book of evidence that the Bible is true. But we ought not to regard the Jews only as witnesses of the truth of Scripture; we should see in them a continual pledge, that the Lord Jesus is coming again one day. Like the sacrament of the Lord's Supper, they witness to the reality of the second advent, as well as of the first. Let us remember this. Let us see in every wandering Jew a proof that the Bible is true, and that Christ will one day return.

Finally, there verses teach us *that our Lord's predictions will certainly be fulfilled.* He says, "Heaven and earth shall pass away, but my words shall not pass away."

and is not open to very serious objections. The word "generation" admits of the sense in which I have taken it, and seems to me to be used in that sense in Matt. xii. 45, xvii. 17, and xxiii. 36; Luke xvi. 8, and xvii. 25: and Philip. ii. 15. The view that I have propounded is not new. It is adopted by Mede, Parœus, Flacius, Illyricus, Calovius, Jansenius, Du Veil, Adam Clarke, and Steir.

Chrysostom, Origen, and Theophylact consider "this generation" to mean "true believers."

Our Lord knew well the natural unbelief of human nature. He knew that "scoffers would arise in the last days, saying, Where is the promise of His coming?" (2 Pet. iii. 4.) He knew that when He came, faith would be rare on the earth. He foresaw how many would contemptuously reject the solemn predictions He had just been delivering, as improbable, unlikely, and absurd. He warns us against such sceptical thoughts, with a caution of peculiar solemnity: He tells us that, whatever man may say or think, His words shall be fulfilled in their season, and shall not "pass away" unaccomplished. May we all lay to heart His warning! We live in an unbelieving age. Few believed the report of our Lord's first coming, and few believe the report of His second. (Isaiah liii. 1.) Let us beware of this infection, and believe to the saving of our souls. We are not reading "cunningly devised fables," but deep and momentous truths: may God give us a heart to believe them!

MATTHEW XXIV. 36—51.

36 But of that day and hour knoweth no *man*, no, not the angels of heaven, but my Father only.

37 But as the days of Noe *were*, so shall also the coming of the Son of man be.

38 For as in the days that were before the flood they were eating and drinking, marrying and giving in marriage, until the day that Noe entered into the ark,

39 And knew not until the flood came, and took them all away; so shall also the coming of the Son of man be.

40 Then shall two be in the field; the one shall be taken, and the other left.

41 Two *women shall* be grinding at the mill; the one shall be taken, and the other left.

42 Watch therefore: for ye know not what hour your Lord doth come.

43 But know this, that if the goodman of the house had known in what watch the thief would come, he would have watched, and would not have suffered his house to be broken up.

44 Therefore be ye also ready: for in such an hour as ye think not the Son of man cometh.

45 Who then is a faithful and wise servant, whom his lord hath made ruler over his household, to give them meat in due season?

46 Blessed *is* that servant, whom his lord when he cometh shall find so doing.

47 Verily I say unto you, That he shall make him ruler over all his goods.
48 But and if that evil servant shall say in his heart, My Lord delayeth his coming;
49 And shall begin to smite *his* fellow-servants, and to eat and drink with the drunken;
50 The Lord of that servant shall come in a day when he looketh not for *him*, and in an hour that he is not aware of.
51 And shall cut him asunder, and appoint *him* his portion with the hypocrites : there shall be weeping and gnashing of teeth.

THERE are verses in this passage which are often much misapplied. "The coming of the Son of man" is frequently spoken of as being the same thing as death; the texts which describe the uncertainty of His coming are used in epitaphs, and thought suitable to the tomb: but there is no solid ground for such an application of this passage. Death is one thing, and the coming of the Son of man is quite another: the subject of these verses is not death, but the second advent of Jesus Christ. Let us remember this. It is a serious thing to wrest Scripture and use it in any but its true meaning.

The first thing that demands our attention in these verses, *is the awful account that they give of the state of the world when the Lord Jesus comes again.*

The world will not be converted when Christ returns: it will be found in the same condition that it was in the day of the flood. When the flood came, men were found "eating and drinking, marrying and giving in marriage," absorbed in their worldly pursuits, and utterly regardless of Noah's repeated warnings. They saw no likelihood of a flood; they would not believe there was any danger: but at last the flood came suddenly and took them all away." All that were not with Noah in the ark were drowned: they were all swept away to their last account, unpardoned, unconverted, and unprepared to meet God. And our Lord says, "So shall also the coming of the Son of man be."

Let us mark this text, and store it up in our minds. There are many strange opinions current on this subject, even among good men. Let us not flatter ourselves that the heathen will all be converted, and the earth filled with the knowledge of God, before the Lord comes; let us not dream that the end of all things cannot be at hand, because there is yet much wickedness both in the Church and in the world. Such views receive a flat contradiction in the passage now before us: the days of Noah are the true type of the days when Christ shall return. Millions of professing Christians will be found thoughtless, unbelieving, Godless, Christless, worldly, and unfit to meet their Judge. Let us take heed that we are not found amongst them.

The second thing that demands our attention is *the awful separation that will take place when the Lord Jesus comes again.* We read twice over, that "One shall be taken and the other left."

The godly and the ungodly at present are mingled together; in the congregation, and in the place of worship, in the city and in the field, the children of God and the children of the world are all side by side: but it shall not be so always. In the day of our Lord's return, there shall at length be a complete division. In a moment, in the twinkling of an eye, at the last trumpet, each party shall be separated from the other for evermore. Wives shall be separated from husbands, parents from children, brothers from sisters, masters from servants, preachers from hearers. There shall be no time for repentance, or a change of mind, when the Lord appears: all shall be taken *as they are*, and reap according as they have sown. Believers shall be caught up to glory, honour, and eternal life; unbelievers shall be left behind to shame and everlasting contempt. Blessed and happy are they who are of one heart in following Christ! Their union alone shall never be broken: it shall last for evermore.—Who can describe the happiness of those who are taken, when the Lord returns? Who can imagine the misery of those who are left behind? May we think on these things, and consider our ways!

The last thing that demands our attention in these verses, is *the practical duty of watchfulness in the prospect of Christ's second coming.* "Watch," says our Lord, "for ye know not what hour your Lord doth come."—"Be ye ready, for in such an hour as ye think not, the Son of man cometh."

This is a point which our blessed Master frequently presses upon our notice: we hardly ever find Him dwelling on the second advent without adding an injunction to "watch." He knows the sleepiness of our nature; He knows how soon we forget the most solemn subjects in religion; He knows how unceasingly Satan labours to obscure the glorious doctrine of His coming again: He arms us with heart-searching exhortations to keep awake, if we would not be ruined for evermore. May we all have an ear to hear them!

True Christians ought to live like watchmen. The day of the Lord so cometh as a thief in the night: they should strive to be always on their guard; they should behave like the sentinel of an army in an enemy's land: they should resolve by God's grace not to sleep at their post. That text of St. Paul's deserves many a thought: "Let us not sleep as do others; but let us watch and be sober." (1 Thes. v. 6.)

True Christians ought to live like good servants, whose master is not at home. They should strive to be always ready for their Master's return: they should never give way to the feeling, "My Lord delayeth His coming;" they should seek to keep their hearts in such a frame, that whenever Christ appears they may at once give Him a warm and loving reception. There is a vast depth in the saying, "Blessed is that servant, whom his Lord when He cometh shall find so doing." We may well doubt whether we are true believers in Jesus if we are not ready at any time to have our faith changed into sight.

Let us close the chapter with solemn feelings. The things we have just been reading call loudly for great searchings of heart. Let us seek to make sure that we are in Christ, and that we shall have an ark of safety when the day of wrath breaks on the world; let us strive so to live that we may be pronounced "blessed" at the last, and not cast off for evermore. Not least, let us dismiss from our minds the common idea that unfulfilled prophecy is a speculative and not a practical thing: if the things we have been considering are not practical, there is no such thing as practical religion at all. Well might St. John say, "Every man that hath *this hope in him* purifieth himself, even as He is pure." (1 John iii. 3.)

MATTHEW XXV. 1—13.

1 Then shall the kingdom of heaven be likened unto ten virgins, which took their lamps, and went forth to meet the bridegroom.

2 And five of them were wise, and five *were* foolish.

3 They that *were* foolish took their lamps, and took no oil with them:

4 But the wise took oil in their vessels with their lamps.

5 While the bridegroom tarried, they all slumbered and slept.

6 And at midnight there was a cry made, Behold, the bridegroom cometh; go ye out to meet him.

7 Then all those virgins arose, and trimmed their lamps.

8 And the foolish said unto the wise, Give us of your oil; for our lamps are gone out.

9 But the wise answered, saying, *Not so*; least there be not enough for us and you: but go ye rather to them that sell, and buy for yourselves.

10 And while they went to buy, the bridegroom came; and they that were ready went in with him to the marriage: and the door was shut.

11 Afterward came also the other virgins, saying, Lord, Lord, open to us.

12 But he answered and said, Verily I say unto you, I know you not.

13 Watch therefore, for ye know neither the day nor the hour wherein the Son of man cometh.

THE chapter we have now begun is a continuation of our Lord's prophetical discourse on the Mount of Olives. The time to which it refers is plain and unmistakable: from first to last, there is a continual reference to the second advent of Christ, and the end of the world. The whole chapter contains three great divisions. In the first, our Lord uses His own second coming as an argument for watchfulness and heart-religion: this He does by the parable of the ten virgins. In the second, He uses His own second coming as an argument for diligence and faithfulness: this He does by the parable of the talents. In the third, He winds up all by a description of the great day of judgment: a passage which for majesty and beauty stands unequalled in the New Testament.

The parable of the ten virgins, which we have now read, contains lessons peculiarly solemn and awakening.

Let us see what they are.

We see, for one thing, that *the second coming of Christ*

will find His Church a mixed body, containing evil as well as good.

The professing Church is compared to "ten virgins, who took their lamps and went forth to meet the bridegroom:" all of them had lamps, but only five had oil in their vessels to feed the flame; all of them professed to have one object in view, but five only were truly "wise," and the rest were foolish. The visible Church of Christ is just in the same condition: all its members are baptized in the name of Christ, but not all really hear His voice and follow Him; all are called Christians, and profess to be of the Christian religion, but not all have the grace of the Spirit in their hearts, and really are what they profess to be. Our own eyes tell us that it is so now: the Lord Jesus tells us that it will be so when He comes again."* Let us mark well this description. It is a humbling picture. After all our preaching and praying,—after

* I think it is fair to say that a different view of this parable is held by some interpreters. They consider that all the ten virgins represent true believers, and that the five foolish ones are believers that fall away,—or believers that are only shut out from certain privileges at the Lord's return, and are finally saved.

I cannot admit the correctness of this view. It appears to me to do great violence to the plain meaning of the conclusion of the parable, to be out of keeping with the general tenor of our Lord's discourse in this place, and to contradict many texts of Scripture.

I believe that the ten virgins represent the two great classes which compose the visible Church of Christ,—the converted and the unconverted,—the false professors and the real Christians —the hypocrites and the true believers,—the foolish builders and the wise builders,—the good fish and the bad,—the living and the dead,—the wheat and the tares.

This view is neither new nor uncommon. It is held in the main, by the following commentators:—Bullinger, Brentius, Gualter, Pellican, Beza, Ferus, Parœus, Piscator, Musculus, Leigh, Baxter, Quesnel, Poole, Manton, Henry, Burkitt, Doddridge, Gill, and Scott.

all our visiting and teaching,—after all our missionary exertions abroad, and means of grace at home, many will be found at last dead in trespasses and sins!" The wickedness and unbelief of human nature is a subject about which we all have much to learn.

We see, for another thing, that *Christ's second coming, whenever it may be, will take men by surprise.*

This is a truth which is set before us in the parable, in a very striking manner. "At midnight," when the virgins were slumbering and sleeping, there was a cry, "The bridegroom cometh; go ye forth to meet him." It will be just the same when Jesus returns to the world. He will find the vast majority of mankind utterly unbelieving and unprepared; He will find the bulk of His believing people in a sleepy and indolent state of soul. Business will be going on in town and country just as it does now; politics, trades, farming, buying, selling, pleasure-seeking, will be taking up men's attention, just as they do now; rich men will still be faring sumptuously, and poor men murmuring and complaining; Churches will still be full of divisions, or wrangling about trifles; theological controversies will be still raging; ministers will still be calling men to repent, and the vast majority in all congregations will be still putting off the day of decision. —In the midst of all this, the Lord Jesus Himself shall suddenly appear. In an hour when no man thinketh, the startled world shall be summoned to break off all its employments, and to stand before its lawful King. There is something unspeakably awful in the idea: but thus it is written, and thus it shall be. Well might a dying minister say, "We are none of us more than half-awake."

We see, in the next place, that *when the Lord comes again many will find out the value of saving religion too late.*

The parable tells us that when the bridegroom came, the foolish virgins said unto the wise, "Give us of your oil; for our lamps are gone out." It tells us further, that as the wise had no oil to spare, the foolish went to "buy for themselves." It tells us finally, that they came when the door was shut, and asked in vain for admission: "Lord, Lord," they cried, "open unto us." All these expressions are striking emblems of things to come. Let us take heed that we do not find them true by experience, to our own eternal ruin.

We may settle it in our minds that there will be an entire change of opinion one day as to the necessity of decided Christianity. At present, we must all be aware, the vast majority of professing Christians care nothing at all about it: they have no sense of sin; they have no love towards Christ; they know nothing of being born again. Repentance, and faith, and grace, and holiness, are mere "words and names" to them; they are subjects which they either dislike, or about which they feel no concern. But this state of things shall one day come to an end. Knowledge, conviction, the value of the soul, the need of a Saviour, shall all burst on men's minds one day like a flash of lightning. But it will be too late! It will be too late to be buying oil when the Lord returns. The mistakes that are not found out till that day are irretrievable.

Are we ever mocked, and persecuted, and thought foolish because of our religion? Let us bear it patiently and pray for those who persecute us: they know not what they are doing; they will certainly alter their minds one day. We may yet hear them confessing that we were "wise" and they were "foolish." The whole world shall one day acknowledge that the saints of God made a wise choice.

We see, lastly, in this parable, *that when Christ returns true Christians shall receive a rich reward for all they have suffered for their Master's sake.* We are told that when the bridegroom came, "they that were ready went in with him to the marriage: and the door was shut."

True Christians shall alone be found ready at the second advent. Washed in the blood of atonement, clothed in Christ's righteousness, renewed by the Spirit, they shall meet their Lord with boldness, and sit down at the marriage supper of the Lamb, to go out no more. Surely this is a blessed prospect.

They shall be with their Lord: with Him who loved them and gave Himself for them; with Him who bore with them, and carried them through their earthly pilgrimage: with Him whom they loved truly and followed faithfully on earth, though with much weakness, and many a tear. Surely this is also a blessed prospect.

The door shall be shut at last: shut on all pain and sorrow; shut on an illnatured and wicked world; shut on a tempting devil; shut on all doubts and fears; shut to be opened again no more. Surely we may again say, this is a blessed prospect.

Let us remember these things: they will bear meditation; they are all true. The believer may have much tribulation, but he has before him abounding consolations. "Weeping may endure for a night, but joy cometh in the morning." (Psalm xxx. 5.) The day of Christ's return shall surely make amends for all.

Let us leave this parable with a settled determination never to be content with anything short of indwelling grace in our hearts. The lamp and the name of Christian, the profession and the ordinances of Christianity, are all well in their way, but they are not the "one thing needful." Let us never rest till we know that we have the oil of the Spirit in our hearts.

MATTHEW XXV. 14—30.

14 For *the kingdom of heaven is* as a man travelling into a far country, *who* called his own servants, and delivered unto them his goods.

15 And unto one he gave five talents, to another two, and to another one; to every man according to his several ability; and straightway took his journey.

16 Then he that had received the five talents went and traded with the same, and made *them* other five talents.

17 And likewise he that had *received* two, he also gained other two.

18 But he that had received one went and digged in the earth, and hid his lord's money.

19 After a long time the lord of those servants cometh, and reckoneth with them.

20 And so he that had received five talents came and brought other five talents, saying, Lord, thou deliveredst unto me five talents: behold, I have gained beside them five talents more.

21 His lord said unto him, Well done, *thou* good and faithful servant: thou hast been faithful over a few things, I will make thee ruler over many things: enter thou into the joy of thy lord.

22 He also that had received two talents came and said, Lord, thou deliveredst unto me two talents: behold, I have gained two other talents beside them.

23 His lord said unto him, Well done, good and faithful servant; thou hast been faithful over a few things, I will make thee ruler over many things: enter thou into the joy of thy lord.

24 Then he which had received the one talent came and said, Lord, I knew thee that thou art an hard man, reaping where thou hast not sown, and gathering where thou hast not strawed:

25 And I was afraid, and went and hid thy talent in the earth: lo, *there* thou hast *that* is thine.

26 His lord answered and said unto him, *Thou* wicked and slothful servant, thou knewest that I reap where I sowed not, and gather where I have not strawed:

27 Thou oughtest therefore to have put my money to the exchangers, and *then* at my coming I should have received mine own with usury.

28 Take therefore the talent from him, and give *it* unto him which hath ten talents.

29 For unto every one that hath shall be given, and he shall have abundance: but from him that hath not shall be taken away even that which he hath.

30 And cast ye the unprofitable servant into outer darkness: there shall be weeping and gnashing of teeth.

THE parable of the talents, which we have now read, is near akin to that of the ten virgins. Both direct our minds to the same important event: the second advent of Jesus Christ. Both bring before us the same persons: the members of the professing Church of Christ. The virgins and the servants are one and the same people,—but the same people regarded from a different point, and viewed on different sides. The practical lesson of each parable is the main point of difference: vigilance is the key note of the first parable; diligence that of the second. The story of the virgins calls on the Church to watch; the story of the talents calls on the Church to work.

We learn, in the first place, from this parable, *that all professing Christians have received something from God.* We are all God's "servants:" we have all "talents" entrusted to our charge.

The word "talents" is an expression that has been curiously turned aside from its original meaning. It is generally applied to none but people of remarkable ability or gifts: they are called "talented" people. Such an use of the expression is a mere modern invention. In the sense in which our Lord used the word in this parable, it applies to all baptized persons without distinction. We have all "talents" in God's sight: we are all talented people.

Anything whereby we may glorify God is "a talent."

Our gifts, our influence, our money, our knowledge, our health, our strength, our time, our senses, our reason, our intellect, our memory, our affections, our privileges as members of Christ's Church, our advantages as possessors of the Bible,—all, all are talents. Whence came these things? What hand bestowed them? Why are we what we are? Why are we not the worms that crawl on the earth? There is only one answer to these questions: all that we have is a loan from God: we are God's stewards; we are God's debtors. Let this thought sink deeply into our hearts.

We learn, in the second place, that *many make a bad use of the privileges and mercies they receive from God.* We are told in the parable of one who "digged in the earth and hid his Lord's money." That man represents a large class of mankind.

To hide our talent is to neglect opportunities of glorifying God, when we have them. The baptized Bible-despiser, the prayer-neglecter, and the Sabbath-breaker; the unbelieving, the sensual, and the earthly-minded; the trifler, the thoughtless and the pleasure-seeker; the money-lover, the covetous, and the self-indulgent,—all, all are alike burying their Lord's money in the ground. They have all light that they do not use: they might all be better than they are. But they are all daily robbing God: He has lent them much, and they make Him no return. The words of Daniel to Belshazzar are strictly applicable to every unconverted person: "The God in whose hand thy breath is, and whose are all thy ways, hast thou not glorified." (Dan. v. 23.)

We learn, in the third place, *that all professing*

Christians must one day have a reckoning with God. The parable tells us that "after a long time the Lord of those servants came, and reckoned with them."

There is a judgment before us all. Words have no meaning in the Bible, if there is none: it is mere trifling with Scripture to deny it. There is a judgment before us according to our works,—certain, strict, and unavoidable. High or low, rich or poor, learned or unlearned, we shall all have to stand at the bar of God and receive our eternal sentence. There will be no escape: concealment will be impossible. We and God must at last meet face to face. We shall have to render an account of every privilege that was granted to us, and of every ray of light that we enjoyed; we shall find that we are dealt with as accountable and responsible creatures, and that to whomsoever much is given, of them much will be required. Let us remember this every day we live: let us "judge ourselves that we be not condemned of the Lord." (1 Cor. ii. 31.)

We learn, in the fourth place, *that true Christians will receive an abundant reward in the great day of reckoning.* The parable tells us that the servants who had used their Lord's money well, were commended as "good and faithful," and told to "enter into the joy of their Lord."

These words are full of comfort to all believers, and may well fill us with wonder and surprise. The best of Christians is a poor frail creature, and needs the blood of atonement every day that he lives; but the least and lowest of believers will find that he is counted among Christ's servants, and that his labour has not been in vain in the Lord. He will discover to his amazement, that his Master's eye saw more beauty in his efforts to please Him, than he ever saw himself; he will find that every hour spent in Christ's service, and every word spoken on Christ's behalf, has been written in a book of remembrance. Let believers remember these things and take courage.—The cross may be heavy now, but the glorious reward shall make amends for all. Well says Leighton, "Here some drops of joy enter into us, but there we shall enter into joy."

We learn, in the last place, that all *unfruitful members of Christ's Church will be condemned and cast away in the day of judgment.* The parable tells us that the servant who buried his master's money, was reminded that he "knew" his master's character and requirements, and was therefore without excuse; it tells us that he was condemned as "wicked," "slothful," and "unprofitable," and cast into "outer darkness:" and our Lord adds the solemn words, "There shall be weeping and gnashing of teeth."

There will be no excuse for an unconverted Christian at the last day. The reasons with which he now pretends to satisfy himself will prove useless and vain: the Judge of all the earth will be found to have done right; the ruin of the lost soul will be found to be his own fault. Those words of our Lord, "thou knewest," are words that ought to ring loudly in many a man's ears, and prick him to the heart. Thousands are living at this day "without Christ" and without conversion, and yet pretending that they cannot help it! And all this time they "*know,*" in their own conscience, that they are guilty. They are burying their talent: they are not doing what they can. Happy are they who find this out betimes! It will all come out at the last day.

Let us leave this parable with a solemn determination, by God's grace, never to be content with a profession of Christianity without practice. Let us not only *talk* about religion, but act; let us not only *feel* the importance of religion, but do something too. We are not told that the unprofitable servant was a murderer, or a thief, or even a waster of his Lord's money: but he *did nothing*, —and this was his ruin! Let us beware of a do-nothing Christianity: such Christianity does not come from the Spirit of God. "To do no harm," says Baxter, "is the praise of a stone, not of a man."

MATTHEW XXV. 31—46.

31 When the Son of man shall come in his glory, and all the holy angels with him, then shall he sit upon the throne of his glory:

32 And before him shall be gathered all nations: and he shall separate them one from another, as a shepherd divideth *his* sheep from the goats:

33 And he shall set the sheep on his right hand, but the goats on the left.

34 Then shall the king say unto them on his right hand, Come, ye blessed of my Father, inherit the kingdom prepared for you from the foundation of the world:

35 For I was an hungred, and ye gave me meat: I was thirsty, and ye gave me drink: I was a stranger, and ye took me in:

36 Naked and ye clothed me: I was sick, and ye visited me: I was in prison, and ye came unto me.

37 Then shall the righteous answer him, saying, Lord, when saw we thee an hungred, and fed *thee?* or thirsty, and gave *thee* drink?

38 When saw we thee a stranger, and took *thee* in? or naked, and clothed *thee?*

39 Or when saw we thee sick, or in prison, and came unto thee?

40 And the King shall answer and say unto them, Verily I say unto you, Inasmuch as ye have done *it* unto one of the least of these my brethren, ye have done *it* unto me.

41 Then shall he say also unto them on the left hand, Depart from me, ye cursed, into everlasting fire, prepared for the devil and his angels:

42 For I was an hungred, and ye gave me no meat: I was thirsty, and ye gave me no drink:

43 I was a stranger, and ye took me not in: naked, and ye clothed me not: sick, and in prison, and ye visited me not.

44 Then shall they also answer him, saying, Lord, when saw we thee an hungred, or athirst, or a stranger, or naked, or sick, or in prison, and did not minister unto thee?

45 Then shall he answer them, saying, Verily, I say unto you, Inasmuch as ye did *it* not to one of the least of these, ye did *it* not to me.

46 And these shall go away into everlasting punishment: but the righteous into life eternal.

IN these verses our Lord Jesus Christ describes the judgment-day, and some of its leading circumstances.

There are few passages in the whole Bible more solemn and heart-searching than this. May we read it with the deep and serious attention which it deserves.

Let us mark, in the first place, *who will be the Judge in the last day.* We read that it will "be the Son of man:" Jesus Christ Himself.

That same Jesus who was born in the manger of Bethlehem, and took upon Him the form of a servant; who was despised and rejected of men, and often had not where to lay His head; who was condemned by the princes of this world, beaten, scourged, and nailed to the cross,—that same Jesus shall Himself judge the world, when he comes in His glory. To Him the Father hath committed all judgment. (John v. 22.) To Him at last every knee shall bow, and every tongue confess that He is Lord. (Philip. ii. 10, 11.)

Let believers think of this, and take comfort. He that sits upon the throne in that great and dreadful day will be their Saviour, their Shepherd, their High Priest, their élder Brother, their Friend. When they see Him, they will have no cause to be alarmed.

Let unconverted people think of this, and be afraid. Their Judge will be that very Christ, whose Gospel they now despise, and whose gracious invitations they refuse to hear. How great will be their confusion at last, if they go on in unbelief and die in their sins! To be condemned in the day of judgment by any one would be awful; but to be condemned by Him who would have saved them will be awful indeed. Well may the psalmist say, "Kiss the Son lest He be angry." (Psalm ii. 12.)

Let us mark, in the second place, *who will be judged*

in the last day. We read that before Christ "shall be gathered all nations."

All that have ever lived shall one day give account of themselves at the bar of Christ: all must obey the summons of the great King, and come forward to receive their sentence. Those who would not come to worship Christ on earth, will find they must come to His great assize, when He returns to judge the world.

All that are judged will be divided into two great classes. There will no longer be any distinction between kings and subjects, or masters and servants, or dissenters and churchmen; there will be no mention of ranks and denominations, for the former things will have passed away. Grace or no grace, conversion or unconversion, faith or no faith, will be the only distinction at the last day. All that are found in Christ will be placed among the sheep "on His right hand;" all that are not found in Christ will be placed among the goats "on the left." Well says Sherlock: "Our separations will avail us nothing, unless we take care to be found in the number of Christ's sheep, when He comes to judgment."

Let us mark, in the third place, *in what manner the judgment will be conducted in the last day.* We read of several striking particulars on this point: let us see what they are.

The last judgment will be a judgment according to evidence. The works of men are the witnesses which will be brought forward, and above all their works of charity. The question to be ascertained will not merely be what we said, but what we did: not merely what we professed, but what we practised. Our works unquestionably will not justify us: we are justified by faith without the deeds of the law; but the truth of our faith will be tested by our lives. Faith which hath not works is dead, being alone. (James ii. 11.)

The last judgment will be a judgment that will bring joy to all true believers. They will hear those precious words, "Come, ye blessed of my Father, inherit the kingdom;" they will be owned and confessed by their Master before His Father and the holy angels; they shall find that the wages He gives to His faithful servants are nothing less than "a kingdom." The least, and lowest, and poorest of the family of God, shall have a crown of glory, and be a king!

The last judgment will be a judgment that will bring confusion on all unconverted people. They will hear those awful words, "Depart, ye cursed, into everlasting fire:" they will be disowned by the great Head of the Church before the assembled world: they will find that as they would "sow to the flesh," so of the flesh they must "reap corruption." (Gal. vi. 8.) They would not hear Christ, when He said, "Come unto Me, and I will give you rest," and now they must hear Him say, "Depart into everlasting fire:" they would not carry His cross, and so they can have no place in His kingdom.

The last judgment will be a judgment that will strikingly bring out the characters both of the lost and saved. They on the right hand, who are Christ's sheep, will still be "clothed with humility" (1 Pet. v. 5): they will marvel to hear any work of their's brought forward and commended.—They on the left hand, who are not Christ's, will still be blind and self-righteous. They will not be sensible of any neglect of Christ: "Lord," they say, "when saw we Thee,—and did not minister unto Thee?" Let this thought sink down into our hearts. Characters on earth will prove an everlasting possession in the world to come: with the same heart that men die, with that heart they will rise again.

Let us mark, in the last place, *what will be the final results of the judgment day.* We are told this in words that ought never to be forgotten: "The wicked shall go away into everlasting punishment; but the righteous into life eternal."

The state of things after the judgment is changeless and without end. The misery of the lost, and the blessedness of the saved, are both alike for ever: let no man deceive us on this point. It is clearly revealed in Scripture: the eternity of God, and heaven, and hell, all stand on the same foundation. As surely as God is eternal, so surely is heaven an endless day without night, and hell an endless night without day.

Who shall describe the blessedness of eternal life? It passes the power of man to conceive: it can only be measured by contrast and comparison. An eternal rest, after warfare and conflict; the eternal company of saints, after buffeting with an evil world; an eternally glorious and painless body, after struggling with weakness and infirmity; an eternal sight of Jesus face to face, after only hearing and believing,—all this is blessedness indeed. And yet the half of it remains untold.

Who shall describe the misery of eternal punishment? It is something utterly indescribable and inconceivable. The eternal pain of body; the eternal sting of an accusing conscience; the eternal society of none but the wicked, the devil and his angels; the eternal remembrance of opportunities neglected and Christ despised; the eternal prospect of a weary, hopeless future,—all this is misery indeed: it is enough to make our ears tingle, and our blood run cold. And yet this picture is nothing compared to the reality.

Let us close these verses with serious self-inquiry. Let us ask ourselves on which side of Christ we are likely to be at the last day. Shall we be on the right hand, or shall we be on the left? Happy is he who never rests till he can give a satisfactory answer to this question.

MATTHEW XXVI. 1—13.

1 And it came to pass, when Jesus had finished all these sayings, he said unto his disciples,
2 Ye know that after two days is *the feast of* the passover, and the Son of man is betrayed to be crucified.
3 Then assembled together the chief priests, and the scribes, and the elders of the people, unto the palace of the high priest, who was called Caiaphas,
4 And consulted that they might take Jesus by subtilty, and kill *him*.
5 But they said, Not on the feast *day*, lest there be an uproar among the people.
6 Now when Jesus was in Bethany, in the house of Simon the leper,
7 There came unto him a woman having an alabaster box of very precious ointment, and poured it on his head, as he sat *at meat*.
8 But when his disciples saw *it*, they had indignation, saying, To what purpose *is* this waste?
9 For this ointment might have been sold for much, and given to the poor.
10 When Jesus understood *it*, he said unto them, Why trouble ye the woman? for she hath wrought a good work upon me.
11 For ye have the poor always with you; but me ye have not always.
12 For in that she hath poured this ointment on my body, she did *it* for my burial.
13 Verily I say unto you, Wheresoever this Gospel shall be preached in the whole world, *there* shall also this, that this woman hath done, be told for a memorial of her.

WE now approach the closing scene of our Lord Jesus Christ's earthly ministry. Hitherto we have read of His sayings and doings: we are now about to read of His sufferings and death. Hitherto we have seen Him as the great Prophet, we are now about to see Him as the great High Priest.

It is a portion of Scripture which ought to be read with peculiar reverence and attention. The place whereon we stand is holy ground. Here we see how the Seed of the woman bruised the Serpent's head; here we see the Great Sacrifice to which all the sacrifices of the Old Testament had long pointed; here we see how the blood was shed which "cleanseth from all sin," and the Lamb slain who "taketh away the sins of the world." (1 John i. 8; John i. 29.) We see, in the death of Christ, the great mystery revealed, how God can be just, and yet justify the ungodly. No wonder that all the four Gospels contain a full account of this wonderful event: on other points in our Lord's history, we often find that when one Evangelist speaks the other three are silent; but when we come to the crucifixion, we find it minutely described by all four.

In the verses we have now read, let us first observe *how careful our Lord is to call the attention of His disciples to His own death.* He said to them, "Ye know that after two days is the feast of the passover, and the Son of man is betrayed to be crucified."

The connection of these words with the preceding chapter is exceedingly striking. Our Lord had just been dwelling on His own second coming in power and glory, at the end of the world; He had been describing the last judgment, and all its awful accompaniments; He had been speaking of Himself as the Judge, before whose throne all nations would be gathered: and then at once, without pause or interval, He goes on to speak of His crucifixion. While the marvellous predictions of His final glory were yet ringing in the ears of His disciples, He tells them once and again of His coming sufferings: He reminds them that He must die as a sin-offering before he reigned as a King; that He must make atonement on the cross, before He took the crown.

We can never attach too much importance to the atoning death of Christ: it is the leading fact in the Word of God, on which the eyes of our soul ought to be ever fixed. Without the shedding of His blood, there is no remission of sin. It is the cardinal truth on which the whole system of Christianity hinges. Without it the Gospel is an arch without a keystone, a fair building without a foundation, a solar system without a sun. Let us make much of our Lord's incarnation, and example, His miracles and His parables, His works and His words, but above all let us make much of His death. Let us delight in the hope of His second personal coming and millennial reign, but let us not think more even of these blessed truths, than of the atonement on the cross. This after all is the master-truth of Scripture,—that "Christ died for our sins." To this let us daily return: on this let us daily feed our souls. Some, like the Greeks of old, may sneer at the doctrine, and call it "foolishness; but let us never be ashamed to say with Paul, "God forbid that I should glory save in the cross of our Lord Jesus Christ." (Gal. vi. 14.)

Let us, observe, in the second place, in these verses, *what honour Christ loves to put on those that honour Him.*

We are told that when He "was in the house of Simon the leper," a certain woman came while He sat at meat, and poured a box of precious ointment on His head. She did it, no doubt, out of reverence and affection: she had received soul-benefit from Him, and she thought no mark of honour too costly to be bestowed on Him in return. But this deed of hers called forth disapprobation from some who saw it: they called it "waste;" they said it might have been better to sell the ointment, and give the money to the poor. At once our Lord rebuked these cold-hearted fault-finders. He tells them that the woman "has wrought a good work," and one that He accepts and approves; and He goes on to make a striking prediction: "Wheresoever this Gospel is preached in the whole world, there shall also this that this woman hath done be told for a memorial of her."

We see, in this little incident, how perfectly our Lord knew things to come, and how easy it is for Him to confer honour. This prophecy of His about this woman is receiving a fulfilment every day before our eyes: wherever the Gospel of St. Matthew is read, the deed that she did is known. The deeds and titles of many a King, and Emperor, and General, are as completely forgotten as if written in the sand; but the grateful act of one humble Christian woman is recorded in one hundred and fifty different languages, and is known all over the globe. The praise of man is but for a few days: the praise of Christ endureth for ever. The pathway to lasting honour is to honour Christ.

Last, but not least, we see in this incident a blessed foretaste of things that will yet take place in the day of judgment. In that great day no honour done to Christ on earth shall be found to have been forgotten.

The speeches of parliamentary orators, the exploits of warriors, the works of poets and painters, shall not be mentioned in that day; but the least work that the weakest Christian woman has done for Christ, or His members, shall be found written in a book of everlasting remembrance. Not a single kind word or deed, not a cup of cold water, or a box of ointment, shall be omitted from the record. Silver and gold she may have had none; rank, power, and influence she may not have possessed; but if she loved Christ, and confessed Christ, and worked for Christ, her memorial shall be found on high: she shall be commended before assembled worlds.

Do we know what it is to work for Christ? If we do, let us take courage, and work on. What greater encouragement can we desire than we see here? We may be laughed at and ridiculed by the world: our motives may be misunderstood; our conduct may be misrepresented; our sacrifices for Christ's sake may be called "waste,"—waste of time, waste of money, waste of strength. Let none of these things move us. The eye of Him who sat in Simon's house at Bethany is upon us: He notes all we do, and is well pleased. Let us be "steadfast, unmoveable, always abounding in the work of the Lord, forasmuch as we know that our labour is not in vain in the Lord." (1 Cor. xv. 58.)

MATTHEW XXVI. 14—25.

14 Then one of the twelve, called Judas Iscariot, went unto the chief priests,

15 And said *unto them*, What will ye give me, and I will deliver him unto you? And they covenanted with him for thirty pieces of silver.

16 And from that time he sought opportunity to betray him.

17 Now the first *day* of the *feast*
of unleavened bread the disciples
came to Jesus, saying unto him,
Where wilt thou that we prepare
for thee to eat the passover?
18 And he said, Go into the city
to such a man, and say unto him,
The Master saith, My time is at
hand; I will keep the passover at
thy house with my disciples.
19 And the disciples did as Jesus
had appointed them; and they
made ready the passover.
20 Now when the even was come,
he sat down with the twelve.
21 And as they did eat, he said,
Verily I say unto you, that one
of you shall betray me.
22 And they were exceeding sorrowful, and began every one of
them to say unto him, Lord, is it I?
23 And he answered and said,
He that dippeth *his* hand with me
in the dish, the same shall betray
me.
24 The Son of man goeth as it is
written of him: but woe unto that
man by whom the Son of man is
betrayed! it had been good for
that man if he had not been born.
25 Then Judas, which betrayed
him, answered and said, Master, is
it I? He said unto him, Thou hast
said.

WE read, in the beginning of this passage, how our Lord Jesus Christ was betrayed into the hands of His deadly enemies. The priests and scribes, however anxious to put Him to death, were at a loss how to effect their purpose, for fear of an uproar among the people: at this juncture a fitting instrument for carrying out their designs, offered himself to them in the person of Judas Iscariot. That false Apostle undertook to deliver his Master into their hands for thirty pieces of silver.

There are few blacker pages in all history than the character and conduct of Judas Iscariot: there is no more awful evidence of the wickedness of man. A poet of our own has said, that "sharper than a serpent's tooth is a thankless child;" but what shall we say of a disciple who would betray his own Master: an apostle who could sell Christ? Surely this was not the least bitter part of the cup of suffering which our Lord drank.

Let us learn, in the first place, from these verses, *that a man may enjoy great privileges, and make a great religious profession, and yet his heart all the time may not be right before God.*

Judas Iscariot had the highest possible religious privileges. He was a chosen apostle, and companion of Christ; He was an eye-witness of our Lord's miracles, and a hearer of His sermons; he saw what Abraham and Moses never saw, and heard what David and Isaiah never heard; he lived in the society of the eleven Apostles; he was a fellow-labourer with Peter, James and John: but for all this his heart was never changed. He clung to one darling sin.

Judas Iscariot made a reputable profession of religion: there was nothing but what was right, and proper, and becoming in his outward conduct. Like the other Apostles, he appeared to believe and to give up all for Christ's sake: like them, he was sent forth to preach and work miracles. No one of the eleven seems to have suspected him of hypocrisy. When our Lord said, "One of you shall betray Me," no one said, "Is it Judas?" Yet all this time his heart was never changed.

We ought to observe these things: they are deeply humbling and instructive. Like Lot's wife, Judas is intended to be a beacon to the whole Church. Let us often think about him, and say, as we think, "Search me, O Lord, and try my heart, and see if there be any wicked way in me." Let us resolve, by God's grace, that we will never be content with anything short of sound and thorough heart conversion.

Let us learn, in the second place from these verses, *that the love of money is one of the greatest snares to a man's soul.* We cannot conceive a clearer proof of this, than the case of Judas. That wretched question, "What will ye give me?" reveals the secret sin which was his ruin. He had given up much for Christ's sake, but he had not given up his covetousness.

The words of the apostle Paul should often ring in our ears: "the love of money is the root of all evil." (2 Tim. vi. 10.) The history of the Church abounds in illustrations of this truth. For money Joseph was sold by his brethren; for money Samson was betrayed to the Philistines; for money Gehazi deceived Naaman, and lied to Elisha; for money Ananias and Sapphira tried to deceive Peter; for money the Son of God was delivered into the hands of wicked men. Wonderful indeed does it seem that the cause of so much evil should be loved so well.

Let us all be on our guard against the love of money. The world is full of it in our days: the plague is abroad. Thousands who would abhor the idea of worshipping Juggernaut, are not ashamed to make an idol of gold. We are all liable to the infection, from the least to the greatest. We may love money without having it, just as we may have money without loving it: it is an evil that works very deceitfully: it carries us captives before we are aware of our chains. Once let it get the mastery, and it will harden, palsy, sear, freeze, blight, and wither our souls. It overthrew an apostle of Christ: let us take heed that it does not overthrow us. One leak may sink a ship: one unmortified sin may ruin a soul.

We ought frequently to call to mind the solemn words, "What shall it profit a man if he gain the whole world, and lose his own soul?" "We brought nothing into this world, and it is certain we can carry nothing out." Our daily prayer should be, "Give me neither poverty nor riches: feed me with food convenient for me." (Prov. xxx. 8.) Our constant aim should be to be rich in grace. They that "*will* be rich" in worldly possessions often find at last that they have made the worst of bargains. (1 Tim. vi. 9.) Like Esau, they have bartered an eternal portion for a little temporary gratification: like Judas Iscariot, they have sold themselves to everlasting perdition.

Let us learn, in the last place, from these verses, *the hopeless condition of all who die unconverted.* The words of our Lord on this subject are peculiarly solemn: He says of Judas, "It had been good for that man if he had not been born."

This saying admits of only one interpretation. It teaches plainly that it is better never to live at all, than to live without faith, and to die without grace. To die in this state is to be ruined for evermore: it is a fall from which there is no rising; it is a loss which is utterly irretrievable. There is no change in hell: the gulf between hell and heaven is one that no man can pass.

This saying could never have been used if there was any truth in the doctrine of universal salvation. If it really was true that all would sooner or later reach heaven, and hell sooner or later be emptied of inhabitants, it never could be said that it would have been "good for a man not to have been born." Hell itself would lose its terrors, if it had an end: hell itself would be endurable, if after millions of ages there was a hope of freedom and of heaven. But universal salvation will find no foot-hold in Scripture: the teaching of the Word of God is plain and express on the subject. There is a worm that never dies, and a fire that is not quenched.

(Mark ix. 44.) "Except a man be born again," he will wish one day he had never been born at all. "Better," says Burkett, "have no being, than not have a being in Christ."

Let us grasp this truth firmly, and not let it go. There are always persons who deny the reality and eternity of hell. We live in a day when a morbid charity induces many to exaggerate God's mercy, at the expense of His justice, and when false teachers are daring to talk of a "love of God lower even than hell." Let us resist such teaching with a holy jealousy, and abide by the doctrine of Holy Scripture: let us not be ashamed to walk in the old paths, and to believe that there is an eternal God, an eternal heaven, and an eternal hell. Once depart from this belief, and we admit the thin edge of the wedge of scepticism, and may at last deny any doctrine of the Gospel. We may rest assured that there is no firm standing ground between a belief in the eternity of hell, and downright infidelity.

MATTHEW XXVI. 26—35.

26 And as they were eating, Jesus took bread, and blessed *it*, and brake *it*, and gave *it* to the disciples, and said, Take, eat; this is my body.

27 And he took the cup, and gave thanks, and gave *it* to them, saying, Drink ye all of it;

28 For this is my blood of the new testament, which is shed for many for the remission of sins.

29 But I say unto you, I will not drink henceforth of this fruit of the vine, until that day when I drink it new with you in my Father's kingdom.

30 And when they had sung an hymn, they went out into the mount of Olives.

31 Then saith Jesus unto them, All ye shall be offended because of me this night: for it is written, I will smite the shepherd, and the sheep of the flock shall be scattered abroad.

32 But after I am risen again, I will go before you into Galilee.

33 Peter answered and said unto him, Though all *men* shall be offended because of thee, *yet* will I never be offended.

34 Jesus said unto him, Verily I say unto thee, That this night, before the cock crow, thou shalt deny me thrice.

35 Peter said unto him, Though I should die with thee, yet will I not deny thee. Likewise also said all the disciples.

THESE verses describe the appointment of the sacrament of the Lord's Supper. Our Lord knew well the things that were before Him, and graciously chose the last quiet evening that He could have before His crucifixion, as an occasion for bestowing a parting gift on His Church. How precious must this ordinance have afterwards appeared to His disciples, when they remembered the events of that night! How mournful is the thought that no ordinance has led to such fierce controversy, and been so grievously misunderstood, as the ordinance of the Lord's Supper! It ought to have united the Church, but our sins have made it a cause of division. The thing which should have been for our welfare, has been too often made an occasion of falling.

The first thing that demands our notice in these verses, *is the right meaning of our Lord's words,* "*This is my body, this is my blood.*"

It is needless to say that this question has divided the visible Church of Christ. It has caused volumes of controversial theology to be written: but we must not shrink from having decided opinions upon it, because theologians have disputed and differed. Unsoundness on this point has given rise to many deplorable superstitions.

The plain meaning of our Lord's words appears to be this: "This bread *represents* my body. This wine represents my blood." He did not mean that the bread He gave to His disciples *was* really and literally His body; He did not mean that the wine He gave to His disciples *was* really and literally His blood. Let us lay firm hold on this interpretation: it may be supported by several grave reasons.*

* "Bishop Law has remarked that there is no term in the

The conduct of the disciples at the Lord's Supper forbids us to believe that the bread they received was Christ's body, and the wine they received was Christ's blood. They were all Jews, taught from their infancy to believe that it was sinful to eat flesh with the blood (Deut. xii. 23—25); yet there is nothing in the narrative to show that they were startled by our Lord's words. They evidently perceived no change in the bread and wine.

Our own senses at the present day forbid us to believe that there is any change in the bread and wine in the Lord's Supper; our own taste tells us that they are really and literally what they appear to be. Things above our reason the Bible requires us to believe; but we are never bid to believe that which contradicts our senses.

The true doctrine about our Lord's human nature forbids us to believe that the bread in the Lord's Supper can be His body, or the wine His blood: the natural body of Christ cannot be at one time in more places than one. If our Lord's body could sit at table, and at the same time be eaten by the disciples, it is perfectly clear that it was not a human body like our own. But this we must never allow for one moment. It is the glory of Christianity that our Redeemer is perfect man as well as perfect God.

Hebrew language, which expresses to *signify* or *denote;* and that the Greek here naturally takes the impress of the Hebrew or Syriac idiom, *it is* being used for *it signifies.* Hence the similar use of the verb in various passages. 'The three branches *are* three days (Gen. xl. 12); 'the seven kine *are* seven years' (Gen. xli. 26); 'the ten horns *are* ten kings' (Dan. vii. 24); 'the field *is* the world' (Matt. xiii. 38); 'the seven stars *are* the angels of the seven Churches, and the seven candlesticks which thou sawest *are* the seven Churches.' (Rev. i. 20.)"—*Watson on Matthew*, p. 386.

Finally, the genius of the language in which our Lord spoke at the Lord's Supper, makes it entirely unnecessary to interpret His word's literally. The Bible is full of expressions of a similar kind, to which no one thinks of giving any but a figurative meaning. Our Lord speaks of Himself as the "door" and the "vine," and we know that He is using emblems and figures when He so speaks : there is therefore no inconsistency in supposing that He used *figurative* language when He appointed the Lord's Supper ; and we have the more right to say so when we remember the grave objections which stand in the way of a literal view of His words.

Let us lay up these things in our minds, and not forget them. In a day of abounding heresy, it is good to be well armed. Ignorant and confused views of the meaning of Scripture language are one great cause of religious error.

The second thing which demands our notice in these verses is *the purpose and object for which the Lord's Supper was appointed.*

This is a subject again on which great darkness prevails. The ordinance of the Lord's Supper has been regarded as something mysterious and past understanding: immense harm has been done to Christianity by the vague and highflown language in which many writers have indulged in treating of the sacrament; there is certainly nothing to warrant such language in the account of its original institution. The more simple our views of its purpose, the more Scriptural they are likely to be.

The Lord's Supper is not a sacrifice. There is no

oblation in it,—no offering up of anything but our prayers, praises, and thanksgivings. From the day that Jesus died there needed no more offering for sin: by one offering He perfected for ever them that are sanctified. (Heb. x. 14.) Priests, altars, and sacrifices, all ceased to be necessary, when the Lamb of God offered up Himself. Their office came to an end: their work was done.

The Lord's Supper has no power to confer benefit on those who come to it, if they do not come to it with faith. The mere formal act of eating the bread and drinking the wine is utterly unprofitable, unless it is done with a right heart. It is eminently an ordinance for the living soul, not for the dead; for the converted, not for the unconverted.

The Lord's Supper was ordained for a continual remembrance of the sacrifice of Christ's death, until He comes again. The benefits it confers are spiritual, not physical: its effects must be looked for in our inward man. It was intended to remind us, by the visible, tangible emblems of bread and wine, that the offering of Christ's body and blood for us on the cross is the only atonement for sin, and the life of a believer's soul; it was meant to help our poor weak faith to closer fellowship with our crucified Saviour, and to assist us in spiritually feeding on Christ's body and blood. It is an ordinance for redeemed sinners, and not for unfallen angels. By receiving it we publicly declare our sense of guilt, and our need of a Saviour,—our trust in Jesus, and our love to Him,—our desire to live upon Him, and our hope to live with Him. Using it in this spirit, we shall find our repentance deepened, our faith increased, our hope brightened, and our love enlarged,—our besetting sins weakened, and our graces strengthened. It will draw us nearer to Christ.

Let us bear these things in mind: they need to be remembered in these latter days. There is nothing in our religion which we are so ready to pervert and misunderstand as those parts which approach our senses. Whatever we can touch with our hand, and see with our eyes, we are apt to exalt into an idol, or to expect good from it as a mere charm: let us specially beware of this tendency in the matter of the Lord's Supper. Above all, "let us take heed," in the words of the Church of England Homily, "lest of the memory it be made a sacrifice."

The last thing which deserves a brief notice in this passage, is the *character of the first communicants.* It is a point full of comfort and instruction.

The little company to which the bread and wine were first administered by our Lord was composed of the Apostles whom He had chosen to accompany Him during His earthly ministry. They were poor and unlearned men, who loved Christ, but were weak alike in faith and knowledge: they knew but little of the full meaning of their Master's sayings and doings; they knew but little of the frailty of their own hearts. They thought they were ready to die with Jesus, and yet that very night they all forsook Him and fled. All this our Lord knew perfectly well: the state of their hearts was not hid from Him; and yet He did not keep back from them the Lord's Supper!

There is something very teaching in this circumstance. It shows us plainly that we must not make great knowledge, and great strength of grace, an indispensable qualification for communicants. A man may know but little, and be no better than a child in spiritual strength, but he is not on that account to be excluded from the Lord's table.—Does he really feel his sins? Does he really love Christ? Does he really desire to serve Him? If this be so, we ought to encourage and receive Him. Doubtless we must do all we can to exclude unworthy communicants: no graceless person ought to come to the Lord's Supper; but we must take heed that we do not reject those whom Christ has not rejected. There is no wisdom in being more strict than our Lord and His disciples.

Let us leave the passage with serious self-inquiry as to our own conduct with respect to the Lord's Supper. Do we turn away from it, when it is administered? If so, how can we justify our conduct?—It will not do to say it is not a necessary ordinance: to say so is to pour contempt on Christ himself and declare that we do not obey Him. It will not do to say that we feel unworthy to come to the Lord's table: to say so is to declare that we are unfit to die, and unprepared to meet God. These are solemn considerations: all non-communicants should ponder them well.

Are we in the habit of coming to the Lord's table? If so, in what frame of mind do we come? Do we draw near intelligently, humbly, and with faith? Do we understand what we are about? Do we really feel our sinfulness, and need of Christ? Do we really desire to live a Christian life, as well as profess the Christian faith? Happy is that soul who can give a satisfactory answer to these questions? Let him go forward, and persevere.

MATTHEW XXVI. 36—46.

36 Then cometh Jesus with them unto a place called Gethsemane, and saith unto the disciples, Sit ye here, while I go and pray yonder.
37 And he took with him Peter and the two sons of Zebedee, and began to be sorrowful and very heavy.
38 Then saith he unto them, My soul is exceeding sorrowful, even unto death: tarry ye here and watch with me.
39 And he went a little further, and fell on his face and prayed, saying, O my Father, if it be possible, let this cup pass from me: nevertheless not as I will, but as thou *wilt*.
40 And he cometh unto the disciples, and findeth them asleep, and saith unto Peter, What, could ye not watch with me one hour?
41 Watch and pray, that ye enter not into temptation: the spirit indeed *is* willing, but the flesh *is* weak.
42 He went away again the second time, and prayed, saying, O my Father, if this cup may not pass away from me, except I drink it, thy will be done.
43 And he came and found them asleep again: for their eyes were heavy.
44 And he left them, and went away again, and prayed the third time, saying the same words.
45 Then cometh he to his disciples, and saith unto them, Sleep on now, and take *your* rest: behold, the hour is at hand, and the Son of man is betrayed into the hands of sinners.
46 Rise, let us be going: behold, he is at hand that doth betray me.

THE verses we have now read describe what is commonly called Christ's agony at Gethsemane. It is a passage which undoubtedly contains deep and mysterious things. We ought to read it with reverence and wonder, for there is much in it which we cannot fully comprehend.

Why do we find our Lord so "sorrowful, and very heavy," as He is here described? What are we to make of His words, "My soul is exceeding sorrowful, even unto death"? Why do we see Him going apart from His disciples, and falling on His face, and crying to His Father with strong cries, and thrice-repeated prayer? Why is the Almighty Son of God, who had worked so many miracles, so heavy and disquieted? Why is Jesus, who came into the world to die, so like one ready to faint at the approach of death? Why is all this?

There is but one reasonable answer to these questions: the weight that pressed down our Lord's soul, was not the fear of death, and its pains. Thousands have endured the most agonizing sufferings of body, and died without a groan, and so, no doubt, might our Lord. But the real weight that bowed down the heart of Jesus was the weight of the sin of the world, which seems to have now pressed down upon Him with peculiar force: it was the burden of our guilt imputed to Him, which was now laid on Him, as on the head of the scape-goat. How great that burden must have been, no heart of man can conceive! it is known only to God. Well may the Greek Litany speak of the "unknown sufferings of Christ." The words of Scott on this subject are probably correct: "Christ at this time endured as much misery of the same kind with that of condemned spirits, as could possibly consist with a pure conscience, perfect love of God and man, and an assured confidence of a glorious event." *

* I believe that the view maintained in this exposition is the only reasonable solution that can be given of our Lord's agony. How any Socinian, or any divine who denies the imputation of man's sin to Christ, and the vicarious nature of Christ's sufferings, can account satisfactorily for the agony in the garden, I am totally at a loss to conceive.—Upon the principle of the Socinian, who utterly denies the doctrine of atonement, and says that our Lord was only a man, and not God, He was one who showed less firmness in suffering than many men have shown! —Upon the principle of some modern divines, who say that our Lord's death was not a propitiation and expiation for sin, but only a great example of self-sacrifice, the intense agony of body and mind here described is equally unaccountable.—Both views appear to me alike dishonouring to our Lord Jesus Christ, and utterly unscriptural and unsatisfactory. I believe the agony in the garden to be a knot that nothing can untie but the old doctrine of our sin being really *imputed* to Christ, and Christ being made sin and a curse for us.

There are deep things in this passage of Scripture, containing the account of the agony, which I purposely leave untouched. They are too deep for man's line to fathom. The extent to which Satan was allowed to tempt our Lord in this hour,—the degree of suffering, both mental and bodily, which an entirely sinless person, like our Lord, would endure in bearing the sin of all

But however mysterious this part of our Lord's history may seem to us, we must not fail to observe the precious lessons of practical instruction which it contains. Let us now see what those lessons are.

Let us learn, in the first place, that *prayer is the best practical remedy that we can use in time of trouble.* We see that Christ Himself prayed, when His soul was sorrowful: all true Christians ought to do the same.

Trouble is a cup that all must drink in this world of sin: we are "born unto trouble as the sparks fly upward" (Job v. 7); we cannot avoid it. Of all creatures, none is so vulnerable as man: our bodies, our minds, our families, our business, our friends, are all so many doors through which trial will come in. The holiest saints can claim no exemption from it: like their Master, they are often "men of sorrow."

But what is the first thing to be done in time of trouble? We must pray.—Like Job, we must fall down and worship (Job i. 20); like Hezekiah, we must spread our matters before the Lord. (2 Kings xix. 14.) The first person we must turn to for help must be our God. We must tell our Father in heaven all our sorrow; we must believe confidently that nothing is too trivial or minute to be laid before Him, so long as we do it with entire submission to His will. It is the mark of faith to keep nothing back from our best Friend: so doing, we may be sure we shall have an answer. "If it be possible," and the thing

mankind,—the manner in which the human and divine wills both operated in our Lord's experience, since He was at all times as really man as God,—all these are points which I prefer to leave alone. It is easy on such questions to "darken counsel by words without knowledge."

we ask is for God's glory, it shall be done: the thorn in the flesh will either be removed, or grace to endure it will be given to us, as it was to St. Paul. (2 Cor. xii. 9.) May we all store up this lesson against the day of need. It is a true saying, that "prayers are the leeches of care."

Let us learn, in the second place, that *entire submission of will to the will of God should be one of our chief aims in this world.* The words of our Lord are a beautiful example of the spirit that we should follow after in this matter: He says, "Not as I will, but as Thou wilt." He says again, "Thy will be done."

A will unsanctified and uncontrolled, is one great cause of unhappiness in life: it may be seen in little infants; it is born with us: we all like our own way. We wish and want many things, and forget that we are entirely ignorant what is for our good, and unfit to choose for ourselves. Happy is he who has learned to have no "wishes," and in every state to be content! It is a lesson which we are slow to learn, and, like St. Paul, we must learn it not in the school of mortal man, but of Christ. (Philip. iv. 11.)

Would we know whether we are born again, and growing in grace? Let us see how it is with us in the matter of our wills. Can we bear disappointment? Can we put up patiently with unexpected trials and vexations? Can we see our favourite plans, and darling schemes crossed, without murmuring and complaint? Can we sit still, and suffer calmly, as well as go up and down and work actively? These are the things that prove whether we have the mind of Christ. It ought never to be forgotten, that warm feelings and joyful frames are not the truest evidences of grace: a mortified will is a far more valuable possession. Even our Lord Himself did not always rejoice; but He could always say, "Thy will be done."

Let us learn, in the last place, that there is *great weakness, even in true disciples of Christ, and that they have need to watch and pray against it.* We see Peter, James, and John, those three chosen apostles, sleeping when they ought to have been watching and praying; and we find our Lord addressing them in these solemn words, "Watch and pray, that ye enter not into temptation: the spirit indeed is willing, but the flesh is weak."

There is a double nature in all believers. Converted, renewed, sanctified as they are, they still carry about with them a mass of indwelling corruption, a body of sin. St. Paul speaks of this, when he says, "I find a law, that, when I would do good, evil is present with me. For I delight in the law of God after the inward man: but I see another law in my members, warring against the law of my mind." (Rom. vii. 21—23.) The experience of all true Christians in every age confirms this. They find within two contrary principles, and a continual strife between the two; to these two principles our Lord alludes when He addresses His half-awakened disciples: He calls the one "flesh," and the other "spirit." He says "the spirit is willing, but the flesh is weak."

But does our Lord excuse this weakness of His disciples? Be it far from us to think so: those who draw this conclusion mistake His meaning. He uses that very weakness as an argument for watchfulness and prayer; He teaches us that the very fact that we are encompassed with infirmity, should stir us up continually to "watch and pray."

If we know anything of true religion, let us never forget this lesson. If we desire to walk with God comfortably, and not to fall, like David or Peter, let us never forget to watch and pray. Let us live like men on enemy's ground, and be always on our guard: we cannot walk too carefully; we cannot be too jealous over our souls. The world is very ensnaring; the devil is very busy: let your Lord's words ring in our ears daily, like a trumpet. Our spirits may sometimes be very willing; but our flesh is also very weak. Then let us always watch and always pray.

MATTHEW XXVI. 47—56.

47 And while he yet spake, lo, Judas, one of the twelve, came, and with him a great multitude with swords and staves, from the chief priests and elders of the people.

48 Now he that betrayed him gave them a sign, saying, Whomsoever I shall kiss, that same is he: hold him fast.

49 And forthwith he came to Jesus, and said, Hail, Master; and kissed him.

50 And Jesus said unto him, Friend, wherefore art thou come? Then came they, and laid hands on Jesus, and took him.

51 And, behold, one of them which were with Jesus stretched out *his* hand, and drew his sword, and struck a servant of the high priest's, and smote off his ear.

52 Then said Jesus unto him, Put up again thy sword into his place: for all they that take the sword shall perish with the sword.

53 Thinkest thou that I cannot now pray to my Father, and he shall presently give me more than twelve legions of angels?

54 But how then shall the scriptures be fulfilled, that thus it must be?

55 In that same hour said Jesus to the multitudes, Are ye come out as against a thief with swords and staves for to take me? I sat daily with you teaching in the temple, and ye laid no hold on me.

56 But all this was done, that the scriptures of the prophets might be fulfilled. Then all the disciples forsook him, and fled.

WE see in these verses, the cup of our Lord Jesus Christ's sufferings beginning to be filled. We see Him betrayed by one of His disciples, forsaken by the rest, and taken prisoner by His deadly enemies. Never surely was there sorrow like His sorrow. Never may we forget, as we read this part of the Bible, that our sins were the cause of these sorrows! Jesus was "delivered for our offences." (Rom. iv. 25.)

Let us notice, for one thing, in these verses, *what gracious condescension marked our Lord's intercourse with His disciples.*

We have this point proved by a deeply touching circumstance at the moment of our Lord's betrayal. When Judas Iscariot undertook to guide the multitude to the place where his Master was, he gave them a sign by which they might distinguish Jesus in the dim moonlight from His disciples: he said, "Whomsoever I shall kiss, that same is He." And so, when he came to Jesus, he said, "Hail, Master; and kissed Him." That simple fact reveals the affectionate terms on which the disciples associated with our Lord. It is an universal custom, in Eastern countries, when friend meets friend, to salute one another with a kiss (Exod. xviii. 7.; 1 Sam. xx. 41); it would seem therefore, that when Judas kissed our Lord, he only did that which all the apostles were accustomed to do, when they met their Master after an absence.

Let us draw comfort from this little circumstance for our own souls. Our Lord Jesus Christ is a most gracious and condescending Saviour. He is not an "austere man," repelling sinners, and keeping them at a distance; He is not a being so different from us in nature, that we must regard Him with awe rather than affection: He would have us rather regard Him as an elder Brother, and a beloved Friend. His heart in heaven is still the same that it was upon earth: He is ever meek, merciful, and condescending to men of low estate. Let us trust Him, and not be afraid.

Let us notice, for another thing, *how our Lord condemns those who think to use carnal weapons in defence of Him and His cause.* He reproves one of His disciples for striking a servant of the high priest: He bids him "put up his sword into its place;" and he adds a solemn declaration of perpetual significance: "All they that take the sword shall perish by the sword."

The sword has a lawful office of its own. It may be used righteously, in the defence of nations against oppression; it may become positively necessary to use it, to prevent confusion, plunder, and rapine upon earth: but the sword is not to be used in the propagation and maintenance of the Gospel. Christianity is not to be enforced by bloodshed, and belief in it extorted by force. Happy would it have been for the Church if this sentence had been more frequently remembered! There are few countries in Christendom where the mistake has not been made of attempting to change men's religious opinions by compulsion, penalties, imprisonment, and death. And with what effect? The pages of history supply an answer. No wars have been so bloody as those which have arisen out of the collision of religious opinions: often, mournfully often, the very men who have been most forward to promote those wars have themselves been slain. May we never forget this! The weapons of the Christian warfare are not carnal, but spiritual. (2 Cor. x. 4.)

Let us notice, for another thing, *how our Lord submitted*

to be made a prisoner of his own free will. He was not taken captive because He could not escape: it would have been easy for Him to scatter His enemies to the winds, if He had thought fit. "Thinkest thou," He says to a disciple, "that I cannot pray to my Father, and He shall presently give Me more than twelve legions of angels? But how then shall the Scriptures be fulfilled, that thus it must be?"

We see in those words the secret of His voluntary submission to His foes. He came on purpose to fulfil the types and promises of Old Testament Scriptures, and by fulfilling them to provide salvation for the world; He came intentionally to be the true Lamb of God, the Passover Lamb; He came voluntarily to be the Scapegoat on whom the iniquities of the people were to be laid. His heart was set on accomplishing this great work. It could not be done without the "hiding of His power," for a time: to do it He became a willing sufferer. He was taken, tried, condemned, and crucified entirely of His own free will.

Let us observe this: there is much encouragement in it. The willing sufferer will surely be a willing Saviour. The Almighty Son of God, who allowed men to bind Him and lead Him away captive, when He might have prevented them with a word, must surely be full of readiness to save the souls that flee to Him. Once more then let us learn to trust Him, and not be afraid.

Let us notice, in the last place, *how little Christians know the weakness of their own hearts, until they are tried.* We have a mournful illustration of this in the conduct of our Lord's Apostles. The verses we have read conclude with the words, "Then all the disciples forsook Him, and fled." They forgot their confident assertions, made a few hours before; they forgot that they had declared their willingness to die with their Master; they forgot everything but the danger that stared them in the face. The fear of death overcame them: they "forsook Him, and fled."

How many professing Christians have done the same! How many, under the influence of excited feelings, have promised that they would never be ashamed of Christ! They have come away from the communion table, or the striking sermon, or the Christian meeting, full of zeal and love, and ready to say to all who caution them against backsliding, "Is thy servant a dog, that he should do this thing?" And yet in a few days these feelings have cooled down and passed away: a trial has come and they have fallen before it. They have forsaken Christ!

Let us learn, from this passage, lessons of humiliation and self-abasement. Let us resolve, by God's grace, to cultivate a spirit of lowliness, and self-distrust. Let us settle it in our minds, that there is nothing too bad for the very best of us to do, unless he watches, prays, and is held up by the grace of God; and let it be one of our daily prayers, "Hold Thou me up, and I shall be safe." (Psalm cxix. 117.)

MATTHEW XXVI. 57—68.

57 And they that had laid hold on Jesus led *him* away to Caiaphas the high priest, where the scribes and the elders were assembled.

58 But Peter followed him afar off unto the high priest's palace, and went in, and sat with the servants, to see the end.

59 Now the chief priests, and elders, and all the council, sought false witness against Jesus, to put him to death;

60 But found none: yea, though many false witnesses came; *yet* found they none. At the last came two false witnesses,
61 And said, This *fellow* said, I am able to destroy the temple of God, and to build it in three days.
62 And the high priest arose, and said unto him, Answerest thou nothing? what *is it which* these witness against thee?
63 But Jesus held his peace. And the high priest answered and said unto him, I adjure thee by the living God, that thou tell us whether thou be the Christ, the Son of God.
64 Jesus saith unto him, Thou hast said: nevertheless I say unto you, Hereafter shall ye see the Son of man sitting on the right hand of power, and coming in the clouds of heaven.
65 Then the high priest rent his clothes, saying, He hath spoken blasphemy; what further need have we of witnesses? behold, now ye have heard his blasphemy.
66 What think ye? They answered and said, He is guilty of death.
67 Then did they spit in his face, and buffeted him; and others smote *him* with the palms of their hands,
68 Saying, Prophecy unto us, thou Christ, Who is he that smote thee?

We read, in these verses, how our Lord Jesus Christ was brought before Caiaphas the high priest, and solemnly pronounced guilty. It was fitting that it should be so. The great day of atonement was come: the wondrous type of the scape-goat was about to be completely fulfilled. It was only suitable that the Jewish high priest should do his part, and declare sin to be upon the head of the victim, before He was led forth to be crucified. (Levit. xvi. 21.) May we ponder these things and understand them. There was a deep meaning in every step of our Lord's passion.

Let us observe, in these verses, that *the chief priests were the principal agents in bringing about our Lord's death.* It was not so much the Jewish people, we must remember, who pushed forward this wicked deed, as Caiaphas and his companions, the chief priests.

This is an instructive fact, and deserves notice. It is a clear proof that high ecclesiastical office exempts no man from gross errors in doctrine, and tremendous sins in practice. The Jewish priests could trace up their pedigree to Aaron, and were his lineal successors; their office was one of pecular sanctity, and entailed peculiar responsibilities: and yet these very men were the murderers of Christ.

Let us beware of regarding any minister of religion as infallible: his orders, however regularly conferred, are no guarantee that he may not lead us astray, and even ruin our souls. The teaching and conduct of all ministers must be tried by the Word of God: they are to be followed so long as they follow the Bible, but no longer. The maxim laid down in Isaiah must be our guide: "To the law and to the testimony: if they speak not according to this word, it is because there is no light in them." (Isaiah viii. 20.)

Let us observe, in the second place, *how fully our Lord declared to the Jewish council His own Messiahship, and His future coming in glory.*

The unconverted Jew can never tell us at the present day that his forefathers were left in ignorance that Jesus was the Messiah. Our Lord's answer to the solemn adjuration of the high priest is a sufficient reply: He tells the council plainly that He is "the Christ, the Son of God." He goes on to warn them that though He had not yet appeared in glory, as they expected Messias would have done, a day would come when He would do so. "Hereafter ye shall see the Son of man sitting on the right hand of power, and coming in the clouds of heaven." They would yet see that very Jesus of Nazareth, whom they had arraigned at their bar, appear in all majesty as King of kings. (Rev. i. 7.)

It is a striking fact which we should not fail to notice, that almost the last word spoken by our Lord to the

Jews, was a warning prediction about His own second advent: He tells them plainly that they would yet see Him in glory. No doubt He referred to the seventh chapter of Daniel, in the language that He used. (Dan. vii. 13.) But He spoke to deaf ears. Unbelief, prejudice, self-righteousness, covered them like a thick cloud: never was there such an instance of spiritual blindness. Well may the Church of England litany contain the prayer, "From all blindness,—and from hardness of heart, Good Lord deliver us."

Let us observe, in the last place, *how much our Lord endured before the council, from false witness and mockery.*

Falsehood and ridicule are old and favourite weapons of the devil. "He is a liar, and the father of it." (John viii. 44.) All through our Lord's earthly ministry we see these weapons continually employed against Him. He was called "a glutton, a winebibber," and "a friend of publicans and sinners;" He was held up to contempt as "a Samaritan." The closing scene of His life was only in keeping with all the past tenor of it. Satan stirred up His enemies to add insult to injury: no sooner was He pronounced guilty, than every sort of mean indignity was heaped upon Him: "they spit in His face, and buffeted Him;" "they smote Him with the palms of their hands;" they said mockingly, "Prophecy unto us, Thou Christ, who is he that smote Thee?"

How wonderful and strange it all sounds! How wonderful that the Holy Son of God should have voluntarily submitted to such indignities, to redeem such miserable sinners as we are! How wonderful, not least, that every tittle of these insults was foretold seven hundred years before they were inflicted! Seven hundred years before Isaiah had written down the words, "I hid not my face from shame and spitting." (Isai. l. 6.)

Let us draw from this passage one practical conclusion. Let it never surprise us if we have to endure mockery, and ridicule, and false reports, because we belong to Christ. "The disciple is not above his Master, nor the servant above his lord." (Matt. x. 24.) If lies and insults were heaped upon our Saviour, we need not wonder if the same weapons are constantly used against His people. It is one of Satan's great devices to blacken the characters of godly men, and bring them into contempt: the lives of Luther, Cranmer, Calvin, and Wesley supply abundant examples of this. If we are ever called upon to suffer in this way, let us bear it patiently. We drink the same cup that was drunk by our beloved Lord. But there is one great difference: at the worst, we only drink a few bitter drops; He drank the cup to the very dregs.

MATTHEW XXVI. 69—75.

69 Now Peter sat without in the palace: and a damsel came unto him, saying, Thou also wast with Jesus of Galilee.

70 But he denied before *them* all, saying, I know not what thou sayest.

71 And when he was gone out into the porch, another *maid* saw him, and said unto them that were there, This *fellow* was also with Jesus of Nazareth.

72 And again he denied with an oath, I do not know the man.

73 And after a while came unto *him* they that stood by, and said to Peter, Surely thou also art *one* of them; for thy speech bewrayeth thee.

74 Then began he to curse and to swear, *saying*, I know not the man. And immediately the cock crew.

75 And Peter remembered the word of Jesus, which said unto him, Before the cock crow, thou shalt deny me thrice. And he went out, and wept bitterly.

THESE verses relate a remarkable and deeply instructive event: the apostle Peter's denial of Christ. It is one of those events, which indirectly prove the truth of the Bible.

If the Gospel had been a mere invention of man, we should never have been told that one of its principal preachers was once so weak and erring, as to deny his Master.

The first thing that demands our notice is *the full nature of the sin of which Peter was guilty.*

It was a great sin. We see a man who had followed Christ for three years, and been forward in professing faith and love towards Him,—a man who had received boundless mercies, and loving-kindness, and been treated by Christ as a familiar friend,—we see this man denying three times that he knows Jesus! This was bad.—It was a sin committed under circumstances of great aggravation: Peter had been warned plainly of his danger, and had heard the warning; he had just been receiving the bread and wine at our Lord's hands, and declaring loudly that though he died with Him, he would not deny Him! This also was bad.—It was a sin committed under apparently small provocation: two weak women made the remark that he was with Jesus; they that stood by say, "Surely thou art one of them." No threat seems to have been used; no violence seems to have been done; but it was enough to overthrow Peter's faith: he denies before all. He denies with an oath: he curses and swears.—Truly it is a humbling picture!

Let us mark this history, and store it up in our minds: it teaches us plainly that the best of saints are only men, and men encompassed with many infirmities. A man may be converted to God, have faith and hope, and love towards Christ, and yet be overtaken in a fault, and have awful falls. It shows us the necessity of humility:

so long as we are in the body, we are in danger. The flesh is weak, and the devil is active: we must never think, "I cannot fall." It points out to us the duty of charity towards erring saints: we must not set down men as graceless reprobates, because they occasionally stumble and err; we must remember Peter, and "restore them in the spirit of meekness." (Gal. vi. 1.)

The second thing that demands our notice is *the series of steps by which Peter was led to deny his Lord.*

These steps are mercifully recorded for our learning. The Spirit of God has taken care to have them written down for the perpetual benefit of the Church of Christ. Let us trace them out one by one.

The first step to Peter's fall was self-confidence: he said, "Though all men should be offended, yet will I never be offended." The second step was indolence: his Master told him to watch and pray; instead of doing so he slept. The third step was cowardly compromising: instead of keeping close to his Master, he first forsook Him, and then "followed Him afar off." The last step was needless venturing into evil company: he went into the priest's palace, and "sat with the servants," like one of themselves. And then came the final fall: the cursing, the swearing, and the three-fold denial. Startling as it appears, his heart had been preparing it: it was the fruit of seeds which he himself had sown. "He ate the fruit of his own ways."

Let us remember this part of Peter's history: it is deeply instructive to all who profess and call themselves Christians. Great illnesses seldom attack the body, without a previous train of premonitory symptoms; great falls seldom happen to a saint, without a previous course of secret backsliding. The Church and the world are sometimes shocked by the sudden misconduct of some great professor of religion; believers are discouraged and stumbled by it; the enemies of God rejoice and blaspheme: but if the truth could be known, the explanation of such cases would generally be found to have been private departure from God. Men fall in private, long before they fall in public. The tree falls with a great crash, but the secret decay which accounts for it, is often not discovered till it is down on the ground.

The last thing which demands our notice is *the sorrow which Peter's sin brought upon him.* We read at the end of the chapter, "He went out, and wept bitterly."

These words deserve more attention than they generally receive. Thousands have read the history of Peter's sin, who have thought little of Peter's tears, and Peter's repentance. May we have an eye to see, and a heart to understand!

We see in Peter's tears, the close connection between unhappiness and departure from God. It is a merciful arrangement of God, that in one sense holiness shall always bring its own reward. A heavy heart and an uneasy conscience, a clouded hope, and an abundant crop of doubts, will always be the consequence of backsliding and inconsistency. The words of Solomon describe the experience of many an inconsistent child of God: "The backslider in heart shall be filled with his own ways." (Prov. xiv. 14.) Let it be a settled principle in our religion that if we love inward peace we must walk closely with God.

We see in Peter's bitter tears the grand mark of difference between the hypocrite and the true believer. When the hypocrite is overtaken by sin, he generally falls to rise no more: he has no principle of life within him to raise him up.—When the child of God is overtaken, he rises again by true repentance, and by the grace of God amends his life. Let no man flatter himself that he may sin with impunity, because David committed adultery, and because Peter denied his Lord. No doubt these holy men sinned greatly: but they did not continue in their sins. They repented greatly; they mourned over their falls; they loathed and abhorred their own wickedness. Well would it be for many, if they would imitate them in their repentance, as well as in their sins! Too many are acquainted with their fall, but not with their recovery. Like David and Peter, they have sinned, but they have not, like David and Peter, repented.

The whole passage is full of lessons that ought never to be forgotten. Do we profess to have a hope in Christ? Let us mark the weakness of a believer, and the steps that lead to a fall.—Have we unhappily backslidden, and left our first love? Let us remember that the Saviour of Peter still lives. There is mercy for us as well as for him: but we must repent, and seek that mercy, if we would find it. Let us turn unto God, and He will turn to us: His compassions fail not. (Lam. iii. 22.)

MATTHEW XXVII. 1—10.

1 When the morning was come, all the chief priests and elders of the people took counsel against Jesus to put him to death:

2 And when they had bound him, they led *him* away, and delivered him to Pontius Pilate the governor.
3 Then Judas, which had betrayed him, when he saw that he was condemned, repented himself, and brought again the thirty pieces of silver to the chief priests and elders,
4 Saying, I have sinned in that I have betrayed the innocent blood. And they said, What *is that* to us? see thou *to that*.
5 And he cast down the pieces of silver in the temple, and departed, and went and hanged himself.
6 And the chief priests took the silver pieces, and said, It is not lawful for to put them into the treasury, because it is the price of blood.
7 And they took counsel, and bought with them the potter's field, to bury strangers in.
8 Wherefore that field was called, The field of blood, unto this day.
9 Then was fulfilled that which was spoken by Jeremy the prophet, saying, And they took the thirty pieces of silver, the price of him that was valued, whom they of the children of Israel did value;
10 And gave them for the potter's field, as the Lord appointed me.

THE opening of this chapter describes the delivery of our Lord Jesus Christ into the hands of the Gentiles. The chief priests and elders of the Jews led Him away to Pontius Pilate, the Roman governor. We may see in this incident the finger of God: it was ordered by His providence, that Gentiles as well as Jews should be concerned in the murder of Christ; it was ordered by His providence, that the priests should publicly confess that the "sceptre had departed from Judah." They were unable to put any one to death, without going to the Romans: the words of Jacob were therefore fulfilled. The Messiah, "Shiloh," had indeed "come." (Gen. xlix. 10.)

The subject that principally occupies the verses we have read, is the melancholy end of the false apostle, Judas Iscariot. It is a subject full of instruction: let us mark well what it contains.

We see, in the end of Judas, *a plain proof of our Lord's innocence of every charge laid against Him.*

If there was any living witness who could give evidence against our Lord Jesus Christ, Judas Iscariot was the man. A chosen apostle of Jesus, a constant companion in all His journeyings, a hearer of all His teaching, both in public and private,—he must have known well if our Lord had done any wrong, either in word or deed. A deserter from our Lord's company, a betrayer of Him into the hands of His enemies, it was his interest for his own character's sake, to prove Jesus guilty. It would extenuate and excuse his own conduct, if he could make out that his former Master was an offender, and an impostor.

Why then did not Judas Iscariot come forward? Why did he not stand forth before the Jewish council, and specify his charges, if he had any to make? Why did he not venture to accompany the chief priests to Pilate, and prove to the Romans that Jesus was a malefactor?—There is but one answer to these questions. Judas did not come forward as a witness, because his conscience would not let him. Bad as he was, he knew he could prove nothing against Christ; wicked as he was, he knew well that his Master was holy, harmless, innocent, blameless, and true. Let this never be forgotten. The absence of Judas Iscariot at our Lord's trial is one among many proofs that the Lamb of God was without blemish,—a sinless man.

We see, for another thing, in the end of Judas, *that there is such a thing as repentance which is too late.* We are told plainly that "Judas repented himself;" we are even told that he went to the priests, and said, "I have sinned:" and yet it is clear that he did not repent unto salvation.

This is a point which deserves special attention. It is a common saying, "that it is never too late to repent."

The saying, no doubt, is true, if repentance be true; but unhappily, late repentance is often not genuine. It is possible for a man to feel his sins, and be sorry for them,—to be under strong convictions of guilt, and express deep remorse,—to be pricked in conscience, and exhibit much distress of mind,—and yet, for all this, not repent with his heart. Present danger, or the fear of death, may account for all his feelings, and the Holy Ghost may have done no work whatever on his soul.

Let us beware of trusting to a late repentance. "Now is the accepted time: to-day is the day of salvation." One penitent thief was saved in the hour of death, that no man might despair; but only one, that no man might presume. Let us put off nothing that concerns our souls, and above all not put off repentance, under the vain idea that it is a thing in our own power. The words of Solomon on this subject are very fearful. He speaks of men who "shall call upon God but He will not answer; who shall seek Him early, and not find Him." (Prov. i. 28.)

Let us see, for another thing, in the end of Judas, *how little comfort ungodliness brings a man at the last.* We are told that he cast down the thirty pieces of silver, for which he had sold his Master, in the temple, and went away in bitterness of soul. That money was dearly earned. It brought him no pleasure, even when he had it:* the "treasures of wickedness profit nothing." (Prov. x. 2.)

* It is a great and undeniable difficulty, that the words quoted as having been used by "Jeremy the prophet," are not to be found in any writings of Jeremiah that we possess, and that they are found in the prophet Zechariah. The following solutions of the difficulty have been suggested.

Sin is, in truth, the hardest of all masters. In its service there is plenty of fair promises, but an utter dearth of performance. Its pleasures are but for a season: its wages are sorrow, remorse, self-accusation, and too often death. They that sow to the flesh, do indeed reap corruption.

Are we tempted to commit sin? Let us remember the

1. Some think that the prophecy quoted by Matthew was really delivered by Jeremiah, though not written, and only handed down and recorded by Zechariah. In favour of this view, we must remember that we have a saying of our Lord's at Acts xx. 35, which is not recorded in the Gospel, and a prophecy of Enoch's in Jude. (Jude 14.)

2. Some think that the name of Jeremiah was applied by the Jews to all that portion of the Old Testament Scripture containing prophecies, and that Matthew did not really mean that Jeremy had delivered the prophecy. This is the view of Lightfoot.

3. Some think that Matthew originally wrote the words "The prophet," without quoting the name of any one in particular, and that the word "Jeremy" was inserted by an ignorant transcriber. In favour of this view, it is fair to say that the Syriac version, one of the oldest extant, simply says "the prophet," and omits Jeremy's name. The Persian version of the Gospels also omits it.

4. Some think that Matthew originally wrote the words "Zechariah the prophet," and that some ignorant transcriber changed the word into Jeremiah. In favour of this view it must be fairly remembered that in manuscripts, names were often written short, and that IOU, and ZOU, are not very unlike.

I offer no opinion on these solutions of the difficulty. A question of this sort, which has puzzled so many interpreters, is not likely to be settled at this period of the world.

One solution of the difficulty I only mention in order to enter my protest against it. That solution is adopted by many modern divines. It is simply this, that "Matthew forgot what he was doing, and made a blunder. He quoted from memory, and inaccurately. He meant Zechariah, and not Jeremiah." I can only say that at this rate we must give up the inspiration of Scripture altogether! If writers of the Bible could make blunders like this, we never know where we are in quoting a text. To use such an argument is putting a sword into the hands of Arians and Socinians, which they well know how to use. Once give up the *verbal* inspiration of Scripture, and we stand on a quicksand.

words of Scripture, "Your sin will find you out," and resist the temptation. (Numbers xxxii. 23.) Let us be sure that sooner or later, in this life or in the life to come, in this world or in the judgment day, sin and the sinner will meet face to face, and have a bitter reckoning. Let us be sure that of all trades sin is the most unprofitable. Judas, Achan, Gehazi, Ananias and Sapphira, all found it so to their cost. Well might St. Paul say, "What fruit had ye in those things whereof ye are now ashamed?" (Rom. vi. 21.)

Finally, let us see in the case of Judas, *to what a miserable end a man may come, if he has great privileges, and does not use them rightly.* We are told that this unhappy man "departed and went and hanged himself." What an awful death to die. An apostle of Christ, a former preacher of the Gospel, a companion of Peter and John, commits suicide, and rushes into God's presence unprepared and unforgiven.

Let us never forget that no sinners are so sinful as sinners against light and knowledge. None are so provoking to God: none, if we look at Scripture, have been so often removed from this world by sudden and fearful visitations. Let us remember Lot's wife, Pharaoh, Korah, Dathan and Abiram, and Saul, King of Israel: they are all cases in point. It is a solemn saying of Bunyan, "that none fall so deep into the pit, as those who fall backward." It is written in Proverbs, "He that being often reproved hardeneth his neck, shall suddenly be destroyed, and that without remedy." (Prov xxix. 1.) May we all strive to live up to our light. There is such a thing as sin against the Holy Ghost: clear knowledge of truth in the head, combined with deliberate love of sin in the heart, go a long way towards it.

And now what is the state of our hearts? Are we ever tempted to rest on our knowledge and profession of religion? Let us remember Judas, and beware.—Are we disposed to cling to the world, and to give money a prominent place in our minds? Again, let us remember Judas, and beware.—Are we trifling with any one sin, and flattering ourselves we may repent by and by? Once more, led us remember Judas, and beware.—He is set up before us as a beacon: let us look well at him, and not make shipwreck.

MATTHEW XXVII. 11—26.

11 And Jesus stood before the governor: and the governor asked him, saying, Art thou the King of the Jews? And Jesus said unto him, Thou sayest.

12 And when he was accused of the chief priests and elders, he answered nothing.

13 Then said Pilate unto him, Hearest thou not how many things they witness against thee?

14 And he answered him to never a word: insomuch that the governor marvelled greatly.

15 Now at *that* feast the governor was wont to release unto the people a prisoner, whom they would.

16 And they had then a notable prisoner, called Barabbas.

17 Therefore when they were gathered together, Pilate said unto them, Whom will ye that I release unto you? Barabbas, or Jesus which is called Christ?

18 For he knew that for envy they had delivered him.

19 When he was set down on the judgment-seat, his wife sent unto him, saying, Have thou nothing to do with that just man: for I have suffered many things this day in a dream because of him.

20 But the chief priests and elders persuaded the multitude that they should ask Barabbas, and destroy Jesus.

21 The governor answered and said unto them, Whether of the twain will ye that I release unto you? They said, Barabbas.

22 Pilate saith unto them, What shall I do then with Jesus which is called Christ? *They* all say unto him, Let him be crucified.

23 And the governor said, Why, what evil hath he done? But they cried out the more, saying, Let him be crucified.

24 When Pilate saw that he could prevail nothing, but *that* rather a tumult was made, he took water, and washed *his* hands before the multitude, saying, I am innocent of the blood of this just person: see ye *to it*.

25 Then answered all the people, and said, His blood *be* on us, and on our children.

26 Then released he Barabbas unto them: and when he had scourged Jesus, he delivered *him* to be crucified.

THESE verses describe our Lord's appearance before Pontius Pilate, the Roman governor. That sight must have been wonderful to the angels of God. He who will one day judge the world allowed Himself to be judged and condemned, though "He had done no violence, neither was any deceit in His mouth." (Isa. liii. 9.) He from whose lips Pilate and Caiaphas will one day receive their eternal sentence, suffered silently an unjust sentence to be passed upon Him. Those silent sufferings fulfilled the words of Isaiah: "As a sheep before her shearers is dumb, so He openeth not His mouth." (Isa. liii. 7.) To those silent sufferings believers owe all their peace and hope.—Through them they will have boldness in the day of judgment, who in themselves would have nothing to say.

Let us learn, from the conduct of Pilate, *how pitiful is the condition of an unprincipled great man.*

Pilate appears to have been inwardly satisfied that our Lord had done nothing worthy of death: we are told distinctly, that "he knew that for envy they had delivered Him." Left to the exercise of his own unbiassed judgment, he would probably have dismissed the charges against our Lord, and let Him go free.

But Pilate was the governor of a jealous and turbulent people; his great desire was to procure favour with them and please them: he cared little how much he sinned against God and conscience, so long as he had the praise of man. Though willing to save our Lord's life, he was afraid to do it if it offended the Jews; and so, after a feeble attempt to divert the fury of the people from Jesus to Barabbas,—and a feebler attempt to satisfy his own conscience, by washing his hands publicly before the people,—he at last condemned One whom he himself called a "just person!" He rejected the strange and mysterious warning which his wife sent to him after her dream: he stifled the remonstrances of his own conscience. He "delivered Jesus to be crucified."

We see in this miserable man a lively emblem of many a ruler of this world! How many there are who know well that their public acts are wrong, and yet have not the courage to act up to their knowledge. They fear the people; they dread being laughed at: they cannot bear being unpopular! Like dead fish, they float with the tide. The praise of man is the idol before which they bow down, and to that idol they sacrifice conscience, inward peace, and an immortal soul.

Whatever our position in life may be, let us seek to be guided by principle, and not by expediency. The praise of man is a poor, feeble, uncertain thing: it is here to-day and gone to-morrow. Let us strive to please God, and then we may care little who else is pleased; let us fear God, and then there is none else of whom we need be afraid.

Let us learn from the conduct of the Jews, described in these verses, *the desperate wickedness of human nature.*

The behaviour of Pilate afforded the chief priests and elders an occasion of reconsidering what they were about. The difficulties he raised about condemning our Lord gave time for second thoughts: but there were no second thoughts in the minds of our Lord's enemies. They pressed on their wicked deed; they rejected the compromise that Pilate offered: they actually preferred having a wretched felon, named Barabbas, set at liberty rather than Jesus. They clamoured loudly for our Lord's crucifixion; and they wound up all by recklessly taking on themselves all the guilt of our Lord's death, in words of portentous meaning: "His blood be on us and on our children."

And what had our Lord done that the Jews should hate Him so? He was no robber, or murderer: He was no blasphemer of their God, or reviler of their prophets. He was one whose life was love: He was one who "went about doing good, and healing all that were oppressed of the devil." (Acts x. 38.) He was innocent of any transgression against the law of God or man; and yet the Jews hated Him, and never rested till He was slain! They hated Him, because He told them the truth; they hated Him, because He testified of their works that they were evil: they hated the light, because it made their own darkness visible. In a word, they hated Christ, because He was righteous and they were wicked,—because He was holy and they were unholy,—because He testified against sin, and they were determined to keep their sins and not let them go.

Let us observe this. There are few things so little believed and realized as the corruption of human nature. Men fancy that if they saw a perfect person they would love and admire him; they flatter themselves that it is the inconsistency of professing Christians which they dislike and not their religion: they forget that when a really perfect man was on earth, in the person of the Son of God, He was hated and put to death. That single fact goes far to prove the truth of an old saying, that "unconverted men would kill God, if they could get at Him."

Let us never be surprised at the wickedness there is in the world. Let us mourn over it, and labour to make it less, but let us never be surprised at its extent. There is nothing which the heart of man is not capable of conceiving, or the hand of man of doing. As long as we live, let us mistrust our own hearts: even when renewed by the Spirit, they are still "deceitful above all things, and desperately wicked." (Jer. xvii. 9.)

MATTHEW XXVII. 27—44.

27 Then the soldiers of the governor took Jesus into the common hall, and gathered unto him the whole band of *soldiers*.

28 And they stripped him, and put on him a scarlet robe.

29 And when they had platted a crown of thorns, they put *it* upon his head, and a reed in his right hand: and they bowed the knee before him, and mocked him saying, Hail, King of the Jews!

30 And they spit upon him, and took the reed, and smote him on the head.

31 And after that they had mocked him, they took the robe off from him, and put his own raiment on him, and led him away to crucify *him*.

32 And as they came out, they found a man of Cyrene, Simon by name: him they compelled to bear his cross.

33 And when they were come unto a place called Golgotha, that is to say, a place of a skull,

34 They gave him vinegar to drink, mingled with gall: and when he had tasted *thereof*, he would not drink.

35 And they crucified him, and parted his garments, casting lots: that it might be fulfilled which was spoken by the prophet, They parted my garments among them, and upon my vesture did they cast lots.

36 And sitting down they watched him there;

37 And set up over his head his accusation written, THIS IS JESUS THE KING OF THE JEWS.

38 Then were there two thieves crucified with him, one on the right hand, and another on the left.

39 And they that passed by reviled him, wagging their heads,

40 And saying, Thou that destroyest the temple, and buildest *it* in three days, save thyself. If thou be the Son of God, come down from the cross.

41 Likewise also the chief priests mocking *him*, with the scribes and elders, said,

42 He saved others: himself he cannot save. If he be the King of Israel, let him now come down from the cross, and we will believe him.

43 He trusted in God; let him deliver him now, if he will have him: for he said, I am the Son of God.

44 The thieves also, which were crucified with him, cast the same in his teeth.

THESE verses describe the sufferings of our Lord Jesus Christ after His condemnation by Pilate,—His sufferings in the hands of the brutal Roman soldiers, and His final sufferings on the cross. They form a marvellous record. They are marvellous when we remember the Sufferer,—the eternal Son of God? They are marvellous when we remember the persons for whom these sufferings were endured. We and our sins were the cause of all this sorrow! He "died for our sins." (1 Cor. xv. 3.)

Let us observe, in the first place, *the extent and reality of our Lord's sufferings.*

The catalogue of all the pains endured by our Lord's body is indeed a fearful one: seldom has such suffering been inflicted on one body in the last few hours of a life. The most savage tribes, in their refinement of cruelty, could hardly have heaped more agonizing tortures on an enemy than were accumulated on the flesh and bones of our beloved Master. Never let it be forgotten that He had a real human body, a body exactly like our own, just as sensitive, just as vulnerable, just as capable of feeling intense pain. And then let us see what that body endured.

Our Lord, we must remember, had already passed a night without sleep, and endured excessive fatigue: He had been taken from Gethsemane to the Jewish council, and from the council to Pilate's judgment hall; He had been twice placed on His trial, and twice unjustly condemned; He had been already scourged and beaten cruelly with rods: and now, after all this suffering, He was delivered up to the Roman soldiers, a body of men no doubt expert in cruelty, and, of all people, least likely to behave with delicacy or compassion.—These hard men at once proceeded to work their will. They "gathered together the whole band;" they stripped our Lord of His raiment, and put on Him, in mockery, a scarlet robe; they "plaited a crown of sharp thorns," and in derision placed it on His head. They then bowed the knee before Him in mockery, as nothing better than a pretended king; they "spit upon Him;" they "smote Him on the head:" and finally, having put His own robe on Him, they led Him out of the city to a place called Golgotha, and there crucified Him between two thieves.

But what was a crucifixion? Let us try to realize it, and understand its misery. The person crucified was laid on his back on a piece of timber, with a cross-piece nailed to it near one end,—or on the trunk of a tree with branching arms, which answered the same purpose: his hands were spread out on the cross-piece, and nails driven through each of them, fastening them to the wood; his feet in like manner were nailed to the upright part of the cross: and then, the body having been securely fastened, the cross was raised up, and fixed firmly in the ground. And there hung the unhappy sufferer, till pain and exhaustion brought him to his end: not dying suddenly, for no vital part of him was injured; but enduring the most excruciating agony from his hands and feet, and unable to move. Such was the death of the cross. Such was the death that Jesus died for us! For six long hours He hung there before a gazing crowd, naked, and bleeding from head to foot,—His head pierced with thorns, His back lacerated with scourging,—His hands and feet torn with nails,—and mocked and reviled by His cruel enemies to the very last.

Let us meditate frequently on these things: let us often read over the story of Christ's cross and passion. Let us remember, not least, that all these horrible sufferings were borne without a murmur: no word of impatience crossed our Lord's lips. In His death, no less than in His life, He was perfect: to the very last Satan found nothing in Him. (John xiv. 30.)

Let us observe, in the second place, that *all our Lord Jesus Christ's sufferings were vicarious.* He suffered not for His own sins, but for our's. He was eminently our substitute in all His passion.

This is a truth of the deepest importance. Without it the story of our Lord's sufferings, with all its minute details, must always seem mysterious snd inexplicable. It is a truth, however, of which the Scriptures speak frequently, and that too with no uncertain sound. We are told that Christ "bare our sins in His own body on the tree,"—that He "suffered for sins, the just for the unjust,"—that "He was made sin for us, who knew no sin, that we might be made the righteousness of God in Him,"—that "He was made a curse for us,"—that "He was offered to bear the sins of many,"—that "He was wounded for our transgressions, and bruised for our iniquities."—and that "the Lord hath laid on Him the iniquity of us all." (1 Peter ii. 22, and iii. 18; 2 Cor. v. 21; Gal. iii. 13; Heb. ix. 28; Isaiah liii. 5, 6.) May we all remember these texts. They are among the foundation stones of the Gospel.

But we must not be content with a vague general belief

that Christ's sufferings on the cross were vicarious. We are intended to see this truth in every part of His passion. We may follow him all through, from the bar of Pilate, to the minute of His death, and see Him at every step as our mighty Substitute, our Representative, our Head, our Surety, our Proxy,—the Divine Friend who undertook to stand in our stead, and by the priceless merit of His sufferings, to purchase our redemption. Was He scourged? It was that "through His stripes we might be healed."—Was He condemned, though innocent? It was that we might be acquitted, though guilty. Did He wear a crown of thorns? It was that we might wear the crown of glory.—Was He stripped of His raiment? It was that we might be clothed in everlasting righteousness.—Was He mocked and reviled? It was that we might be honoured and blessed.—Was He reckoned a malefactor, and numbered among transgressors? It was that we might be reckoned innocent, and justified from all sin.—Was He declared unable to save Himself? It was that He might be able to save others to the uttermost.—Did He die at last, and that the most painful and disgraceful of deaths? It was that we might live for evermore, and be exalted to the highest glory,—Let us ponder these things well: they are worth remembering. The very key to peace is a right apprehension of the vicarious sufferings of Christ.

Let us leave the story of our Lord's passion with feelings of deep thankfulness. Our sins are many and great: but a great atonement has been made for them. There was an infinite merit in all Christ's sufferings: they were the sufferings of One who was God as well as man. Surely it is meet, right, and our bounden duty, to praise God daily because Christ has died.

Last, but not least, let us ever learn from the story of the passion, to hate sin with a great hatred. Sin was the cause of all our Saviour's suffering. Our sins plaited the crown of thorns: our sins drove the nails into His hands and feet; on account of our sins His blood was shed. Surely the thought of Christ crucified should make us loathe all sin. Well says the Church of England Homily of the Passion: "Let this image of Christ crucified be always printed in our hearts. Let it stir us up to the hatred of sin, and provoke our minds to the earnest love of Almighty God."

MATTHEW XXVII. 45—56.

45 Now from the sixth hour there was darkness over all the land unto the ninth hour.

46 And about the ninth hour Jesus cried with a loud voice, saying, Eli, Eli, lama sabachthani? that is to say, My God, my God, why hast thou forsaken me?

47 Some of them that stood there, when they heard *that*, said, This *man* calleth for Elias.

48 And straightway one of them ran, and took a sponge, and filled *it* with vinegar, and put *it* on a reed, and gave him to drink.

49 The rest said, Let be, let us see whether Elias will come to save him.

50 Jesus, when he had cried again with a loud voice, yielded up the ghost.

51 And, behold, the veil of the temple was rent in twain from the top to the bottom; and the earth did quake, and the rocks rent;

52 And the graves were opened; and many bodies of the saints which slept arose,

53 And came out of the graves after his resurrection, and went into the holy city, and appeared unto many.

54 Now when the centurion, and they that were with him, watching Jesus, saw the earthquake, and those things that were done, they feared greatly, saying, Truly this was the Son of God.

55 And many women were there beholding afar off, which followed Jesus from Galilee, ministering unto him.

56 Among which was Mary Magdalene, and Mary the mother of James and Joses, and the mother of Zebedee's children.

IN these verses we read the conclusion of our Lord Jesus Christ's passion. After six hours of agonizing suffering, He became obedient even unto death, and "yielded up the ghost." Three points in the narrative demand a special notice: to them let us confine our attention.

Let us observe, in the first place, *the remarkable words which Jesus uttered shortly before His death:* "My God, my God, why has Thou forsaken Me!"

There is a deep mystery in these words, which no mortal man can fathom. No doubt they were not wrung from our Lord by mere bodily pain: such an explanation is utterly unsatisfactory, and dishonourable to our blessed Saviour. They were meant to express the real pressure on His soul of the enormous burden of a world's sins; they were meant to show how truly and literally He was our substitute,—was made sin, and a curse for us, and endured God's righteous anger against a world's sin in his own person. At that awful moment the iniquity of us all was laid upon Him to the uttermost. It pleased the Lord to bruise Him, and put Him to grief. (Isaiah liii. 10.) He bore our sins: He carried our transgressions. Heavy must have been that burden, real and literal must have been our Lord's substitution for us, when He, the eternal Son of God, could speak of Himself as for a time "forsaken."

Let the expression sink down into our hearts, and not be forgotten. We can have no stronger proof of the sinfulness of sin, or of the vicarious nature of Christ's sufferings, than His cry, "My God, my God, why hast Thou forsaken Me!" It is a cry that should stir us up to hate sin, and encourage us to trust in Christ.*

* The following quotations deserve notice, and throw light on this peculiarly solemn portion of Scripture.

"Our Lord said this under a deep sense of His Father's

Let us observe, in the second place, *how much is contained in the words which describe our Lord's end.* We are simply told "He yielded up the Ghost."

There never was a last breath drawn of such deep import as this: there never was an event on which so much depended. The Roman soldiers, and the gaping crowd around the cross, saw nothing remarkable: they only saw a person dying as others die, with all the usual agony and suffering which attend a crucifixion. But they knew nothing of the eternal interests which were involved in the whole transaction.

That death discharged in full the mighty debt which sinners owe to God, and threw open the door of life to every believer; that death satisfied the righteous claims of God's holy law, and enabled God to be "just, and yet the Justifier" of the ungodly (Rom. iii. 26); that death was no mere example of self-sacrifice, but a complete atonement and propitiation for man's sin, affecting the condition and prospects of all mankind; that death solved the hard problem, how God could be perfectly holy, and yet perfectly merciful. It opened to the world a fountain for all sin and uncleanness; it was a complete victory over Satan, and spoiled him openly; "it finished

wrath unto mankind, in whose stead he now underwent that which was due for the sins of the whole world. When He said 'Why hast Thou forsaken Me?' He implied that God had for the time withdrawn from Him the sense and vision of His comfortable presence. When He said 'My God,' He implied the strength of His faith whereby He did firmly apprehend the sure and gracious aid of His eternal Father."—*Bishop Hall.*

"All the wailings and howlings of the damned to all eternity, will fall infinitely short of expressing the evil and bitterness of sin with such emphasis as these few words, 'My God, my God, why hast Thou forsaken me.'"—*Jamieson.*

the transgression, made an end of sins, made reconciliation for iniquity, and brought in everlasting righteousness" (Dan. ix. 24); it proved the sinfulness of sin, when it needed such a sacrifice to atone for it; it proved the love of God to sinners, when He sent His own Son to make the atonement. Never, in fact, was there, or could there be again, such a death. No wonder that the earth quaked, when Jesus died in our stead on the accursed tree: the solid frame of the world might well tremble and be amazed, when the soul of Christ was made "an offering for sin." (Isaiah liii. 10.)

Let us observe, in the last place, *what a remarkable miracle occurred at the hour of our Lord's death, in the very midst of the Jewish temple.* We are told that "the veil of the temple was rent in twain." The curtain which separated the holy of holies from the rest of the temple, and through which the high priest alone might pass, was suddenly "split from top to bottom."

Of all the wonderful signs which accompanied our Lord's death, none was more significant than this. The mid-day darkness, for three hours, must needs have been a startling event; the earthquake, which rent the rocks, must have been a tremendous shock: but there was a meaning in the sudden "rending of the veil from top to bottom," which must have pricked the heart of any intelligent Jew. The conscience of Caiaphas, the high priest, must have been hard indeed, if the tidings of that rent veil did not fill him with dismay.

That rending of the veil proclaimed the termination and passing away of the ceremonial law: it was a sign that the old dispensation of sacrifices and ordinances was no longer needed: its work was done; its occupation was gone, from the moment that Christ died. There was no more need of an earthly high priest, and a mercy-seat, and a sprinkling of blood, and an offering up of incense, and a day of atonement: the true High Priest had at length appeared; the true Lamb of God had been slain; the true mercy-seat was at length revealed. The figures and shadows were no longer wanted. May we all remember this! To set up an altar, and a sacrifice, and a priesthood *now*, is to light a candle at noon-day.

That rending of the veil proclaimed the opening of the way of salvation to all mankind. The way into the presence of God was unknown to the Gentile, and only seen dimly by the Jew, until Christ died; but Christ having now offered up a perfect sacrifice, and obtained eternal redemption, the darkness and mystery were to pass away. All were to be invited now to draw near to God with boldness, and approach Him with confidence, by faith in Jesus. A door was thrown open, and a way of life set before the whole world. May we all remember this! From the time that Jesus died, the way of peace was never meant to be shrouded in mystery: there was to be no reserve. The Gospel was the revelation of a mystery, which had been hid from ages and generations: to clothe religion *now* with mystery, is to mistake the grand characteristic of Christianity.

Let us turn from the story of the crucifixion, every time we read it with hearts full of praise. Let us praise God for the confidence it gives us, as to the ground of our hope of pardon. Our sins may be many and great, but the payment made by our Great Substitute far outweighs them all.—Let us praise God for the view it gives us of the love of our Father in heaven. He that spared not His own Son, but delivered Him up for us all, will surely with Him give us all things. (Rom. viii. 32.) Not least, let us praise God for the view it gives us of the sympathy of Jesus with all His believing people. He can be touched with the feeling of our infirmities; He knows what suffering is: He is just the Saviour that an infirm body, with a weak heart, in an evil world, requires.

MATTHEW XXVII. 57—66.

57 When the even was come, there came a rich man of Arimathæa, named Joseph, who also himself was Jesus' disciple:
58 He went to Pilate, and begged the body of Jesus. Then Pilate commanded the body to be delivered.
59 And when Joseph had taken the body, he wrapped it in a clean linen cloth,
60 And laid it in his own new tomb, which he had hewn out in the rock: and he rolled a great stone to the door of the sepulchre, and departed.
61 And there was Mary Magdalene, and the other Mary, sitting over against the sepulchre.
62 Now the next day, that followed the day of the preparation, the chief priests and Pharisees came together unto Pilate,
63 Saying, Sir, we remember that that deceiver said, while he was yet alive, After three days I will rise again.
64 Command therefore that the sepulchre be made sure until the third day, lest his disciples come by night, and steal him away, and say unto the people, He is risen from the dead: so the last error shall be worse than the first.
65 Pilate said unto them, Ye have a watch: go your way, make *it* as sure as ye can.
66 So they went, and made the sepulchre sure, sealing the stone, and setting a watch.

THESE verses contain the history of our Lord Jesus Christ's burial. There was yet one thing needful, in order to make it certain that our Redeemer accomplished that great work of redemption which He undertook. That holy body, in which He bore our sins on the cross, must actually be laid in the grave, and rise again. His resurrection was to be the seal and head-stone of all the work.

The infinite wisdom of God foresaw the objections of unbelievers and infidels, and provided against them.—Did the Son of God really die? Did He really rise again? Might there not have been some delusion as to the reality of His death? Might there not have been imposition or deception, as to the reality of His resurrection?—All these, and many more objections, would doubtless have been raised, if opportunity had been given. But He who knows the end from the beginning, prevented the possibility of such objections being made: by His over-ruling providence He ordered things so that the death and burial of Jesus were placed beyond a doubt.—Pilate gives consent to His burial: a loving disciple wraps the body in linen, and lays it in a new tomb hewn out of a rock, "wherein was never man yet laid:" the chief priests themselves set a guard over the place where His body was deposited. Jews and Gentiles, friends and enemies, all alike testify to the great fact, that Christ did really and actually die, and was laid in a grave. It is a fact that can never be questioned.—He was really "bruised;" He really suffered;" He really "died;" He was really "buried." Let us mark this well: it deserves recollection.

Let us learn, for one thing, from these verses, that *our Lord Jesus Christ has friends of whom little is known.*

We cannot have a more striking example of this truth than we see in the passage now before us. A man named Joseph, of Arimathæa, comes forward, when our Lord was dead, and asks permission to bury Him. We have never heard of this man at any former period of our Lord's earthly ministry: we never hear of him again. We know nothing, but that he was a disciple who loved Christ, and did Him honour. At a time when the Apostles had forsaken our Lord,—at a time when it was a dangerous thing to profess regard for Him,—at a time when there seemed to be no earthly advantage to be gained by confessing his discipleship,—at such a time as this, Joseph comes forward boldly, and begs the body of Jesus, and lays it in his own new tomb.

This fact is full of comfort and encouragement. It shows us that there are some quiet, retiring souls on earth, who know the Lord, and the Lord knows them, and yet they are little known by the Church. It shows us that there are "diversities of gifts" among Christ's people: there are some who glorify Christ passively, and some who glorify Him actively; there are some whose vocation it is to build the Church, and fill a public place, and there are some who only come forward, like Joseph, in times of special need. But each and all are led by one Spirit, and each and all glorify God in their several ways.

Let these things teach us to be more hopeful. Let us believe that "many shall yet come from the east and west, and sit down with Abraham, and Isaac, and Jacob, in the kingdom of heaven." (Matt. viii. 11.) There may be in some dark corners of Christendom many, who, like Simeon, and Anna, and Joseph of Arimathæa, are at present little known, who shall shine brightly among the Lord's jewels in the day of His appearing.

Let us learn, for another thing, from these verses, *that*

God can make the devices of wicked men work round to His own glory.

We are taught that lesson in a striking manner, by the conduct of the priests and Pharisees, after our Lord was buried. The restless enmity of these unhappy men could not sleep, even when the body of Jesus was in the grave. They called to mind the words, which they remembered He had spoken, about "rising again:" they resolved, as they thought, to make His rising again impossible. They went to Pilate: they obtained from him a guard of Roman soldiers; they set a watch over the tomb of our Lord; they placed a seal upon the stone. In short they did all they could to "make the sepulchre sure."

They little thought what they were doing; they little thought that unwittingly they were providing the most complete evidence of the truth of Christ's coming resurrection. They were actually making it impossible to prove that there was any deception or imposition. Their seal, their guard, their precautions, were all to become witnesses, in a few hours, that Christ had risen. They might as well have tried to stop the tides of the sea, or to prevent the sun rising, as to prevent Jesus coming forth from the tomb. They were taken in their own craftiness (1 Cor. iii. 19): their own devices became instruments to show forth God's glory.

The history of the Church of Christ is full of examples of a similar kind. The very things that have seemed most unfavourable to God's people, have often turned out to be for their good. What harm did the "persecution which arose about Stephen" do to the

Church of Christ? They that were scattered "went everywhere, preaching the Word." (Acts vii. 4.)—What harm did imprisonment do St. Paul? It gave him time to write many of those Epistles which are now read all over the world.—What real harm did the persecution of bloody Mary do to the cause of the English Reformation? The blood of the Martyrs became the seed of the Church.—What harm does persecution do the people of God at this very day? It only drives them nearer to Christ: it only makes them cling more closely to the throne of grace, the Bible, and prayer.

Let all true Christians lay these things to heart, and take courage. We live in a world where all things are ordered by a hand of perfect wisdom, and where all things are working together continually for the good of the body of Christ. The powers of this world are only tools in the hand of God: He is ever using them for His own purposes, however little they may be aware of it. They are the instruments by which He is ever squaring and polishing the living stones of His spiritual temple, and all their schemes and plans will only turn to His praise. Let us be patient in days of trouble and darkness, and look forward. The very things which now seem against us are all working together for God's glory. We see but half now: yet a little, we shall see all; and we shall then discover that all the persecution we now endure was, like "the seal" and "the guard," tending to God's glory. God can make the "wrath of man praise Him." (Psalm lxxvii. 10.)

MATTHEW XXVIII. 1—10.

1 In the end of the sabbath, as
it began to dawn toward the first
day of the week, came Mary Magdalene and the other Mary to see
the sepulchre.
2 And, behold, there was a great
earthquake: for the angel of the
Lord descended from heaven, and
came and rolled back the stone
from the door, and sat upon it.
3 His countenance was like
lightning, and his raiment white
as snow:
4 And for fear of him the keepers
did shake, and became as dead *men*.
5 And the angel answered and
said unto the women, Fear not
ye: for I know that ye seek Jesus,
which was crucified.
6 He is not here: for he is risen,
as he said. Come, see the place
where the Lord lay.
7 And go quickly, and tell his
disciples that he is risen from the
dead: and behold, he goeth before
you into Galilee; there shall ye
see him: lo, I have told you.
8 And they departed quickly
from the sepulchre with fear and
great joy; and did run to bring
his disciples word.
9 And as they went to tell his
disciples, behold, Jesus met them,
saying, All hail. And they came
and held him by the feet, and worshipped him.
10 Then said Jesus unto them,
Be not afraid: go tell my brethren
that they go into Galilee, and
there shall they see me.

The principal subject of these verses is the resurrection of our Lord Jesus Christ from the dead. It is one of those truths which lie at the very foundation of Christianity, and has therefore received special attention in the four Gospels. All four Evangelists describe minutely how our Lord was crucified: all four relate, with no less clearness, that He rose again.

We need not wonder that so much importance is attached to our Lord's resurrection: it is the seal and headstone of the great work of redemption, which He came to do; it is the crowning proof that He has paid the debt which He undertook to pay on our behalf, won the battle which He fought to deliver us from hell, and is accepted as our Surety and our Substitute by our Father in heaven. Had He never come forth from the prison of the grave, how could we ever have been sure that our ransom had been fully paid? (1 Cor. xv. 17.) Had He never risen from His conflict with the last enemy, how could we have felt confident that He has overcome death, and him that had the power of death, that is the devil? (Heb. ii. 14.) But thanks be unto God, we are not left in doubt: the Lord Jesus really "rose again for our justification." True Christians are "begotten again unto a lively hope by the resurrection of Jesus Christ from the dead;" they may boldly say with Paul, "Who is he that condemneth: it is Christ that died, yea rather that is risen again." (Rom. viii. 34; Rom. iv. 25; 1 Peter i. 3.)

We have reason to be very thankful that this wonderful truth of our religion is so clearly and fully proved. It is a striking circumstance, that of all the facts of our Lord's earthly ministry, none are so incontrovertibly established as the fact that He rose again. The wisdom of God, who knows the unbelief of human nature, has provided a great cloud of witnesses on the subject. Never was there a fact which the friends of God were so slow to believe, as the resurrection of Christ; never was there a fact which the enemies of God were so anxious to disprove: and yet, in spite of the unbelief of friends, and the enmity of foes, the fact was thoroughly established. Its evidences will always appear to a fair and impartial mind unanswerable: it would be impossible to prove anything in the world, if we refuse to believe that Jesus rose again.

Let us notice in these verses, *the glory and majesty with which Christ rose from the dead.* We are told that "there was a great earthquake." We are told that "the angel of the Lord descended from heaven, and came and rolled back the stone from the door of the sepulchre, and sat upon it." We need not suppose that our blessed Lord needed the help of any angel, when He came forth from the grave; we need not for a moment doubt that He rose again by His own power: but it pleased God, that His resurrection should be accompanied and followed by signs and wonders. It seemed good that the earth should shake, and a glorious angel appear, when the Son of God arose from the dead as a conqueror.

Let us not fail to see in the manner of our Lord's resurrection, a type and pledge of the resurrection of His believing people. The grave could not hold Him beyond the appointed time, and it shall not be able to hold them; a glorious angel was a witness of His rising, and glorious angels shall be the messengers who shall gather believers when they rise again: He rose with a renewed body, and yet a body, real, true, and material, and so also shall His people have a glorious body, and be like their Head. "When we see Him we shall be like Him." (1 John iii. 2.)

Let us take comfort in this thought. Trial, sorrow, and persecution are often the portion of God's people; sickness, weakness, and pain often hurt and wear their poor earthly tabernacle: but their good time is yet to come. Let them wait patiently, and they shall have a glorious resurrection. When we die, and where we are buried, and what kind of a funeral we have, matters little: the great question to be asked is this, "How shall we rise again?"

Let us notice, in the next place, *the terror which Christ's enemies felt at the period of His resurrection.*

We are told that, at the sight of the angel, "the keepers did shake, and became as dead men." Those hardy Roman soldiers, though not unused to dreadful sights, saw a sight which made them quail. Their courage melted at once at the appearance of one angel of God.

Let us again see in this fact, a type and emblem of things yet to come. What will the ungodly and the wicked do at the last day, when the trumpet shall sound, and Christ shall come in glory to judge the world? What will they do, when they see *all* the dead, both small and great, coming forth from their graves, and *all* the angels of God assembled round the great white throne? What fears and terrors will possess their souls, when they find they can no longer avoid God's presence, and must at length meet Him face to face? Oh, that men were wise, and would consider their latter end! Oh, that they would remember that there is a resurrection and a judgment, and that there is such a thing as "the wrath of the Lamb!" (Rev. vi. 16.)

Let us notice, in the next place, *the words of comfort which the angel addressed to the friends of Christ.* We read that he said, "Fear not ye: for I know that ye seek Jesus, which was crucified."

These words were spoken with a deep meaning. They were meant to cheer the hearts of believers in every age, in the prospect of the resurrection; they were intended to remind us, that true Christians have no cause for alarm in the last day, whatever may come on the world. The Lord shall appear in the clouds of heaven and the earth be burned up; the graves shall give up the dead that are in them, and the sea shall give up the dead that are in it; the judgment shall be set, and the books shall be opened; the angels shall sift the wheat from the chaff, and divide between the good fish and the bad: but in all this there is nothing that need make believers afraid. Clothed in the righteousness of Christ, they shall be found without spot and blameless; safe in the one true ark, they shall not be hurt when the flood of God's wrath breaks on the earth. Then shall the words of the Lord receive their complete fulfilment: "When these things begin to come to pass, lift up your heads, for your redemption draweth nigh." Then shall the wicked and unbelieving see how true was that word: "Blessed are the people whose God is the Lord." (Psalm xxxiii. 12.)

Let us notice, finally, *the gracious message which the Lord sent to the disciples after His resurrection.* He appeared in person to the women who had come to do honour to His body. Last at the cross and first at the tomb, they were the first privileged to see Him after He rose; and to them He gives commission to carry tidings to His disciples. His first thought is for His little scattered flock: "Go, tell my brethren."

There is something deeply touching in those simple words, "My brethren:" they deserve a thousand thoughts. Weak, frail, erring as the disciples were, Jesus still calls them His "brethren." He comforts them, as Joseph did his brethren who had sold him, saying, "I am your brother Joseph." Much as they had come short of their profession, sadly as they had yielded to the fear of man, they are still His "brethren." Glorious as He was in Himself,—a conqueror over death and hell, and the grave, the Son of God is still "meek and lowly of heart." He calls His disciples "brethren."

Let us turn from the passage with comfortable thoughts, if we know anything of true religion. Let us see in these words of Christ an encouragement to trust and not be afraid. Our Saviour is one who never forgets His people; He pities their infirmities: He does not despise them. He knows their weakness, and yet does not cast them away. Our great High Priest is also our elder brother.

MATTHEW XXVIII. 11—20.

11 Now when they were going, behold, some of the watch came into the city, and shewed unto the chief priests all the things that were done.

12 And when they were assembled with the elders, and had taken counsel, they gave large money unto the soldiers.

13 Saying, Say ye, His disciples came by night and stole him *away* while we slept.

14 And if this come to the governor's ears, we will persuade him, and secure you.

15 So they took the money, and did as they were taught: and this saying is commonly reported among the Jews until this day.

16 Then the eleven disciples went away into Galilee, into a mountain where Jesus had appointed them.

17 And when they saw him, they worshipped him: but some doubted.

18 And Jesus came and spake unto them, saying, All power is given unto me in heaven and in earth.

19 Go ye therefore, and teach all nations, baptizing them in the name of the Father, and of the Son, and of the Holy Ghost:

20 Teaching them to observe all things whatsoever I have commanded you: and, lo, I am with you alway, *even* unto the end of the world. Amen.

THESE verses form the conclusion of the Gospel of St. Matthew. They begin by showing us what absurdities blind prejudice will believe, rather than believe the truth; they go on to show us what weakness there is in the hearts of some disciples, and how slow they are to believe; they finish by telling us some of the last words spoken by our Lord upon earth,—words so remarkable that they demand and deserve all our attention.

Let us observe, in the first place, *the honour which God has put on our Lord Jesus Christ.* Our Lord says, "All power is given unto Me in heaven and earth."

This is a truth which is declared by St. Paul to the Philippians: "God hath highly exalted Him and given Him a name, which is above every name." (Phil. ii. 9.) It is a truth which in nowise takes away from the true notion of Christ's divinity, as some have ignorantly supposed. It is simply a declaration, that, in the counsels of the eternal Trinity, Jesus, as Son of man, is appointed heir of all things; that He is the Mediator between God and man; that the salvation of all who are saved is laid upon Him, and that He is the great fountain of mercy, grace, life, and peace. It was for this "joy set before Him that He endured the cross." (Heb. xii. 2.)

Let us embrace this truth reverently, and cling to it firmly. Christ is He who has the keys of death and hell; Christ is the anointed Priest, who alone can absolve sinners; Christ is the Fountain of living waters, in whom alone we can be cleansed; Christ is the Prince and Saviour, who alone can give repentance and remission of sins. In Him all fulness dwells. He is the way, the door, the light, the life, the Shepherd, the Altar of Refuge. "He that hath the Son hath life; and he that hath not the Son of God hath not life." (1 John v. 12.) May we all strive to understand this! No doubt men may easily think too little of God the Father, and God the Spirit; but no man ever thought too much of Christ.

Let us observe, in the second place, *the duty which Jesus lays on His disciples.* He bids them "go and teach all nations." They were not to confine their knowledge to themselves, but communicate it to others; they were not to suppose that salvation was revealed only to the Jews, but to make it known to all the world; they were to strive to make disciples of all nations, and to tell the whole earth that Christ had died for sinners.

Let us never forget that this solemn injunction is still in full force. It is still the bounden duty of every disciple of Christ to do all he can in person, and by prayer, to make others acquainted with Jesus. Where is our faith, if we neglect this duty? Where is our charity? It may well be questioned whether a man knows the value of the Gospel himself, if he does not desire to make it known to all the world.

Let us observe, in the third place, *the public profession which Jesus requires of those who believe His Gospel.* He tells His apostles to "baptize" those whom they received as disciples.

It is very difficult to conceive, when we read this last command of our Lord's, how men can avoid the conclusion that baptism is necessary, when it may be had. It seems impossible to explain the word that we have here of any but an outward ordinance, to be administered to all who join His Church.—That outward baptism is not absolutely necessary to salvation, the case of the penitent thief plainly shows: he went to paradise unbaptized. That outward baptism alone often confers no benefit, the case of Simon Magus plainly shows: although baptized he remained "in the gall of bitterness and bond of iniquity." (Acts iii. 23.) But that baptism is a matter of entire indifference, and need not be used at all, is an assertion which seems at variance with our Lord's words in this place.*

The plain practical lesson of the words is the necessity of a public confession of faith in Christ. It is not enough to be a secret disciple: we must not be ashamed to let men see whose we are, and whom we serve. We must not behave as if we did not like to be thought Christians; but take up our cross, and confess our Master before the world. His words are very solemn: "Whosoever shall be ashamed of Me,...of him also shall the Son of man be ashamed, when He cometh in the glory of His Father with the holy angels." (Mark viii. 38.)

Let us observe, in the fourth place, the *obedience which Jesus requires of all who profess themselves His disciples.* He bids the Apostles teach them to observe all things, whatsoever He has commanded them.

This is a searching expression. It shows the uselessness of a mere name and form of Christianity; it shows that they only are to be counted true Christians who live in a practical obedience to His word, and strive to do the things that He has commanded. The water of baptism, and the bread and wine of the Lord's Supper

* I purposely abstain from saying anything on the subject of infant baptism.

There is nothing in this text which can be fairly used either way in settling this much-vexed controversy.

It is certain that the missionaries of the Church of England carry out the meaning of this text as fully and thoroughly as the missionaries of Baptist Churches.

The point settled by the text is not so much what ought to be done with the *children* of Christians, as what ought to be done with heathens when converted.

alone will save no man's soul. It profits nothing that we go to a place of worship and hear Christ's ministers, and approve of the Gospel, if our religion goes no further than this.—What are our lives? What is our daily conduct at home and abroad? Is the Sermon on the Mount our rule and standard? Do we strive to copy Christ's example? Do we seek to do the things that He commanded?—These are questions that must be answered in the affirmative, if we would prove ourselves born again, and children of God. Obedience is the only proof of reality. "Faith without works is dead," being alone. (James ii. 17, 20, 26.) "Ye are my friends," says Jesus, "if ye do whatsoever I command you." (John xv. 14.)

Let us observe, in the fifth place, the *solemn mention of the blessed Trinity which our Lord makes in these verses.* He bids the Apostles to baptize "in the name of the Father, and of the Son, and of the Holy Ghost."

This is one of those great plain texts which directly teach the mighty doctrine of the Trinity. It speaks of Father, Son, and Holy Ghost, as Three distinct persons, and speaks of all Three as co-equal. Such as the Father is, such is the Son, and such is the Holy Ghost. And yet these Three are One.

This truth is a great mystery. Let it be enough to receive and believe it, and let us ever abstain from all attempts at explanation. It is childish folly to refuse assent to things that we do not understand. We are poor crawling worms of a day, and know little at our best about God and eternity: suffice it for us to receive the doctrine of the Trinity in unity, with humility and reverence, and to ask no vain questions. Let us believe that no sinful soul can be saved without the work of all three Persons in the blessed Trinity, and let us rejoice that Father, Son, and Holy Ghost, who co-operated to make man, do also co-operate to save him. Here let us pause: we may receive practically what we cannot explain theoretically.

Finally, let us observe in these verses, *the gracious promise with which Jesus closes His words.* He says to His disciples, "I am with you alway, even unto the end of the world."

It is impossible to conceive words more comforting, strengthening, cheering, and sanctifying than these. Though left alone, like orphan children in a cold unkind world, the disciples were not to think they were deserted: their Master would be ever "with them." Though commissioned to do a work as hard as that of Moses when sent to Pharaoh, they were not to be discouraged: their Master would certainly be "with them." No words could be more suited to the position of those to whom they were first spoken; no words could be imagined more consolatory to believers in every age of the world.

Let all true Christians lay hold on these words and keep them in mind. Christ is "with us" always: Christ is "with us" wherever we go. He came to be "Emmanuel, God with us," when He first came into the world: He declares that He is ever Emmanuel, "with us," when He comes to the end of His earthly ministry and is about to leave the world. He is with us daily to pardon and forgive, with us daily to sanctify and strengthen, with us daily to defend and keep, with us daily to lead and to guide: with us in sorrow and with us in joy, with us in sickness and with us in health, with us in life and with us in death, with us in time and with us in eternity.

What stronger consolation could believers desire than this? Whatever happens, they at least are never completely friendless and alone: Christ is ever with them. They may look into the grave, and say with David, "Though I walk through the valley of the shadow of death I will fear no evil, for Thou art with me." They may look forward beyond the grave, and say with Paul, "We shall ever be with the Lord." (Psalm xxiii. 4; 1 Thess. iv. 17.) He has said it, and He will stand to it: "I am with you alway, even unto the end of the world." "I will never leave you and never forsake you."—We could ask nothing more. Let us go on believing, and not be afraid. It is everything to be a real Christian. None have such a King, such a Priest, such a constant Companion, and such an unfailing Friend, as the true servants of Christ.